Volume 1: South-eastern Europe

Denied a future?

the right to education of
Roma/Gypsy & Traveller children in Europe

Save the Children

Save the Children is the UK's leading international children's charity. Working in more than 70 countries, we run emergency relief alongside long-term development and prevention work to help children, their families and communities to be self-sufficient.

Drawing on this practical experience, Save the Children also seeks to influence policy and practice to achieve lasting benefits for children within their communities. In all its work, Save the Children endeavours to make children's rights a reality.

Published by
Save the Children
17 Grove Lane
London SE5 8RD
UK

Tel: (0) 20 7703 5400
Fax: (0) 20 7708 2508
www.savethechildren.org.uk

First published 2001
Reprinted 2002

© The Save the Children Fund 2001
Registered Charity No. 213890

ISBN 1 84187 058 7

Designed and typeset by Neil Adams, Grasshopper Design Company

Contents

List of tables

Denied a Future? Volume 1: Summary

The countries covered in this volume represent what can be seen as the heartland of Roma/Gypsies in Europe – the Balkans. This area has the highest concentration of Roma/Gypsy communities and is also the region that provides most of the continent's native Romani speakers. However, there is considerable linguistic and cultural diversity amongst Roma/Gypsy populations even within this region. This is reflected in the various names that communities have for each of the Romani dialects used, and in the many different types of relationships that exist between the communities and wider society.

The region has faced enormous problems since the end of the Cold War. All the countries (with the exception of Slovenia – not included in this report) have experienced severe recession and an accompanying rise in social tensions. Most dramatically, the countries of the former Yugoslavia have undergone a decade of war. Although Roma/Gypsy populations have not been directly part of the ethnic fragmentation of the region, they have often suffered considerably from violence and insecurity. This has led to considerable migration both within the region and to countries further afield. Another effect of war has been that over the last ten years, Roma/Gypsies have not received the levels of attention and resources that populations have enjoyed in other countries. This is reflected in the considerable difficulties that exist in obtaining precise data about their numbers and circumstances.

In countries such as Croatia, the effect of internal displacement and the introduction of procedures to define membership of the new state have had a negative impact on the ability of many Roma/Gypsy parents to register their children for schooling. The creation of new political units has also increased complexity, best shown in Bosnia and Herzegovina, which, divided between the Federation and Republika Srpska, limits access to international and even domestic rights to education. The Roma/Gypsy minority in Kosovo suffered considerably as a result of the conflict there (even though Roma/Gypsies were not directly party to it) with the majority of the population fleeing to surrounding regions.

War and conflict more generally has seen the destruction of infrastructure, including schools. Many Roma/Gypsy populations live in relatively isolated settlements and have found themselves either far from a school or having to attend schools which offer very low-quality accommodation. Unsurprisingly, little progress has been made in reforming mainstream educational systems and in enabling teachers to adopt a more positive approach to Roma/Gypsy pupils. In addition to this, although a significant number of Roma/Gypsies in the region speak one or other dialect of Romanes as their mother tongue, there is practically no provision for study in this language.

In general, attendance rates of Roma/Gypsy children in schools are low, and they rarely attend beyond primary school. The social status of Roma/Gypsies is equally low, and cultural and physical isolation has been compounded over the last decade by increasing impoverishment, economic marginalisation and conflict. Relations with wider society, at best, have not improved within a climate of strengthening "majority'" national identities. One exception is the Former Yugoslav Republic of Macedonia. There, while the Roma/Gypsy minority experiences similar problems to those throughout the former Yugoslavia, the existence of very large communities, notably the municipality of Shutka, has led to relatively greater attention being paid to Roma/Gypsy language and education, especially by NGOs.

In those states not directly involved in armed conflict (Romania, Bulgaria and Albania) the situation of Roma/Gypsies has been characterised by the effects of post-communist transition. As in other countries in Eastern Europe, the abandonment of communist integration/assimilation policies has produced high levels of unemployment, particularly for those with fewer skills, having a disproportionate effect on Roma/Gypsies. Assessing the situation of Roma/Gypsies in Romania is made difficult by the extensive diversity that exists within the population coupled with the lack of any comprehensive data about them. Romania has produced large numbers of Roma/Gypsy refugees throughout the 1990s, partly as a result of the economic circumstances, but also due to waves of violence at the local level. The Romanian state has been slow to address formally Roma/Gypsy issues, including education, and has preferred to allow the NGO sector to develop initiatives rather than to allocate its own resources.

In Bulgaria NGOs have also played a prominent (though sometimes controversial) role in relation to Roma/Gypsy education. A significant problem revolves around the high number of Roma/Gypsy children placed in segregated schools that developed during the communist period. However, the effect of two recessions and the persistence of strong negative attitudes towards Roma/Gypsies on the part of much of the wider population has resulted in slow progress and the intensification of problems such as the growing number of street children, many of whom are Roma/Gypsies.

Albania has not been directly affected by war. However, the Albanian population has suffered as a result of economic collapse and political instability, further reinforcing the marginalisation of Roma/Gypsies within society. Unlike in Bulgaria and Romania, where a small number of Roma/Gypsies have succeeded within the educational system, in Albania, Roma/Gypsies remain a largely isolated, low-status group with little political presence.

Since the current circumstances of Roma/Gypsy minorities in the region have been heavily shaped by conflict, it can be assumed that the end of conflict will bring opportunities for Roma/Gypsies, local and national governments and the non-governmental sector to develop strategies that will enable all citizens to enjoy their right to education. Greater progress has been made in Romania and Bulgaria, not least because both are candidate countries for membership of the EU. Perhaps more than in any other region, those shaping educational change in the Balkans need to consider not only issues relating to economic and social marginalisation, but also issues surrounding language provision.

Terms used

Each of the terms below is understood differently by different people. This list describes how we are using them in this report:

Preschool – sometimes referred to as nursery or kindergarten. This refers to the non-compulsory stage of schooling immediately prior to primary education.

Primary education – sometimes referred to as basic or elementary education. This refers to the foundation stages of a child's school education. In the Central and South Eastern Europe context this means the compulsory element of schooling, which in most cases caters for children between 6/7 and 14/15 years of age. In the Western European context it refers to the stage of schooling that comes after pre-school and before secondary. It can start for children as young as 4/5 years and usually goes up to the age of 10/11 years.

Secondary education – sometimes referred to as further education according to context. In Central and South Eastern Europe, further education is the non-compulsory stage of schooling that immediately follows primary education. It caters

for young people aged from 14/15 years up to 18 years. In Western Europe, secondary education also follows on from primary education (ie, starting from 10/11 years), but is compulsory up to the age of 16 years. Pupils then have the option of continuing in further education up to the age of 18 years and in higher education post 18 years.

Community – a group of people who live within a defined context (eg, a Roma/Gypsy community in a remote rural area). When talking about "consulting with Roma/Gypsy communities", we do not assume they are cohesive or that there is an organised structure to work through.

NGO (Non-governmental organisation) – this can be anything from a small voluntary group to a large development agency. More specifically:

Local NGO – a group working within a particular country, run by nationals, but who may be "outsiders" to the local communities with which they work

INGO – an international non-governmental organisation

Abbreviations used

ADRA	Adventist Development and Relief Agency
AEDP	Albanian Education Development Project
AOR	Area of Responsibility (Kosovo)
BiH	Bosnia and Herzegovina (a state comprising two entities: the Federation of Bosnia and Herzegovina and the Republic of Srpska).
BSP	Bulgarian Socialist Party
CEGI	Chamber of Commerce and Industry of Romania and Bucharest
CIP	Centre for Interactive Pedagogy (Serbia)
COOPI	*Cooperazione Internazionale* (Italian International Co-operation)
CPS	Central European University Centre for Policy Studies
CRCA	Children's Rights Centre of Albania
CRS	Catholic Relief Services
CSCE	Conference on Security and Co-operation in Europe
DCA	Dan Church Aid (Danish)
DM	Deutschmark
DPNM	Department for the Protection of National Minorities (Romania)
ECRI	European Commission Against Racism and Intolerance
ERRC	European Roma Rights Centre
EU	European Union
FBiH	the Federation of Bosnia and Herzegovina (one of the two Entities in BiH)
FID	Forum for Democratisation (Kosovo)
FOC	*Fundatia Familia Si Ocrotireas Copilului* (Romania)
FOSIM	Foundation Open Society Macedonia
FRY	Federal Republic of Yugoslavia
FSD	Open Society Foundation Romania
FYR	Former Yugoslav Republic
FYROM	Former Yugoslav Republic of Macedonia
GDP	Gross Domestic Product
GTZ	*Deutsche Gesellschaft für Technische Zusammenarbeit* (German Development Agency)
HDZ	Croatian Democratic Union (political party)
HLC	Humanitarian Law Centre (Serbia)
HRK	Croatian Kuna (12 HRK = £GB1)
IDP	Internally Displaced Person
IEP	Institute for Educational Policy, Open Society Institute
IOM	International Organisation for Migration
IRC	International Rescue Committee

KFOR	NATO-led military security force, deployed in Kosovo
KLA	Kosovo Liberation Army
KPC	Kosovo Protection Corps
LCO	Local Community Officer (Kosovo)
MATRA	'MATRA' Programme of the Ministry of Foreign Affairs of the Netherlands
MES	Ministry of Education and Sport (Albania)
	Ministry of Education and Science (Bulgaria)
NGO	Non-Governmental Organisation
NORAD	Norwegian Development Agency
NPA	Norwegian People's Aid
ODIHR	OSCE Office for Democratic Institutions and Human Rights
ODW	Operation Days Work (Danish organisation)
OECD	Organisation for Economic Co-operation and Development
OHR	Office of the High Representative in Bosnia and Herzegovina
OSCE	Organisation for Security and Co-operation in Europe
OSF	Open Society Foundation
OSI	Open Society Institute
RS	The Republic of Srpska (one of the two Entities in BiH)
SME	Small and Medium-sized Enterprise
SOCO	'Social Consequences of Economic Transformation in East Central Europe' Programme
SPOLU	Spolu International (NGO)
SPS	Socialist Party of Serbia
SRSG	Special Representative of the Secretary-General (Kosovo)
SURH	*Savez Udruženja Roma Hrvatske* (Union of the Associations of Roma in Croatia)
UDF	Union of Democratic Forces (Bulgaria)
UNDP	United Nations Development Programme
UNESCO	United Nations Educational, Scientific and Cultural Organisation
UNHCR	United Nations High Commissioner for Refugees
UNICEF	United Nations Children's Fund
UNMIK	United Nations Interim Administration Mission in Kosovo
USAID	US Agency for International Development
UXO	Unexploded ordnance
WWI	World War One
WWII	World War Two
$US	US dollars
£GB	Pounds sterling

Preface

Why *Denied a Future?* was produced

The idea for the *Denied a Future?* report emerged at the 1999 session of the UN Commission on Human Rights. Save the Children presented information about the ways in which the right to education of Roma/Gypsy and Traveller* children was being compromised or violated in a number of European countries. Various people were interested in finding out more and asked us to recommend publications that they could refer to. We discovered that there were very few of these. While there was a lot of information available, from research institutes, from governmental sources, from organisations working with Roma/Gypsy and Traveller communities and from activists in those communities, this information was in libraries, archives and in people's heads, in many different locations and languages.

Large sums of money are being spent by governments, intergovernmental agencies and international NGOs on programmes that aim to reform education provision in Central and South-Eastern Europe and to improve the situation of Roma/Gypsy and Traveller children in Western Europe. The absence of an accessible text describing the starting point against which

* Given the vast number of names applied to the people who are the subject of this report, the term "Roma/Gypsies" is employed in accordance with Liégeois and Gheorghe's *Roma/Gypsies: a European Minority* (Minority Rights Group, 1995). In some Western European countries, the term "Traveller" is preferred. Therefore, in this report we employ the term "Roma/Gypsies and Travellers" or "Roma/Gypsy and Traveller" when we are referring also to countries with populations whose preferred term is "Traveller".

the impact of this expenditure could be measured meant that it was difficult to assess whether these programmes were actually bringing about positive changes for Roma/Gypsy and Traveller children. There appeared to be hundreds of small projects, many of which were highly innovative and successful. But it was hard to tell whether these successful pilot initiatives were having any significant impact in the long term or on a wider scale. In other words, was expenditure on pilots and experimental initiatives leading to any systemic change?

Save the Children decided that there was a need for a basic text that described legislation, policy and practice with regard to education provision for Roma/Gypsy and Traveller children in a number of European countries. *Denied a Future?* therefore describes law, policy and practice in the period June 2000 to June 2001. We intend the report to serve as a benchmark against which the impact of current and future investments by the World Bank, the European Union, national and local governments and other agencies can be assessed.

The issues addressed in *Denied a Future?* are of growing significance and relevance in contemporary Europe. They feature in the debates leading up to the enlargement of the European Union and in the work of the Working Table on Democratisation and Human Rights of the Stability Pact for South-Eastern Europe. The failure to safeguard the right to education of large numbers of Roma/Gypsy and Traveller children was highlighted at the UNESCO Education for All 2000 regional meeting for Europe and North America. It was also

highlighted at the European Conference against Racism, which was organised by the Council of Europe in preparation for the UN World Conference against Racism.

How *Denied a Future?* was produced

Each *Denied a Future?* country report was co-ordinated by a single author or editor. However, the authors/editors drew upon a wide range of written and verbal contributions in the countries concerned. The drafts were widely circulated by the co-ordinating team, and comments were particularly sought from individuals in Roma/Gypsy and Traveller communities who are clients and users of the education services under discussion. The views and experiences of Roma/Gypsy and Traveller children, young people, parents and teachers are central to the conclusions and recommendations of *Denied a Future?*

Who *Denied a Future?* is for

Denied a Future? comprises a Summary, an International Legislation Handbook and two volumes of country reports. The International Legislation Handbook describes the international and regional legal frameworks guaranteeing the right to education of children of minority groups. Volume One of the country reports covers South-Eastern Europe and Volume Two covers Central and Western Europe. There are summaries for each country report as well as volume summaries to allow for quick reference and ease of navigation. The Summary identifies the main findings of the 14 country reports, Save the Children's conclusions and recommendations for future action.

We expect different types of reader to use *Denied a Future?* in different ways. For international and locally based NGOs, we hope it will be useful as an advocacy tool. In the International Legislation Handbook, the relevant laws and articles are explained and analysed, and the "control mechanisms" related to them are described. Each country report contains a section outlining the international legal instruments that have been ratified in that country. As a practical advocacy tool, *Denied a Future?* contains most of the information needed by NGOs that are interested in using international law to lobby for change at national and community level.

We hope that *Denied a Future?* will be widely used as a planning and briefing resource by staff and volunteers of intergovernmental agencies and international NGOs. The individual country reports provide an overview of law and policy, and also a detailed description of the situation in schools and communities and the views of pupils, parents and teachers. They also provide information about the different Roma/Gypsy and Traveller communities, their histories and the languages they speak. Within each country report there is a set of recommendations that Save the Children believes should be the focus for further attention and action.

We hope that policy-makers will find *Denied a Future?* a useful source of information about developments in other European countries. A great deal of good practice has been developed that can be scaled up and built upon. Although some of the country reports are critical of the records of governments to date, the intent in producing *Denied a Future?* is constructive. We are aware that there are significant financial and other barriers impeding policy implementation and also that a number of positive initiatives are underway, but have been instituted so recently that it is too early to discern results. Our aim in producing *Denied a Future?* is to demonstrate where governments need to focus their efforts because their actions are such an important part of the solution. However, the country reports also indicate where action is needed by professionals, practitioners, NGOs, community leaders and activists.

The limitations of *Denied a Future?*

We should acknowledge from the outset that *Denied a Future?* is not the final word in the issue of the right to education of Roma/Gypsy and Traveller children. In some countries, it has proved difficult to get reliable information. However, in cases where we believed there was a possibility of bias, or where we were given information that was contentious or possibly out of date, we commissioned additional research and sought alternative views. We have not succeeded in getting as much information as we would have liked about how a child's gender influences decisions about education. Also, the important issue of labour-market discrimination falls outside the parameters of this report.

Denied a Future? presents a "snapshot" in a dynamic period. Although every effort has been made by the project's co-ordinators to ensure that the information is up to date, it is possible that, even in the few months between conducting research and going to print, new policies or initiatives will have been introduced. This is to be welcomed. We hope that the existence of *Denied a Future?* will make it easier for people to identify where and how things are changing for the better.

How we selected countries for *Denied a Future?*

A number of people have asked us how we selected the 14 countries that feature in the *Denied a Future?* report. Save the Children's UK and Europe Programme works in the United Kingdom and South-Eastern Europe. For our own purposes we were, of course, particularly interested in the situation in those countries. We wanted to include reports from other member states of the European Union in order to draw attention to issues which need to be addressed there too – the denial of the right to education of children who are labelled as "Gypsies" is often wrongly perceived as a problem limited to Central and South-Eastern Europe. Partner organisations in Italy, Finland and Greece were able to assist us in producing reports for these countries. Unfortunately, with the time and resources available to us, we were unable to extend the scope of the report to, for example, Spain, Germany, Ireland, Poland, Slovenia, the Baltic States or Russia. We have included reports on the Czech Republic, Slovakia and Hungary because, in these countries, segregation of Roma/Gypsy children and the practice of educating them in special schools for the mentally disabled present particular challenges.

Who are the children in the photographs?

Most of the photographs that appear in *Denied a Future?* were taken in Roma/Gypsy and Traveller communities in Bosnia and Herzegovina, Hungary, Italy, Serbia, Romania and Wales in the summer of 2001. The reports also feature images from the photographer's archive of work from other countries including the Czech Republic, England, Poland and Slovakia.

As a rule, the children and young people were closely involved in directing how they would be portrayed in the photographs. In many cases, they chose to be photographed alongside things and people that were important to them: brothers and sisters, friends, pets, toys, places where they play and work.

The photographer, Poppy Szaybo, has worked as a documentary photographer and organiser of cultural and educational projects with Roma/Gypsies and Travellers throughout Europe for over a decade. She extends her thanks to all of the communities she visited in summer 2001 for their kindness, hospitality and generosity. In particular, she would like to thank the young people that she worked with and photographed for sharing with her their humour, energy, vitality and warmth, making *Denied a Future?* an unforgettable and inspiring project with which to be involved.

1 Roma/Gypsy and Traveller education in Europe: an overview of the issues

Introduction

The people to whom the term "Roma/Gypsy and Traveller" has been attached represent a unique phenomenon in European history and culture. From their first appearance in the historical record over 600 years ago, the relationship between Roma/Gypsies and mainstream societies has been marked by many tensions and changes. Roma/Gypsies are now widely considered to be Europe's largest ethnic minority. The continental population is estimated to be between 7 to 8.5 million and rising. There are Roma/Gypsy and Traveller communities in practically every European country.*

This report examines educational policy and provision in relation to Roma/Gypsy and Traveller people from a child rights perspective. Access to formal education is more important than ever in enabling individuals to maintain and develop living standards in Europe's increasingly knowledge-based economy. Formal education also plays an important role in promoting awareness of the diversity within society, as well as the recognition of our common humanity, providing the basis for our concepts of democracy and human rights. This report reflects growing concern in recent years about the failures of educational provision to Roma/Gypsy and Traveller people. In 1984 the European Commission instigated research into Roma/Gypsy and Traveller education, on the basis of which in 1989 the Council and Ministers of

Education passed Resolution 89/C 153/02 "On School Provision for Gypsy and Traveller Children".

As its title suggests, the 1989 Resolution was drafted with reference to the circumstances and needs of the more mobile Roma/Gypsy and Traveller populations of the member states of the European Union (EU) at that time. The emphasis was on developing innovative practice to meet the needs of children and young people whose lifestyles presented practical and cultural challenges to service providers. The Resolution sought improvement rather than the achievement of any final aim and did not refer directly to rights. Over the following decade dramatic changes occurred both in terms of how Roma/Gypsies were perceived (to include the whole European diaspora), and in terms of how practice was developed, including the increasing importance of a human rights framework. This report aims to provide a basis for ongoing research into the relationship between rights and Roma/Gypsy and Traveller education. By gathering data on educational services and initiatives specifically targeted at Roma/Gypsies, and by compiling a summary of relevant national and international legal instruments, the report will provide a resource for all those involved in the field of Roma/Gypsy and Traveller education, including authorities with statutory duties to make appropriate provision. The need for such work is underlined by the recognition that the report comes at a time of rapid social, economic, cultural and political change, not only for Roma/Gypsy and Traveller people, but also for European society as a whole.

*It is important to note that Roma/Gypsies are not unique to Europe, but can be found in continents throughout the globe, including the Americas and Australia for example.

East and West

Since 1989, policy approaches towards the overwhelming majority of Roma/Gypsies and their access to public services, including education, have undergone dramatic changes as a result of the collapse of communism and the process of European reintegration. Over three-quarters of the continent's Roma/Gypsies live in the former communist countries of Central and South-Eastern Europe. There are considerable differences between Roma/Gypsies in Central and Eastern Europe, Roma/Gypsies in South-Eastern Europe and Roma/Gypsies and Travellers in Western Europe, in terms of their demographic distribution, and their historical, social, economic and cultural circumstances. Yet such divisions in themselves are arbitrary; there are just as many differences within countries as there are between countries.

Cultural and linguistic diversity

The inclusion of Roma/Gypsies from Central and South-Eastern Europe into Europe-wide policy initiatives emphasises all the more the need for policy-makers to consider the full range of cultural and linguistic diversities that exist. Central and South-Eastern Europe contain the overwhelming majority of Romani speakers in the whole of Europe, yet Romani speakers account for only around 40 per cent of Roma/Gypsies in the region. Furthermore, native Romani speakers use a wide variety of dialects. Most Roma/Gypsies speak the language of the surrounding society as their main language, and different communities represent different stages of the transition from Romani to mainstream languages as mother tongue. Although the majority of Roma/Gypsies in Central and South-Eastern Europe live in the countryside, the region also has more and larger urban Roma/Gypsy populations than Western Europe. Finally, historically the relatively greater integration of Roma/Gypsies in the former communist states means that Roma/Gypsies in Central and South-Eastern Europe have been more exposed to majority cultural norms than their Western European counterparts.

A growing population

Roma/Gypsy populations in both parts of Europe differ in terms of their absolute and relative size. The often subjective nature of ethno-cultural identities, combined with the diversity and spread of Roma/Gypsy and Traveller communities, means that population figures should be treated as estimates. It is broadly accepted that approximately 4.2 million Roma/Gypsies live in eight Central and Eastern European states (which have a total population of 56 million). Only 1.5 million Roma/Gypsies live in the five largest Western European states (which have populations of between 30 and 80 million each) – over half of these live in Spain.

Table 1.1 Estimated size of Roma/Gypsy populations and GDP per head in selected EU and post-communist countries

Country	Total population	GDP per head ($US)	Roma/Gypsy population (est.)	Roma/Gypsy % of total population
EU members				
France	59.3m	$23,000	340,000	0.6%
Germany	82.8m	$22,700	130,000	0.2%
Italy	57.6m	$21,400	100,000	0.2%
Spain	40.0m	$17,300	800,000	2.0%
UK	59.5m	$21,800	120,000	0.2%
Post-communist states				
Bulgaria	7.8m	$4,300	800,000	10.3%
Czech Republic	10.3m	$11,700	300,000	2.9%
Hungary	10.1m	$7,800	600,000	5.9%
Romania	22.4m	$3,900	2,000,000	8.9%
Slovakia	5.4m	$8,500	520,000	9.6%

Sources: Jean-Pierre Liégeois and Nicolae Gheorghe, *Roma/Gypsies: A European Minority*, Minority Rights Group International, London, 1995; *CIA Fact Book*, 2000

The context of transition

As well as considerable differences in wealth between the two halves of the continent, differences in economic development also have a major effect on the opportunities of Roma/Gypsy people and populations. Whereas Western European states generally allowed Roma/Gypsies and Travellers to develop traditional practices (for example, as private traders or seasonal farm labourers), in the communist states Roma/Gypsies were usually targeted for relatively low-skilled employment within the centrally planned economy, in both agriculture and industry.

The transition in Central and South-Eastern Europe to a market economy has dramatically undermined the formerly state-owned extractive, manufacturing and agricultural concerns that provided the main employment opportunities for most Roma/Gypsies in this region. The result has been widespread long-term structural unemployment and a deepening dependence on dwindling state benefits and services. Economic difficulties for Roma/Gypsies are exacerbated by slow economic recovery in some countries, coupled with the emergence of widening gaps between the more- and less-developed areas both within countries and between Northern Europe and South, East and Central Europe.

The importance of children

Within this wider context, the situation of Roma/Gypsy and Traveller children and young people is particularly important. Throughout Europe national populations are in greater or lesser decline, and there is growing concern about the implications of an increasingly ageing population. However, the age profile of Roma/Gypsy and Traveller communities diverges considerably from the national average in many states. A combination of higher fertility and lower life expectancy means that young people constitute a majority in most Roma/Gypsy communities and the percentage of Roma/Gypsies of school age is greater than that of the Roma/Gypsies as a whole within national populations. Addressing the educational disadvantages of Roma/Gypsy and Traveller children is therefore a matter of particular urgency in order, firstly, to ensure that a growing number of individuals can enjoy their human rights and equality of opportunity, secondly, to contribute to the development of Roma/Gypsy communities and cultures, and finally, to ensure the economic development and social cohesion of Europe and its individual countries.

In Western Europe the main challenge has been to connect mobile or socially isolated Roma/Gypsy and Traveller children to the education system. By contrast, in Central and Eastern Europe the vast majority of Roma/Gypsies are settled, with most children enrolled in primary school (although this is not necessarily the case in South-Eastern Europe). The question for many countries in Central and Eastern Europe is more one of the quality of education received rather than one of access. Currently about half of Roma/Gypsy and Traveller children in the EU never attend school, although the situation varies from country to country and between communities. In Central and Eastern Europe attendance rates (especially in primary school) are at least 50 per cent higher, although again with wide variations within the region.

A European issue

In spite of such huge diversities among Roma/Gypsy and Traveller communities across Europe, one feature is more or less ubiquitous: the persistence of prejudice and discrimination. This in turn reinforces their relative lack of success within mainstream institutions and processes and, in particular, in formal education. This focuses attention on the importance of tackling anti-Roma/Gypsy and Traveller prejudice. However, there are a variety of other factors that also affect the access of Roma/Gypsy and Traveller people to education. This demands that policy-makers be aware of the diversity that exists within the pan-European Roma/Gypsy and Traveller diaspora. This has proved particularly difficult to achieve, given the inherent tendency in all policy-making to over-simplify issues in order to make the policy-making task both manageable and cost-effective.

During the Cold War division of Europe, policy towards Roma/Gypsies was almost exclusively framed within national boundaries. Since 1990, there has been a dramatic increase in the levels of attention and in the number of initiatives focusing on Roma/Gypsies drawn up by supra-national European institutions. Their number is so great (and rapidly increasing) that the timeline (see pages 22 and 23) indicates only the main developments explicitly relating to or directly affecting Roma/Gypsies.

European institutions with a pan-European membership (Council of Europe, OSCE) have shown particular interest in Roma/Gypsies. To date, their activities have largely centred on information gathering, including the establishment of offices to provide continual monitoring and information exchange on Roma/Gypsy-related developments within individual countries. EU activity has been divided between the provision of ongoing support for initiatives aimed at improving the educational opportunities of Roma/Gypsy and Traveller children and voicing concerns about the human rights situation of Roma/Gypsies in candidate countries within negotiations on EU enlargement.

Table 1.2 Timeline of main European initiatives aimed at Roma/Gypsies and Travellers

1969	Council of Europe Recommendation 563 (1969) "On the Situation of Gypsies and other Travellers in Europe".
1975	Council of Europe Resolution (75)13 "Containing Recommendations on the Social Situation of Nomads in Europe".
1983	Council of Europe Recommendation R(83)1 "On Stateless Nomads and Nomads of Undetermined Nationality".
1984	Resolution C172/153 "On the Situation of Gypsies in the Community" was passed in the European Parliament. It recommended that national governments of member states co-ordinate their approach to the reception of Gypsies.
1987	EU Report "School provision for Gypsy and Traveller Children". The report was extended until 1989 to take account of new member states (Spain, Portugal, Greece). The full report was published as "School Provision for Ethnic Minorities: The Gypsy Paradigm" in 1998 (Interface Collection).
1989	EU Council Resolution No. 89/C 153/02 (No. C 153/3) "On School Provision for Gypsy and Traveller Children".
1991	Paris Charter for a New Europe (CSCE) – which made specific reference to the need to address the "particular problems" of Roma/Gypsies and also developed a framework of explicit minority rights.
1992	Office of High Commissioner on National Minorities established in the Conference on Security and Co-operation in Europe (CSCE) (since renamed the Organisation for Security and Co-operation in Europe – OSCE) with responsibility for monitoring and resolving potential ethnic conflicts. The High Commissioner has taken particular interest in the situation of Roma/Gypsies.
1992	Council of Europe European Charter for Regional or Minority Languages – provisions of which may be applied in respect of "non-territorial languages" such as Romani.
1993	High Commissioner on National Minorities (CSCE) first report on "Roma (Gypsies) in the CSCE region".
1993	Council of Europe Recommendation 1203 (1993) "On the Situation of Roma in Europe".
1993	Standing Conference of Local and Regional Authorities in Europe, Resolution 249 (1993) "On Gypsies in Europe: the Role and Responsibilities of Local and Regional Authorities".

More broadly, the OSCE and the Council of Europe have been active in developing the concept of minority rights and proactive engagement to encourage the preservation and promotion of distinctive minority languages, cultures and identities. The EU has concentrated more on anti-discrimination and equal opportunities measures. Overall, in the 1990s, there has been a significant increase of interest in issues of racism and inequality and a number of fora have emerged through which interested parties, including Roma/Gypsies and their organisations, can contribute to debate and policy-making at the European level.

Table 1.2 Timeline *continued*

1994	Appointment of a Co-ordinator of Activities on Roma/Gypsies, Directorate of Social and Economic Affairs – Council of Europe.
1995	Council of Europe – Framework Convention for the Protection of National Minorities – requiring states to develop a proactive approach to enabling minority communities to develop and promote their culture and identity.
1995	Specialist Group on Roma/Gypsies established in the European Committee on Migration (CDMG) – Council of Europe.
1996	Contact Point for Roma and Sinti Issues established in the Office for Democratic Institutions and Human Rights – OSCE. The Contact Point's role is to co-ordinate Roma/Gypsy-related initiatives within European institutions, to monitor relevant legislative and political developments in individual countries and to promote Roma/Gypsy self-organisation/representation.
1997	EU – Amsterdam Treaty, Article 13 of which provides the basis for the EU (and member states) to develop initiatives aimed at combating racial discrimination and promoting equal opportunities.
1997	Accession negotiation for membership of the EU opened with Poland, the Czech Republic, Slovakia, Hungary, Bulgaria, Romania and Slovenia. The situation of Roma/Gypsies is dealt with under Political Criteria, and the EU's annual "Opinions on Progress towards Accession" includes specific reference to the situation of Roma/Gypsy minorities in individual countries.
1998	EU – European Monitoring Centre on Racism and Xenophobia established to monitor development in race relations throughout Europe, publishing annual reports on each of the member states of the Council of Europe. Since its inception, it has taken a special interest in the situation of Roma/Gypsies.
1999	EU adopts "Guiding principles for improving the situation of Roma" in Candidate Countries that includes a large number of recommendations in the field of education.
2000	EU Race Directive 2000/43/EC, making provisions for equal treatment, regardless of ethnic origin, binding on member states.
2000	Second report by the High Commissioner on National Minorities (OSCE) "On the Situation of Roma and Sinti in the OSCE Area".

Information and policy-making

The way that Roma/Gypsies are viewed by policy-makers shapes how policy towards them is formed and implemented. The current lack of success of Roma/Gypsies and Travellers within mainstream educational systems reflects a long history of governments failing to adopt appropriate and effective policies towards Roma/Gypsies in general. This failure is rooted in the inability and, in most cases, the reluctance of policy-makers and decision-takers to fully appreciate the history, circumstances, aspirations and capabilities of Roma/Gypsy and Traveller people. There are few, if any, other population groups in Europe against which regular racist pronouncements and actions still pass largely unremarked. The tendency has been for

Roma/Gypsies to be seen as "the problem" rather than the key to the solution, and it is still unusual to come across acknowledgements that "the problem" could be the outcome of personal or institutional racism or well-meaning but ill-advised policies. The consequences of failed governmental initiatives have been deepening misunderstanding, fear and suspicion, contributing to the generation and reproduction of prejudice on both sides. The end result is frequently to apportion blame to Roma/Gypsy and Traveller people themselves for policies and practices that were derived without any consultation with, or involvement of, their end users.

Problems of accountability

Being aware of the reasons for past policy mistakes may help to avoid their repetition. In recent years this process has been greatly facilitated by the unprecedented degree of self-organisation displayed by Roma/Gypsy and Traveller people, and their desire to engage in decision-making processes that affect them. There are still significant obstacles to the development of reliable mechanisms of accountability between those who represent (especially at national and international levels) and those who are represented. Every activity in which Roma/Gypsies and Travellers come into contact with mainstream institutions (such as education) should have a basis of dialogue and consultation. It is increasingly recognised (at least in Central and Eastern Europe) that government policy cannot be implemented without the consent of Roma/Gypsy and Traveller people. Underpinning

this is the need to develop a dialogue that does not reinforce a Roma/Gypsy elite, but that reflects their diversity. The question is not only to what extent decision-takers invite and understand the views of Roma/Gypsies, but also to what extent they take into account these representations when decisions are made. It is important that supra-national institutions, governments, NGOs and other organisations are able to evaluate the growing data on Roma/Gypsies and their circumstances in order to avoid joining the long list of those who have failed to find an answer to the "Gypsy Question".

A "common European home"

The movement towards the greater internationalisation of Roma/Gypsy and Traveller policy began in 1984 with the passage in the European Parliament of Resolution C172/153 "On the Situation of Gypsies in the Community", which recommended that governments of member states co-ordinate their approach to the reception of Gypsies. The collapse of communism and the continuing process of EU enlargement have served to increase the diversity of legal instruments which can be deployed in relation to the education of Roma/Gypsy and Traveller children and young people. Indeed, the creation of a "common European home" could have particular significance for Roma/Gypsies. By making Roma/Gypsies and Travellers citizens of a multicultural Europe rather than minorities within nation states, they may finally be able to overcome some of the many problems they face. However, at the same time, the debate on EU enlargement has created scope for some national governments to seek to evade their responsibilities towards their Roma/Gypsy populations by portraying Roma/Gypsies as a stateless "European problem" for whom no national government need take responsibility.

The rights framework

In addition to the current context of changing policy approaches to Roma/Gypsies, this report is being compiled at a time when large-scale political changes in Europe are creating new fora and an enhanced role for the discourse on human rights. For much of the post-war period, international law and the domestic legislation of European states have dealt with the rights of ethnocultural minorities by guaranteeing their right not to be discriminated against. Policy affecting Roma/Gypsies – including education policy – was developed and implemented within individual states and is therefore subject to domestic political and cultural considerations. Since they had little political influence at this level, Roma/Gypsy and Traveller people and their interests were rarely taken into account.

European enlargement has strengthened the position of international agreements with regard to domestic legislation through the process of legal harmonisation. In addition, new bodies have been established to monitor political developments within states and to check compliance with international agreements. In 1993 the Parliamentary Assembly of the Council of Europe endorsed Recommendation 1203 "On the situation of Roma in Europe", which explicitly requested that governments

implement international agreements relating to Roma/Gypsies. Offices have been established within the Council of Europe (Specialist Group) and the OSCE (Contact Point) to monitor and advise on policy towards Roma/Gypsies against a rights background. Furthermore, the OSCE's High Commissioner on National Minorities has conducted two detailed investigations into the circumstances of Roma/Gypsies (1993 and 2000). In respect of post-communist states (many of which have large Roma/Gypsy populations), their aspirations to join the EU are conditioned by the Copenhagen Criteria, which demand the "stability of institutions guaranteeing democracy, the rule of law, human rights and respect for and protection of minorities".

Minority rights

As a result of these developments there are now accessible institutions, charged with collating data and facilitating good policy and practice across Europe, working to a more rights-oriented agenda. The process of Europeanisation also means that more Roma/Gypsies are able to promote their interests at a wide range of international fora and may seek remedies at the European Court of Human Rights.

A key change in the rights discourse has been the development of special rights for ethnocultural groups, known collectively as minority rights. The degree to which minority rights will evolve, and the extent of their application with regard to Roma/Gypsies, is a matter of conjecture and will be decided ultimately by how useful they are perceived to be in different local contexts and at

the regional (European) level. In 1991, minority rights achieved detailed expression in the Paris Charter (CSCE/OSCE). This was followed, in 1995, by the Council of Europe's Framework Convention for the Protection of National Minorities, which implicitly recognises minorities as collective entities with legal entitlements. Given the wider debates about Roma/Gypsies, and most recently Travellers, as ethnic minorities, minority rights have an important bearing on Roma/Gypsy and Traveller education.

The primary justification of minority rights lies in the acknowledgement that the right not to be discriminated against has not ended discrimination. Their justification also lies in the recognition that minorities possess certain characteristics that are not dealt with by anti-discrimination and often require additional institutional or legal support to maintain. Whereas anti-discrimination rights seek to make sure that members of minorities can access mainstream resources, services and individual remedies, minority rights focus on enabling the minority community to develop and reproduce itself as a distinct cultural community.

Extensive linguistic and cultural diversity and the wide variation in relationships with extra-communal institutions, societies and cultures that characterise Roma/Gypsy and Traveller communities pose fundamental challenges to the development of a distinct cultural community. However, it is precisely because the Roma/Gypsy diaspora exhibits diverse circumstances and needs that minority rights may well prove to be the most useful instrument in addressing a particular issue or situation.

Human rights

Human rights mechanisms have also dealt with rights for Roma/Gypsies and Travellers. The UN Commission on Human Rights, the UN Sub-Commission for the Promotion and Protection of Human Rights and its Working Group on Minorities are examples of fora where the issue of Roma/Gypsy rights have been made explicit. For example, in 1999 the Sub-Commission entrusted one of its members to prepare a working paper on the human rights problems and protection of Roma/Gypsies. In addition, the reports of the Special Rapporteur on Contemporary Forms of Racism, Racial Discrimination, Xenophobia and Related Intolerance have frequently referred to discrimination encountered by Roma/Gypsies and Travellers.

Child rights

Finally, the existence of the United Nations Convention on the Rights of the Child and its almost universal ratification by governments across the globe has helped to reduce the invisibility of children and establish their value in their own right. The establishment of formal mechanisms to monitor child rights and in particular the UN Committee on the Rights of the Child have been instrumental in holding countries to account on a number of issues, some of them specific to Roma/Gypsy and Traveller children.

A voice for Roma/Gypsies and Travellers

The development of appropriate and effective policy and other initiatives targeting Roma/Gypsy and Traveller education has been facilitated by improved channels of communication between Roma/Gypsy and Traveller people and mainstream society, resulting from the unprecedented growth in formal Roma/Gypsy self-organisation. Since 1970, five World Gypsy Congresses have been held, with a continually expanding number of affiliated organisations. Since 1979, the International Romany Union has enjoyed Consultative Status at the UN (enhanced in 1993). European institutions have proved less enthusiastic about supporting the establishment of a permanent representative body for Roma/Gypsies; however, the Specialist Group and the Contact Point (see page 15) encourage both national and international Roma/Gypsy and Traveller organisations to play a greater role in decision-making.

At the national level, the steady growth in the number of Roma/Gypsy and Traveller organisations in Western Europe since the 1960s has been enhanced by Roma/Gypsies in Central and South-Eastern Europe exploring new opportunities to adopt a public role with the development of civil society in this region and the end of one-party political systems. Roma/Gypsy and Traveller representation currently plays a mediator role, allowing Roma/Gypsy and Traveller people to transmit information up to Government as well as providing policy-makers with a means of disseminating information and explaining policy to Roma/Gypsy and Traveller communities. The balance in these relations varies according to the political context, ie, the degree of political authority that Roma/Gypsy and Traveller representation can command in any situation, and the extent to which policy-makers are interested in taking on board what Roma/Gypsies might have to say.

Decisions taken at local-government level often have direct significance for Roma/Gypsies and Travellers, especially in the field of education. Local authorities usually have the primary role in allocating resources and monitoring the quality of educational provision. As Roma/Gypsies and Travellers perceive the need to develop mechanisms for representing their view to local decision-makers, the response of authorities ranges from conflictual to co-opting. Roma self-organisation can also take cultural or religious forms and manifests itself within the activities of mainstream NGOs and other organisations. The development of Roma/Gypsy and Traveller media throughout Europe also provides means by which Roma/Gypsy and Traveller people and mainstream actors can establish a dialogue and aim for greater mutual understanding.

Finally, there are the Roma/Gypsy and Traveller individuals themselves, including children and young people. The arena of education is naturally favourable to identifying and establishing dialogue with those targeted by educational initiatives. In respect of education, it is particularly important to identify, understand and take account of the views of those most directly affected by education: children themselves.

Therefore, the Denied a Future? report includes many direct quotations from school pupils and other young people in which they explain their experiences and aspirations.

The diversity of Roma/Gypsies and Travellers, their long history and the continued pervasiveness of anti-Roma/Gypsy and Traveller prejudice means that governments and NGOs must be aware of the need to establish confidence in themselves and their activities among Roma/ Gypsy and Traveller communities. Such confidence is best achieved through the representatives of mainstream bodies demonstrating their ability to understand the concerns of Roma/Gypsy and Traveller people, including those of children, and to establish a consensus on how Roma/Gypsy and Traveller people can enjoy their educational and other rights.

2 Albania

"Until 1991, there were two kindergartens here in M. One of them was in the Roma/Gypsy neighbourhood. In 1991, when the local co-operative to which it belonged was closed, they simply closed the kindergarten too... the teachers who used to work there tried to reopen it for a year. The other kindergarten was threatened with the same fate, but the authorities found a solution to save it."

Primary-school teacher

"We would like a school nearby, but not one separated from *gadje*. We want an integrated school. We are against racial prejudice here."

Roma community leader

Summary

Context

Since 1990, Albania has experienced severe economic recession resulting in widespread impoverishment and the destruction of public buildings, including schools. Political instability has meant that the state has largely neglected the Roma population, exemplified by the absence of efforts to develop policy directed towards the Roma minority during the post-communist period.

Roma population

The situation of the Roma population is characterised by a dearth of reliable information. Official census figures (1989) put the Roma population at a little over 1,000 whilst NGOs claim between 100,000 and 120,000. Prior to 1945, Roma were nomadic, but many settled during the communist regime. Some communities migrate within the country and others travel abroad in search of seasonal work. There are at least four dialects of Romanes spoken in Albania. The small number of Roma organisations are operating primarily in relation with NGOs rather than pursuing an explicit political course.

Roma and education

Roma make up a high proportion of those not attending compulsory school. This is partly due to the non-registration of migrants, but also due to experiences of discrimination in school as well the declining accessibility of schools due to infrastructure decay. Very few Roma attend preschool classes, due to cost, problems of accessibility and the high rate of female unemployment. Officials appear unwilling to enforce compulsory education on Roma and can only levy fines, which are not a viable tool given the levels of poverty among Roma/Gypsies.

Language provision

In school, Roma pupils learn alongside non-Roma pupils. Despite constitutional and legal opportunities for Roma minority classes and Romani teaching, a lack of materials and teachers mean these have not been utilised.

Balance of NGO and government activity

To date, the main initiatives to help Roma children have been carried out by NGOs and include Romani summer camps, curriculum development and vocational-skills training for disadvantaged young people.

Albania report contents

Introduction – The Roma/Gypsy minority

Albania shares borders with the Federal Republic of Yugoslavia and Greece. It has a number of ethnic minorities, which mainly consist of: Greeks (by far the largest and found mainly in southern parts of Albania); Roma (some who are settled and some who are semi-nomadic); Egyptians (who claim Egyptian origins and are referred to as *Gjupci, Egjupci, Jupci, Ejupci* and *Ojupci*); and a small group of Macedonians who live in a cluster of fewer than 15 villages in the east. Other minorities include Montenegrin, Jewish and Armenian groups.

Although it is recognised that Roma and Egyptians[1] have been in Albania for many centuries, it is difficult to estimate when they first began to arrive. Before WWII, Roma in Albania were largely nomadic. The effects of communism and a number of other factors forced most of them to settle in various parts of the country. Roma form several distinct groups and, according to some scholars, can be grouped into a number of Romani dialectal divisions.[2] The Egyptian minority speaks the language of the surrounding population – Albanian. They are predominantly endogamous and are a settled population with no history of nomadism, mainly living in central or market parts of cities and villages.[3]

The 1989 census figures indicate that there were approximately 1,300 Roma (including Egyptians) living in Albania, although most people consider this to be a gross underestimate. Some people report that there are as many as 100,000 Roma alone in Albania. According to Roma NGOs established in Tirana in the early 1990s, the overall number of Roma living in Albania is even higher at 120,000. These sources also claim that over half of the Roma population is under 18 years of age.

Although there is no legislated discrimination against the Roma/Gypsy minority in Albania, it is generally accepted that in practice racial discrimination against these groups can be found in most aspects of everyday life. Evidence of discrimination in formal schooling is discussed later in this report. Although Roma/Gypsy and non-Roma/Gypsy communities engage with each other on a number of levels, such as in commerce and the exchange of goods, both Roma and Egyptian communities generally live separately from the majority society.

International legislation

The Albanian government has not yet presented an initial or periodical report on the implementation of its obligations under the various Conventions. For example, Albania ratified the Convention on the Rights of the Child (CRC) in 1992. Article 44 of the Convention provides that, within two years of ratification, the State Parties must submit a report to the Committee on the Rights of the Child, indicating the progress made towards implementation. Further reporting is required after five years. At the end of 1997 the Albanian government nominated a commission to draft the first periodic report on the CRC. However, at the time of writing the report had not yet been submitted.

Further to the ratification of the CRC by the Albanian government, new legislation for the protection of children's rights was expected. A draft law on children's rights was prepared by the Children's Rights Centre of Albania (CRCA), with funding from the EU. This draft has been submitted for the attention of some MPs because NGOs are entitled to present draft legislation. However, this draft is still being discussed by the parliament's Preparatory Commission.[4] Article 18 of the Draft Law states that the government has an obligation to protect and develop children's education in public and private schools.[5] Furthermore, it should ensure the construction of new schools, the development of school curricula and teacher training. In addition, the Draft Law provides for the establishment of a Commissioner for Children's Rights.[6]

Article 5 of the Albanian Constitution, adopted on 21 October 1998, provides that the Republic of Albania shall apply those international laws that are binding upon it. Article 122 of the Constitution states that, after its publication in the Official Journal, any ratified international agreement constitutes part of the internal legal system. International agreements are directly applicable in the internal legal system, except when they are not self-executing. They are not self-executing when the adoption of further legislation is required. Furthermore, the second paragraph of this Article states that an international agreement ratified by law has priority over laws of the country that are incompatible with it.

Minority rights

Article 18 of the Albanian Constitution guarantees equality for all its citizens before the law free from discrimination. It gives a comprehensive list of criteria including gender, race, ethnicity, language, political and religious affiliation, income and social status. Article 20 of the Albanian Constitution provides that:

1 *Persons who belong to national minorities exercise in full equality before the law their human rights and freedoms.*
2 *They have the right to freely express, without prohibition or compulsion, their ethnic, cultural, religious and linguistic belonging. They have the right to preserve and develop it, to study and to be taught in their mother tongue, as well as unite in organisations and associations for the protection of their interests and identity.*

Different levels of attention have been given to the educational needs of these populations. For example, the Council of Ministers Decision No. 502 of 5 August 1996 stipulates that in the cities of Saranda, Delvine and Gjirokastra, parents from the Greek minority can request school units for their children in order to learn in their mother tongue. Instruction No. 12 of 13 August 1996 of the Ministry of Education and Sport (MES) sets out the details of this provision in these three cities. It was decided that in one existing primary school there should be a Greek-language class for Greek-minority children. Order No. 83 of 16 December 1998 further stipulates that upon demand from members of Greek and Macedonian minorities, subjects such as the history of Greece and Macedonia may be added to the curriculum.

The Council of Ministers Decision No. 396 of 22 August 1994 deals more generally with elementary education for minorities. It stipulates that individuals belonging to minority groups have the right to be taught in their own language, according to plans and programmes determined by the Ministry of Education. This decision regulates the procedure for setting up school units for minority languages. The process is initiated by a request from the minority group, which is then examined by the Ministry of Education and the relevant mayor. The establishment of such units is granted only if certain criteria are met, such as a specific number of children from the minority. In addition to this, the Decision of the Ministry of Education No. 14 of 3 September 1994 regulates in which language subjects will be taught and exams held, ie, Albanian or the minority language.

The right to education

Article 57 of the Constitution provides that everyone has the right to education. It states that compulsory education is determined by law; that general high-school public education is open to all; and that professional high-school education and higher education are conditional upon merit alone. Article 57 also guarantees that compulsory education and general high-school education in public schools are free of charge. The Constitution also protects the right of students at all levels to be educated in private schools, which must operate according to the relevant legislation.

Article 10 of the Law on the Pre-University Education System, No. 7952 of 21 June 1995, provides that national minorities are entitled to learn in their own language and about their history and culture. Such subjects should be included in mainstream teaching plans and programmes. Article 10 also states that facilities must be created for national minorities to learn the Albanian language, history and culture. The last paragraph of Article 10 states that education for minorities is to be carried out in schools and specific education institutions, which must function according to particular procedures determined by the Council of Ministers. However, it seems that there is no specific budget law to implement this article. The National Budget Law allocates funds to the MES, which is then responsible for distributing them according to its priorities.

The Pre-University Education Law regulates the whole education system. Article 19 establishes that registration of children aged between three and six in kindergartens is optional. In terms of basic schooling, however, Article 24 states that it is compulsory and Article 59 provides for sanctions in case of violations. Article 22 sets out the structure of basic schooling. It states that basic schooling is made up of two levels: primary (from first to fourth grade) and advanced (from fifth to eighth grade), lasting eight years in total. Those students aged 16 years who have not yet completed basic schooling can attend either full time or part time. Pupils have the option after the eighth grade of continuing onto further education.

Article 25 provides that birth and vaccination certificates must accompany the registration of children in basic school. Articles 26 to 29 contain the general principles of the medium school, which is equivalent to secondary school. This is made up of high school and vocational training, both of which are regulated by the Pre-University Education Law.

Chapter 3 of this Law deals with Special Public Education, which is provided for children with a physical, mental or emotional disability. It is not clear what is meant by "emotional disability", nor what form it may take. Special education is free of charge and depends on the consent of parents. Paragraph 2 provides for the establishment of special classes and institutions for those children with specific needs that cannot be met by the

mainstream school system. The Council of Ministers is responsible for deciding the criteria for diagnosing children with special needs.

Although various institutions in the governmental structure are responsible for education matters, MES is the central institution charged with the management of education. The Parliamentary Commission on Culture and Education is the key legislative body responsible for education matters. A National Commission on Education is the formal advisory body to the Minister of Education. The Institute for Pedagogical Studies forms a unit within the MES and provides technical support and advice. It is responsible for curriculum development, evaluation, education research and analysis, and staff development. It can also make recommendations to the MES on various programmes and policy issues. There are seven University-based teacher-education programmes and training institutions that provide pre-service training for most Albanian primary- and secondary-school teachers.

In the 37 districts and municipalities of Albania, Local Education Authorities (LEAs) are particularly important mid-level institutions with primary responsibility for:
- monitoring and evaluation (including inspection and supervision)
- the allocation of financial and staff resources
- the execution of directives from the MES.

Moreover, they have recently been made responsible for in-service teacher training. Various *ad hoc* working groups assist the LEAs in their efforts. Each district and municipality has a functioning Commission for Social and Cultural Problems as an entity of its legislative body. These Commissions are responsible for overseeing educational matters, and are the local-government agencies that debate and recommend allocations from the local budget. They are also entitled to inquire into education programmes and management. Finally, school directors are responsible for implementing programmes, staff deployment and evaluation, and financial management in each school.

Preschool

Albania entered the transition period with a satisfactory level of education according to the per-capita income level. This was a reflection of the priority accorded this sector by the communist regime. However, the education system developed under the communist regime has not fitted well with market reform. Consequently, school enrolment has been falling, and public investment in the sector has been insufficient to effectively address children's right to education. The most affected educational institutions have been preschools. Data from MES show that before 1999 there were 3,426 daycare schools across Albania, and that since then this number has dropped to 2,330. There are a number of reasons for this decline in the number of preschools. One main reason is simply the closing down of many daycare centres in cities and villages which, as part of the civil unrest associated with the collapse of the communist regime, took place between 1990 and 1992. During this period, 5,330 school buildings were destroyed or damaged. Those school buildings that have remained are often in very bad condition, with no heating or windows. Many schools simply do not function during the winter.[7]

Preschool attendance has also fallen by over a third, from 58 per cent in 1990 to 35 per cent in 1997. The extremely poor physical conditions and the lack of materials and teacher training are certainly important factors to consider. The high level of unemployment, especially among females, is also seen as a contributing factor. Families have to pay a considerable amount of money to register their children at preschool, and in schools where children receive lunch the fees may be higher. Many families simply cannot afford such fees. Many mothers who have lost their jobs during the transition prefer to keep their children at home. Attendance is further undermined by a fear felt by many parents of their daughters being abducted for trafficking abroad. As highlighted in a Save the Children report *Child Trafficking in Albania*, there has been a dramatic decrease in the number of girls over the age of 14 years attending high school. Research carried out for the report revealed that in some areas, both north and south, where pupils have to walk for over an hour to get to school as many as 90 per cent of girls no longer attend high-school education. Although research into this area is just beginning, it does appear that Roma/Gypsy children are most susceptible. According to the Albanian NGO *Ndihmë për Fëmijët* (Help for Children), most children trafficked to Greece for forced labour are Roma/Gypsies.[8]

According to the MES, the overall number of children in preschool is 75,371. More children attend nurseries in rural areas (around 42,353) than in urban areas (around 33,018). While it was estimated that 27 per cent (8,836) of the latter are provided with food, very few children, if any, receive this service in rural areas.

Primary school

In 1990, according to official statistics, all children aged from six to fourteen years attended school. By 1997, primary school enrolment had fallen to 94 per cent. To what extent the decline in enrolment is a result of recent internal and international migration, or of an increase in drop-out rates, is still to be determined. However, it seems that migration is one of the main reasons for children not attending school. The Institute of Pedagogical Studies estimates that only seven per cent of those who migrate within the country enrol in schools in the new area of residence.

The completion rate for primary school was only 66.3 per cent in the school year 1993-94. In 1996-97 the number of children who completed the eight-grade compulsory cycle represented 71.2 per cent of those who enrolled for the first time in the first grade. As well as problems of migration and dropping out, many primary-school buildings (as with preschool buildings) were destroyed between 1990 and 1992 and have yet to be rebuilt.

In practice

The right to education for Roma/Gypsy children

Currently, there are no accurate data to determine to what extent Roma and Egyptian children aged seven upwards attend compulsory education.[9] However, according to *Amaro Drom*, an NGO working on Roma issues, it is clear that the number of illiterate Roma children is increasing, indicating that Roma children are not benefiting to the same degree as other children from the education system.

School abandonment and dropping out

Most Roma/Gypsy children study in mainstream public schools together with non-Roma/Gypsy children. However, the numbers of children dropping out of school have risen gradually in recent years, and for Roma/Gypsy children this rise has been particularly steep. It is estimated that only one to two per cent of Roma/Gypsy children attend pre-school education. Article 59 of the Law on Pre-University Education provides for sanctions against parents who do not send their children to school. However, it seems that this provision has never been applied by courts or other state institutions, on the basis that families cannot afford to pay such fines.

The reasons for the high drop-out rates among Roma/Gypsies are numerous. Not the least important is the extremely poor condition of schools. There are also reasons specific to the situation of Roma/Gypsy children. Anti-Roma/Gypsy bullying is common among pupils and according to *Amaro Drom*, an NGO working with Roma/Gypsies, there are also examples of teachers being discriminatory against Roma/Gypsy children. Many Roma/Gypsy children are separated from their classmates, for example, by being made to sit at the back of the classroom. The European Roma Rights Centre (ERRC) has reported further examples of discriminatory practices in relation to the education of Roma/Gypsy children in Albania. In a town near Korce in south-eastern Albania, a Romani woman told the ERRC:

"In school, Roma kids are treated differently from the others now. Two years ago, when my daughter L was eight years old, she had some problems in school. She was not a very good pupil, but instead of helping her, they sent her home. She was no longer accepted. They do not try to teach our kids... Now my daughter does not want to go back to school. She is afraid of the other children and does not trust the teacher. The other kids in her class used to beat her sometimes and call her 'dirty Gypsy'. She was the only Romani kid in her class."[10]

The woman's father said that his brother's two children had dropped out of school for the same reasons. He thought that a separate school for Roma/Gypsies in Maliq was the only solution to their problem.

In Berat, the school is only 200 metres away from the ghetto-like settlement to which the Roma/Gypsies in this town have been forced to move. The majority of Roma/Gypsy children do not attend school here either, however, because they have strongly negative associations with schools, teachers and other children. Forty-year-old AX, mother of 12 children, explained:

"Most *gadje* [non-Roma] are good when they are young, but as they grow up, they change, and their hearts turn to stone. There are some *gadje* kids who come here to play with our children, but then again, not all kids are good. In school, our kids have been beaten up and now they are afraid to go to school. Some of the children here go to school, but most of them have stopped."

In May 1996, in Tirana, nine-year-old VD was expelled from school one month before the end of the school year because he went to school without his exercise book. He said that the day before he had quarrelled with his younger sister because she wanted to play with the exercise book, and that their mother had solved the fight by throwing away the exercise book.

Mrs MR, a primary school teacher of Roma origin in a community approximately 5km from Berat, explained:

> "In M, Roma/Gypsies constitute around four per cent of the population. Despite the fact that there are about 400 children here who should be in school, only about 250 of them attend school. This means that most of the Roma/Gypsies are not in school. Younger Roma/Gypsy children of kindergarten age also stay at home. Until 1991, there were two kindergartens here in M. One of them was in the Roma/Gypsy neighbourhood. In 1991, when the local co-operative to which it belonged was closed, they simply closed the kindergarten too. The state did not do anything to ensure its continuity, despite the fact that the teachers who used to work there tried to reopen it for a year. The other kindergarten was threatened with the same fate, but the authorities found a solution to save it. The problem now is that this one remaining kindergarten is too far away from the Roma/Gypsy settlement. Also, there are just too many children here for only one kindergarten."

The situation in the community of LA in Fier in southern Albania is typical. Parents are reluctant to send their children to school since several of them have been beaten by other pupils. They also complain about the long distance (3km) to the nearest school, and that they were afraid of their children being hit by cars or trains on their way to school. HZ, head of the LA community, said that although the community of Baltez – one of the other large Roma/Gypsy communities around Fier – has its own Roma/Gypsy school, they do not want this arrangement at LA:

> "We would like a school nearby, but not one separated from *gadje*. We want an integrated school. We are against racial prejudice here."

In a community on the outskirts of Gjirokaster, children missed school because, as residents explained, every year the entire community leaves for Greece from April to October to take on seasonal work such as picking tomatoes and oranges. Similarly, in a south-eastern community near Korce, 16-year-old KD dropped out of school after the fourth grade because he preferred to work with horses, a traditional Roma/Gypsy practice. However, his seven-year-old sister A said she liked school and did not want to stop going.

Despite legal mandate, local authorities responsible for educational issues do not seem to have taken firm steps to fight the ever-increasing drop-out rate of Roma/Gypsy children from school. Local authorities defend their passivity by arguing that, "Roma do not want to send their kids to school, so why should we force them?" The Mayor of FK, at the time, explained his response to the high level of non-attendance by Roma/Gypsy children in his school district in the following terms: "I could fine them, but they are too poor to pay the fines, so there is not much I can do."

Language provision

In terms of minority language provision, Greek-minority children may be educated in their mother tongue regardless of their place of residence. In addition, the Greek government has funded some education support for students and for teacher training. Students of Macedonian descent – an extremely small group – receive modest assistance from the Macedonian government to support their education and cultural needs. According to Article 10 of the Law on Pre-University Education, Roma/Gypsy children should have the right to learn their own language, history and culture; however, Roma/Gypsies, although representing a larger proportion of the population, do not receive any such support. They do not receive any education in their own language, or on their own history or culture. According to Mina Qirici of *Amaro Dives* – an organisation working on Roma/Gypsy issues:

> "It is very difficult to establish schools for Roma children because there are no books, no teachers who know the Romani language, and few Roma know how to write in their language. So it is not possible to find teachers for Roma schools."

For all three groups, little is known about their curricula or about their special learning needs. While changes have been made in the Social Studies and Civics curriculum to emphasise democratic values, little attention has been given to addressing tolerance and respect for diversity in the context of ethnic difference. Furthermore, within the MES there is no one specifically responsible for the education of national ethnic minorities.[11]

It is alleged that so far the Albanian government has made no effort to establish policies for the development of Roma/Gypsy communities in Albania. It seems there are no plans or other measures for the protection of Roma/Gypsy children.[12] The government may be supportive of some isolated activity, but it does not normally initiate anything to ameliorate the problems of Roma/Gypsy children. Education of these children does not yet seem to be a government priority.

NGO practice in the area

In the village of Baltëz, close to Fier, a local Roma/Gypsy established a summer school for Roma/Gypsy children aimed specifically at teaching the Romani language and history. Thirty children currently attend. A summer school for some 100 Roma/Gypsy children based along similar lines was also set up in the small town of Fushë-Krujë, 25km from Tirana. This was developed by a Roma/Gypsy teacher. In 1999, *Amaro Drom* also set up a summer school, which was attended by 30 Roma/Gypsy children.

The Open Society Foundation (OSF) has also been active in Albania. It established a programme designed to assist NGOs working on Roma/Gypsy issues in Albania, as it has in other countries in Central and Eastern Europe. At the time of writing, the annual budget for this programme ranged from US$25,000 to US$30,000. One such NGO funded by OSF is the Albanian Education Development Project (AEDP). This is a long-term project working on the education of Roma/Gypsy children. Its activities include conducting research, introducing multicultural curricula, training teachers who teach Roma/Gypsy students and establishing resource centres in some schools for the Roma/Gypsy community. As part of its research programme, AEDP has distributed questionnaires to Roma/Gypsy and non-Roma/Gypsy teachers, students and others. It has also conducted structured and semi-structured interviews in order to gather background information on the education of Roma/Gypsy children. In partnership with Roma/Gypsy organisations, AEDP has visited several districts where large Roma/Gypsy communities live.

AEDP has also initiated teacher training in the Tirana area. Together with the Institute for Pedagogical Research, it has started revising curricula in order to include Roma/Gypsy history and culture. AEDP will submit its proposal to the Ministry of Education. Finally, AEDP recently opened a community centre in the Bairam Curri school, where most of the pupils are Roma/Gypsy children. They are now planning a calendar of activities there, with the involvement of the community. On 26 and 27 November 1999, AEDP organised a national workshop on the education of Roma/Gypsy children, in which teachers, head teachers, local education inspectors, Roma/Gypsy parents and representatives of Roma/Gypsy associations participated. The workshop emphasised that education is the key mechanism for integrating marginalised groups in society. The participants' evaluation of the workshop – the first in Albania – was very positive. For the first time, teachers were given useful information related to Roma/Gypsies.

The Save the Children Alliance also plans to develop work in the area of integrated education. It plans to work in Diber, a district in the north-eastern part of Albania, and Korca in a south-eastern district. Roma/Gypsy populations are particularly numerous in the latter district, and will therefore play a major part in the project. An internal strategy workshop is scheduled for July 2001, during which such plans will be made more concrete.

Another positive experience is that of the *Fondacioni Ndihme per Femijet* in Korcia (southern Albania), which has been running two education projects in three towns – Korcia, Elbasan and Berat. The projects target children who are disadvantaged for socio-economic reasons. Most of them are Roma/Gypsies: 80 per cent in the first project and 60 per cent in the second. The first project is aimed at children aged from 12 to 16 years, who have not attended school regularly because they have dropped out, mostly for socio-economic reasons. It offers general classes to help children fill in the gap, and additional classes which support the children by building up the relationship between the school and their families. These children also follow vocational training classes (hairdressing, mechanics, carpentry, for example) with local people. However, children do not attend vocational courses in all towns, because it is not always easy to find specialised staff locally, and some families do not allow children to go very far from the area where they live.

This project holds two classes, each of 25 children, in each of the three towns where it operates. Each class has two teachers, who are

paid from the project's budget, which is funded by the Swiss government. The vocational trainers are paid from the same budget. The project started in 1998 and was expected to terminate in July 2000. Depending on their circumstances, families who have continued to send their children to the classes will be allowed to receive food aid. All children receive school materials and clothes free of charge. The project has been very successful so far, with only three children dropping out: two left for Greece and one girl got married. It was reported that the children who went to Greece were taken by trafficking gangs. The project manager went there to learn their whereabouts and to bring them back. The most difficult period is the spring, when families start travelling. To counteract this, it has been necessary to explain to them the importance of their children's regular attendance at school.

UNICEF and Care have funded a number of summer camps during which children go on excursions and prepare for the following school year.

The second project, funded by UNICEF, is aimed at children aged 6 to 12 who have dropped out of school, or who are at risk of dropping out and do not attend regularly for socio-economic reasons. These children receive extra support from teachers in mainstream schools through additional courses held for them. This project also grants food aid to families that send their children to school, as well as school materials and clothes. In addition, project staff and teachers visit the families regularly, offering advice on babycare and providing financial assistance for family planning and other essentials (a stove, a heater, the making of a door, for example). A hundred children in each town are involved in this project. The success rate so far has been 80 per cent.

In the early stages these projects experienced problems concerning the lack of information about the children. Because of overcrowding and subtle discrimination, head teachers and teachers would not recognise that there are children who do not attend school. The projects have not enjoyed government support. In some cases the relationship with the Director of Education at the local level is very difficult. The Albanian government does not seem to be committed to tackling these children's problems effectively, nor to including positive experiences, like these projects, in its national policy.

Recommendations

Given that Albania has ratified:
- the International Covenant on Civil and Political Rights (ratified 4 October 1991, entered into force 4 January 1992)
- the International Covenant on Economic, Social and Cultural Rights (ratified 4 October 1991, entered into force 4 January 1992)
- the International Convention on the Elimination of All Forms of Racial Discrimination (ratified 11 May 1994, entered into force 10 June 1994)
- the Convention on the Rights of the Child (ratified 27 February 1992, entered into force 28 March 1992)
- the UNESCO Convention against Discrimination in Education (However, Albania did not ratify the Protocol, instituting a Conciliation and Good Offices Commission to be responsible for seeking the settlement of any dispute which may arise between States Parties to the Convention against Discrimination in Education.)
- the European Convention for the Protection of Human Rights and Fundamental Freedoms (ratified 2 October 1996, entered into force the same day)
- the First Protocol to the European Convention on Human Rights and Fundamental Freedoms (ratified 2 October 1996, entered into force the same day)
- the Framework Convention for the Protection of National Minorities (ratified 28 September 1999, entered into force 1 January 2000; ratification published in the Official Journal, *Fletorja Zyrtare*, on 3 June 1999 (Issue No. 21, Law No. 8496))

Save the Children recommends that:

The Government of Albania

- Submits its first report to the Committee on the Rights of the Child, highlighting the educational problems particularly in relation to Roma/Gypsy children.
- Invites the Special Rapporteur on the Right to Education to conduct a field mission in order to assess the shortcomings of the Albanian education system, in particular with regard to the right to education of Roma/Gypsy children.
- Produces sound statistics on Roma/Gypsies, including educational data on access of Roma/Gypsy children to school, and on their attainment.
- Supports morally and financially those projects which have so far demonstrated a positive outcome and could be included in a national policy plan for implementing the right to education of Roma/Gypsy children.
- Addresses related problems, such as child labour, parents' employment and living conditions, which inevitably affect the equal access of Roma/Gypsy children to their right to education.

The Albanian NGOs

- Actively engage in and monitor the reporting process of the government to the Committee on the Rights of the Child and any other international obligation.

The international organisations, including the UN Commission on Human Rights, the Special Rapporteur on the Right to Education and the Special Rapporteur on Contemporary Forms of Racism, Racial Discrimination, Xenophobia and Related Intolerance, and the European Union

- Closely monitor the international obligations undertaken by the Albanian government in respect of the right to education with particular attention to the right to education of Roma/Gypsy children.
- Strongly encourage the Albanian government to comply with its international reporting obligations under the main international human rights instruments, taking into consideration children's rights, and including information on children from ethnic minorities.

Albania: Notes on the text

1 "Roma/Gypsy" is used to refer to both the Roma and Egyptian populations in Albania. Where we wish to refer to just Roma, then 'Roma' is used.

2 Human Rights Watch/Helsinki, *Human Rights in Post-Communist Albania*, March 1996.

3 Elena Marushiakova and Vesselin Popov, *Identity Formation among Minorities in the Balkans: the cases of Roms, Egyptians and Ashkali in Kosovo*, Minority Studies Society Studii Romani, Sofia, 2000.

4 A. Hazizaj, "A New Law for the Protection of Children's Rights in Albania", in CRCA *Revista*, No. 3, January 1999, pp. 58-63.

5 For a copy of the Draft Law see CRCA *Bulletin* No. 4, May 1999, pp. 77-90.

6 It is worth noting that a law establishing an Ombudsperson for Human Rights has been adopted and that the Ombudsperson has now been nominated and is operational.

7 UNICEF, *Children's Situation in Albania*, 1999.

8 Daniel Renton, *Child Trafficking in Albania*, Save the Children, March 2001.

9 Dr M. Gjokutaj, "The Needs of Roma Children for Education", in *Se Bashku*, AEDP Newsletter, 1999, pp. 18–24.

10 See ERRC. "No record of the case. Roma in Albania", *Country Reports*, No. 5, June 1997, p. 65.

11 This information has been drawn from the paper "An Education Development Strategy for Albania" of the Albanian Education Development Project (AEDP), 1999.

12 This information has been drawn from the report entitled *The Forgotten Children*, 1999, by the Children's Human Rights Centre of Albania; a local partner of Save the Children Alliance.

3 Bosnia and Herzegovina

"I wanted to go to school this year too, but I have to take care of my sister. She is eight and cannot walk. Mother works at the market, and my sister Z got married. I know how to read and write. It was nice to go to school. The teacher was good."

Roma girl, 11 years old

"My son will continue attending school even when I do not have the bread to eat. He rides a bicycle to school now. It is 6km to get there. But how will he go in the winter? It gets dark early in the afternoon... I am afraid for him."

Roma mother

Summary

Context
The state of Bosnia and Herzegovina (BiH) was born in a war during which it is estimated up to a quarter of a million people died (from a pre-war population of 4.4m), with many more people displaced, either internally or abroad. Following the Dayton Agreement, the state has been effectively divided between the Federation of Bosnia and Herzegovina (FBiH) and the Republic of Srpska (RS). Roma are not explicitly recognised in the state's Constitution or considered a "constituent people" in either of the Entities, which effectively precludes Roma engagement in public life or enjoyment of minority rights. In recent years a number of Roma organisations have emerged, mainly in FBiH. Before the war almost 9,000 people declared themselves to be Roma, yet other estimates put the Roma population up to 80,000. During the war, in addition to those killed, there was considerable displacement within the country (including between the two Entities) and abroad. However, Roma still constitute the country's largest ethnic minority.

Roma population
These events mean that it is difficult to obtain accurate information about the Roma population. In FBiH many Roma are still nomadic, but many are well integrated with majority communities. Most speak Romanes.

Majority nationalism and widespread impoverishment have strengthened the marginalisation of Roma and reduced living standards. The Roma population of RS is smaller than in FBiH and divided along religious lines as well as between long-standing residents and refugees from the Bosnian and wider conflicts. The lives of many Roma are shaped by coping with the dislocation and material destruction caused by war.

Roma and education

It is equally difficult to obtain accurate information on the educational circumstances of Roma, and there is considerable complexity in respect of educational provision and authority. While the central state applies international agreements, responsibility for educational provision is handled by the two Entities (and subdivisions within them). In FBiH different curricula apply in areas with Bosniak and Croat majorities, and responsibility for education is exercised at either canton or municipal level depending on the ethnic composition of the locality. Authorities apply different rules in respect of language, alphabet and religion used in schools. There are differences in the applicability of rights to education between authorities, there are no Roma classes, and there is no teaching in Romanes. In RS, education policy is consistent across the Entity as it is handled at Entity level.

The low social status of Roma across BiH is reflected in bullying in school. Educational statistics do not include Roma ethnicity, but surveys show high levels of illiteracy (23 per cent of households in BiH). Preschool and primary-school attendance in FBiH is low and there is practically no attendance at secondary and tertiary levels. In RS, practically no Roma attend preschool. Though Roma primary-school attendance is unknown, it is recognised that few complete this level of education and thus Roma participation in secondary and higher education is negligible. Roma were over-represented in special schools before the war, but this no longer appears to be the case.

Balance of NGO and government activity

NGO and community groups have been active in terms of establishing preparatory classes, for example, in the Tuzla and Sarajevo Cantons. More recently, a Step-by-Step programme has been introduced for Romani children in FBiH. National and international NGOs have also set up projects aimed at integrating children with disabilities into mainstream schools.

Bosnia and Herzegovina report contents

Introduction

Bosnia and Herzegovina (BiH) is a country still coming to terms with its recent conflict. Children have been affected more than most and are struggling to survive in a post-war environment. They are faced with a multitude of problems related to, for example, internal displacement, returning after having been a refugee and high unemployment, in particular of parents and other care-givers. These difficulties are compounded by a weak infrastructure and a state of transition within education systems and youth services more generally. The multiple layers of government that lack a clear hierarchy in terms of areas of responsibility and the constitutional inequalities of people within each Entity of Bosnia and Herzegovina further undermine the overall situation.[1a] In addition to these problems there are those specific to Romani children, contributing to their low levels of participation in the education system.[1b] These include poverty, irrelevance of mainstream education, discrimination and harassment at school, mistrust of government, travelling culture, war and displacement, language, cultural beliefs and practices, and a lack of educated leaders or role models.

BiH is bordered on the north, west and south by Croatia, on the east and south-east by the Yugoslav republics of Serbia and Montenegro and on the south-west by the Adriatic Sea. BiH is one of five states created after the dissolution of Yugoslavia in 1991, declaring its sovereignty in October 1991. It held a referendum for independence from Yugoslavia in 1992. This was one of the factors that sparked the war in BiH, when those who sought to maintain the republic

within Yugoslavia responded with armed resistance. In March 1994, Bosnian Croats and Bosniaks united to create the joint Bosniak/Croat Federation of Bosnia and Herzegovina, thereby reducing the number of parties to the conflict in BiH to two. In November 1995, the warring factions signed a peace agreement in Dayton, Ohio, which brought the conflict to an end. The effects of the conflict – which, at the time of writing, ended a mere five years ago – were devastating for the people of BiH. Over two million people, slightly more than half of the population, left their homes, being displaced internally or seeking refuge outside the country. It has been reported that as many as 250,000 were killed or are missing. Children lost their parents, friends, teachers and homes.

The two Entities of BiH

BiH obtained its present state structure through the Dayton Peace Agreement of 1995. The agreement divided BiH into two territorial - administrative units known as "Entities", namely

the Federation of Bosnia and Herzegovina (the Federation – FBiH) and the Serb Republic (Republika Srpska – RS).[2] The Dayton Agreement has resulted in BiH having a complicated state structure within which the two Entities have a high level of autonomy in the performance of the functions of the state authorities. Article III of the Constitution of BiH grants the central state legislative power over a number of areas including foreign policy and inter-Entity transportation. Any area not expressly assigned to the central state authorities, such as education, is devolved to the Entities. However, the Constitution of BiH makes a number of international legal instruments directly applicable in BiH. Those instruments contain obligations in areas other than those expressly assigned to the central state. The consequence of this is that the central state has the ability to implement international obligations only for those areas within its responsibility. Although it retains responsibility over international obligations in other areas, it has no enforcement mechanism to ensure implementation of those obligations.

The organisation of state authority differs markedly between FBiH and RS. Power is decentralised within FBiH according to the Constitution of the Federation of Bosnia and Herzegovina, but this decentralisation is inconsistently implemented as it is based on the dominating position of cantons (the federal units of FBiH) and the vague and uncertain position of municipalities. There are four vertical levels of functioning of the authorities: the respective levels of municipality, town, canton and the federation, in ascending order. As will be shown, this creates a great deal of confusion and inconsistency. By contrast, the Constitution of Republika Srpska contains only two functional levels of authority, at municipality and Entity level.

As a result of this new framework, public administration in BiH functions on three levels: the central state, the Entities (FBiH and RS) and various local levels within the Entities. The myriad of institutions, each with differing levels of power, leaves administrators and citizens alike confused as to which institution has the power to perform which function.[3] When considering the implementation and realisation of human rights, it is not sufficient simply to refer to law and practice in BiH. Rather, we need to consider all levels of government in BiH and how they interact. This underlying complexity, together with the post-conflict difficulties of reconciliation and reconstruction, must form the basis for any analysis of BiH, especially with regard to the issue of the right to education of Romani children.

The Roma population in Bosnia and Herzegovina

Demography

Official data on the number of Roma in BiH is only available for the years before the war, as the last census was conducted in 1991. As noted, during the war, many people were forced to leave their houses and were either internally displaced or left the country entirely. While there have been returns, it is impossible to know precisely how many people returned to where they had been living before the war. Therefore, while the 1991 statistics may be indicative of the position of Roma in BiH generally – although this is in itself by no means certain – it cannot give an accurate idea of the distribution of the population between FBiH and RS since the war.

When the 1991 census was conducted, 4,377,033 citizens were registered in Bosnia and Herzegovina, during which citizens also declared their nationality/ethnicity (*nacionalna pripadnost*). On this question, 35,670 citizens were registered as those whose nationality/ethnicity was unknown, 17,592 were "others", 14,585 did not declare themselves as members of a specific ethnic group and 8,864 citizens declared themselves to be Roma. The following table compiles data from censuses conducted between 1961 and 1991 in relation to persons with permanent residence in BiH. Statistics for "unknown", "other" or "undeclared" nationality could, among others, include Roma covered by the census who may not have wished to declare themselves as Roma. Roma may also have declared themselves first as Serbs or Muslims, for example. There were perceived and real benefits

Table 3.1 Population of BiH grouped according to nationality/ethnicity, by censuses 1961 – 1991

Nationality/ethnicity	Total				Distribution in %			
	1961	1971	1981	1991	1961	1971	1981	1991
TOTAL	3,277,948	3,746,111	4,124,256	4,377,033				
Muslim	842,248	1,482,430	1,630,033	1,902,956	25.7	39.6	39.5	43.5
Serb	1,406,057	1,393,148	1,320,738	1,366,104	42.9	37.2	32.0	31.2
Croat	711,665	772,491	758,140	760,852	21.7	20.6	18.4	17.4
Yugoslav	275,883	43,796	326,316	242,682	8.4	1.2	7.9	5.6
Montenegrin	12,828	13,021	14,114	10,071	0.4	0.4	0.4	0.2
Roma	588	1,456	7,251	8,864	0.0	0.0	0.2	0.2
Albanian	3,642	3,764	4,396	4,925	0.1	0.1	0.1	0.1
Ukrainian	...	5,333	4,502	3,929	...	0.2	0.1	0.1
Slovene	5,939	4,053	2,755	2,190	0.2	0.1	0.1	0.1
Macedonian	2,391	1,773	1,892	1,596	0.1	0.1	0.1	0.1
Hungarian	1,415	1,262	945	893	0.1	0.0	0.0	0.0
Italian	717	673	616	732	0.0	0.0	0.0	0.0
Czech	1,083	871	690	590	0.0	0.0	0.0	0.0
Polish	801	757	609	526	0.0	0.0	0.0	0.0
German	347	300	460	470	0.0	0.0	0.0	0.0
Jewish	381	708	343	426	0.0	0.0	0.0	0.0
Russian	934	507	295	297	0.0	0.0	0.0	0.0
Slovak	272	279	350	297	0.0	0.0	0.0	0.0
Turkish	1,812	477	277	267	0.1	0.0	0.0	0.0
Romanian	113	189	302	162	0.0	0.0	0.0	0.0
Ruthenian	6,136	141	111	133	0.2	0.0	0.0	0.0
Other	811	602	946	17,592	0.0	0.0	0.0	0.4
Undeclared	...	8,482	17,950	14,585	...	0.2	0.4	0.3
Regional affiliation	...	...	3,649	224	...	...	0.1	0.0
Unknown	1,885	9,598	26,576	35,670	0.1	0.3	0.7	0.8

Source: Federation Office of Statistics, Statistical Yearbook of the Federation of Bosnia and Herzegovina, 1999, Chapter 4 – Population, Table 4–6;
Federalni zavod za statistiku, Statististički godišnjak/ljetopis Federacije Bosne i Hercegovine, 1999, poglavlje 4 – Stanovništvo, tabela 4–6.

(and detriments) to declaring oneself as such, depending on where one lived.

According to the 1981 census, the number of Roma living in municipalities where there were 50 or more Roma was 6,838 out of a total of 7,251 Roma in BiH. Of the 1981 total, 3,703 Roma lived in towns/municipalities in RS and 3,135 lived in towns/municipalities in FBiH.[4] It is important to be clear that these statistics show a particular point in history and do not provide a realistic picture for the current situation.

There is a wide disparity between the official statistics on the number of Roma in BiH and those obtained from Roma Associations. According to some Roma Associations, approximately 17,000 Roma lived in BiH in 1991, while others have cited the far larger number of 80,000.[5] According to the Centre for Protection of the Rights of Minorities, Sarajevo, the actual number of Roma in BiH should be placed somewhere between the official and unofficial sources. There are many reasons for the vagueness of such estimates. For example, many Roma live a nomadic lifestyle, making it difficult to count them in any one place. Many Roma communities also have a lack of interest in, or mistrust of, the census. Finally, many Roma are also well integrated into mainstream society and identify themselves first as members of one of the three constituent groups.

According to the Roma Association *Bahtale Roma*, which operates in the area of Travnik and Turbe, approximately ten per cent of the Roma in that area declare themselves to be members of other ethnic groups, believing that by doing so they will have better status in society. Taking data from other sources into account, it is evident that the real number of Roma living in BiH is far larger than indicated by the official census.

Displacement

As a consequence of the war, Roma communities were displaced within and between Entities and also abroad, primarily to Germany and Italy. Return of BiH citizens to their pre-war places of residence is one of the largest problems for normalisation of relations in the post-war period. Roma who were displaced internally and externally are facing the challenge of return to their places of origin. Political problems have created obstructions to returns, and these present a significant obstacle alongside practical problems resulting from the devastation of housing and economic facilities and their reconstruction.

Different Roma groups in the Federation of BiH

The Roma minority in FBiH comprises a complex mix of different groups. They include:

- **Domicile Roma populations** who have been in the FBiH over many generations.
- **Internally displaced persons (IDPs)** from what is now Republika Srpska.
- **Refugees** from Kosovo and the rest of Serbia who fled either during the air strikes or as the Kosovo Albanian population returned and conflicts emerged between the returnees and the Roma.[6]
- **Returnees** who have returned from abroad after fleeing during the war in BiH.

Romanes is the first language of most Roma in FBiH, although this varies between regions. Research by the Centre for Protection of the Rights of Minorities showed that Romanes was the first language of 86 per cent of the Roma surveyed. The majority of those who do not speak Romanes as their first language are from the younger age-group. The survey also revealed that the Romani language was better preserved among the populations in Tuzla, Bijeljina and Brčko. In Travnik, just one-third of Roma declared the Romani language as their mother tongue and in Sarajevo, almost half of the Roma interviewed stated that they did not speak the Romani language.[7]

Different Roma groups in Republika Srpska

Before the war, there were two main Roma communities in RS, who had little contact with each other: Muslim communities, who settled mainly in urban areas and their outskirts, and Orthodox Christian communities, who called themselves *Karavlahs*, and lived mainly in rural areas.[8] The Muslim Roma communities were relatively isolated, maintaining little contact with mainstream populations. However, most of their children did attend school. The *Karavlahs* worked on the land and dealt in crafts such as wooden dishes and cutlery. Many of them also worked abroad. Before the war, children from these communities regularly attended primary and secondary school or craft apprenticeships. At the same time, it was common for Romani children to marry and start families young, thus cutting short their school careers.

Following the war, however, it would be more accurate to describe Roma communities in RS as falling into four general groups.

- **Domicile Roma communities**, including both the Muslim and *Karavlah* communities who stayed during the war and whose circumstances remain practically the same as before the war, though affected by and struggling with post-war circumstances.
- **Internally displaced persons (IDPs)**, mostly Roma families originally from FBiH. This group consists of Muslim Roma who left Sanski Most and settled in Prijedor in 1995. Their children continue to attend school, despite living in hard conditions in an improvised settlement near Prijedor.
- **Refugees**, including those who fled from Croatia in 1992, and from Serbia, including Kosovo, in 1999. The Christian Roma from Croatia settled in the area of Srpski Brod and Srbac, in vacated Croat houses, although they are expecting relocation. They live mainly on paid employment, cultivating the land, collecting and reselling waste material, begging and, sometimes, modest social welfare. Most Romani children who are refugees from Croatia attend school, but there is an increasing tendency to drop out of school due to severe poverty. The Orthodox Christian Roma from Serbia, fleeing from the NATO bombing, have neither a regulated status nor resident permits and reside in established settlements for Roma, although they are often forced to move from location to location, and generally do not have steady employment. Children from these communities live in very hard conditions and tend not to attend school. The Roma who are refugees from Kosovo live with their relatives

in Prijedor, where they have no official status, have not been registered, and cannot return to Kosovo, for various reasons.

- **Returnees**, approximately 384 families who have returned to their pre-war homes either from FBiH or from abroad. Most of the returned families are now in Bijeljina, in the area of Modriča and on the outskirts of Brčko. While some houses have been built using humanitarian donations, most families live in tents on assistance from UNHCR, although they did receive some assistance from local authorities when they returned. Given that they live in very difficult conditions where mere survival is the priority, some Roma regard the issue of schooling for children as of relatively less importance.

Socio-economic status of Roma in Bosnia and Herzegovina

Roma usually live in private houses, whose quality and size depend on their material means, ranging from structures made of whatever materials can be gathered to solid, large houses. Usually, several families are accommodated in one house (immediate and extended families). Within most Roma communities, the problems of infrastructure – such as sewerage, water and electricity supply systems, and access roads – have not been resolved. This is particularly acute in rural and peripheral communities.

The Association of the Roma Citizens, *Naša budućnost – Sarajevo*, has produced data on Roma receiving welfare support: 80 people residing in Sarajevo (two per cent), 110 in Zenica (three per cent), 15 in Kakanj (less than one per cent) and 30 in Travnik (two per cent). This support includes minimum funds for heating and electricity, but does not cover basic living requirements. Most Roma are unaware of their rights to social welfare and even if they are sufficiently informed, many are unable to fulfil the necessary administrative conditions to exercise those rights. In some instances, Roma do not declare births in their family, particularly in larger families. In other cases, their documents were lost or destroyed during the war and have not been replaced for a number of reasons, including the fees for replacement documents, which are often prohibitive for Roma. There have been few organisations with the necessary will, knowledge and experience in the particular problems facing Roma to assist them both in knowing their rights and navigating the bureaucracy. This may change, however, as Roma associations are being formed and gaining strength.

The situation of Roma is very difficult due to a number of factors. They belong to the poorest part of the BiH population and rarely have steady permanent employment, instead earning money by gathering secondary raw material and having occasional seasonal jobs.[9] Research undertaken by the Centre for Protection of the Rights of Minorities in 1999 showed that 80 per cent of the surveyed Roma families did not have a single member who was permanently employed.[10] This can also be seen from data obtained from the Roma Association *Naša budućnost – Sarajevo*, which includes Roma from Alipašino Polje in Novi Grad municipality.

The Constitution and laws of BiH declare that all BiH citizens are equal under the law. However, in practice, some citizens, Roma in particular, are disadvantaged due to a number of factors. The economic and political aftermath of war and transition have affected the lives of all of BiH's citizens. However, the lower economic 'starting point' of many Roma has left them particularly adversely affected. Regardless of the fact that they are formally afforded most of the same rights as all other citizens, Roma live at or, more frequently, below the minimum standards necessary for survival and generally lack the means to adequately support their families or to secure education for their children.

Minority rights in Bosnia and Herzegovina

The Constitutional Court of BiH recently issued a number of decisions stipulating that several provisions of the Constitutions of the FBiH and RS were inconsistent with the Constitution of BiH. These provisions concern, *inter alia*, the ethnic origin of the constituent people of each Entity and the official use of languages and alphabets in each Entity. Decisions of the Constitutional Court of BiH create a legal obligation on the Entity Constitutions to initiate appropriate provisions. Although the decisions have yet to be implemented, they will entail a critical reconsideration of a number of constitutional provisions for both Entities, which place people in legally different positions according to their ethnicity. Even if the Entity Constitutions are amended, however, the BiH Constitution still retains several provisions whose import is identical (and more explicit) to those which have been proclaimed unconstitutional in the Entity Constitutions.

According to a declaration in the preamble of the Constitution, BiH is composed of "constituent peoples", namely "Bosniaks, Croats, and Serbs... (along with Others)" as well as citizens of BiH. It appears that a basic characteristic of the constitutional framework of BiH is that the organisation of both the state and its power is based on explicit domination by national factors. This is further reflected in the Constitutions of FBiH and RS, which provide respectively that the Bosniaks and Croats, without Serbs, are the constituent people in FBiH, and that Serbs, without Bosniaks and Croats, are the constituent people in RS. Therefore, despite the declaration in the preamble of the BiH Constitution according to which the Bosniaks, Serbs and Croats are the constituent peoples of BiH, the members of these groups are only constituent peoples in half of the territory. In other words, any of these three peoples has equal rights only in half of the territory of BiH (in one Entity), while their members who are living in the other Entity are restricted or prevented from the realisation of many constitutional rights. In accordance with the Constitution, in order to exercise rights the citizen must live within the Entity in which his/her people are a constituent. Otherwise, a person's civil right to be elected to public office is either fully eliminated (within some bodies) or restricted (within other bodies). The right of citizens of BiH to participate fully in public life, particularly within the political process as elected officials, shows a weakness in the constitutional treatment of citizens on the basis of national grouping.

Given this constitutional situation and the fact that the national parties of Bosniaks, Serbs and Croats have divided all state power among themselves, members of minorities are practically out of the sight and care of the actual state and political authorities. This is equally true in each of the Entities, where minorities always fall within the category of "Other". Therefore, a member of a minority cannot be elected to several state functions in BiH regardless of where he/she lives. Even if the authorities were to seek out members of minorities, their status would still be subject to discrimination, given that they are defined as a "citizen" rather than a "constituent people".

Given that the Constitution of BiH is based explicitly on the national factor, minority rights remain unacknowledged. Although international instruments guaranteeing minority rights have been signed and ratified by BiH, national minorities, including Roma, are not granted equal status and do not have scope for political power.

The right to education

The right to education in Bosnia and Herzegovina

The situation before the war

Before the war, the Assembly of Bosnia and Herzegovina was responsible for regulating education at all levels across BiH as a whole. Article 3 of the Law on Primary Schools (*Official Gazette of SR BiH*, No. 39/90) states that teaching was to be provided in Serbo-Croat (*jekavian* dialect) and that children in the first three grades were to learn both alphabets (Cyrillic and Latin), which were to be used equally. The School Assembly was supposed to determine which alphabet was to be learned first, on the basis of a proposal by the Council of Teachers and taking into account parental opinion and the

environment in which children lived. Article 36 of the Law on Primary Schools mandated the republic body responsible for education to approve the textbooks and teaching methods that could be used in primary schools. While classes were to be taught in Serbo-Croat, Article 4 provided that if there were at least 20 pupils in a class from a particular ethnic group, whose mother tongue was not Serbo-Croat, additional classes of the mother tongue were also to be organised. In primary schools attended by pupils belonging to only one ethnic group, the entire teaching process was to be performed in the language of that particular ethnic group, with additional compulsory classes of the Serbo-Croat language.

On the basis of a motion passed by the Republic Pedagogical Institute and on the decision of a committee appointed by the Republic Administration Body for Education, the secondary-school curriculum was issued by the republic body responsible for education. Teaching in these schools was in Serbo-Croat (*jekavian* dialect) and both alphabets (Latin and Cyrillic) were equally used. The Law on Secondary School also prescribed that where the mother tongue of at least 30 pupils in a school was not Serbo-Croat, additional classes of that mother tongue should be organised.

During the war and post-war

In November 1993, at the beginning of the war in BiH, the Republic of BiH Presidency (whose authority was recognised only in Bosniak-administered areas) issued a Decree by which the Laws on Primary and Secondary Schools were amended. Among other things, the provisions on the use of language in primary and secondary schools were amended to prescribe that the teaching process was to be performed in a standard language, *jekavian* dialect, of the constituent peoples of Bosnia and Herzegovina, namely Bosnian, Serb, and Croatian. Equal use of both alphabets (Latin and Cyrillic) was prescribed for secondary schools, while for primary schools, Steering Boards were to determine which of these two alphabets would be learned first, taking into account the parents' opinion and the background of the children.

Following Dayton, however, the central state authorities of BiH no longer have competence over the field of education *per se*. The Entities are entirely responsible for this issue. The Constitution of FBiH devolves the responsibility down to cantonal level. While this does not in itself present difficulties, the basic paradox (not only in this field) is that the state of BiH is responsible for international legal obligations such as for education while, at the same time, it is deprived of the authority to ensure the Entities meet those responsibilities.

The post-war situation with respect to education in BiH is extremely complex and burdened with large problems. Strong national interests considerably burden the curriculum and the mere organisation of education. BiH is a post-war country and this is reflected in every aspect of life. As already mentioned, there are two separate education systems in BiH, one in FBiH and one in RS, with different curricula. Further, in FBiH it could be said that two separate curricula exist, one used in the areas with the Bosniak majority and one used in the areas with the Croat majority.

At present, the international community is currently working with the Entity ministries of education to forge a common approach to education out of the different curricula, school systems, textbooks and laws. In addition, educational textbooks are being revised under the supervision of the international community.

The right to education in the Federation of Bosnia and Herzegovina

Article III.4(b) of the FBiH Constitution explicitly prescribes that the determination of educational policy, including the regulation and provision of education, is a cantonal responsibility. Presently therefore, education falls within the sphere of competence of the cantonal ministries of education. Article V.2(2) of the Constitution allows cantons to transfer their responsibilities related to education to municipalities within their territories. Where the majority population in a municipality is not from the same group as the majority population in the canton as a whole, cantons are obliged to transfer responsibility to the municipalities. In addition to this, Articles III.2(a) and III.3 of the Constitution ensure that FBiH authorities, jointly or separately or through the cantons co-ordinated by them, are responsible for guaranteeing and enforcing human rights.

Cantons have each developed laws for all levels of education from pre-school to university, where relevant. These laws have been enacted in ten different locations, without basic common principles being agreed at the Federation level. An examination of the content and form of the cantonal regulations and the curricula reveals that

inter-cantonal co-operation in the development and enactment of such laws has taken place on an *ad hoc* basis, for example, between those that have common national characteristics. In general, cantonal laws prescribe that teaching is to be carried out in the Bosnian and Croatian languages, using the Latin alphabet. Only a few cantons have imposed the obligation that, during the first three years of school, pupils attending primary school should also learn Cyrillic to a functional level (eg, Article 3 of the Law on Primary School in the Tuzla canton, *Official Gazette of TPC*, No. 4/96 and 9/97).

Likewise, the issue of religion and religious practice in schools is treated differently from one canton to another. Whereas most laws do not include any declaration on this matter, some stipulate specific measures on religious practice in schools. For example, the Laws on Changes and Amendments to the Laws on Primary School and Secondary School (*Official Gazette of Una-Sana Canton*, No. 11/98) in the Una-Sana Canton provides that religious education shall be included in the curriculum as a compulsory subject for pupils of primary and secondary schools. However, Article 1 of the Laws on Changes and Amendments to the Laws on Primary School and Secondary School provides that at the parents' request, a pupil may be released from their obligation to attend these classes.

The various cantonal laws on education also differ in their regulation of the treatment of national minorities in the educational system. A number of the cantonal laws do not touch upon the rights of national minorities in the educational system at all (for example, the laws in the cantons of Podrinje, West Herzegovina, Herzeg-Bosnia and Posavina). Other cantons (for example, Tuzla, Zenica-Doboj and Una-Sana) regulate this issue with just one article, which is essentially the same as the regulation that existed prior to and during the war. These laws differ from each other only in terminology: Tuzla and Zenica-Doboj cantons refer to "a member of a people and ethnic group", while the Una-Sana canton refers to "members of national minorities". The laws generally prescribe that in the case of primary schools, if there are at least 20 pupils in a class who belong to an ethnic group whose mother tongue is neither Bosnian nor Croatian, additional classes of their mother tongue shall be organised. Article 4 of the Law on Primary Schools in the Tuzla canton further states that in primary schools attended by pupils who belong to only one ethnic group, the entire teaching process shall be performed in the language of that ethnic group, with compulsory Bosnian language instruction. If in a secondary-school there are at least 30 pupils who belong to an ethnic group whose mother tongue is neither Bosnian nor Croatian, additional classes of their mother tongue shall be organised. Article 7 of the Law on Secondary Schools in the Tuzla canton states that in secondary schools attended by pupils who belong to only one ethnic group, the entire teaching process shall be performed in the language of that ethnic group, with compulsory learning of Bosnian/Croatian.

Although many cantonal education laws are similar, if not identical, across FBiH, ultimately there is no single system of policy formation and regulation, leading to inconsistencies in implementation. In theory, the laws allow for equal rights in access to education at all levels and even allow for teaching of minorities in their mother tongue. However, for Romani children this does not translate into practice.

The right to education in Republika Srpska

Education policy is formed and implemented at the Entity level in RS, and not at a municipal level. This ensures that policy remains consistent throughout RS, though differs from that in FBiH. Article 38 of the RS Constitution states that among the basic human rights there is the right to education under equal conditions including compulsory and free primary schooling. It also states that education at the secondary and higher levels shall be accessible to everyone under equal conditions.

Article 4 of the Law on Primary School (*Official Gazette of Republika Srpska*, No. 4/93) prescribes that the curriculum shall be taught and developed in the Serbian language. When there are at least 20 pupils in the same class belonging to an ethnic group whose mother tongue is not Serbian, classes of their mother tongue shall be organised for them at school. In a primary school attended by pupils belonging to only one ethnic group, the entire teaching process shall be performed in the language of that particular ethnic group, with compulsory Serbian-language classes. Article 4 of the Law on Secondary School (*Official Gazette of Republika Srpska*, No. 4/93) includes provisions almost identical to those on primary schools, although increasing the number of pupils to 30 in the same class in order for classes in their mother tongue to be organised. According to Article 8 of the Law on University (*Official Gazette of Republika*

Srpska, No. 12/93), the teaching process at the University and Institution of Higher Education shall be in the Serb language only.

Article 7(1) of the RS Constitution sets Serbian, written in Cyrillic, as the official language, a prescription that applies equally in the field of education. However, Article 7(2) of the Constitution goes on to state that where there are minority groups that speak other languages, their respective languages and alphabets may be used in an official capacity, in accordance with the respective law. The Law on Official Use of Language and Alphabet (*Official Gazette of Republika Srpska*, No. 15/96) prescribes that an official use of the language and alphabet shall mean use in, *inter alia*, all educational institutions, including textbooks, school forms and public signs, and in official records and correspondence. Article 3 of the Law provides that in the second to fourth classes of primary school and in addition to Cyrillic, Latin shall be compulsorily learned and used once a week. Article 5(3) of the Law allows religious communities and national cultural-educational associations that preserve the linguistic tradition of the people and national minorities in RS to use both standard dialects (*jekavian* and *ekavian*) and both alphabets (Cyrillic and Latin). Although stating that the right to use one's own language is a citizen's special personal right, the RS Constitutional Court held that only those provisions of the law prescribing compulsory use of the *ekavian* dialect are unconstitutional.

In theory, the law allows for equal access to education for all children across Republika Srpska, including provision for organisation of classes in a child's mother tongue. However, as with FBiH, for Romani children this does not translate into practice.

In practice

The right to education of Roma children in Bosnia and Herzegovina

Before the war, a high percentage of children attended school (96-98 per cent in the 1980s), with approximately equal enrolment of male and female children. Of those enrolled in primary school, approximately 99 per cent finished school while some 80 per cent were enrolled in secondary schools. In the 1990/91 school year in BiH, 736,069 pupils attended 2,484 educational institutions. Within this period, approximately 800,000 citizens were involved in the education and educational process, that is, 34 per cent of the total population.[11]

Despite the impressive results in attendance in education before the war, there was still significant illiteracy, particularly among older people (see Table 3.2). It should be noted that government censuses do not include data on the number of Romani children in preschool, primary-school, secondary-school or university education. Further still, the censuses do not include the age structure of the BiH population by nationality or ethnicity. However, research by the Centre for Protection of the Rights of Minorities from 1999 shows that in the surveyed sample only 30 per cent of Roma families were without illiterate members. It further showed that almost a quarter of Roma families (23 per cent) have four or more illiterate members.[12]

Table 3.2 BiH population older than ten years, by age, literacy and gender, according to censuses (totals and percentage illiteracy)

Age group		1981			1991		
		Total	Male	Female	Total	Male	Female
All ages	Total	3,383,159	1,672,135	1,711,024	3,697,232	1,835,272	1,861,960
	Illiterate	491,044 14.5%	92,694 5.5%	398,350 23.3%	367,733 9.9%	62,659 3.4%	305,074 16.4%
10-19	Total	826,328	423,719	402,609	707,598	363,224	344,374
	Illiterate	7,859 1.0%	2,707 0.6%	5,152 1.3%	5,722 0.8%	2,728 0.7%	2,994 0.9%
20-34	Total	1,057,026	546,008	511,018	1,093,621	569,408	524,213
	Illiterate	32,244 3.1%	5,434 1.0%	26,810 5.2%	12,538 1.1%	3,868 0.7%	8,670 1.7%
35-64	Total	1,239,532	591,602	647,930	1,509,186	745,673	763,513
	Illiterate	293,397 23.7%	40,402 6.8%	252,995 39.0%	196,135 13.0%	27,083 3.6%	169,052 22.1%
65 + or unknown	Total	260,273	110,806	149,467	386,827	156,967	229,860
	Illiterate	157,544 60.5%	44,151 39.8%	113,393 75.9%	153,338 39.6%	28,980 18.5%	124,358 54.1%

Source: Federation Office of Statistics, Statistical Yearbook of the Federation of Bosnia and Herzegovina, 1999, Chapter 4 – Population, Table 4-7.

While the situation regarding education is considered below in the context of each Entity, some general observations can be made about the overall position of Roma in BiH, which impacts upon the ability of Roma to exercise the right to education. Particularly during the last ten years, the ruling parties have focused their attention on the interpretation and representation of the interests of their "own" people. Consequently, their concern for ethnic minorities, including the Roma, has been considerably reduced. This is compounded by the marginalisation of Roma from mainstream communities on account of differences in culture, traditions and lifestyles. The prevailing view of Roma in almost all mainstream communities consists primarily of stereotypes, rather than a real knowledge, expressed in beliefs that most or all Roma beg, deal in contraband and are generally undisciplined. A distinction is rarely made between practices that result from poverty and practices that are traditionally associated with Roma. Behaviour that evolves out of necessity among most people living in poverty (for example, children needing to work to support the family, children not being able to attend school, a lack of adequate nutrition and of potable water) is perceived as being traditionally and voluntarily Roma, rather than behaviour that is a result of the pervasive poverty experienced by generations of Roma.

The right to education of Roma children in the Federation of Bosnia and Herzegovina

In FBiH, the relevant ministries, offices in the field of education and official statistics bureaux do not maintain records on the school attendance rates according to the nationality of pupils and students. Therefore there are no official data on the numbers of Romani children attending school. The only possible sources of information on this issue are Roma associations and individual schools. Perhaps the only official acknowledgement of the lack of school attendance by Romani children has been by the Ombudsman Institution for the FBiH and its Division for the Rights of the Child. The ombudsman reported that a significant proportion of those children who had not been enrolled in primary schooling were Romani children with unknown permanent residence.[13] Research by the Centre for Protection of the Rights of Minorities shows that it is more common than not for Roma to drop out of school before completing the first four grades of primary school. Furthermore, very few Romani children attend secondary school and even fewer attend college or university. The research also

shows that, with respect to the surveyed sample, one or more children from 37 per cent of families attend some level of schooling.[14] Data from *Naša budućnost – Sarajevo* giving Roma by age in Sarajevo, Zenica, Kakanj and Travnik-Turbe in 1999-2000 is shown in Table 3.3. According to *Naša budućnost – Sarajevo*, at all locations covered by its survey, 1,430 children of preschool, primary- and secondary-school age (10 per cent of the eligible population) were regularly attending school. However, the organisation also noted that in Sarajevo canton there are no Romani children attending preschool within the existing mainstream network of kindergartens. Again it is important to be aware that such data is problematic given the huge shifts in populations.

In the early 1980s, the first primer in the Romani language was developed by Roma themselves and was published in preparation for the introduction of the study of Romanes by Romani children at schools. However, this was never implemented, due to the outbreak of war, and has not yet been reintroduced.

Table 3.3 Roma population in some towns in FBiH, by age-groups

Location	From 1 to 15 years	From 15 to 20 years	From 20 to 50 years	From 50 to 70 years	Total
Sarajevo	1,700	1,250	1,700	400	5,050
Zenica	1,300	1,000	1,400	300	4,000
Kakanj	1,200	600	1,500	100	3,400
Travnik-Turbe	200	700	600	105	1,605
Total	4,400	3,550	5,200	905	14,055

Source: Roma Association *Naša budućnost – Sarajevo*, 1999/2000.

Roma and preschool education in FBiH

Preschool education is organised for children from one year of age until school age, although it is not compulsory. The structure of the educational programme for preschool children includes the care and upbringing of children aged two and three (infant nursery age) and preschool upbringing and education from three years of age until school age. In addition to these two programmes, there is also a programme for children with "mild disabilities", which may be conducted in preschools if there is a child in need of such a programme. The existing laws in FBiH also enable the introduction and realisation of shorter, more specialised programmes intended for various groups of children with specific needs, such as music and art, according to the affinity of the child.

Following the end of the war, the percentage of children in preschool institutions within FBiH decreased considerably, from about ten per cent of the eligible population before the war to about five per cent. The public institutions for preschool upbringing and education are partly funded from the cantonal budget, but the main source of income is payments by parents whose children attend preschool. Local and international organisations, as well as individuals, are also able to set up preschools.

All children, according to the law, have equal opportunities to enrol in preschool institutions. However, realistically, there are a number of factors limiting equal access, including the payment of fees. This is amply illustrated by the fact that, both during and after the war, no Romani child has been involved in preschool institutions in Sarajevo canton. Indeed, in the 1995-96 school year, the Roma Association *Naša budućnost* registered 119 Romani children under seven years in the Sarajevo canton, of whom none were enrolled in a preschool institution.

Roma and primary school education in the FBiH

Primary school education and upbringing in FBiH lasts 8 years, from 7 to 15 years of age, and is compulsory for all children regardless of their sex and ethnicity. This includes children with disabilities, who are expected to attend special classes or schools (though children of rural areas are rarely able to afford the transportation to these schools or classes, which are predominantly in urban centres). In the 1995-96 school year in Sarajevo canton, there were, according to *Naša budućnost* approximately 582 Romani children in total aged from 7 to 18 years, of whom only 189, or 33 per cent, attended regular school. According to the Law on Primary Education and Upbringing, children who have turned 16 and have not finished primary school or have not attended primary school at all can take extraordinary exams for grades of primary school. However, the preparatory classes for this are not organised, and there is a fee to take the examinations.

Beginning in the school year 2000/01, some cantons, notably Sarajevo and Mostar, have initiated preparatory classes for children from five and a half to six and a half years. The establishment of the preparatory classes is aimed at enlarging children's experiences, language skills, development and socialisation to prepare them for entry into the formal schooling system. There are also examples of preparatory classes taking place through activities of community groups and NGOs, as in the Biberovići Romani community in Tuzla canton, Sapna municipality, where preparatory classes were organised for a group of Romani children during 1998-99. The classes were

the initiative of the adult members of the Roma community in conjunction with an unofficial Roma association *Kate Acha* and with support in equipment and supplies from the local school. The classes took place in one of the private houses in the Roma community and were delivered by the adult Romani members of the community. In the school years 1999 to 2002, the NGO *Budi moj prijatelj*/Be my Friend, Sarajevo, in partnership with Save the Children UK, has organised preparatory classes for Romani children in three Roma communities in the Sarajevo canton. More recently, a Step-by-Step programme has been introduced for Romani children in FBiH.

A large number of school facilities were severely damaged during the war and some of them were completely destroyed. In addition to this, some school buildings temporarily housed soldiers and displaced people, which contributed to the destruction of school equipment and furniture. During the war, therefore, in some locations the teaching process was performed in flats, shops and other premises. However, in the post-war period, foreign donors have used their funds to renovate school buildings, and a large proportion of school buildings have been rebuilt and refurbished and sometimes are even in a better condition than before the war. Nonetheless, a shortage of teaching aids and equipment remains a problem in primary schools.

Given the large numbers of children displaced or killed during the war, it is difficult to calculate general attendance at primary school compared with the total number of children of primary-school age in the FBiH.[15] For the time being, it is

Table 3.4 Situation in primary-school education from 1990/91 to 1998/99, BiH/FBiH & RS

Year	Area	Schools	Classes	Pupils	Female pupils %	Teachers	Female teachers %
1990/91	BiH	2,202	19,280	532,468	47%	23,664	57%
1991/92	BiH	2,195	19,533	537,256	48%	23,486	59%
1992/93	FBiH	510	8,197	232,612	46%	9,179	61%
1993/94	FBiH	662	8,065	224,479	48%	8,822	66%
1994/95	FBiH	830	8,461	236,933	48%	10,026	64%
1995/96	FBiH	898	8,982	252,332	48%	10,821	64%
	RS	657	4,920	126,487	49%	6,086	
	BiH	1,555	13,902	378,819	49%	16,907	
1996/97	FBiH	943	9,572	259,882	49%	11,830	64%
	RS	734	5,414	130,517	49%	6,879	
	BiH	1,677	14,986	390,399	49%	18,709	
1997/98	FBiH	951	9,956	266,918	49%	12,382	63%
	RS	737	5,414	127,736	49%	6,842	
	BiH	1,688	15,370	394,654	49%	19,224	

Source: UNDP, Human development report: Bosnia and Herzegovina 1998, Chapter VII – Education, Table 18 (Compiled using the data from the Statistical Almanac 1993/1998, Statistical Bulletin no. 269, Statistics Bureau of FBiH and Statistics Bureau of the RS).

only possible to discuss existing data on the absolute number of children who are enrolled in and attend primary school.

Primary school education in state primary schools is free, with funding coming from the cantonal budgets. After the war, local and international entities have been able to open private primary schools, which was not possible prior to the war. There are now six private schools in Sarajevo and two requests for opening further schools have been submitted. Generally, private schools are not free, although there is a private primary school for children without parental care that does not charge either school or residential fees. Another new development in primary education has been the opening of boarding schools in FBiH.

In recent years, the primary-school curriculum has changed, and it continues to change, as the aims of primary school education have shifted. There has been a move away from developing a child's capacity to serve collective aims towards a focus on the development of individual capability, taking into account factors such as psychological and physical capacities and upbringing. The alteration of the aims should encourage, in theory at least, increased attendance by enabling all children to come to school, including Roma.

There are no official data on Romani children enrolled in primary school education. However, an illustration of the small number of Romani children included in the education system is provided in data taken from the *Analysis on the Current Status of the Roma Returnees to the Tuzla Canton*.[16] For that 1999 report, 798 Roma returnees (189 Roma families) were interviewed, and it was established that only ten families (5 per cent) enrolled their children in school. Similar results were found during August 2000, when Save the Children UK conducted

preliminary research into the situation of Romani children and their communities in Tuzla canton (see Table 3.5). As noted, primary school education is compulsory for all children regardless of sex or ethnicity. The Law on Primary School Education and Upbringing prescribes sanctions for parents whose children irregularly attend classes or do not attend them at all, which are seldom, if ever, applied.

According to information obtained through contact with Roma Associations, it is evident that few Roma finished primary school or even four classes in primary school. As illustrated in Table 3.5, only a small number of Roma continue their education and attend secondary schools, and it is rare that someone attends higher education beyond the secondary level. In addition, Romani

Table 3.5 Data on population, children and education of Roma communities in Tuzla canton

Location	No. of population	No. of families	No. of children	Attendance at:			
				Preschool	Primary	Secondary	College & university
Biberovići community (Sapna municipality)	180	36	50	–	6	–	–
Živinice municipality	1450	304	448	–	123	11	–
Poljice community (Lukavac municipality)	300	50	140	–	n/a (at least 3)	–	–
Veseli Brijeg community (Gračanica municipality)	100	25	35	–	5	–	–
Ćubrić community (Banovići municipality)	253	52	114	–	15	1	–
Kiseljak community (Tuzla municipality)	309	72	210	–	94	–	–

Source: Information collected in support of preliminary research into the situation of Romani children and their communities in Tuzla Canton by Save the Children UK, August 2000. Information was collected from Roma associations and Romani communities. Data given in the table are approximate only and should be viewed as such.

children often do not attend classes regularly and drop out of school before completing their education, most often between the 3rd and 5th grade.

Roma and secondary school and higher education in FBiH

In the FBiH school system, secondary school education is not compulsory. In the pre-war period, approximately 80 per cent of pupils went on to attend secondary school after primary school. In the post-war period, the authorities responsible for education estimate that attendance at secondary school has not considerably changed from pre-war enrolment levels.

There are three types of secondary schools: general high schools, technical and related schools and vocational schools. Education in the general high schools and technical and related schools lasts for four years, and enrolment is based on an entrance examination. There is no entrance examination for vocational schools, and pupils are enrolled on the basis of their primary-school performance until a pre-established quota of pupils is reached.

Following completion of secondary education at a general high school, pupils may enter the college or university of their choice upon passing the entrance examination. Pupils who finish technical and related schools may apply to the faculties related to the school they finished (for example, from a secondary medical school to the faculties of medicine, dental medicine, pharmacy and veterinary medicine) and pass an entrance examination for acceptance onto that faculty.

According to research carried out by the Roma Association *Naša budućnost* in 1995/96, there were 582 school-age Romani children living in Sarajevo canton, of whom just 13 (two per cent) were enrolled in secondary schools and four (one per cent) in universities. Given that Sarajevo is an urban area with higher levels of enrolment in secondary and university education than in other regions, this data indicates that in the rest of FBiH, such figures would be even lower.

Roma and special schools and institutions in the FBiH

Special schools in FBiH provide education for children with disabilities as a part of the school system. There are special institutions with residential placements for children with disabilities that are considered special schools (see Table 3.6). At the same time, there are also special classes within some mainstream schools where education is provided to children with disabilities. More recently, daycare centres for children with disabilities have been established. Projects aimed at integrating children with disabilities into mainstream schools have also been set up, in co-operation with national and international NGOs. A child can be placed in a special institution or included in a special class or school, following a disability assessment ("categorisation") that assesses the child as disabled. There is no known practice of placing children in special institutions with residential care for other reasons, such as social, ethnic and linguistic.

Since the FBiH Ministry of Social Welfare does not keep a national/ethnic breakdown of beneficiaries of social-welfare institutions, there

Table 3.6 Special primary and secondary schools in FBiH

Year	Level	Number of schools	Number of classes	Total pupils	Girls
1993/94	Primary	10	68	505	173
1994/95	Primary	12	66	524	206
1995/96	Primary	16	77	610	252
1996/97	Primary	21	111	819	321
1997/98	Primary	25	122	937	348
1993/94	Secondary	8	28	190	66
1994/95	Secondary	9	30	185	54
1995/96	Secondary	11	36	226	66
1996/97	Secondary	13	42	299	97
1997/98	Secondary	11	38	288	112

Source: Federation Office of Statistics, Statistical Yearbook of the Federation of Bosnia and Herzegovina, 1999, Chapter 18 – Education, Table 18-1.

are no official data on the current number of Romani children in institutions such as children's homes, institutions for disabled children or institutions for young offenders. Research conducted for this report suggests, however, that Roma are not disproportionately represented in the special-school system (see Table 3.7).

The right to education of Roma children in Republika Srpska

According to a field assessment in 2000 by Save the Children UK, there are currently 741 Roma families with 1,761 children in RS, though this number is changing due to returns to the Entity. There are no accurate data on how many Romani children attend school in RS. However, in the former Yugoslavia before the war, although many Romani children did not complete their schooling, a reasonably high percentage of Romani children overall did attend primary and secondary schools.

In the Centre for Social Work in Banja Luka, a Romani social worker stated that higher levels of education, employment and participation in social-community life for Roma parents could increase the chances of Romani children regularly attending and completing primary and secondary schools. However, such families form a very small proportion of the total number of Roma families. This social worker also argued that the education system both before and since the war is not conducive to Romani children successfully getting a basic education.

Table 3.7 Survey of some special/social institutions in FBiH, with respect to the number of Romani children in these institutions

Location	Name of institution	Type of institution	Number of Romani children Female	Male
Sarajevo	Centre for upbringing, education, vocational training and employment of children with mental disabilities, children with autism and cerebral palsy "Vladimir Nazor"	Secondary special school without residential care	2	4
Sarajevo	Institute for special upbringing and education of children "Mjedenica"	Primary special school and social institution with residential care	–	1
Sarajevo	Centre for hearing and speech rehabilitation	Special school without residential care	–	–
Sarajevo	Centre for blind and partially sighted children	Special school with residential care	–	–
Pazarić	Institute for protection of children and the youth	Special social institution with residential care	–	–
Tuzla	Special school for hearing-impaired children	Special school without residential care	–	–
Sarajevo	Institute for upbringing of male children and the youth of Sarajevo (known as "Hum")	Social institution for young offenders with residential care	–	–

Source: Data collected during research for this report relating to the 1999/2000 school year.

Roma and preschool education in RS

Pre-school education is organised for children from two to six years of age in government facilities. These are funded through the local community budget and fees are paid by parents. More recently, some private preschools have opened. The Ministry of Education, which draws up school curricula and monitors teaching in the preschool facilities, regulates the functioning and legal status of preschools according to the Act on Children's Protection. While general preschool education is not free, children of poor financial status, those without parental care, those with special needs and disabled children can have a free or sponsored stay in preschool facilities. Fewer than five per cent of children attend preschool, which is generally considered a "privilege" of the urban, developed population. There are no specific data available on the attendance of Romani children, but it can be extrapolated from the general situation of Roma in RS and the difficulties faced by those Roma who attend primary school (see below) that very few, if any, Romani children go to preschool.

Roma and primary school education in RS

Primary education is obligatory and free for all children from 7 to 14 years of age. It is organised in state schools and funded from the RS budget fund. In addition to regular education in state schools, there are special schools for children with special needs/disabilities and classes in primary education for adults, namely persons over 16 years of age.

There are currently very few Romani children attending primary school in RS, although there are no official data to indicate this. Furthermore, of those Romani children who do attend primary school, most tend to discontinue their schooling at a very early stage. Although there are no reliable data, girls more than boys tend to leave school before completing their primary education. Indeed, most Romani children who do attend primary school are refugees from Croatia, who now live in Srpski Brod and Mali Sitneš near Srbac. Some domicile Romani children in Prijedor, Ostružnja near Doboj, and in Teslić also attend

school. Among the returned Romani children there are very few who continued schooling. In Bijeljina there are five children who continued schooling after their parents returned. Three of them still regularly attend, but two have dropped out, which according to their parents is due to the problem of constant discrimination on the part of peers and schoolteachers. In the community of returnees in Modrički Lug, one father daily drives his five children to a school in Odžak in FBiH. According to him, conditions are not suitable in the school in Jakeš, although it is closer and is the school that the children attended before the war. This family can afford education for their children because they were refugees in Germany, and used their savings to build a house, buy a van and have enough for the fuel for transport. Most families do not live in comparable circumstances. In Prijedor only a small number of settled Romani children attend school. While at least some Roma living in very harsh conditions are able to regularly attend school, this is not true for returnees, refugees or those who are internally displaced.

Roma and secondary and higher education in Republika Srpska

Secondary education is free and a part of the total education system. It is organised in secondary schools, schools of art, technical schools, military schools and schools of theology. Secondary schools are state schools. New school construction and teachers' salaries are funded from the state budget fund with the local community providing money for teaching materials.

Roma and special schools and institutions in the RS

Information on special schools in RS is only available for the pre-war situation, ie, for BiH as a whole, including what is now the FBiH. In the pre-war period, approximately 20 per cent of Romani children attending the Esad Midžić school in Banja Luka (now the Branko Radičević school) were placed into special classes for children with minor disabilities. Staff at the school believed that Romani children were more likely to be characterised as "disabled" than children belonging to the majority, due to a lack of

pre-school education for Romani children and their insufficient knowledge of the official language rather than because of any disability.

The procedure for placing children in the school started with the school's referral of the child for categorisation to the local Centre for Social Work, which is a local office for the Commission for Disability Categorisation. Parents whose children were referred had the legal right to refuse or stop the categorisation without further sanctions or measures either towards child, them or the school. However, according to social workers in the Banja Luka Centre of Social Work, Roma parents usually did not oppose either the school's referral to categorisation or the results of the disability categorisation. According to one school psychologist, Roma parents mostly did not object to their children attending these "special classes", because they believed their children would complete their schooling sooner and more easily due to the reduced programme, as well as being less exposed to harassment from other children.

In three schools for disabled children (for children with moderate learning disability, hearing impairments and sight impairments), it seems that before the war more Roma children were enrolled than are today. According to the principals of these schools there were no cases of non-disabled children being referred to these schools, because of the nature and level of the disability of children attending them.

Voices of Roma children and parents in BiH

Children

S, Romani girl, 11 years old, completed the first class but no longer attends school

"I wanted to go to school this year too, but I have to take care of my sister. She is eight and cannot walk. Mother works at the market, and my sister Z got married. I know how to read and write. It was nice to go to school. The teacher was good."

E, Romani boy, 11 years old, attends second grade of primary school

"At the beginning of the first class, children usually hit, teased and called me ugly names and I cried for that. My mama came to see our teacher and complain and he said that he would take care of this. Mainly, there have been no larger problems since that time. I would like to have a young, female teacher who would smile all the time, as our male teacher is often gloomy. I would like more flowers around the school, for the school to have football goals and basketball hoops and the interior of our school to be painted green. I often help pupils who have a poor school performance with mathematics and Bosnian. No one has ever helped me as I have never asked anyone for assistance as I know how to do all the school tasks myself. I would like to become a teacher when I grow up. Children would only sing to me."

Ž, Romani girl, 15 years old, attends sixth grade of primary school

"I attend school on a regular basis. I have problems with the Bosnian language, so a girl friend of mine who is not Roma helps me with it."

R, Romani boy, ten years old, attends first class for the first time

"It is nice to got to school, but there is no-one in the family to wake me up in the morning. My mum goes to the market to work at four o'clock in the morning and I often oversleep. When I wake up it is already late and I feel ashamed to enter in my classroom so late. But I will not stop going to school, so I will ask my mum to buy me a clock."

A, Romani boy, nine years old, attends second grade of primary school

"I like going to school and I like mathematics most. Our teacher teaches us well. However, he sometimes hits us when we are disobedient. I like my teacher and regardless of anything, I would not change him. When I grow up, I would like to become a policeman and help people when they cannot do something themselves."

A, Romani girl, 14 years old

"I finished the 1st class and dropped out of school. My teacher liked me. I did not feel good in school. Some children were teasing me."

NS, Romani boy, 14 years old
"I completed three grades in the primary school "Petar Kočić" in Prijedor. When the war began I stopped going to school because my parents were afraid, they feared some problems may occur, I don't know. So I didn't go on. But now I don't have the opportunity, and how can I attend the third grade with small children?"

N, Romani boy, 12 years old, attends third grade of primary school
"My first day at school and meeting with my teacher remained etched on my mind as fond memories... On several occasions, children who are not Roma were teasing and insulting me."

D, non-Romani young man, 17 years old
"I personally feel that it would be better for the Roma to attend school, because this is what the world is like today – if you don't know anything, they treat you as a complete idiot and moron, I don't know... It is true for them that they should continue schooling. Here, in Prijedor they are treated... I don't know, like, 'Ha, look, Gypsies, what do they want now? Don't pay attention to them. They are stupid.' and so... I personally don't feel this is so. What they do, they do it OK. What they are doing here (in the youth centre) is really OK. I think here they are really accepted."

S, Romani boy, 12 years old
"I do not attend and I have never attended a regular school. I do not want to go to school. Now I am too old to attend the 1st class. However, I would like to finish school and become a driver."

D, Romani young man, 16 years old, attends seventh grade of primary school
"I have a nice time in school. I have not experienced any larger unpleasant things. I have been enrolled in school. However I have to pay. I felt best at a judo contest where I won the first prize. I got a cup and that was the most beautiful. I felt good because I won. Teachers and my coach were also there. I would like to buy a motorcycle to make my going to market-place easier."

S, Romani boy, 12 years old
"I never attended school. I can't read, nor write, and I would like to."

M, Romani girl, ten years old
"I go to school on a regular basis. I have a nice time with my girl friends who are not Roma. I felt so nice when I was in a choir and the director came and praised us saying that we sang nice and that we were nicely dressed. When we have our holiday (Đurđevdan/ St. George's Day), we talk with our teacher about it. She wants to know how we celebrated it. Our friends also talk to us about it. They want us to invite them to celebrate the holiday with us next time. When I grow up, I would like to become a hairdresser."

N, Romani young man, 17 years old, dropped out after the third grade of primary school

"I finished the third class. My father did not allow me to go to school during the war and I also was not keen on going. Later, the director told me that I did not have the right to continue to go to school because I was 16. Sometimes, the company you keep influences you and you want to be like them and not go to school. And in school some teachers are good to you. My brother and I work at the market-place to survive. I would like to finish primary school. If I did not work at the market-place, I would become a thief or dealer. If someone does not have money, he becomes a dealer."

M, non-Romani girl, 12 years old

"I would always take care that I do not hurt them. I would share my snack with them. If someone attacked them, I would take [the Roma child's] side."

C, Romani young man, 16 years old

"Before, I lived in Sanski Most and there I went to school. I completed four grades, but could not continue here because I haven't had the opportunity. I would like to continue, but my parents don't have enough money for the books and everything else I need."

E, Romani young man, from Sarajevo, 16 years old

"At school, they called me a Gypsy. I do not go to school. I finished some classes. I am selling goods by going from one door to another and on the street. When I come to a door, some drive me away and some just slam the door.

I earn well, when I earn some money. That's the way it is. One can lose everything today, and you start from the beginning. Why do I need school?! There are professors who work at the market-place. There are more of them at the market-place than in companies. Just go there and count!"

Parents

Returnee Romani mother of three school-age children

"My children do not go to school. I am not sure that it is safe for them to attend the school in Jakeš and they are too small to go on feet even to Odžak. Let them open our school here in village, or organise some transport for the older ones, then I will let them attend. Now I will not let them attend. I am not sure that they would be safe."

Romani father

"I cannot provide the school books nor clothes for them. Older ones must take care of the younger children while my wife and I work. Also, you see that there is no place for them to study."

Romani mother

"My son will continue attending school even when I do not have the bread to eat. He rides a bicycle to school now. It is 6km to get there. But how will he go in the winter? It gets dark early in the afternoon... I am afraid for him."

Romani father

"My son has completed the sixth grade in the Federation, but he had problems with his classmates. The director of the school was not ready to help us just because we are the Roma. Now we are preparing the documents to enrol him in the school here."

Romani mother of six children, three of whom attend school

"Like my brothers and sisters, I never attended school. Therefore, I am trying to have my children regularly attend school. Some schoolmates of my children tease them and insult them calling them Gypsies – because of their clothes."

Conclusion

A number of factors need to be considered in order fully to understand the situation of Roma regarding education. Improving the standard of education among the Roma population is not simply a matter of improving access to education *per se*; it also requires a general improvement in the standard of living among Roma. This would enable Roma to take advantage of the education system. Among the many reasons behind low levels of participation in the education system on the part of Roma children are the following:

Poverty: the inability to pay for clothes, school supplies and other school requirements; the need for children to contribute to the family's income through work; the inability to provide children with an adequate environment for study at home; lack of lighting for study; lack of water and the consequences this has for hygiene and clean clothes for school.

Irrelevance of mainstream education: the lack of relevant studies for children that would prepare them for adulthood as contributing members of their Roma community; pervasive discrimination that would (potentially) preclude employment even if Romani children were educated; parents' experience of being capable and contributing members of the community without having any formal education, and their consequent perception that mainstream education is not important for their children.

Discrimination and harassment at school: One Romani parent in one of our projects with Romani children (outside the context of this report) remarked: "Why would I send my child to a place where they might be beaten just because they are Roma?"

Mistrust of government: The relationships of Roma people with the authorities have not historically engendered a feeling of confidence in agencies of the government, including the education system; Many Romani children do not possess documents required by school authorities, such as birth certificates or other identity documents.

War and displacement: Thousands of Romani children (recently including Romani children from Kosovo) have been displaced by the wars of this region and have not been able to return to communities where they might have a greater sense of belonging and be able to plan their futures, including the formal education of their children.

Cultural beliefs and practices: Children assume adult responsibilities much earlier in many Roma communities than in non-Roma communities. Children are often married and have children themselves in their teen years. Household and other work responsibilities accordingly increase, providing children with little time for formal education.

Language: Many Romani children are not proficient in written or spoken non-Roma languages to the extent that they would be able to learn effectively in the local languages in which classes are taught in BiH.

Lack of an educated leadership or role models: There are few educated Romani leaders who have managed to succeed in spite of all else in BiH and who can provide inspiration to Romani children, making them believe that they too can have a promising future if they complete their education.

Recommendations

Given that the following international instruments are directly applicable in Bosnia and Herzegovina either through ratification or, since December 1995, by virtue of Annex I of the Constitution of Bosnia and Herzegovina, in Annex IV of the General Framework Agreement for Peace (the Dayton Agreement):

- the European Convention on the Protection of Human Rights and Fundamental Freedoms 1950 (The Convention and its Protocols take priority over all other law in BiH – BiH Constitution, Article II.2)

- the International Convention on the Elimination of All Forms of Racial Discrimination 1965
- the International Covenant on Civil and Political Rights 1966
- the International Covenant on Economic, Social and Cultural Rights 1966
- the UN Convention on the Rights of the Child 1989
- the European Charter for Regional or Minority Languages 1992
- the Framework Convention for the Protection of National Minorities 1994

Save the Children recommends that:

The Authorities of BiH and the Federation of BiH and Republika Srpska

- Intensifies efforts to reform legislation, including the Constitutions of the country to be in compliance with BiH's international legal obligations under human rights instruments, including the UN Convention on the Rights of the Child.
- Has an open dialogue with the various Roma communities, including children, and develops a response that reflects the concerns and realities of the Roma communities themselves.
- In consultation with Roma communities:
  - Organises preparatory classes for Romani children of preschool age to prepare them for primary school, including teaching in the Romani language and the language used at primary school.
  - Implements a system of part-time education for children and young people who did not complete school grades at the appropriate

age, and for children who must also work to support their families.

– Allows for children who have dropped out of or never attended school to sit extra-ordinary exams to complete primary school, even if under the age of 16, when they would normally be required to attend full time to complete classes.

– Sets up a body to assess and monitor the education of Romani children, within the government system, that includes Romani participants and/or advisers.

– Ensures that a systematic study of the status of Roma in Bosnia and Herzegovina, including their numbers, regional patterns and social status is carried out. Such a study could then be used in planning for challenging disadvantage over the next decade. If appropriate protective measures can be assured, there should be a breakdown of data on the basis of ethnicity, age and gender with particular attention paid to ensuring that data on ethnicity are not misused and are based on self-identification.

– Introduces measures for raising awareness about Roma among educational institutions and society in general.
– Provides funding to enable children to attend school, including funds for books and equipment, and either transport fees or organised free transport to school.

The OHR, UNESCO, other international intergovernmental agencies and government authorities

• Oversee consistent educational policy across the whole territory of BiH that specifically addresses the right of Romani children to education, taking into account the human rights obligations applicable in BiH.
• Actively engage with Romani communities, including children, to determine jointly ways in which the international community could support priorities with respect to the education of Romani children.
• Ensure that poverty analysis and alleviation measures specifically engage Romani communities.

Bosnia and Herzegovina: Notes on the text

1a The Constitutional Court of Bosnia and Herzegovina has recently taken the decision that the constitutional inequalities of people within the two Entities are to be rectified but how to implement this is still being discussed.

1b The term Roma (adjective: Romani) is used in the BiH report as opposed to Roma/Gypsy as this is the preferred self-appellation.

2 The Dayton Agreement included as a third area the administrative region of Brcko, a former municipality that will be considered in the context of RS for the purposes of this report. According to Annex V of the Dayton Peace Agreement, the status of Brcko was to be decided by arbitration. In 1999, following the eventual submission of the issue to arbitration, Brcko was declared to be a "shared condominium" between FBiH and RS, although in practice it continues to be a self-governing administrative unit and its future integration remains to be decided: see *Is Dayton Failing?*, International Crisis Group, 1999, pp. 35-6.

3 For an analysis of the problems of public administration in BiH in general, see *Rule of Law in Public Administration*, International Crisis Group, 1999.

4 Source: *The Population Nationality Structure of the SFR Yugoslavia According to the Settlements and Municipalities: Book I*, 1981, Federal Bureau of Statistics of Yugoslavia and *Statistical Yearbook of the Republic of BiH*, 1992.

5 Centre for Protection of the Rights of Minorities, Sarajevo, *Status of the Roma in Bosnia and Herzegovina (Survey Results)*, Sarajevo, 1999; Analysis by Prof. Dr Slavo Slavko Kukić, p. 14.

6 Roma who remained in Kosovo during the war in 1999 were often perceived to have collaborated with the Serbs by returning Kosovar Albanians.

7 Centre for Protection of the Rights of Minorities, Sarajevo, *Status of the Roma in Bosnia and Herzegovina (Survey Results)*, Sarajevo, 1999. Analysis by Prof. Dr Slavo Slavko Kukić. See further the UNDP *Human Development Report Bosnia and Herzegovina 2000: Youth*, which specifically refers to an alarming situation with respect to knowledge of the Romani language among young Roma.

8 *Karavlahs* are one of the groups of Romanian speaking Gypsies (often with a non-Romani consciousness) that are found throughout Europe. They are also referred to in other contexts as Rudara/Rudari, Beasha (variant Boyasha/Boyashi).

9 In the UNDP *Human Development Report Bosnia and Herzegovina 1998*, the unemployment rate in BiH is estimated at 36.21%.

10 Centre for Protection of the Rights of Minorities, Sarajevo, *Status of the Roma in Bosnia and Herzegovina (Survey Results)*, Sarajevo, 1999. Analysis by Prof. Dr Slavo Slavko Kukić.

11 UNDP *Human Development Report Bosnia and Herzegovina 1998*, Chapter VII – Education.

12 Centre for Protection of the Rights of Minorities, Sarajevo, *Status of the Roma in Bosnia and Herzegovina (Survey Results)*, Sarajevo, 1999. Analysis by Prof. Dr Slavo Slavko Kukić.

13 *Report on Human Rights Situation in the Federation of BiH for 1999*, Sarajevo, February 2000, Ombudsmen of the Federation of Bosnia and Herzegovina, Chapter VII – Protection of the Rights of the Child.

14 Centre for Protection of the Rights of Minorities, Sarajevo, *Status of the Roma in Bosnia and Herzegovina (Survey Results)*, Sarajevo, 1999. Analysis by Prof. Dr Slavo Slavko Kukić.

15 UNDP *Human Development Report Bosnia and Herzegovina 1998*, Chapter VII – Education.

16 Helsinki Citizen's Assembly and Roma Associations from Tuzla Canton, *Analysis on the Current Status of the Roma Returnees to Tuzla Canton*, 1999.

4 Bulgaria

Many Roma children continue to attend overcrowded "Gypsy Schools" first established in the 1940s and 1950s, and cannot enrol in many half-empty Bulgarian schools which have higher standards.

"The buses come here every week, collect the Gypsy children and take them all the way to Rozovets, where there is a school for them. The teachers here don't want any Gypsy children"

Roma child, 13 years old

Summary

Context

Bulgaria has been hit particularly hard by transition to a market economy, suffering severe economic recession both when communism collapsed and again in 1995. Government expenditure on education has declined and Roma/Gypsies have been disproportionately affected by the increased costs of schooling due to widespread unemployment and impoverishment. Post-communist governments were slow to develop a comprehensive strategy towards the Roma/Gypsy minority. This is reflected in the insensitivity of many aspects of the mainstream education system, including outdated teaching methods based on a mono-ethnic conception of Bulgaria, a lack of materials and teacher training in Roma/ Gypsy issues and Romanes, and a failure to tackle the low social status of Roma/Gypsies and discrimination.

Roma/Gypsy population

The last official household census (1992) found over 300,000 Roma/Gypsies, but other estimates put the size of the Roma/Gypsy minority at up to 800,000, nearly ten per cent of the country's population. The youthful profile of the Roma/Gypsy minority means its absolute and relative size is certain to increase in coming years. The Roma/Gypsy population is distributed throughout the country, in both urban and rural areas, and is also differentiated by language (Bulgarian, different dialects of Romanes and Romanian are all spoken as mother tongues) and religion (Orthodox/Muslim).

Roma/Gypsies and education

Figures on educational attainment are broken down by ethnicity and show very few Roma/Gypsies with tertiary qualifications, small numbers graduating from vocational secondary schools and a far higher proportion than the national average who are illiterate. The insensitivity of the school system is shown by high drop-out rates amongst Roma/Gypsies, though cultural and economic factors also contribute.

Segregated provision

Segregation is a major factor in low educational attainment. Almost 20,000 Roma/Gypsy children attend separate "Gypsy schools" where the quality of education is low. There is often strong local resistance to plans to integrate Roma/Gypsies into mainstream schools. Roma/Gypsies are also grossly over-represented amongst pupils in special schools for the mentally handicapped. Many of Bulgaria's thousands of street children are Roma/Gypsies. The Constitution does not recognise any collective minority identities and it was not until 1997 that the government made its first attempt to develop a Roma policy. These proposals were rejected by Romani NGOs who lobbied for a programme which was finally approved in 1999. Since then, some steps have been taken to end educational segregation, though without government funding. A programme to train Roma/Gypsy teaching assistants appears to reinforce lower standards for Roma/Gypsy pupils.

Language provision

Governments have been unwilling to develop teaching in Romanes, citing the multitude of dialects and absence of skills and materials on the subject.

Balance of NGO and government activity

NGOs have become a dominant force on Roma/Gypsy issues, particularly at the level of developing ideas such as on multicultural education, curriculum development and teacher training, as well as helping with the development of educational infrastructure. NGOs have become a focus for the activity of the growing number of Roma/Gypsy organisations. Together with international institutions, they have sought to influence government policies. However, problems have emerged such as the inconsistency and short-termism of projects and with the perception that some NGO activities effectively absolve the state from its responsibilities and are not accountable to their Roma/Gypsy users. NGOs have largely occupied a space vacated by the state and it is still too early to evaluate their actual contribution to improving the education of Roma/Gypsy people.

Bulgaria report contents

Introduction – Roma/Gypsies in Bulgaria

Demography

There are no precise and comprehensive official statistical data on ethnic minorities in Bulgaria, such as indicators on demography and education. At the time of writing, the only official source of demographic data with an ethnic breakdown is the most recent *Population and Housing Census*, conducted on 4 December 1992. This states that, the total population of Bulgaria was 8,487,317. Of these, 7,271,185 were Bulgarian, 800,052 were Turkish and 313,396 were Roma/Gypsy.[1]

However, this information should not be taken to be precise and comprehensive. Due to the imperfection of the census methods used, and a number of other factors, the figures do not reflect accurately the actual situation. Inaccuracies are especially striking for Roma/Gypsies.
The discrepancy between the number of people who declare themselves as Roma/Gypsies and the actual number of Roma/Gypsies is a well-known phenomenon, which exists in many countries. In the 1976 population census, conducted during the Socialist era (the information has not been officially published), 373,200 people were registered as Roma/Gypsies. However, in 1980 the Ministry of Internal Affairs conducted a second census with the assistance of the Fatherland Front for the needs of the Central Committee of the Bulgarian Communist Party. This was a special census of the Roma/Gypsy population based on a different principle – it registered not only the people who had declared themselves as Roma/Gypsies, but also all people

perceived as Roma/Gypsies by the surrounding population. This perception was based on anthropological type, lifestyle, cultural and other characteristics. The 1980 census listed 523,519 Roma/Gypsies – nearly one-third more than in the previous census.

The Ministry of Internal Affairs continued for some time to conduct undeclared secret population censuses (of Roma/Gypsy population in particular). A similar one was conducted in January 1989, for the needs of the so-called *Process of Revival*. This registered 576,927 Roma/Gypsies (6.45 per cent of the then population of Bulgaria). The latest census conducted by the regional offices of the Ministry of Internal Affairs was in May 1992 (during the government of the Union of Democratic Forces). It was incomplete (not all regional offices of the Ministry of Internal Affairs submitted the required information), but registered 533,466 Roma/Gypsies (see Table 3.1).

The information provided by the Ministry of Internal Affairs censuses should not be perceived as comprehensive, since these censuses were often a mere formality and the information given was incomplete and imprecise. Were we to compare this information with that gained from other sources and from observation, we could say tentatively that the overall number of people of Roma/Gypsy origin in Bulgaria is between 700,000 and 800,000. For various reasons (mostly because of the predominant negative social attitudes and prejudices), many people do not wish to declare themselves as Roma/Gypsies.

When calculating the number of people in the minority communities of Bulgaria, and more specifically the number of Roma/Gypsies, we have to consider a number of factors, including the phenomenon of "preferred ethnic identity" – a public declaration of a different identity that a person prefers. Such instances are common among many of the Turkish-speaking Roma/Gypsies, who prefer to present themselves as "Turks". Other Roma/Gypsy Muslims prefer the neutral (and ethnically unclear) category of *millet'* ('nation' or 'people'). The Romanian-speaking Roma/Gypsies prefer to declare themselves as Wallachians, Romanians or ethnically neutral "Rudara" and others. Clearly, official data from the census (and from Bulgarian statistics in general) on the number of Roma/Gypsies in Bulgaria, and their demographic characteristics must be treated with reservation.

The age pyramid of the major minorities in Bulgaria (Turks and Roma/Gypsies) reveals a very significant characteristic feature – the relatively higher number of children and young people compared to those among ethnic Bulgarians (see Table 3.2).

However incomplete the census may be, these figures reveal an indisputable trend – the share of Roma/Gypsy children of school age will grow because of the higher percentage of Turks and Roma/Gypsies of child-bearing age (especially since some of those registered as Turks in the census are actually Roma/Gypsies with a preferred Turkish identity). This adds force to the fact that the Roma/Gypsy minority must be considered in the preparation of new educational strategies.

Table 4.1 Bulgaria's Roma/Gypsy population, 1992[2]

Regional Directorate of the Ministry of Internal Affairs (MI) (formerly District)	Jan 1989 (MI)	May 1992 (MI)	Dec 1992 (Census[1])	Dec 1992 (Census[2])
Sofia (city)	38,000	n/a	10,797	13,902
Sofia (district)	14,136	17,077	10,812	11,684
Blagoevgrad	16,100	18,000	7,652	8,216
Burgas	37,894	38,453	16,365	16,120
Varna	20,682	35,000	14,313	17,077
Veliko Târnovo	20,880	n/a	2,750	7,236
Vidin	15,115	12,000	6,142	7,965
Vratsa	22,160	23,715	9,924	11,927
Gabrovo	5,920	114	2,314	1,585
Dobrich (Tolbuhin)	23,665	18,000	17,210	18,449
Kârdzhali	9,024	9,843	1,562	1,899
Kyustendil	8,463	12,762	6,248	6,057
Lovech	17,746	12,490	5,581	6,384
Montana (Mihailovgrad)	28,813	29,480	8,867	19,079
Pazardzhik	45,705	50,000	22,124	21,810
Pernik	38	6,600	1,604	2,142
Pleven	24,870	27,747	6,559	7,111
Plovdiv	45,333	61,585	24,403	21,139
Razgrad	5,213	16,468	7,639	7,464
Russe	16,306	16,306	8,917	11,934
Silistra	12,826	12,826	4,570	6,519
Sliven	46,491	40,590	17,170	18,183
Smolyan	548	1,225	n/a	514
Stara Zagora	28,289	38,000	22,309	24,143
Târgovishte	17,035	n/a	6,487	9,474
Haskovo	13,488	26,100	12,135	14,014
Shumen	20,128	15,823	15,760	14,727
Yambol	11,240	12,762	8,515	6,669
Total	576,927	553,466	287,732	313,396

Note: (1) 2% representative sample. (2) Final census data.

Table 4.2 Structure of Bulgaria's population by age and ethnic group, 1992[3]

Age	All ethnic groups	Ethnic Bulgarians	Turks	Roma/Gypsies
0-9	12.0%	10.9%	16.8%	25.4%
10-19	14.5%	13.7%	18.1%	23.2%
20-29	13.3%	12.7%	16.5%	17.4%
30-39	13.7%	13.4%	14.9%	13.9%
40-49	14.0%	14.4%	12.2%	9.2%
50-59	12.1%	12.7%	9.9%	5.8%
60 and over	20.4%	22.2%	11.6%	5.1%

A brief historical overview

Roma/Gypsies have lived in Bulgarian lands for centuries. Most historians think that the first big settlements of Roma/Gypsies in the Balkans, and more specifically in Thrace, can be dated back to the beginning of the ninth century AD. Abundant historical evidence points to the presence of Roma/Gypsies in the Byzantine Empire and their entry into Serbia, Wallachia and Moldova from the eleventh to the fourteenth century. This wide timeframe (from the ninth to the fourteenth century) also includes the lasting settlement of Roma/Gypsies in Bulgarian lands (the first Gypsy wave of migration).

There is a wealth of information about Roma/Gypsy presence in Bulgaria at the time of the Ottoman Empire. They were mentioned in many laws and other official documents, mostly tax registers, under the names *cengene* or *kıpts* (ie, Copts). Roma/Gypsies in the Ottoman Empire were actively settling in towns and villages. A new type of semi-nomadic way of life was established too – the Roma/Gypsies had a permanent winter residence and an active nomadic season. Often some Roma/Gypsies would break away from the traditional Roma/Gypsy occupations and take up farming or menial labour in the towns.

Roma/Gypsies had a special place in the overall social and administrative organisation of the Ottoman Empire. They were differentiated on the grounds of ethnicity (something rather unusual for the Ottoman Empire), with no sharp differentiation between Muslims and Christians in social status and the payment of taxes. Roma/Gypsies were similar in status to the local subject population, with some small privileges for the Muslim Roma/Gypsies and bigger privileges for those who served in the army. In this environment the Roma/Gypsies were able to preserve a number of their specific ethnic and cultural features, such as the nomadic lifestyle and traditional occupations. From a comparative point of view their civil status in the Ottoman Empire was more favourable than the status of Roma/Gypsies in Western Europe at that time.

In the seventeenth and eighteenth centuries many Roma/Gypsies left the Danubian principalities (Wallachia and Moldova) and entered the Ottoman Empire (the second wave of Roma/Gypsy migration in Bulgarian lands). Other Roma/Gypsy groups (the third wave of Roma/Gypsy migration) came to Bulgaria in the second half of the nineteenth century and the beginning of the twentieth, leaving Romania after the end of Roma/Gypsy slavery. Roma/Gypsy migrations from the neighbouring countries (Romania, Yugoslavia, Greece and Turkey) continued in the twentieth century as well, and were usually related to the change of state borders after the wars and subsequent population migrations (the two Balkan wars, WWI and WWII).

More than two-thirds of Roma/Gypsies in the newly independent Bulgarian state (1878) were living in villages. This number also included a lot of nomads (most of whom had permanent winter residences). In the 1920s and 1930s some nomadic Roma/Gypsy groups began to settle down and go to the big city neighbourhoods (*mahalas*). These processes continued after WWII as well, when the Roma/Gypsies were the target of the purposeful, though rather inconsistent and superficial, state policy of the new government. In the middle of the 1950s the Council of Ministers issued several decrees for sedentarisation (Decree 1216, 8/10/1957, "On solving the problem of the Roma/Gypsy minority in the People's Republic of Bulgaria" and Decree 258, 17/10/1958, "On settling the problems of the Roma/Gypsy population in the People's Republic of Bulgaria"). All nomadic Roma/Gypsies had to adopt a sedentary lifestyle and obtain permanent residence. The overall change in the economic environment during socialism forced many Roma/Gypsy groups to abandon their traditional occupations and way of life. Many Roma/Gypsies moved from small villages to big cities as part of the general processes of migration in the country.

The collapse of the Eastern European socialist system in 1989 was followed by a long and still uncompleted period of transition in Bulgaria. This has had a powerful influence on the situation of Roma/Gypsies in Bulgaria. Economic hardship has very often resulted in a return to traditional Roma/Gypsy occupations and a semi-nomadic lifestyle, a transformation or modification of the traditional professional specialisation or migration abroad. At present, Roma/Gypsies are living in a wide range of economic circumstances due to a number of factors, including the internal subdivisions in the Roma/Gypsy community itself.

Different Roma/Gypsy groups in Bulgaria

Roma/Gypsies in Bulgaria, like Roma/Gypsies all over the world, are not a homogeneous community. They have many internal divisions – groups, meta-group units and subgroup divisions. The most numerous and varied Roma/Gypsy community is the meta-group community of the so-called *Yerlia* (ie, local). They are the descendants of the first Roma/Gypsy wave of migration and speak different dialects of the Balkan group of Romanes (the Roma/Gypsy language). The Balkan group of Romanes is divided into two main groups – *Erlides* and *Drandari* dialects. Some Roma/Gypsies from this meta-group community speak Turkish or use both languages – Turkish and Romanes.

As well as having these dialect/language groups, the *Yerlia* community is also divided on religious grounds into two main subdivisions: *Dasikane Roma* (Bulgarian Roma/Gypsies, ie, Christians) and *Xoraxane/Xoroxane Roma* (Turkish Roma/Gypsies, ie, Muslims). Within the framework of these main subdivisions there are more or less preserved endogamous groups, whose members are aware of their group identity and some of whom still practise traditional occupations. There are also large Roma/Gypsy communities whose members remember the old-time occupations and the group divisions which are no longer relevant. The group divisions have been mostly obliterated, and there is a shift within the borders of the larger communities (*Dasikane Roma* or *Xoraxane Roma*). In general, *Dasikane Roma* live mostly in western Bulgaria, while *Xoraxane Roma* live mostly in eastern Bulgaria, but sometimes parts of these communities may merge into one another. These processes are typical of the big city *mahalas*, where the memories of old groups have faded.

Roma/Gypsies in Bulgaria have another large subdivision, which is now a part of the big *Yerlia* community. It includes the communities of the so-called *Vlaxichki* (versions *Vlaxoria, Laxo*, etc). These communities speak the so-called Old Vlax dialects of Romanes. They settled in Bulgaria during the second wave of Roma/Gypsy migration (17th-18th century). In the 1920s, 1930s and later some of them gradually adopted a settled lifestyle (mainly in the urban *mahalas*) and some changed their religion (for example, they are Muslims in eastern Bulgaria now), gradually merging with the major group communities (*Dasikane Roma* and *Xoraxane Roma*). Today, living with other Roma/Gypsy groups from these subdivisions and intermarrying with them is considered normal, but their different group origin is still remembered.

Some members of the two main communities (Bulgarian and Turkish Roma/Gypsies) gradually separated themselves from the others on the basis of their preferred ethnic identities. This is the case with many Turkish Roma/Gypsies, who lost most of their group characteristics, are mostly bilingual (speaking both Turkish and Romanes), or only Turkish-speaking, and prefer to declare themselves as Turks or only as *millet'* (ie, people).

The second main meta-group of the Roma/Gypsy community in Bulgaria is very clearly distinct from the rest. This is the group of the so-called *Kardarasha* (self-appellation *Rom Ciganjaka*, in sense "true Gypsies"), descendants of the third wave of Roma/Gypsy migration (19th-20th century). They were nomads until 1958 and now are living mostly in villages and smaller towns and less often in the big cities. They speak the so-called New Vlax dialect of Romanes. *Kardarasha* are strictly endogamous within their meta-group community and differentiate themselves from the other Roma/Gypsies.

The "Thracian" *Kalajdzhia* [ie, tinsmiths] (self-appellation *Vlaxos*) are semi-nomads, permanently settled in small villages on the Thracian Plain. They are endogamous and rigorously distinguish themselves from other Roma/Gypsy communities. They speak an Old Vlax dialect of Romanes.

The third main meta-group is the one of *Rudara*, often called *Vlasi* (ie, Wallachians) or Wallachian Gypsies by the surrounding population.[4] They speak a Romanian dialect and they vehemently distinguish themselves from the Roma. In the past they were mostly nomads, settling in Bulgaria mainly in the nineteenth and twentieth centuries. The *Rudara* community has two main subdivisions: *Lingurara* (ie, spoon-makers, also called *Kopanari* – ie, trough-makers), who are wood carvers, and *Ursara* (bear-trainers, monkey-trainers). The *Rudara* are endogamous within their large community and scattered all over the country. They live mostly in villages and small towns.

Minority rights

After the transition from communism in 1989, the situation of Bulgaria's minorities changed. In August 1991 a new Constitution was adopted, which was based on the presumption of individual civil rights and the denial of some collective minority rights. The most frequently cited article from this Constitution is Article 6, paragraph 2, which does not allow for "any limitations of the rights or privileges based on race, nationality, ethnic belonging". This text has some harmful implications for minorities – whenever their problems have to be solved, the typical reply is that, according to the Constitution, all Bulgarian citizens are equal and there can be no privileges. In November 1992 the Constitutional Court elaborated on this text, allowing for "certain socially justified privileges" for "groups of citizens" who are in "an unfavourable social situation", thus opening the way for the state to adopt a policy in regard to minorities.

However, the situation in the system of executive government remained almost unchanged, despite changes of cabinets and political leadership. For several years, there were discussions about instituting a special body of the Council of Ministers, with representatives of various ministries who would implement a co-ordinated state policy in respect of minorities. Finally, an Inter-departmental Council on Ethnic Problems was organised in 1994. The following year the Bulgarian Socialist Party (BSP) came to power, and the council was transformed into an Inter-administrative Council on Social and Demographic Issues. However, it was inactive. In early 1997 the new government of the Union of Democratic Forces (UDF) declared a new approach to the minorities, and established a new government body – the National Council on the Ethnic and Demographic Issues at the Council of Ministers. In the same year President Stoyanov signed the Framework Convention for Protection of National Minorities. This was ratified in parliament on 18 February 1999, with a special declaration according to which Bulgaria is obliged to maintain a policy of human-rights protection and tolerance of minorities and to ensure their complete integration into Bulgarian society.

Yet despite the changes brought about in 1989, and the political ideologies of the various governments since then, there has been no real policy implementation concerning the education of minorities in Bulgaria. The past decade has seen governments of all the major political groupings, including the government formed with the mandate of the Movement for Rights and Freedoms (uniting Bulgarian Turks and Muslims). However, nothing tangible has been done about the education of minorities (except for the study of mother-tongue languages as discussed below).

There are some essential differences in the views of the major political groupings regarding the education of minorities, not at the level of general strategy, but in relation to specific measures concerning individual aspects of education. These differences are especially clear in the comparison of two governmental programmes aimed at Roma/Gypsies and the subsequent chapters on education adopted by the UDF and the BSP.

The right to education in Bulgaria

Primary, secondary and further education

The 1991 Constitution was promulgated in the Official Gazette No. 56 of 13 July 1991. Article 53 guarantees the right to education of every citizen. It states that education is compulsory for all children under the age of sixteen, and there is a right to free primary and secondary education. The Bulgarian language is compulsory in schools because Article 3 of the Constitution proclaims that it is the Republic's official language. Article 36/1 stipulates that:

> "The study and use of the Bulgarian language shall be the right and obligation of every Bulgarian citizen."

Article 36/2 proclaims that:

"Citizens whose mother tongue is not Bulgarian shall have the right to study and use their own mother tongue together with the mandatory study of the Bulgarian language."

Education is free and compulsory for all those aged between 7/8 years and 15/16 years. Compulsory education is broken down into primary education (grades one to four) and secondary education (grades five to eight). Primary and secondary education is predominantly government-funded through local authorities, with a small percentage of schools being privately run, more so at primary than at secondary level (less than five per cent).[5]

In addition, there are a number of optional stages in the schooling career. These include, preschool care and education, and kindergartens catering for young children aged from nine/ten months. Kindergartens are partially subsidised by local authorities, and lower-income families pay lower fees. Although this is optional, many children do attend. However, exact figures do not exist on how many attend and to what extent minority groups are represented.

Further education is also provided for those aged between 16 and 18 years. This is delivered through three types of institutions: profile-oriented colleges, gymnasiums and vocational/technical colleges. Profile-oriented colleges cover topics such as the natural sciences, mathematics, and the humanities, which are studied over a four-year period. This type of college can be attended on

completion of grade eight. Gymnasiums focus on modern languages and can be attended on completion of grade seven, for a total of five years. Finally, vocational/technical colleges are available for those who have completed grade eight, the course taking three years to complete. On completing further education, those aged 18 and over are entitled to go on to higher education in universities and equivalent institutions.

According to Article 5 of the Public Education Act, adopted in 1991, education in Bulgaria is secular. Article 4 guarantees the right to education and the ongoing development of education and attainment of qualifications. No restrictions or privileges based on race, nationality, gender, ethnic or social origin, faith or social status are admissible. In the past, the Ministry of Education and Science (MES) supplied all students from grades one to eight with textbooks and obligatory manuals free of charge. This provision has been amended, and now textbooks are free only for those children who are identified as poor. Parents have to request free textbooks from the school authorities and submit evidence of their income. Preparatory classes are compulsory for children aged six years or over who have a poor command of the Bulgarian language and who have not previously attended a kindergarten. However, as will be shown later, this provision is seldom implemented. Likewise, Article 8/2 of the National Education Law, and the 1992 Council of Ministers Decree No. 223 provides practical arrangements for the study of minority languages in municipal schools. However, the teaching of such languages has not been made compulsory, but instead remains optional. Consequently, such languages are only studied if the option has been made available in individual state and municipal schools or through private schooling.

In recent years, several legislative instruments have been adopted for the development of the private school sector. For example, the Ordinance on Private Schools of the Ministry of Education, Science and Technologies (now the Ministry of Education and Science – MES) states that the government, and in particular the MES, must create the necessary conditions and preconditions for the development of private school systems. The Ministry's position is that, in a context of economic, political, social and cultural change, private schools have a specific role to play in the system of formal education. They present an extra opportunity for ensuring the constitutional right of all citizens to choose freely the kind of school and education they wish.

Higher education

A new structure of higher education was introduced at the end of 1995, enacted by the Higher Education Act and adopted by the National Assembly. In line with Chapter ten of this Act, the setting up of a National Agency for Evaluation and Accreditation of Higher Education Establishments is intended to contribute to the development and application of criteria for the evaluation of profitability in different education establishments. The Law on Academic Autonomy states that all universities and higher education institutions must determine independently all matters relating to their curricula, structure, teaching, research, qualifications and certification.

Laws established for the higher-education sector remain largely distinct from those that underpin compulsory education in so far as the Law on Academic Autonomy relates only to universities and the prime focus of the National Agency for Evaluation and Accreditation is that of issuing academic titles.

At the beginning of 1995, an Ordinance on Unified Government Norms for Higher Education of Teachers was adopted by Decree No. 12 of the Council of Ministers. The Ordinance establishes obligatory forms for the practical training of future teachers, guaranteeing the minimum level of their teaching competence, and regulates the pedagogical and methodological elements in the study plans for teacher training. However, the Ordinance does not inform the entire content of teacher training, thus giving scope for variation between colleges on what aspects are covered. Teaching of equal opportunities or multicultural education, for example, is not compulsory, and therefore it is possible to find only a few examples of these topics being included in teacher-training courses. Shumen University has courses on bilingual education and Sofia University on multicultural education. With such limited examples, however, the impact on the segregated school system is minimal.

In practice

The right to education of Roma/Gypsy children

According to official census data, the levels of education of the main minority groups are shown in Tables 3.3 and 3.4:

Table 4.3 Population aged seven and above, according to ethnic group and primary education

	Total	Primary	Elementary	Incomplete elementary	Illiterate	Not indicated
Bulgarian	6,735,540	1,978,680	969,696	395,113	69,479	
Turks	708,107	287,891	171,741	75,612	52,599	
Roma/Gypsies	257,840	83,410	80,179	51,892	28,897	
Total	7,797,602	2,370,214	1,231,727	527,392	152,955	7,876

Table 4.4 Population aged seven and above, according to ethnic group and post-primary education[6]

	Total	University	College	Specialised College	Gymnasium
Bulgarian	6,735,540	602,204	258,077	1,253,549	1,208,742
Turks	708,107	2,798	5,523	38,416	73,527
Roma/Gypsies	257,840	464	274	4,210	8,514
Total	7,797,602	619,294	266,907	1,311,652	1,309,585

According to the Bulgarian report for the Education for All 2000 Assessment, the relative share of education expenditure within overall GDP declined in the period between 1992 and 1994.[7] However, the Education for All country report makes no reference to education arrangements and legislation for children belonging to minority ethnic communities, including Roma/Gypsy children. This is despite the fact that, in its 1997 concluding observations on Bulgaria, the UN Committee on the Elimination of Racial Discrimination notes as a matter of serious concern the persistent marginalisation of the large Roma/Gypsy population, in spite of continuing efforts by the government. The observations make reference to inadequate training and education for the Roma/Gypsy minority.[8]

The 1999 Enlargement Commission Report for Bulgaria on progress towards accession to the EU similarly deplores the fact that a disproportionate number of Roma/Gypsy children are sent to special schools for the so-called mentally handicapped.[9] Furthermore, it notes that the health and housing conditions of Roma/Gypsies remain considerably lower than for the rest of the population. The 1999 concluding observations on the Bulgarian report by the United Nations Committee on Economic, Social and Cultural Rights also expresses concern over the issue of multiple discrimination against the Roma/Gypsy minority, including in the field of education.[10]

The most persistent problem concerning the education of minority ethnic communities in

Bulgaria is the low level of education among the largest minority communities (ie, Turks, Roma/Gypsies, and Bulgarian Muslims, otherwise referred to as *Pomaks*) leading to basic inequalities. Smaller minority groups are affected to a lesser degree, due to their size and the fact that their level of education does not differ as much from that of the majority. In some instances, the educational level of smaller minorities, for example, the Jewish minority, in fact exceeds the national average. In contrast, the level of education among Roma/Gypsies is the most far removed from the national average, causing additional problems of poor professional qualifications, unemployment and poor living standards.

The reasons for the lower level of education among the Roma/Gypsy minority are complicated. To a certain extent they are related to the unequal status of this minority in Bulgarian society, but there are other important factors at play, which vary in influence. These include (not in order of importance):

• ineffective and outdated teaching methods of minority children in an educational system which so far has been a mono-ethnic (Bulgarian) system and is intended for the needs of an ethno-national (one-nation) state
• lack of consideration for minorities in the principles and teaching methods of the current educational system

- lack of consideration of their ethnic and cultural characteristics, and for varying levels of bilingualism
- widespread and persistent negative attitudes towards certain minorities (especially Roma/Gypsies) in Bulgarian society, which are often reflected in the attitude towards Roma/Gypsy children in Bulgarian schools
- specific peculiarities in the ethnic, cultural and religious characteristics of the Roma/Gypsy minority, which determine their different values, and especially their attitude towards education
- the hardship during the period of transition from communism and the economic crisis, which has had an impact on the social and economic situation of the Roma/Gypsy minority and in turn hindered the access of their children to school.

These, as well as a number of other, factors are obstacles to equal education for the Roma/Gypsy minority, and must always be considered against the backdrop of their specific environment – the region, town or village, type of school, etc – along with the specific internal community subdivision of this minority.

In recent years, there has been a misuse and even open abuse (at the state level as well as in the NGO sector) of the economic hardship of Roma/Gypsies, which has often been aimed at shifting the emphasis away from this problem and postponing attempts at its solution. The standard explanation that "children have no shoes and that is why they do not go to school" is universally applied to Eastern European Roma/Gypsies and has existed for some time.[11] Ultimately,

government programmes and NGO projects that focus on the distribution of free breakfasts or shoes for Roma/Gypsy children, do not automatically result in a higher quality of education, even if they yield a higher percentage of school attendance.

School abandonment

Directly related to the low level of minority education (especially among the Roma/Gypsy minority) is the problem of high drop-out rates. Unfortunately, there is no precise information about this phenomenon, but the MES, based on figures drawn up by Regional Inspectorates, registers some 30,000-40,000 drop-outs each year, most of whom are Roma/Gypsy children. NGOs usually give different numbers, ranging from 45,000 to 120,000 children, but such figures are unsubstantiated and generalised. As well as disparities between official and non-official estimates, there are significant gaps in knowledge in terms of how these drop-out rates link with age, ethnicity and religion. Furthermore, there is the need to establish to what extent "dropping out" among Roma/Gypsy pupils is due to family migration (labour, seasonal or abroad) and whether the children ever go back to school. Connected to this is also the question of whether children continue their education in another form after a temporary break, such as in another school, a specialised school, private tuition or even abroad.

The 1999 UNICEF Report *Out-of-School Youth in Bulgaria* indicates that widespread poverty and the return of minorities to their cultural traditions do not in themselves explain the school drop-out rates.[12] Even if the family situation places demands upon young people, such as pressure to contribute to household income and/or to marry young, these circumstances should not automatically disqualify young people from enjoying their right to education. Ultimately, a failure on the part of both policy-makers and practitioners to respond to the reality of children's circumstances contributes to high drop-out rates. In the new market economy, schools in Bulgaria are struggling to survive financially and are competing with each other to maintain overall student numbers as well as to attract "good students". (In 1998, more than 300 schools were closed because of reduced numbers.) Social prestige is important for schools, as parents endeavour to enrol their children in schools offering a 'modern' curriculum (particularly featuring language instruction and IT skills). While this situation could result in an increase in drop-out rates as neighbourhood schools are closed, it also provides an incentive for schools to try to attract pupils by offering innovative and relevant curricula.

Bulgarian schools are often perceived as being detached from the social, economic and cultural needs of today's youth, lacking in activities that appeal to children, and failing to provide opportunities for students to acquire vocational, social and basic professional skills. It is felt that the schools are losing their multidimensional vocational education role, and are modifying the learning process to a simple transfer of a huge amount of academic information. The UNICEF report draws attention to the fact that MES does not systematically collect data of its own, but makes use of data transmitted by the National Institute of Statistics to the Department of Finance. Such data is not intended for educational and pedagogical purposes, but mainly for the management of schools and staff. Furthermore, neither the National Institute of Education nor the 28 MES Regional Inspectorates collect data about school attendance on a regular basis. They may collect specific data at the request of MES for some special purpose, or for certain surveys. Finally, the report highlights the lack of communication and co-operation among the diverse institutions and partners dealing with education at all levels, which does not serve the interests of students.

Roma/Gypsies and segregated schooling

Another very important issue specifically related to the quality of education of Roma/Gypsy children, is that of the so-called "Gypsy schools". These schools have predominantly or only Roma/Gypsy children, and their learning conditions and quality of education are considerably poorer than mainstream schools in Bulgaria. Gypsy schools were built in the 1940s and 1950s in separated Roma/Gypsy neighbourhoods. At the time they had a positive influence on the education of Roma/Gypsy children in that it was the first time that Roma/Gypsies had received any formal schooling. However, over the years, the quality of education in these schools suffered a drastic decline. In particular, during the 1970s and 1980s, with the breaking up of the school system into differentiated parts, these schools began to deteriorate. Official policy was to gather all Roma/Gypsy children into the Gypsy schools. Some of the schools were given the special status of primary schools with 'specialised labour' education at the expense of general education. According to MES, in 1991 there were 31 such schools with 17,800 children and another 77 schools which were euphemistically defined, in the terminology of the past Socialist era, as schools for children with a "lower level of lifestyle and culture". In 1992, MES cancelled the special status of labour schools, and introduced the national curriculum. However, due to the lack of any ministerial backing, the absence of new teachers, the reluctance to invest resources and a general lack of interest on the part of the population, the educational environment has remained unchanged.

In the first few years after the changes, the state institutions avoided taking a stand on the problems in Gypsy schools. Their excuse was the existing territorial principle of the distribution of students. This principle is no longer mandatory, but its abolition in the early 1990s did not change the *status quo*, and Roma/Gypsy children are still not allowed (for different "reasons") to enrol in many of the half-empty Bulgarian schools. Instead they are sent to the overcrowded Gypsy schools (even where a Bulgarian and a Gypsy school are next to each other). When the decreased number of ethnic Bulgarian children and increased number of Roma/Gypsy children requires the transfer of students from a Gypsy school to a Bulgarian school, the process is often accompanied by widespread protests from Bulgarian parents or the segregation of Roma/Gypsy children into different classes. For example, in Yambol in autumn 1999, due to insufficient places, Roma/Gypsy children were transferred without prior notice and little preparation to a neighbouring school. This led to problems of non-compliance on the part of the receiving school and to protests from the

non-Roma/Gypsy parents. More recently, in September 2000, in the Nov Pat Romani neighbourhood in Vidin, a more organised and well-prepared process of desegregation was initiated, which is discussed in more detail in the following section.

Roma/Gypsy children and special schools

The problems of the so-called "special schools" are related to the educational problems of the minorities in Bulgaria. According to MES, on 31 December 1997, there were 299 special schools in Bulgaria. These were of 12 kinds, including educational boarding schools; social-pedagogical boarding schools; homes for children and youth (orphans or children who were temporarily abandoned by their parents); schools for children with learning disabilities; schools for the speech-impaired, and schools for children with health problems (see Table 3.6). In 1997, a total of 27,148 children attended these special schools, with the highest numbers being in schools for children with learning disabilities (34 per cent in 85 schools) and homes for children and youth (25.5 per cent in 87 homes), which together accommodated more than half of these children. At the end of 1999, there were a total of 34,122 children, or 1.8 per cent of Bulgaria's child population, in specialised institutions under the Ministries of Health, Education and Science, Labour and Social Policy and the Ministry of Justice.

The majority of children in special schools are of minority origin. Many are children from Roma/Gypsy communities who have expressed this as a preferred ethnic identity. The problems of these schools are often seen in terms of the problems

Table 4.5 Social institutions in Bulgaria, 1997

Type of institution	Number of institutions	Number of children	As percentage of all children in special schools
Reform boarding schools	11	782	2.9%
Social-pedagogical boarding schools	25	2,428	8.9%
Schools for children with learning disabilities	85	9,228	34.0%
Schools for children with impaired hearing	4	767	2.8%
Schools for children with impaired vision	2	303	1.1%
Schools for children with speech problems	5	262	1.0%
Schools for children with health problems	35	3,909	14.4%
Sanatoria-type schools	6	477	1.8%
Hospital schools	3	508	1.9%
Homes for children and young people	87	6,933	25.5%
Family homes	2	7	0.0%
Homes for children of pre-school age	34	1,544	5.7%
Total	299	27,148	100.0

Source: Ministry of Education, 31 December 1997.

of minority education, which is by no means justified. There are no precise data about the number of minority children in special schools. Moreover, most of the children with minority origins in these schools belong to communities with no preserved ethnic and cultural traditions and no clear identity.

The problems of special schools are many and diverse, and to a great extent they are related to the economic situation in Bulgaria. The unclear legal status of these schools and the complicated mechanisms for their financial support brought about by the transition to a market economy result in extremely hard living conditions for the students. For example, laws and regulations issued before and after 1989 often overlap, making it difficult to determine where responsibility lies for issues such as payments for school maintenance. As a result, both municipal and state authorities have evaded payments for basic resources for individual schools.

The economic crisis has presented some elements of Roma/Gypsy society with difficult decisions about their children's welfare. For example, it has led to a growing number of parents temporarily leaving their children in homes for children and youth, whilst maintaining parental rights. Others have sent normal and healthy children to schools for children with learning disabilities where they are at least provided with meals. Teachers who actively seek out pupils in Roma/Gypsy districts further encourage this. This is the case in other countries too, including the Czech Republic, for example. (See the chapter on the Czech Republic in Volume Two of this report.)

Officially, there are certain procedures for deciding which children should attend schools for those with learning disabilities. According to existing legislation, the decision must be taken by a special committee – consisting of a psychologist, an educator and the child's teacher – elected by the regional educational office, or by the issuing of a medical certificate showing the child's psychological status. In reality, however, the majority of Roma/Gypsy children are sent to such schools upon parental request only, thus demonstrating that the decision is not based on the existence of mental disability or learning difficulties, but that it is a "social" one.

Educational provision for street children

Somewhat similar is the problem of the so-called "street children". This euphemism describes children who have left their homes for long or short periods of time, or have been abandoned by their parents, and have neither homes nor parental supervision. The category of "street children" is ill-defined, and the number of children it encompasses is subject to discussion. According to the Ministry of Internal Affairs, which discloses information about street children on a regular basis, their number across Bulgaria fluctuates between 2,000 and 3,000.

NGOs working in this area, however, provide much higher estimates, ranging between 20,000 and 30,000 children. It is certain that most street children are of Roma/Gypsy origin. However, as with the special-school situation, this does not justify treating street children as an ethnic problem. To focus on street children ultimately distracts from the bigger underlying issue that the educational system is failing Roma/Gypsy children.

The state continues to justify its lack of concern with the problems of "street children" by transferring their care to the NGO sector. In many respects, the NGO sector has certain advantages over the state in terms of its potential for greater flexibility and innovation. However, for the NGO sector to be effective, the government must provide financial support and a means for monitoring NGO work to ensure child-protection and other standards. At present, the Bulgarian government, and in particular the MES, must be informed of any project activity in the area of education and in turn offer expertise in the implementation of projects such as those aimed at Roma/Gypsy education. However, this "in-kind" contribution does not make up for the lack of direct financial support. For example, it has been NGOs, not the government, that have established temporary accommodation for street children, such as *Nadezhda* in Sofia and *Gavrauche* in Varna. Ultimately, the establishment of temporary homes by NGOs alone is not a solution.

The lack of adequate legislation is the routine and often reiterated excuse offered by the Bulgarian government for its failure to act on a number of social issues. However, in June 2000, at its 38th National Assembly, the Bulgarian government ratified the Child Protection Act. This piece of legislation, together with the possible introduction of foster families and a series of proposed amendments to the Family Code, potentially has huge implications for the rights of Roma/Gypsy children.

The study of Romanes by Roma/Gypsy children

A constant issue concerning the education of minorities is the study of their mother tongue. This has often been the subject of heated political and public debate, and has acquired symbolic significance for many minorities in Bulgaria. The 1991 Bulgarian Constitution declared "the right of citizens, whose mother tongue is not Bulgarian... to study and use their mother tongue, together with the mandatory study of Bulgarian" (Article 35, paragraph 2). Decree No. 232 of the Council of Ministers of 10 December 1991 specified how this constitutional right should be implemented within the educational system. Turks, Roma/Gypsies, Armenians and Jews were allowed to study their mother tongue as an "elective" subject (ie, outside the regular curriculum) for two hours a week. Decree No. 183 of 5 September 1994 expanded the time to four hours a week. After lengthy public debate, and with pressure from the Movement for Rights and Freedoms, as well as other minority parties and NGOs, there was a major breakthrough in the law that established a minimum standard in primary and secondary education. The study of one's mother-tongue language became a "mandatory elective", with a view to including all stages of education after the respective laws and curricula had been approved.

At present, the study of a mother-tongue language in Bulgarian schools varies substantially between different minority groups. There are a number of factors behind this, such as the demographic characteristics of a minority or the manner of their settlement, whether it is according to regions or the type of towns or villages that they live in.

The study of Romanes (the Romani/Gypsy language) is extremely complicated. After the 1991 decree, the study of Romanes was rejected by the Bulgarian institutions on the grounds that there was no standardised written form of Romanes – only a multitude of dialects. Furthermore, there were no teachers in this subject. Hristo Kyuchukov, who at the time was appointed as a Romanes expert in the Ministry of Education, did manage to develop and publish a series of teaching materials and to train part-time Romanes teachers. As a result, many schools across Bulgaria started teaching Romanes in the following school year. However, since his departure, the government has refused to appoint a new Romanes expert. The unresolved status of part-time teachers, the fact that universities do not cover Romanes as part of their teacher training and the resistance (or lack of co-operation) on the part of school boards, regional educational inspectors and MES have combined to mean that Romanes is currently not studied in Bulgaria. Under pressure from Roma/Gypsy-led NGOs, the present government has promised to engage with this issue within the Framework Programme. As yet, however, no tangible activity has been observed.

Government initiatives

In its last days in power, in January 1997, the government of Zhan Videnov (BSP) approved a "Programme for solving the problems of Roma in the Republic of Bulgaria", which failed to recognise the existing segregation of the vast majority of Roma/Gypsy children in special Gypsy schools. Indeed, the programme emphasised the preservation of these schools and the need to ensure regular attendance of all Roma/Gypsy children. It was believed that this would fulfil the proposed objective that all pupils should receive a vocational qualification by the age of sixteen. The BSP programme largely reproduced the underlying educational philosophy of socialist primary schools, ie, labour training. It also combined a number of methods used in the "Let's bring the children back to school" project run by the International Centre for Minority Studies and Intercultural Relations (described below). Other educational problems of Roma/Gypsy children, such as the need for bilingual education and preparatory Bulgarian-language classes, were merely noted, with no specific ideas for their implementation.

Similar in philosophy and trends was the Draft Programme (the so-called "Spanish Programme"), prepared in 1999 by the new UDF government with the assistance of experts from the Council of Europe. The programme was not accepted, due to pressure from Roma/Gypsy-led NGOs. Their main objections were that, firstly, Roma/Gypsies were not consulted or allowed to participate during the preparation of the programme and, secondly, the proposed strategy was not applicable to the Bulgarian context. These factors resulted in the programme failing to reflect issues already identified by Roma/Gypsy organisations, such as the desegregation of schools. Instead the programme spoke of the "double discrimination" of Roma/Gypsy women and the need to create schools that catered for nomadic populations.

In April 1999, with the support of a number of international institutions, and after a long series of negotiations, a number of Roma/Gypsy-led NGOs obliged the government to accept their own "Framework Programme for Equal Integration of Roma/Gypsies in Bulgarian Social Life". This programme's philosophy for the solution of the educational problems of Roma/Gypsy children was radically different. Its goal is to guarantee the right to (and opportunities for) equal education of Roma/Gypsy children. The most important elements of the Framework Programme are:

- the need for desegregated education
- the gradual abolition of the so-called Roma/Gypsy schools
- the gradual abolition of all forms of specialised education on an ethnic basis (including the special schools).

The Framework Programme includes the introduction of preparatory classes for children who do not speak Bulgarian, and additional teacher training for teachers of Roma/Gypsy children.

Although the Framework Programme was accepted by the Bulgarian government, there has been no indication of any financial support, or indeed any indication of how the MES has been working on it, if at all. For example, an important first step towards desegregation began in

September 2000, in the Nov Pat Romani quarter in Vidin. This was a process initiated by Rumyan Russinov, chair of the Roma Participation Programme of the Open Society Institute, and a Vidin-based Romani NGO, DROM, as part of the framework programme. Unlike previous attempts, such as those in Yambol (previously discussed), there were many months of preparation; parents and teachers were consulted, and an agreement was reached with the school inspectorate. The process was also closely monitored and proper support given to the Roma families and children during the transfer process. Around 300 children were transported to a number of mixed schools in Vidin, and it is now estimated that three-quarters of the school population in this area are participating in the initiative.[13] Although this initiative is part of the Framework Programme, there has been neither government funding nor indeed any support offered of any kind. Instead, external funding and support has come through the Roma Participation Programme of the Open Society Institute. The institute will also fund processes of desegregation in the towns of Montana, Pleven, Stara Zagora, Haskovo and Sliven in the school year 2001-02.[14]

Once again this raises the issue of the unwillingness (or lack of ability) on the part of all Bulgarian governments since 1989 to tackle the problems of Roma/Gypsy children and education. It seems possible, with the approval of a primary-school curriculum that seeks to establish a minimum standard of attainment (and primarily aimed at securing students' early vocational training), that the segregated

Roma/Gypsy schools will remain in existence *de facto*, even if they no longer exist *de jure*.

A current violation of the principles of the Framework Programme is the recent announcement made by the National Council of Ethnic and Demographic Issues to finance selected NGOs with an EU (PHARE) grant to train teaching assistants of Roma/Gypsy origin. In many respects this serves to consolidate rather than challenge the principle of specialised education for Roma/Gypsy children, especially in light of the fact that the position of teaching assistant does not currently exist in the Bulgarian educational system. It also encourages increased segregation, in that the training required is considerably less than is required for full members of staff and in turn would restrict the professional potential for such assistants. The introduction of Roma/Gypsy teaching assistants via the NGO sector, without any state back-up, is another example of the way in which the state attempts to transfer its obligations to the NGO sector, through half measures and temporary solutions.

NGO practice in the area

It must be emphasised that Roma/Gypsy-led NGOs have a specific role to play in the development of state policy on the education of Roma/Gypsy children. With the help of international institutions and other NGOs they are able to exert pressure on the government, and to have a number of their concepts and specific ideas accepted. The Framework Programme, which prioritises education, is the best example of this. It was developed under the initiative of the Human Rights Project prior to negotiations with the government. Central to its development was extensive discussion with Roma/Gypsy-led NGOs throughout the country and their support during the difficult negotiations with the government.

Since the "transition" from communism in 1989, the NGO sector has grown rapidly and emerged as an important factor for the development of society. Over a short period of time, it has found a stable place in various aspects of Bulgarian public life, where it now occupies key positions. In times of state crises, the NGO sector has often taken upon itself the duties of the state. The NGO sector is dynamic and has become a generator of new ideas in many aspects of Bulgarian society. In the context of the Bulgarian economy, where the average monthly salary is 224 Bulgarian Leva (£GB72), the NGO sector is also relatively well funded.[15] It is estimated that salaries in the NGO sector far exceed those in other more traditional spheres such as the university sector and the law.

The NGO sector has been instrumental in the development of debates around the education of minorities. NGO actors have been able to fill the gaps that have eluded the attention (and abilities) of the state. The support of foreign donors and, in particular, their prioritising of Roma/Gypsy issues has been a major contributing factor.

In reviewing the NGO sector's major education projects targeting Roma/Gypsy children, we are concerned not with problems of implementation (or the lack of it), but rather with overall concepts and possibilities for their adaptation into the state education system (or at least co-operation between these two sectors). Some NGO projects are not specifically targeted towards Roma/Gypsies, but towards minorities in general. However, the situation in Bulgaria is such that their emphasis tends to fall on the "Roma/Gypsy issue".

One of the first projects on minority education came from the Bulgarian National Committee of UNICEF, and was implemented in 1991-93 in a number of schools and kindergartens around the country in which Roma/Gypsy children were a majority. This project included the preparation of special teaching materials introducing bilingual teaching methods and an introduction to Roma/Gypsy language, history and cultural traditions. The PHARE Programme Project for Intercultural Education, implemented in 1995-98 by the Minority Rights Group (London) and the Interethnic Initiative for Human Rights Foundation was to a great extent a repetition of the UNICEF project, with the following differences:

- a wider range of schools were included in the project (35 schools)
- a more extended programme was implemented for the different levels of education (primary and secondary)
- kindergartens were not included
- the study of Romanes was not included
- there was more extensive and expensive printing of teaching materials, which included samples of Roma/Gypsy folklore and Roma/Gypsy music.

A series of projects under the Step-By-Step Programme of the Open Society Fund has been implemented in rapid succession since the early 1990s. These projects are dedicated to different forms of minority integration through special (intercultural and multicultural) education in kindergartens. Another series of projects based on the principle of intercultural and multicultural education is currently being implemented by the Open Education Centre (initially a part of the Open Society Fund). It includes various training courses and teacher-training seminars.

The project "Let's Bring the Children Back to School" has become very popular. It was implemented by the International Centre for Minority Studies and Intercultural Relations in a selection of schools in Bulgaria (14 schools at the last stage of the project) and initially funded by UNESCO (other sponsors contributed later). This project started in 1993 and has been modified many times in the course of its development. It is dedicated to the inclusion in the school system (initially within the regular curriculum and later as extracurricular activities) of a number of elements (music, fine arts, choreography, sports) designed to attract Roma/Gypsy children to the school and, importantly, to keep them there.

NGO-sector projects are very often oriented towards the solution of specific problems, such as building additional wings of schools in Roma/Gypsy neighbourhoods. An example is the project to extend the school building in Fakulteta, Sofia (the Bulgarian Helsinki Committee).

The Balkan Foundation for Cross-Cultural Education and Understanding "Diversity" has been very active in the last few years. It has implemented a series of projects related to the publication and dissemination of academic literature, methodological writings and teaching materials for the bilingual education of minority children (especially Roma/Gypsy children), and teaching materials for the study of Romanes. The Foundation's other projects are dedicated to the study of the conditions and forms of education for Roma/Gypsy children in the various types of special schools as discussed above.

A new element was introduced into the Bulgarian education system as part of a project run by the Interethnic Initiative for Human Rights Foundation funded by the Council of Europe. The project consisted of a short training course organised by the Nova Skola Foundation in the Czech Republic in 1998. Although based in the Czech Republic, this course trained young Roma/Gypsies as teaching assistants for Roma/Gypsy children in Bulgaria. The methods used and outcomes achieved are unclear, in so far as many of those who underwent the training could not speak Czech, English or Romanes. The MES promised to employ these teaching assistants in the Bulgarian education system even though, as mentioned above, no such position exists in Bulgaria. Further still, the teaching-assistant salaries come exclusively from Council of Europe funds, rather than from the MES budget. The project has since come to an end, and consequently no funding is now available for the payment of salaries. As a result, none of the participants who were trained for these positions is currently employed in schools.

Roma/Gypsy teaching assistants are also important in the ongoing projects of the Creating Effective Grassroots Alternatives Foundation in many towns and villages. The difference is that the teaching assistants are trained in Bulgaria and they take part in the education process in special preparatory classes (a year before 1st grade of school) where Roma/Gypsy children study Bulgarian. The projects include the active participation of Roma/Gypsy communities in these activities and events. As a result, new forms of project implementation are being developed, including the participation of local Roma/Gypsy organisations. The Catholic Remedial Services project is also directed at encouraging community (Roma/Gypsy and Turkish) participation in the education of their children. It includes the participation of community members on the school boards of trustees, which will be registered as juridical bodies according to new legislation.

In 1998/99 the Open Society Fund's Programme for Reform of Education's mega-project "Education" entered its pilot stage. Its purpose was to make recommendations to the MES by summarising the results of the various minority education projects of the NGO sector and outlining the achievements and faults of their implementation. The overall aim was to enhance co-operation between the state and the NGO sector with a view to achieving the best possible results.

On the whole, it is not possible to conclude either way whether NGO projects dealing with education and Roma/Gypsy children have been successful or, indeed, detrimental. While evaluation reports produced for the donors by the NGO very rarely highlight negative aspects of a given project for fear of losing vital funding, we cannot ignore their low efficiency relative to the funds invested in them. In measuring the effectiveness of such projects, a number of indicators need to be established. For example, one very important indicator is to look at what a given NGO is actually advocating. A worrying trend is that many projects emphasise the special education of Roma/Gypsy children, rather than their general education, thus helping to increase rather than challenge the existing segregation of Roma/Gypsy children in the Bulgarian education system. Another important indicator is how well NGO materials are used and distributed. The bibliography at the end of this volume lists some examples of publications that have been produced by NGOs in Bulgaria, none of which are currently used in mainstream schools. This is particularly significant given the high costs of such publications, which may include costs of surveys, writing, printing, salaries, office maintenance, seminars and workshops. More specific data on the effectiveness of NGOs is dealt with in annual reports. However, in order to prevent the fuelling of negative attitudes towards NGOs and Roma/Gypsies in particular, these reports tend to remain confidential.

The attitudes of state institutions towards NGO minority-education projects have varied a great deal in the years since 1989. In general, the MES has tended to accept education projects as proposed by the NGO sector and has not created any major obstacles to their implementation (even during the BSP government). However, when it comes to the expansion or continuation of a project, the MES and its regional inspectorates fail to deliver. For example, as discussed above, the MES has not helped in the dissemination of NGO-produced materials, such as Romanes teaching materials. Most NGO projects therefore lack the potential for genuine development and the means for directly influencing the education system.

It has become standard practice for the MES (in all governments to date) to offer mainly "in-kind" support (whatever form this may take) rather than any substantial financial backing. In 1992-93, the MES did fund the development and publication of textbooks for the learning of Romanes. The Bulgarian state, however, has tended to embark on more general programmes aimed at improving the lot of Roma/Gypsies. These programmes are often ill-informed, poorly prepared and sporadic, demonstrating little evidence of thorough preparation or follow-up. As a result, they often fail to be implemented in the first place, or if they do get implemented, fail to fulfil original objectives, thus remaining just "one-off" projects. For example, in 1993-94 the Ministry of Labour and Social Affairs embarked on a pilot programme in Stolipinovo, a Roma/Gypsy neighbourhood in Plovdiv, for the development of literacy, professional qualifications and employment among the Roma/Gypsy population. Unofficially, it was admitted that it had failed to reach most of its targets. Only a few dozen people gained employment (and that was not even permanent), and participation in training courses had deprived Roma/Gypsies of unemployment benefits, leaving many participants in fact worse off. Because of its "in-kind" contribution, the MES is able to take credit for gains made by the NGO sector, even when there has been little or no financial input. Conversely, if the MES is subject to criticism for any such activities, it is quick to place the responsibility back with the NGO sector.

In some cases, NGO projects are approved without criticism and presented as the basis for an entire programme, such as the project "Let's Bring the Children Back to School." For example, the "Programme for Solving the Problems of Roma/Gypsies in the Republic of Bulgaria" was approved by the BSP government, and an ongoing programme, "School for Everyone", has been implemented by MES in 13 regions. The approval of such projects, however, represents more a gesture than funding *per se*. The "School for Everyone" programme, for example, distributes free breakfasts and lunches to schools, as well as offering various courses, such as in music. Although the MES has approved this programme, various foreign donors actually provide the funding.

NGO activities in the field of minority education are perceived differently by the political parties and organisations of the minorities themselves. The initial euphoria of Roma/Gypsy-led NGOs caused by the growth of interest in them has given way to disappointment, and even to confrontation with NGOs run by non-Roma/Gypsies. The latter type of NGO is increasingly perceived as a parasite feeding on Roma/Gypsy problems without displaying any real attempt at trying to solve them. Such confrontations influenced the discussion and approval of the "Framework Programme for Equal Integration of Roma/Gypsies in Bulgarian Public Life". Through their organisations,

Roma/Gypsies were able to express their desire to cease being the passive object of state and NGO interventions, and instead to become active agents of change. This desire has received almost no support from the wider NGO sector. The confrontation is most explicit when you compare the approach of Roma/Gypsy-led NGOs with that of the various Roma/Gypsy-oriented educational projects of the wider NGO sector. Whereas for Roma/Gypsy-led organisations, the most important element of the Framework Programme is the right to equal education for Roma/Gypsy children through desegregation, the vast majority of NGO projects emphasise the differentiation of Roma/Gypsy children, the end result of which is segregation. This fundamental contradiction, which is reflected in each individual project evaluation, has led to a negative attitude among Roma/Gypsy-led organisations towards such projects.

On the other hand, there are some non-Roma/Gypsy NGOs that, in co-operation with partner Roma/Gypsy NGOs and with the involvement of Roma/Gypsy participants, do carry out important work that represents the interests of this minority. The sheer volume of projects dedicated to issues connected with Roma/Gypsies, together with their high turnover, however, makes it difficult to monitor them all. While some Roma/Gypsy NGOs may approve of certain projects, others may not. The emphasis, therefore, in selecting examples of good practice, should be more on measuring the extent to which there is, or is not, a clear contradiction between the objectives of a given project and the needs of the community as represented (where possible) by Roma/Gypsy organisations.

Finally, a very important aspect of the education process, which must not be overlooked, is the role of teachers, and especially their professional organisations (including the most popular one, the Union of Bulgarian Teachers). So far they have not developed a clear-cut approach to the education of minorities. Individual speeches by members of the teachers' unions have been limited to generalisations and politically correct phrases, or to expressing the desire for additional payment for work with minority children (ie, the restoration of some socialist practices).

Voices of Roma/Gypsy children

TNV, 15 years old, from kv. Fakulteta, Sofia
"You can't learn anything in this school. There aren't enough rooms, we study in three shifts, the rooms are overcrowded – 30-40 people. Some feel like studying, others don't. The teachers don't care. Whoever managed to go to a Bulgarian school almost always finished it, while here only a few students finish the eighth grade every year... They may ask you for money to send your child to a Bulgarian school... They choose their students there and when they don't like someone they don't tell you that they don't want the child because you are a Gypsy, but they tell you that there are no vacancies, the classes are full and there is nothing you can tell them. How can you check if this is true or not, who can you complain to?"

AVH, 14 years old, from kv. Istok, Pazardjik
"I was lucky that years ago I was accepted in a Bulgarian school. They accept about 10-15 of our children every year. They want to have only three or four Roma/Gypsy children in a classroom in order to fulfil the requirement, and they tell the rest that we have a Roma/Gypsy school... The two schools are about 100 metres away one from the other, but the classes in the Gypsy school are two times bigger, and you can see that the students there have not learned anything. You can immediately tell who goes to which school."

KTG, 13 years old, from kv. Nikola Kotchev, Sliven
"It is not hard to study in our school at all. They give you a C whether you know something or you don't in order to get rid of you. There are some students who cannot read until the fifth grade... Otherwise they are not strict, the teacher sends you to do her shopping for her or to do something else for her, and you don't have to come back before the end of the lessons."

APY, 15 years old, from kv. Nov Pat, Vidin

"When I was in the fourth grade we studied the 'mother tongue'. It was very nice. The teacher was talking to us in Romanes, she told us stories and she told us about our history. We were studying our letters... But we don't have this any more. We haven't had it for four years, I don't know why."

HSR, 14 years old, from kv. Trite Kuli, Russe

"Some people came here from a foundation and made us study Gypsy language. What do you mean, Gypsy language? We are Turks[16] and we want to study Turkish, maybe also English, and let the Gypsies study Gypsy language. Our parents went to the school to argue about it."

ONV, 14 years old, from kv. Istok, Kustendil

"We have a school here in the neighbourhood, so why would we go to the town to look for another school... We all study here. There is also a school for the mentally handicapped – it is elsewhere. Their teachers come here every fall before the beginning of the school year to make their classes full – they go around the neighbourhood, telling the people to send their children there because it is like a boarding school and they don't have to think how to feed and clothe them. And the poorer people agree, they can't help it, and thus the mental school gets enough students. It is not difficult to send your child to a mental school, you need a note from the local clinic, from a psychiatrist, but even if you only sign a request they will accept them."

TNF, 13 years old, from Rakovski, Plovdiv region

"The buses come here every week, collect the Gypsy children and take them all the way to Rozovets, where there is a school for them. The teachers here don't want any Gypsy children... The parents agree because they cannot help it – they cannot feed them here. Others send their children to orphanages to be raised there, not that they give them up, but they want the state to raise them and they will have them back when they grow up. They can't afford to do it now."

GBJ, 11 years old, Orphanage, Plovdiv region

"We are mostly Gypsies here, and when people come to adopt children no one wants us... The foreigners take Gypsy children but only few foreigners come. They take two to three children every year, younger children, the lucky ones."

ANM, 12 years old, Temporary Accommodation Home, Sofia

"It's good that we have this place, at least we don't have to sleep in the train station... What can we do here all day? We wander around... They give us new clothes when foreigners come."

These interviews were conducted for the purpose of this study. Their text in full is in the archive of the Minority Studies Society, *Studii Romani*. Interviewees' initials are used instead of their names, in order to preserve their privacy.

Recommendations

Given that Bulgaria has ratified:

- the International Covenant on Civil and Political Rights (ratified 21 September 1970, entered into force 23 March 1976)
- the International Covenant on Economic, Social and Cultural Rights (ratified 21 September 1970, entered into force 3 January 1976)
- the International Convention on the Elimination of All Forms of Racial Discrimination (ratified 8 August 1966, entered into force 4 January 1969)
- the Convention on the Rights of the Child (ratified 3 June 1991, entered into force 3 July 1991)
- the UNESCO Convention against Discrimination in Education. (The UNESCO Protocol instituting a Conciliation and Good Offices Commission to be responsible for seeking the settlement of any disputes which may arise between States Parties to the Convention against Discrimination in Education has not yet been ratified.)
- the European Convention for the Protection of Human Rights and Fundamental Freedoms (ratified 7 September 1992, entered into force 7 September 1992)
- the First Protocol to the European Convention for the Protection of Human Rights and Fundamental Freedoms (ratified 7 September 1992, entered into force 7 September 1992)
- the European Framework Convention for the Protection of National Minorities (ratified 7 May 1999, entered into force 1 September 1999)

and has signed but not ratified:

- the European Charter for Regional or Minority Languages

Save the Children recommends that:

The Government of Bulgaria
- Ratifies the European Charter for Regional or Minority Languages
- Initiates a policy of equal education of Roma/Gypsy children as its basic philosophy and primary goal – this should constitute the basis for MES to develop its "General Strategy for the Education of Roma/Gypsy Children" and implement it through specific programmes.
- Adapts existing laws and regulations in the field of education to this General Strategy.
- Adopts a flexible approach to the implementation of the new General Strategy, which should always take into consideration the characteristics of each internal group and subgroup of Roma/Gypsy community, region, town or village and school. At the same time this approach should remain within the framework of the main principles of the General Strategy.
- Accords priority to the principle of integrated, equal and generally accessible education for everyone – the different forms of special education should be used only in the context of this principle as a means of achieving the common goal and not to segregate minority groups.
- Establishes an extensive system of preparatory classes for Roma/Gypsy children before first grade for the study of Bulgarian and, where necessary, provides for the application

of the methods of bilingual education in the primary education system.

- Bases education on the principles of intercultural and multicultural education, through a modification of the curricula, which should be enriched with lessons on the history and culture of Roma/Gypsies as an integral part of Bulgarian history and culture.
- Improves the training system for teachers and other educational staff, with the aim of teaching the teachers about the major ethnic and cultural characteristics (including language, at least at a basic level) of the Roma/Gypsy community. The presence of highly qualified teachers will render redundant the teaching assistants (whose status, qualification and obligations are unclear).
- Instructs the MES and the regional inspectorates to help actively in the implementation of the constitutional right of Roma/Gypsy children to study their mother tongue. The study of the mother tongue should be made more extensive in terms of content, and should include the study of minority history and culture. The MES should, in addition, develop the necessary teaching materials and build a comprehensive university-based system for the preparation and professional qualification of teachers in Romanes.

- Establishes an efficient system for interaction in the field of minority education between governmental institutions, the different NGO types within the sector (ie, the Roma/Gypsy-led organisations and those run by non-Roma/Gypsies). This system should work on different levels – national, regional and local – and should also make active use of the potential of school boards of trustees.

The international organisations, including the UN Commission on Human Rights, the Special Rapporteur on the Right to Education and the Special Rapporteur on Contemporary Forms of Racism, Racial Discrimination, Xenophobia and Related Intolerance, and the European Union:

- Closely monitor the international obligations undertaken by the Bulgarian government in respect of the right to education, paying particular attention to the right to education of Roma/Gypsy children.

Bulgaria: Notes on the text

1 In the census, citizens gave answers to specially trained census takers, who wrote the information in categories prepared in advance; these were according to ethnic group, religion and mother tongue. Data from the 2001 census were beginning to be made available at the time of writing, but with no ethnic breakdown. According to this census (01/03/2001), the overall population in Bulgaria was 7,973,671.

2 E Marushiakova and V Popov, *Gypsies (Roma) in Bulgaria*, Frankfurt am Main, Berlin, Bern, New York, Paris, Wien, Peter Lang Verlag, 1997, pp. 41-2; *Rezultati ot prebroyavaneto na naselenieto, Tom I – Demografski charakteristiki* (The results of the population census, Vol. 1 – Demographic characteristics), Sofia, Natsionalen statisticheski institut, 1994, p. 194; *Demografska charakteristika na Bulgaria (rezultati ot 2% izvadka)* (Demographic characteristics of Bulgaria (results from a 2 per cent sample)), Sofia, Natsionalen statisticheski institut, 1993; D Dimitrov, B Chakalov, K Dechev, Iv Georgieva and P Georgiev, *Utvâr-zhdavane na socialisticheskia nachin na zhivot sred bulgarskite grazhdani ot tsiganski proizhod* (The affirmation of socialist lifestyle among Bulgarian citizens of Roma/Gypsy origin), Sofia, CK na BKP, 1980.

3 *Rezultati ot prebroyavaneto na naselenieto, Tom I – Demografski charakteristiki* (The results of the population census, Vol. 1 – Demographic characteristics), Sofia, Natsionalen statisticheski institut, 1994.

4 Rudara/Rudari are one of the groups of Romanian-speaking Gypsies (often with a non-Romani consciousness) that are found throughout Europe. They are also referred to in other contexts as *Karavlahs* (in Bosnia and Herzegovina, for example) and Beasha (variant Boyasha/Boyashi) (in Croatia, for example).

5 Ministry of Education, Science and Technologies, Institute for Education and Science, *Development of Education 1994-1996*, (National report presented to the 45th session of the International Conference on Education in Geneva, 30 September – 5 October 1996), Sofia, 1996.

6 *Rezultati ot prebroyavaneto na naselenieto, Tom I – Demografski charakteristiki* (The results of the population census, Vol. 1 – Demographic characteristics), Sofia: Natsionalen statisticheski institut, 1994, p. 303.

7 National Institute for Education, Republic of Bulgaria, *Education For All, The Year 2000 Assessment National Report*, Sofia, 1999.

8 In the context of Bulgaria, we recognise that Roma/Gypsy, as a term, may not always be appropriate. For example, Turkish- and Romanian-speaking Gypsies and/or Gypsies with a preferred Turkish or Romanian identity refer to themselves and are referred to by others specifically as Gypsies, *not* Roma.

9 Commission on Bulgaria's Progress Towards Accession, *Second Regular Report*, Enlargement Commission Report, October 1999.

10 Concluding Observations of the Committee on Economic, Social and Cultural Rights: Bulgaria. 08/12/99 E/C.12/1/ADD.37.

11 The same explanation could be heard during the years of communism. For example, I Kemeny *Beszamolo a magyarorszagi ciganyok helyzeteve foglalkozo; 1971 ben vegzett kutatasrol* (Information from the 1971 survey on the situation of Gypsies in Hungary), Budapest, 1976.

12 UNICEF, Regional Office for CEE, CIS and the Baltics, *Out-of-School Youth in Bulgaria: Mission Report*, Sofia, February 1999.

13 ERRC, '"Desegregation effort begins in Bulgaria", Snapshots from around Europe', *Roma Rights*, 4/2001.

14 The successful implementation of the Vidin programme, which today includes some 460 Romani children, has prompted a debate about using it throughout Bulgaria. It was the focus of a conference held in Sofia on 27 April 2001, entitled "The Desegregation of the 'Romani Schools' A Condition for an Equal Start for Roma". The conference was co-organised by the Open Society Institute's Roma Participation Programme, the European Roma Rights Centre, the Bulgarian Helsinki Committee and the Human Rights Project. The conference was the first major forum focusing on Roma and school integration in Bulgaria, and it allowed Romani education experts and activists, government officials, diplomats and representatives of the World Bank and human rights organisations to discuss the implications of desegregation in Vidin.

15 National Statistical Institute, April 2000. Exchange rate 3.10BLeva/£GB1.

16 As discussed at the beginning of this report, many "Turkish" Roma/Gypsies, are Turkish-speaking and prefer to declare themselves only as Turks or *millet'* (ie, "people").

5 Republic of Croatia

Primary school education is compulsory between the ages of 7 and 14. It is estimated that 50 per cent of all Roma/Gypsy children enrol in primary school and that 25 per cent of all Roma/Gypsy children complete primary school education.

"My other brothers and sisters are not enrolled in school. School is useful because it develops our brain, we do not fight, we learn to calculate and not to use drugs. I think there should be some Roma language in the school. The teacher treats me differently from other children and this is why I have to learn more. I am not good in maths and do not want to continue schooling."

Romani boy, ten years old

"The problems are large. The enrolled children range from 7 to 11 years of age and none of them have a good-enough command of the Croatian language to follow the classes normally."

School pedagogue

Summary

Context

Croatia was declared an independent state in 1990, but it was not until the end of the war with the Yugoslav Federation, in 1995, that the government obtained full control over the country's territory. Until 1999, Croatian politics was dominated by Franjo Tuđman and, despite the development of a sophisticated structure of minority-related institutions, the Roma/Gypsy population (officially considered an "ethnic community") received little government attention and is "represented" in parliament by the MP for the Italian minority. There are few official data on the Roma/Gypsy population, though steps have been taken recently to include Roma/Gypsies in official minority-representative institutions and, in 1998, a government committee was formed to improve Roma/Gypsy educational opportunities and to develop a broader Roma/Gypsy policy.

Roma/Gypsy population

Historically, the Croatian lands have had a relatively small Roma/Gypsy population. The 1991 census recorded fewer than 7,000 Roma/Gypsies, though other estimates put the population at around 40,000. The current picture is even more uncertain, due to large movements both in and out of Croatia during the war years and afterwards, including Roma/Gypsy refugees from other conflicts. In 1991, over two-thirds of Roma/Gypsies were permanently settled. At least two dialects of Romani are spoken, and Roma/Gypsies are differentiated by religion (Catholic, Orthodox, Muslim). Many Roma/Gypsies have failed to obtain Croatian citizenship. They suffer high rates of unemployment, welfare dependency and job insecurity. Most Roma/Gypsies live in marginal settlements in poor-quality accommodation often lacking basic infrastructure. This has led to conflicts with local authorities and social tensions.

Roma/Gypsies and education

Small-scale surveys indicate around half of Roma/Gypsies of school age don't enrol in (compulsory) primary school. In part this is due to their not possessing the necessary documents, but also lack of fluency in the language of instruction, Croatian, is a factor. Fewer than five per cent attend a secondary school, demonstrating a high dropout rate between the two stages. Schools are often far from Roma/Gypsy settlements, and high Roma/Gypsy absenteeism can be due to illness or family obligations. Antipathy towards the presence of Roma/Gypsy children in mainstream classes remains a problem. Some authorities have sought to address Roma/Gypsy disadvantage through separate classes, but this has been criticised by the Ombudsman.

Balance of NGO and government activity

Government activity is still at the stage of information gathering and a pilot project involving a small number of Roma/Gypsy classroom assistants. Broader government proposals are yet to be implemented, and it is unclear to what extent Roma/Gypsies will be able to use new opportunities for minority education and language teaching. Given the slow pace of state activities, NGOs have taken a leading role in developing educational initiatives for Roma/Gypsies, including summer schools, course development and training Roma/Gypsy educators. Projects have also been developed to help prepare Roma/Gypsy children for school and to raise awareness amongst Roma/Gypsy parents about the school system. However, Roma/Gypsy NGOs have proved less successful in constructing an effective political lobby and in exerting pressure on the state to allocate sufficient resources to address Roma/Gypsy educational disadvantage.

Croatia report contents

Introduction

With a population of some 4.5 million, Croatia was formerly one of the more developed republics in the Yugoslav Federation. Before the onset of war, its *per capita* GDP was approximately $US5000.[1] Following Croatia's declaration of independence in 1990 and in the wake of democratic elections, full-scale war broke out in 1991. Between 1991 and 1995, about a quarter of the country was not under government control, and the GDP halved. Military actions in 1995 restored three of the four United Nations Protected Areas to Croatian control, leading to the exodus of over 250,000 ethnic Serbs. The Eastern Slavonia region was peacefully reintegrated into Croatia later, after being administered by a UN transitional authority. From 1990 to 1999, Croatia's government was led by the Croatian Democratic Union, with its leader Dr Franjo Tuđman as President. The government's record on minority rights, refugee return and on wider human rights was problematic, and internationally, the country was relatively isolated.

Following Dr Tuđman's death in December 1999, the general election held on 3 January 2000 produced a decisive victory for two opposition groupings: one bloc formed by the Croatian Social Democratic Party and the Croatian Social-Liberal Party (which secured some 40 per cent of the popular vote) and another formed by the Croatian Peasants' Party, the Croatian Liberal Party, the Istrian Democratic Party and the Croatian People's Party (which secured 16 per cent). The result led to the formation of a coalition government of six parties (the *šestorka*) headed by Social Democratic Party leader Ivica Račan as Prime Minister. The new government has embarked on an ambitious programme of returning Croatia to the mainstream of the international community, and offers the opportunity for a renewed dialogue and commitment to minority rights. However, the sheer scale of the task facing it has led to the postponement of many key initiatives. In addition, until local elections scheduled for May 2001, the Croatian Democratic Union retained control of many municipalities.

Roma/Gypsies in Croatia

Demography

The last census in Croatia was in 1991, when the republic was still part of the Yugoslav Federation. Whilst republic-specific data were recorded, there are real problems with the census in giving an accurate picture of the total number of Roma/Gypsies in Croatia. A new census is due to be undertaken in 2001. Given the complexities of "ethnic" identification in Croatia, and the stigma attached to self-identification as Roma/Gypsy, it is likely that the 1991 census considerably underestimates the magnitude of the Roma/Gypsy population. In any case, the impact of the war between 1991 and 1995, with large-scale migration into and out of Croatia, further undermines the reliability of the census figures from 1991.

According to the 1991 census, Croatia had a total population of 4,784,265, of whom only 6,695 (or 0.14 per cent) of the population identified themselves as Roma/Gypsies.[2] Excluding those who identified themselves as Yugoslav, this made Roma/Gypsies the tenth-largest nationality in Croatia. The underestimation that this number represents is illustrated by another census statistic: namely that some 7,657 people (or 0.16 per cent) stated that their mother tongue was Roma, an increase of almost a thousand on the Roma/Gypsy nationality figure. In any case, the figure represents a significant increase from those who identified themselves as Roma/Gypsies in previous censuses (only 405 in the 1948 census; 1,263 in 1953; 313 in 1961; 1,257 in 1971; and 3,858 in 1981).[3]

The census also indicates clearly that Roma/Gypsies are concentrated in certain parts of Croatia, with over 70 per cent of the recorded Roma/Gypsy population in seven municipalities, towns and cities, namely: Čakovec (1,930), Zagreb (1,105), Pula (575), Rijeka (445), Varaždin (245), Osijek (221) and Slavonski Brod (208).[4] The scale of underestimation is illustrated by the fact that the Municipal Centre for Social Work in Čakovec, in 1996, had 2,957 Roma/Gypsies registered as users of their services, 1,000 more than the census suggested as living there.[5] Indeed, within many of these municipalities, there are individual Roma/Gypsy settlements which themselves have a population in excess of the 1991 census figure for the municipality as a whole. For example, in the municipality of Pitomaca in Podravina county, only 28 people declared themselves as Roma/Gypsies in the 1991 census, whereas the Ivo Pilar research study estimated, on the basis of birth records, that there were up to 200 Roma/Gypsies in just one settlement in 1998.[6]

It is generally accepted that the 1991 census seriously underestimates the number of Roma/ Gypsies living in the Republic of Croatia at that time. In any case, the number of Roma/Gypsies has since increased dramatically because of immigrants from other post-Yugoslav Republics or territories, notably from Bosnia and Herzegovina and from Kosovo, some of whom have joined family members who had arrived in Croatia before the wars. As most Roma/Gypsies were not concentrated in the war-affected parts of Croatia, with the exception of those in Eastern Slavonia/Baranja, there was no corresponding outward migration in the same period.

In the absence of accurate statistics, there are a number of more or less informed estimates on the present size of the Roma/Gypsy population. Whilst some Roma/Gypsy leaders have suggested figures as high as 150,000, the most common and respected estimate, given by both the Council of Europe and the European Roma Rights Centre (ERRC), is between 30,000 and 40,000 – over six times the 1991 census figure and representing close to 1 per cent of the Croatian population.[7] This would make them, alongside Muslims, the second or third largest minority in Croatia. Whilst it is extremely likely that the 2001 census will continue to understate the figures, there is some evidence of a recognition of this higher number by some key policy-makers. However, there have as yet been no systematic attempts to obtain reliable figures upon which to base policies.

Different Roma/Gypsy groups in Croatia

In 1998, the Ivo Pilar research institute carried out a small-scale survey of 126 Roma/Gypsy heads of households in five different Roma/

Gypsy settlements on the outskirts of large towns throughout Croatia. The survey found that Roma/Gypsies spoke two major dialects: *Romani Chib* and a dialect of the Romanian language (*Ljimba d'bjaš*).[8] Speakers of *Ljimba d'bjaš*, quite a significant group in Croatia, are also known as Boyashi (*Bajaši*), and are thought to have travelled from Romania hundreds of years ago.[9] Roma/Gypsies can also be differentiated in terms of religious affiliation with three distinct groupings: Roman Catholic, Orthodox Christian and Muslim. The survey also looked at family size and concluded that there is an above average number of children in Roma/Gypsy households in Croatia (see Table 5.1).

As previously stated, there was large-scale migration within the republics of former Yugoslavia before its break-up in 1991. According to the 1991 census, before internal barriers to movement had been set up, about 68 per cent of Roma/Gypsies in Croatia were long-term sedentary inhabitants. Some 27 per cent had come to Croatia from other parts of Yugoslavia.

Table 5.1 Sample survey of Roma/Gypsies in Croatia: family size

Families with:	% of families
No children	9%
One child	22%
Two children	18%
Three children	22%
Four children	15%
Five children	14%

Source: Štambuk, "Roma in Croatia in the Nineties", *Journal for General Social Issues (Društvena istraživanja)*, 2000, 9: 2-3; Table 9.

The socio-economic status of Roma/Gypsies

Survey evidence suggests that Roma/Gypsies are in a disadvantaged socio-economic position in Croatia, with high levels of unemployment. The Ivo Pilar survey notes unemployment at 73 per cent, with 21 per cent of households having one member employed, only 6 per cent with two members employed and just under 1 per cent with three or more employed members.[10] Of those employed and pensioners, the majority are "unqualified workers" (37 per cent) or "collectors of scrap iron and other materials" (21 per cent).[11] A similar majority were in temporary or seasonal, rather than permanent employment, with most engaged in trade, in the construction industry or in agriculture. Given that Roma/Gypsies often lack the papers required for legal employment, much of this participation is in the grey economy, thus compounding their marginalisation.

There has been no systematic study of poverty amongst the Roma/Gypsy community in Croatia, although the cumulative disadvantage noted above is highly likely to have created large numbers of families living in poverty. It has been noted that Roma/Gypsies in Croatia are no different from their Central and Eastern European counterparts: "Roma are both poorer than other population groups and more likely to fall into poverty".[12] This thesis is borne out by the Ivo Pilar survey, which found that the most often-mentioned problem was the "weak material situation of the family" affecting between 67 per cent and 91 per cent of households.[13] The survey also showed that 47 per cent of households relied on social support from the state as a major source of income.[14]

There are many issues concerning the relationship between Roma/Gypsies and Centres for Social Work in Croatia that are beyond the scope of this report.[15] However, evidence shows that Roma/Gypsies are over-represented as users of social services but underrepresented as recipients of cash support. For example, in Čakovec, around which there is the largest concentration of Roma/Gypsies, the Centre for Social Work has established a special office for Roma/Gypsy issues. A social worker from this office stated, in a conference held in 1997:[16]

> "We do not give them all financial assistance in cash, 70 per cent of it goes directly to the shops where they can get food and 30 per cent we give them in cash. Of course, Roma are not satisfied with this form of support. However, the regulations allow us to deliver assistance in the way we consider to be most useful for Roma."

One of the most serious problems that Roma/Gypsies face in Croatia, and the one which has attracted the most media attention in recent years, is that of housing and property rights. Most Roma/Gypsy settlements are on the edges of large towns and, whilst some of these indicate a clear intention to settle in one place, many houses were constructed without building permission. In recent years, both past and present governments have sought to clamp down on such illegal building, and the threat of demolition hangs over many Roma/Gypsy settlements – some houses have already been demolished. Many settlements lack essential infrastructure. According to the Ivo Pilar survey, while over 70 per cent of Roma/Gypsies lived in houses and 11.9 per cent in flats, most of these were extremely small, lacked water and electricity and had no functioning sewerage system.

Such settlements are often the targets of resentment from other communities and from sections of the local authorities. In some cases, government attempts to build sewerage and water connections have been opposed locally. There is now a system by which the government can make available matching funds to local authorities, which will fund infrastructure programmes. This has had positive results in some parts of the country, for example, the establishment of a drinking fountain in Drnje, near Koprivnica, and electrification of two villages in Sisak Municipality. However, in other cases, for example, in Čakovec, the local authority has blocked essential infrastructure programmes, which would raise the standards of Roma/Gypsy settlements, presumably for fear of a backlash from the majority community. Where such programmes are in place, they represent an important step forward, not least since Roma/Gypsy communities are involved in consultations about priorities.

The 1998 ERRC field report also focuses on police mistreatment of Roma/Gypsies in Croatia, as well as the growing problem of civilian violence against Roma. The latter appears particularly pronounced in eastern Slavonia, where many Roma/Gypsies sought to return after the war, but who were sometimes attacked as "Serbs" by local Croats. In Našice, the ERRC also report that the chair of the municipal council had made racist comments about Roma/Gypsies and sought to restrict their movement.

The legal status of Roma/Gypsies

As a result of the war, the issue of Roma/Gypsies in Croatia has rarely been discussed or systematically addressed, outside specialist arenas or policy forums. In addition, the complexities of minority policies are such that Roma/Gypsies are not treated as a fully constitutive "national minority", but rather as an "ethnic community" in Croatia. This is partly demonstrated by the fact that Roma/Gypsies have been left out of the preamble to the Constitution. Although this does not mean an abrogation of rights, it does mean that the identification of Roma/Gypsies remains merely symbolic.

With the break-up, and the independence of Croatia in 1991, it became important for Roma/Gypsies in Croatia to obtain Croatian citizenship (*domovnica*). However, the legal, administrative and practical regulation of citizenship was extremely complex and, in effect,

discriminatory against Roma/Gypsies. The June 1991 Law on Citizenship of the Republic of Croatia granted citizenship automatically to those former Yugoslav citizens who also held citizenship of the Republic of Croatia. In fact, this Republic-based citizenship had not previously been widely regarded as important. Without this, citizenship could only be obtained by those who had been registered residents of Croatia for at least ten years. In addition, a statement of "belonging to Croatia" had to be submitted within six months of the enacting of the law, at a local police station. This tended to restrict citizenship to "ethnic Croats". In May 1992, the law was amended: the ten-year rule was removed but no new regulations more favourable to wider citizenship rights were added. As a result, few Roma/Gypsies obtained citizenship through this route and had to seek it, effectively, as foreigners. Articles 8 and 9 of the law set criteria for this, including proficiency in the Croatian language and Latin script, and "attachment to the laws and customs of Croatia", further compounding discrimination against Roma/Gypsies.

Although there are no accurate statistics available, after its field visit to Croatia in 1998, the ERRC concluded that probably most Roma/Gypsies in Croatia do not have Croatian citizenship, and that the vast majority of them are stateless.[17] If we accept the estimates above of the numbers of Roma/Gypsies in Croatia, this could amount to as many as 30,000 people. Roma/Gypsies who do have documents are, effectively, foreigners with limited rights to stay in Croatia. This, of course, seriously jeopardises the right of access of Roma/Gypsy children to education since these same documents are required for enrolment.

Minority rights

The Croatian Constitution inherited a model of minorities from the Federal Republic of Yugoslavia, in which there were constitutive peoples (*narodi*) in the Federal Republic as a whole, who might be numerical minorities in specific republics. These had more rights than "other" groups, constitutionally minorities, including Italians and Czechs, whose "nation" was considered to be outside the Federal Republic of Yugoslavia. Groups such as Roma/Gypsies fall outside both of these categories. With the break-up of Yugoslavia, grave problems emerged as some of the nations previously recognised as a majority became a minority (eg, Serbs in Croatia). Given the huge tensions caused by these changes, the problems faced by smaller minority and ethnic communities were not included as priorities in debate. Indeed, the Croatian Constitution introduced after independence reflected some of the political preferences and shifts of the time. For example, the preamble of the Constitution not only omits Roma/Gypsies as a national minority, but also omits Slovenes and Bosniaks (Muslims). This has led to the formation of an alliance of Bosniaks and Roma/Gypsies to lobby to be included in the preamble.

The status of minorities has been mainly regulated through the following national legal documents:
- the Constitution
- the Constitutional Law on Human Rights and Freedoms and on the Rights of Ethnic and National Communities or Minorities in the Republic of Croatia
- the Law on the Use of Language and Script of National Minorities in the Republic of Croatia
- the Law on Upbringing and Education in the Languages of National Minorities.

There are numerous other laws and legal acts that also have provisions regarding minority and human rights.

Under Articles 14 to 20, the Constitution establishes basic rights and freedoms: the equality of all people and citizens before the law; and equal rights and freedoms regardless of race, skin colour, gender, language, religion, political or other beliefs, national or social background, property, birth, education, social position or other characteristics. As well as equality before the law, the Constitution guarantees the equality of members of all national minorities, with full freedom to express their national belonging, freedom to use their language and script, and cultural autonomy.

In order to promote and protect human rights, the following governmental bodies have been formed at national level:
- Co-ordination for Social Affairs and Human Rights. This discusses cultural, scientific and social issues, health and pension rights, protection and promotion of human rights, and the rights of ethnic and national communities. It resolves complaints and encourages the state administration in solving certain problems. The president is selected from one of the vice-presidents of the government. The members consist of Ministers of Culture; Education and Sport;

Labour and Social Care; Health; Science and Technology; War Veterans; Justice and Local Government; and Finance.

- The National Committee on Human Rights. Its goal is to educate citizens and raise awareness on the principles of equality and freedom of all.

- The Committee on Issues of Equality. The goal of this committee is to co-ordinate and act as an umbrella for all activities connected with the implementation of the documents of the Fourth World Conference on the Rights of Women, held in 1995.

- The National Committee for the Development of a National Plan of Action for Children in the Republic of Croatia. The goal of this committee is to develop a National Plan compatible with the action plan of the World Summit for Children, which took place in 1990.

- The Committee for Children. This is a co-ordinating body consisting of representatives of state authorities, MPs, NGOs, experts and media representatives. Its main goal is to monitor the implementation of the National Programme.

- The Office for National Minorities. The goal of this office is to monitor and protect human rights in Croatia, to formulate policies in relation to minorities and to distribute funds from the state budget to associations of national minorities. It was established in 1991 as The Office for Ethnic and National Communities or Minorities.

There are also specific bodies within the parliamentary structure, which seek to ensure representation of minority interests in policy-making. Within the parliament there is a Committee for Human Rights, and within that committee there is a Subcommittee for National Minorities, which monitors policy implementation and participates in the process of passing laws. It has all the rights and obligations of the working body. Another important parliamentary body is the Council for Minorities, formed in 1997, as required by the Council of Europe, on which each of the 16 minorities has its own representative. The council co-operates with minority MPs and exists as an institution complementary to the MPs. It supervises the policies on the preservation and promotion of minority rights, comments on laws and other acts with provisions for minorities, makes proposals and forms requests to parliament, government and other bodies, and co-operates with governmental bodies and the international community. Perhaps one of the most important of the council's achievements was the recent recommendation that a Roma/Gypsy representative, for the first time, be included in the Parliamentary Subcommittee for National Minorities.

At a general election, members of national minorities have a choice as to whether to vote with the majority of the population for a majority list, or to cast their vote within a section of the parliament reserved for minorities. However, there is no obstacle to mainstream parties including minority candidates within the majority list. The system of representation is complex, and has also

been changed to reduce the number of MPs for minorities to eight. This was designed to reflect the decline in the Serbian population, the result of the exodus during the war. National minorities are grouped according to their proportion in the population, and can vote and be candidates on that particular list. In practice, those elected are likely to be from the larger minorities, but are still meant to represent the interests of smaller minorities and ethnic communities from the same list. Currently, of the eight minority seats, three are held by candidates from the Serb minority, one by Hungarians, one by an Italian, one by Czechs and Slovaks, one by Ruthenians and Ukrainians, and one by Germans and Austrians. At the moment, the Italian minority MP, as the President of the Parliamentary Committee on Human Rights, is also meant to represent the Roma/Gypsy community.

In practice

The right to education of Roma/Gypsy children

There are no accurate figures on current rates of enrolment and achievement of Roma/Gypsies in the school system in Croatia. From our discussions, observations and experiences, we would suggest the following as very approximate figures:

- 50 per cent of Roma/Gypsy children enrol in primary education
- 50 per cent of these pupils finish primary education (25 per cent of all Roma/Gypsy children)
- No more than 10 per cent of these pupils enrol in secondary education (2.5 per cent of the total)
- 50 per cent of these finish secondary education (1.25 per cent of the total)
- 1 per cent or fewer go on to higher education (0.01 per cent of the total).

An illustration of the long-standing nature of the issue can be gleaned from the experience in Međimurje County. The Municipality of Čakovec, with the largest concentration of Roma/Gypsies in Croatia, developed a plan as early as 1972 to co-ordinate activities in favour of improved social and educational support for the Roma/Gypsy population. There are reports that, by 1978, up to three-quarters of Roma/Gypsy children were enrolled in the primary schools. Subsequently, there was a relative neglect of the issue, and there are now figures which suggest that far fewer (around 45 per cent) now register and only 7 per cent actually complete primary education. Different schools now implement their own approaches, and any idea of a co-ordinated plan, based on consultations with the Roma/Gypsy community, has been lost. In addition, there have never been additional resources provided to promote the integration of Roma/Gypsy children into the educational system, for instance, through additional staff. Indeed, the fact that, in recent years, only seven Roma/Gypsies finished secondary school in the entire county, gives further cause for concern.[18]

There is little evidence available on the quality of education experienced by Roma/Gypsy children. From our interviews and discussions, there appear to be many causes for concern, perhaps best expressed by the following quote from an interview with a representative of the Association of Roma in the County of Međimurje:

"Children here are discriminated against in school. Parents of non-Roma children are against their children sharing the class with Roma children – they say that they would rather kill their children than let them sit together with Roma children. They all complain that our children are dirty. They are not dirty because they want to be, but because of the poverty they live in. They have nowhere to wash themselves. Children themselves are not aware that they are being discriminated against. Also, they are being educated according to the shortened programme, similar to the programme for those with learning difficulties, and then, later on, they have problems if they want to enrol in the secondary school. Children are told that this is best for them... We feel powerless."

Roma/Gypsies and primary school

Primary school education is compulsory between the ages of 7 and 14. Secondary education for ages 14 to 18 is not compulsory. According to UNICEF's TransMONEE Index, Croatia has a gross enrolment rate in secondary education of 19.0 per cent. Access of Roma/Gypsy children to the educational system of Croatia in practice remains quite limited, mainly because most do not have the documents needed for enrolment. Currently, school authorities require a birth certificate, a police residence permit and proof of citizenship (*domovnica*). There are numerous examples of Roma/Gypsy children and their parents finding it very difficult to register and being deterred by what can be quite complex bureaucratic procedures. This may change, since there appears to be a strand in the government, particularly in the Ministry of Labour and Social Affairs and the Ministry of Education and Sport, supporting a more permissive and relaxed approach towards Roma/Gypsies in terms of citizenship and personal documentation.[19]

Table 5.2 Educational levels of households

Family members with...	Kozari Bok	Capraške Poljane	Kotoriba	Bjelovar	Vodnjan	Total
No schooling	45.8%	83.9%	61.5%	61.9%	56.5%	62.7%
Primary incomplete	62.5%	38.7%	84.6%	52.4%	78.3%	61.9%
Completed primary	20.8%	32.3%	30.8%	52.4%	78.3%	42.1%
Secondary education	20.8%	3.2%	7.7%	19.0%	17.4%	13.5%
Higher education	8.3%	0	0	4.8%	0	2.4%

Source: Štambuk, "Roma in Croatia in the Nineties", *Journal for General Social Issues (Društvena istraživanja)*, 2000, 9: 2-3; Table 11.

However, given that much is left to local discretion, practice will continue to be problematic even if there is a new emphasis on inclusion at the centre of power.

As with many other issues noted in this report, there have been no systematic studies of school enrolment of Roma/Gypsies throughout Croatia. It is possible to refer to only small-scale local studies. In the Ivo Pilar survey, 47 per cent of families had no member enrolled in primary education (ranging from 27 per cent in Kotoriba to 71 per cent in Capraške Poljane) and 95 per cent had no one in secondary education.[20] These rates are particularly worrying given that most families surveyed had school-age children. It suggests a national picture of a massive drop-out among Roma/Gypsy children before the stage of secondary education and of limited, although very geographically varied, enrolment in primary education.

A more nuanced picture of the situation can be gleaned from interviews carried out by a group of students at the School of Social Work in Zagreb with 40 Roma/Gypsy children: 30 boys and 10 girls, all enrolled in primary education in one school in Kutina.[21] The study included a control group of non-Roma. In the study, 43 per cent of Roma/Gypsy pupils stated that they are absent from school several times a month but, unlike the control group, none skip classes. This was confirmed by the school pedagogue who "expressly stated that the Romani children do not 'skip' classes; they either come and stay the whole day, or simply do not show up at all".[22] Most Roma/Gypsy children were absent from school as a result of illness, although a significant minority (40 per cent) stated that their absence was a result of other obligations, such as helping at home or working at the market.

In addition, none of the girls and only a quarter of the boys had brothers or sisters enrolled in school, indicating that school enrolment varied within the same family. Also, far fewer of the girls (20 per cent as opposed to 57 per cent of the boys) could speak Croatian well before going to school. The vast majority of the Roma/Gypsy children have to walk a long way to school (taking about an hour), and most do not intend to continue beyond primary education (63 per cent of Roma/Gypsy children compared to none of the non-Roma/Gypsy children). The students conclude that Roma/Gypsy children's relative failure in education is a product of poor socio-economic conditions, distance from school and inappropriate curriculum in schools.

The Ivo Pilar survey provides a snapshot of the educational levels of Roma/Gypsy families in five settlements, concluding that a majority of Roma/Gypsy children remain outside the primary education system. The figures are complex to interpret, however, given their reliance on heads of households as respondents.

Roma/Gypsies and segregated education

The problems which schools face in adjusting to the presence of Roma/Gypsy children are illustrated by the comments of a school pedagogue from Drnje in Koprivnica-Križevci County, where a quarter of the pupils in two annexes of the school are Roma/Gypsies:[23]

"This year, 14 Romani and 11 other children were enrolled in the 1st grade (two of them are repeating the grade and one of them is following the adjusted programme). There are no parallel classes and there are no legal possibilities of opening any (an insufficient number of children). The problems are large. The enrolled children range from 7 to 11 years of age and none of them have a good enough command of the Croatian language to follow the classes normally. The conditions at home are not conducive to learning – the majority of

their parents are illiterate. The adjustment to the school and the process of socialisation are very slow. They received textbooks free of charge because many of them possess social-welfare cards, but they do not have any other material needed. The textbooks and notebooks remain at school because if they take them home, they get ruined in a short period of time. We cannot assist the teacher legally or financially... Children are, at the moment, regularly attending school and their biggest motivation is a free hot meal. Another problem is tardiness – they have no clocks at home, so they come whenever they like... The best solution would be to separate the first grade into two classes, although this is legally impossible. The hygienic and work habits, as well as the knowledge level of these two groups cannot be compared and it is impossible to work with one group at the expense of the other. The new law on primary education should introduce the provision that would make this possible even in the cases when the number of pupils is insufficient for two classes."

Whilst clearly seeking to address the wider context, the solution proposed of separate classes for Roma/Gypsy children is controversial and open to many objections, as it would compound rather than solve the problems. Recently, there have been 13 cases from Međimurje and Varaždin counties in which separate classes have been formed exclusively for Roma/Gypsy children. The issue has come to public attention because of the interest of the Office of the Ombudsperson of Croatia in the case.[24] The violation of the human rights of Roma/Gypsy children is highlighted by some cases. In one school in Međimurje County, there are separate entrances for Roma/Gypsy children and, in another, Roma/Gypsy children who could not afford school meals were allowed into the dining room afterwards to eat the leftovers of other children. Following an investigation, the Ombudsperson's office asked for a report from the Ministry of Education and Sport. However, the office considered the report to be insufficient, whereupon it made the cases public. Beyond a brief public debate, however, nothing changed as a result of this and, to our knowledge, both situations remain.

As early as 1994, Neven Hrvatić, of the Department of Pedagogy of the University of Zagreb, summarised the problems for Roma/Gypsies "lost within the educational system", and sought a holistic approach based on both integrative and specific measures.[25] He outlined the need for:

- greater inclusion of Roma/Gypsy children in kindergartens, both inside and outside Roma/Gypsy settlements, preparing Roma/Gypsy children for enrolment in primary education
- complete inclusion of Roma/Gypsy children in primary schools as the key area for Roma/Gypsy education, to be accompanied by social measures encouraging parents to have closer links with schools – where Roma/Gypsy children comprise 50 per cent or more of the school population, there should be teaching in Croatian and in Romani languages, with the possibility of specific teaching on Romani language and culture

- a commitment to increased Roma/Gypsy participation at the secondary-school level, through granting of scholarships to Roma/Gypsy children – this would then allow for the possibility of introducing specialist topics into the curricula
- at university level, introduction of Romani language into teacher training, and the establishment of an Institute for Romology.
- appointment of an adviser for Romani education in the Ministry of Education
- specific extra-scholastic institutional provision, such as a summer school for Roma/Gypsies.

Looked at in the light of Hrvatić's framework, it is much easier to concur with the ERRC's conclusion that "the education of Romani children is a grave problem", with little or no progress made in terms of the first five of his objectives.[26] In a sense, there has been little reform of mainstream educational provision, other than a reinforcement of separate provision based on the notion that Romani pupils are the problem. An emphasis has instead been placed on supporting initiatives from NGOs. Whether this has, itself, further marginalised and discriminated against Roma/Gypsy children, is an open question, discussed below when we look at the work of NGOs.

Language provision

The issue of language as a barrier to education is referred to in Croatia's 1994 report to the Committee on the Rights of the Child:[27]

"The schooling of the Romani children poses a number of specific problems, ranging from the lack of Romani teachers to the fact that the Romani children have extreme difficulties in following the school courses in the Croatian language."

However, since this report, little has been done to tackle this issue. The new government, however, did bring in a series of laws on minority rights in May 2000, which appear to offer a more permissive framework for a progressive approach. According to the new Law on Education in the Languages and Script of National Minorities, national minorities have the right to receive education in their first language in pre-school institutions, primary and secondary schools.[28] This right can be implemented through special language schools or separate classes for national-minority pupils. The curriculum in minority languages and script can cover both the general curriculum for all pupils, and specific, relevant teaching in the mother tongue itself, literature, history, geography and cultural heritage of the national minority. Curricula should be developed by the Ministry of Education and Sport on the basis of consultations with associations representing minority communities.

The law goes on to state that any such educational programme should be taught by teachers who have perfect command of the minority language, whether or not drawn from the minority community itself. As a framework for reform, the law is excellent. However, real problems remain in translating this law into practice for Roma/Gypsy children, not least in terms of ongoing debates about the nature and status of Romani languages, and the need for systematic institutional reform and recruitment of teachers and counsellors fluent in these languages.

Government initiatives

Until relatively recently, there has been little government and state concern about the plight of Roma/Gypsies in Croatia, beyond a stereotypical perception of Roma/Gypsies as an intractable social problem. The many factors behind this neglect include more pressing problems as a result of war and a refugee crisis, an unwillingness to address minority rights issues, and the lack of Roma/Gypsy political strength. Since 1997, as war problems have eased somewhat and, perhaps more importantly, as Croatia signs up to membership of a number of international bodies, including the Council of Europe, there has been more evidence of strategic thinking and planning. In 1997, members of national minorities elected representatives into the Council of National Minorities, which established a permanent dialogue between national minorities and government on subjects including its administration.

In 1998, as part of this thinking, the government financed a programme "...[aimed] at supporting the Roma/Gypsy population which, because of its long-term marginalisation, remains in a neglected position".[29] Funds were provided for two seminars, one implemented by the Ministry of

Education and Sport for Roma/Gypsy assistants in schools; and the other by the Ministry of Labour and Social Affairs for Roma/Gypsy mediators in social work and social care.

Subsequently, in 1998, a Committee for the Inclusion of the Roma Population in the Educational System of the Republic of Croatia was established, with representatives from the Ministries of Education and Sport; Labour and Social Affairs; Reconstruction and Public Works and Internal Affairs; as well as the Office for National Minorities, and Roma/Gypsy associations. According to a key driving force behind this initiative, a representative from the Ministry for Public Works, this committee was a deliberate attempt to shift the focus away from only supporting Roma/Gypsy cultural initiatives and, also, to address access to education in a wider context. Hence, whilst one of the three main aspects of the Committee's work is to support Roma/Gypsy children to enter and continue in mainstream education, this is linked to an attempt to improve standards of living in Roma/Gypsy communities and to improve relationships between Roma/Gypsy communities and social support services.[30]

An attempt is also being made to create a National Developmental Programme for Roma/Gypsies in Croatia (*Nacionalni razvojni program za rome u RH*), involving the same groups. Whilst only at the conceptual stage so far, the approach adopted appears to be one which seeks to look at the situation of Roma/Gypsies in a holistic manner. It recognises that one problem cannot be solved in isolation from other issues, and that there is a need for simultaneous and co-ordinated action from all relevant agents in society. The programme outline shows that there will first be a consideration of the historical aspects, the general position of Roma/Gypsies in Croatia, their heritage. Then, based on an assessment of the existing infrastructure of the major Roma/Gypsy settlements, as well as the status of Roma/Gypsies in regard to health, social care and education, there will be a clear attempt to prescribe concerted action. The aim is to discuss the role of all levels of government, state, local authority and local communities. Whilst not itself a financing mechanism, the programme seeks to steer existing sources of finance, as well as to attract international donors to fund publications (newsletters, bulletins and a first textbook for Roma/Gypsies), projects of Roma/Gypsy associations and Roma/Gypsy cultural centres. Whilst this is clearly a step forward, there is a noticeable lack of detail in terms of how much finance it plans to generate, sources of finance, what exactly it plans to spend money on and over what period.

The concept represents a clear statement both of the developmental potential of Roma/Gypsies and a clear signal of the willingness on the part of the new government to work with Roma/Gypsies and improve their situation. The authors of the concept document are aware of the limiting factors that exist in terms of basic misunderstandings between the majority population and the Roma/Gypsy population. The first misunderstanding is general, and follows from the perception of the majority population that Roma/Gypsies are deeply attached to their way of life, and changes that bring their lifestyles closer to those of the majority society can never happen successfully. For their part, Roma/Gypsies are anxious about what 'integration' entails, because of the extent of misunderstanding and lack of awareness. The second misunderstanding arises from the perception that Roma/Gypsies until now have had a "separate destiny", based on their oral tradition and their fear of an imposed majority culture.[31] The authors of the concept document hope to present it to the government and have it approved as a national strategy. However, given that its completion has, already, been delayed by some six months, the extent to which the government sees this as a high priority is open to question.

The majority of Roma/Gypsy associations offered support for the document, welcoming its holistic approach and seeing it as an opportunity to contribute to development through their own projects. It is also hoped that the government will, through the programme, be able to finance projects that already exist, especially those in the area of culture and education.

The European Commission against Racism and Intolerance (ECRI) of the Council of Europe, in its report on Croatia in November 1999 based on field visits in 1998, stated with regard to the "Roma/Gypsy community" that:[32]

"Progress has been made in the field of education... through the publication of studies on the subject of Romani education, initiatives related to the organisation and financing of Roma children, (and) training of Roma teachers..."

The judgement appears overly optimistic and, perhaps, was influenced by a pilot programme, in 1998, by the Ministry of Education and Sport, funded by the Office for National Minorities. The programme consisted of a series of seminars for Roma/Gypsies wishing to become classroom assistants. The basic idea was to train some of the more highly educated and motivated Roma/Gypsies, mainly those who had begun, and preferably completed, secondary education, to act as aids to non-Roma/Gypsy teachers in classrooms where Roma/Gypsy children were present. These aids would provide additional help to children with homework, Croatian and Romani languages and culture. It was planned that their role would also be to raise awareness in the Roma/Gypsy community about the need for education.

The seminar was organised two years ago for 12 Roma/Gypsy participants from different parts of Croatia, including one of the authors of this report. However, given that the law on education does not support such provisions, there are no legal grounds for the introduction of assistants in the classrooms, so those who attended could not do what they were trained for in any of the state institutions. As a result, only two of four planned seminars were actually held. Even so, the programme can be considered to be partially successful because it had an unintended outcome: a number of the participants went on to form NGOs, some of which have initiated programmes on education.

The optimism in the ECRI report might also have derived from a document entitled *A Programme of Integration of Romani Children in the Educational and School System of the Republic of Croatia*, also written in 1998. The programme outline promises:

- to elaborate and devise experimental programmes for kindergartens for Romani children within state-run kindergartens, or through the formation of special groups if necessary
- experimental supplementary programmes for the education of Romani children in primary schools
- a supplementary programme for training of teachers
- tolerance education of other school children
- a mentorship programme, through which school personnel would be more engaged in monitoring and supporting Roma/Gypsy children to attend school and would liaise with centres for social work and NGOs.

More than two years on, there has been no systematic implementation of this programme, and only a piecemeal approach has been adopted. Indeed, the provisions for education have been less developed than those on infrastructure, for example. With the change of government, a new approach is being developed.

NGO practice in the area

In recent years, the most innovative approaches to the education of Roma/Gypsies in Croatia have come from local NGOs, most of which have been established since 1991. All of the initiatives noted below have sought to promote new forms of educational provision for Roma/Gypsy children as a supplement and corrective to the mainstream educational system. There have been many other initiatives which we do not have space to mention. Notwithstanding the energy and creativity of the NGOs, these initiatives have sometimes been beset by various kinds of politics, both internally and in relation to governmental institutions, and few have been able to consolidate their work in terms of influence over mainstream provision.

One of the earliest and most important initiatives was the summer school for Roma/Gypsy Children in Croatia, which was first organised in 1994 by the Union of the Associations of Roma in Croatia (*Savez Udruženja Roma Hrvatske*, SURH). The school was supported by the Committee for Pastoral Care of Roma of the Croatian Archbishops' Conference and financed by the Ministry of Education and Culture. The idea of the programme was to act as a supplementary curriculum for Roma/Gypsy children from all over Croatia who are enrolled in schools. The programme addressed two extremely important issues simultaneously: the provision of a relatively intensive programme on the Romani language, culture, history and art; and the introduction of Roma/Gypsies as teachers. The core objectives of the summer school were: to raise awareness about Roma/Gypsy national identity; to promote use of *Romani Chib* and other Romani dialects spoken in Croatia; and to explore Roma/Gypsy history and tradition.[33] The initiative gained the support of some within the formal educational system and gathered a group of experts from the Department of Pedagogy in the University of Zagreb, who supported the concept and developed the content.

It also used the event as an opportunity to develop a systematic approach to the education of Roma/Gypsy children in the mainstream educational system, as well as additional programmes aimed at specific education on Roma/Gypsy national identity and culture.

A similar initiative, also called the Roma Summer School, was started in 1996 and was held in 1997 and 1998, organised by the Union of Roma of Croatia (*Zajednica Roma Hrvatske*). In its first year, the school attracted some 35 attendees aged 7-15 years old. The programme introduced Roma/Gypsy history, literature, the basics of *Romani Chib*, music, art and health education. Between 1995 and 1997, summer programmes were also organised by the Croatian Archbishops' Conference for Roma/Gypsy and non-Roma/ Gypsy children to meet together and learn about Roma/Gypsy culture. Roma/Gypsy children from Međimurje County, as well as from the towns of Nova Gradiöka, Bjelovar, Karlovac and Zagreb attended.

In 1996, SURH also developed a mentorship programme which, through seminars, aimed to mobilise and educate community members to work with parents and children to raise awareness on the importance of schooling. Within this programme, the "A Hundred for A Hundred" initiative was planned. The idea was that for each of the one hundred mentors, there would be at least one hundred children who would be encouraged to go to school. To our knowledge, the programme was never implemented, for various reasons, including financial ones.

The first preschool initiative for Roma/Gypsies was organised in the Kozari Put settlement on the edge of Zagreb in 1996, by the Association of Roma of Zagreb and Zagreb County. Entirely conceptualised and implemented by Roma/ Gypsies, the programme sought to prepare Roma/Gypsy children to enter the mainstream educational system. In the house of a leading community member and his family, which functioned as a kind of community centre, the programme also introduced literacy classes for those children who had not attended school and, for whatever reason, were unlikely to be enrolled. The initiative also expanded to include art and cultural programmes, courses for parents, and literacy and computing classes for adults. Some of those programmes were carried out in co-operation with other NGOs, mostly non-Roma/Gypsy, although this co-operation tended to be temporary rather than permanent. The preschool centre and related activities have attracted considerable media and public attention, and are currently funded by Zagreb Municipality. Some 40-50 children attend classes led by Roma/Gypsy educators, some of whom had training in pedagogy. However, staffing of the centre seems to be a permanent problem, given the shortage of Roma/Gypsy educators with appropriate training/education. There have been attempts to compensate for that shortage through co-operation with non-Roma/Gypsy teachers. The programme itself raised quite significant debates within the Roma/Gypsy community, whilst it was widely accepted and praised by the non-Roma/Gypsy community. Critics of the initiative contend that it contributes to the further ghettoisation of Roma/Gypsies since they are not being included in the educational opportunities

133

offered to the wider community. They say that there has been little attention paid to the integration of the pupils into the mainstream system, an original goal of the project.

One example of a non-Roma/Gypsy NGO working on preschool education is Children First (*Djeca prva*) which, in 1997, implemented the programme "Psycho-Social Support with Educational Elements for Preschool Children and their Mothers", also in the Kozari Bok/Kozari Put communities. The programme sought to address issues of socialisation of children, non-violent communication and co-operation, as well as tolerance towards differences amongst people. Some 120 children, of whom 80 were Roma/Gypsies, were included in the programme.

According to the Office for National Minorities, there are some 17 Roma/Gypsy associations in Croatia. To our knowledge, many of them place the education of Roma/Gypsy children as one of their priorities and most have developed, at least in part, activities which seek to contribute to a resolution of education-related problems. The Roma Women's organisation Better Future (*Bolja budućnost*) has a programme of awareness-raising about the need for children to attend school, and its activists sometimes play the role of mediators between the Roma/Gypsy community and school authorities.

There has been little evidence of more co-ordinated efforts or attempts to lobby jointly the relevant ministries and government authorities. This disunity, or lack of co-ordinated action, might be one of the reasons that pressure has recently been put on Roma/Gypsy NGOs

to work more closely together. Some of the funding currently earmarked for Roma/Gypsy associations has been made conditional on Roma/Gypsy associations forming an umbrella organisation; a similar condition does not exist for human rights, women's rights, and child rights organisations.

Funding for minority associations comes mainly from the Office for National Minorities rather than through the annual governmental competition organised by the Office for Co-operation with NGOs (*Ured za udruge*), which has a much larger funding pool. In 2000, the Office for Co-operation with NGOs gave grants totalling some HRK20.5m (about £GB1.7 m).

The approach of the Office for National Minorities is not without its critics. In its report, it states: "The schooling of the children of the Roma/Gypsy minority is specific and encounters problems uncharacteristic of other national minorities. For the majority of Roma/Gypsy children the basic problem is not an inability to learn about their language and culture, it is rather not attending mandatory education. This part of the Roma/Gypsy population is illiterate, which means that their chances for inclusion into civilised life are smaller." In 1998, the government earmarked HRK556,728 (about £GB46,000), routed through the Office for the programme of inclusion of Roma/Gypsy children into the educational and school system. The money was spent on the seminars already mentioned, two organised by the Ministry of Labour and Social Affairs and two by the Ministry of Education and Sport. A drinking-water system has also been financed in one of the Roma/Gypsy settlements near Čakovec. A much smaller amount was given for the funding of Roma/Gypsy magazines, although, as the ERRC report notes, this was given on the condition that the Office appointed the editors of the magazines.[34]

As mentioned above, currently the Office appears to want to link financial support to the setting up of an umbrella organisation of Roma/Gypsy NGOs and associations, through which all the funding can be channelled. The debate about the formation of an umbrella organisation is not new and in recent years has raised a lot of debate amongst Roma/Gypsy associations and between them and governmental authorities. Although some associations support the proposal (including the strongest, albeit only on paper) most Roma/Gypsy associations consider that forming such an organisation would be very difficult, taking into account all the differences that exist. This impasse is currently preventing any systematic state funding being administered to Roma/Gypsy NGOs.

Voices of Roma/Gypsy children

Children from two counties, Istria in the north-west, and from a settlement in the County of Zagreb, participated in group discussions, giving their own input for the report. In total, some 40 children and young people provided their views on many aspects of the report. In addition, a number of adults were also consulted, including leaders of the associations of Roma/Gypsies in two other counties: Primorsko Goranska County and the County of Međimurje. The four counties

together were chosen because they account for a significant proportion of the entire Roma/Gypsy population in Croatia.

Međimurje County

The largest group of Roma/Gypsies in Croatia live in Međimurje County, mainly on the edge of ten towns and villages where spatial segregation is often accompanied by a different nickname for the "Roma part of the town". The village of Kotoriba is somewhat typical:[35]

"In the beginning Roma used to live in the village itself, but since their presence was said to impede the development of the village, ie, its expansion, they were given a location some 200 metres away from the village. It is disconnected from Kotoriba village by a canal, over which the Roma built an improvised bridge... In order to compensate for resettlement, the village gave to the Roma some building materials... The settlement now needs to expand because of the growing number of inhabitants."

All the children we had contact with were quite open and frank about their experiences in education and in schools. They often made efforts to point out what they felt was good about school, as well as difficulties, especially with respect to language. Many children found school difficult because they could not understand fully what was going on in the classroom. In addition, Roma/Gypsy children often pointed out that other, non-Roma/Gypsy children did not accept them. When asked if they thought would it be useful to have some Romani language spoken in school, the children seemed surprised at such an idea. It was as if it was commonly accepted that Croatian is the sole scholastic language and that they had never considered the possibility that a Romani language could be taught.

There was a widespread recognition that, although school can be somewhat boring, it was worth attending since it might be useful for coping with the environment in the future. Older children were more forthcoming on the issue of enrolment and the pressures they faced. We were told that sometimes it might be necessary for pressure to be put on parents to enrol children. There was a definite sense from those children we spoke with who were not attending school that they were missing out. Most of them stated that they did not have the documentation required for enrolment and that the school did not want to receive them without this. Many said that they wanted to be like other children, and it was their great wish to learn to read and write.

Istria

The County of Istria has, we estimate, some 1,000 Roma/Gypsy inhabitants, with the majority of the population working in trade, benefiting from the area being close to Italy and, in addition, from seasonal summer work related to the tourist industry. One of the biggest problems faced by Roma/Gypsies in Istria is the issue of citizenship. Roma/Gypsies in Istria are nevertheless relatively well organised, willing and able to put pressure on state and local bodies to respond more positively to their needs.

Preschool children

We spoke with three preschool children, all of whom were attending a daycare programme in a state-run kindergarten. They liked their teachers, were having fun with other children, and felt that they were not treated any differently from other children.

Primary-school children

Girl, nine years old

"Kindergarten is better than school. There were no tests and we could play. My parents enrolled me into school. When I finish the school, I will be a kindergarten teacher."

Boy, ten years old

"My other brothers and sisters are not enrolled in school. School is useful because it develops our brain, we do not fight, we learn to calculate and not to use drugs. I think there should be some Roma language in the school. The teacher treats me differently from other children and this is why I have to learn more. I am not good in maths and do not want to continue schooling."

Girl, ten years old

"School can be useful in the future, we can teach our own children once we have them. When I started school, the teachers accepted me, but other children did not. They were calling me Gypsy."

Girl, 12 years old

"When I started school, I did not know the Croatian language. Children were making fun of me. There should be some classes in Roma language in school."

Girl, 12 years old

"School is good for the future, we can achieve something. My sister finished school. She is a tailor."

Kozari Bok/Putevi

Within the County of Zagreb, Kozari Bok and Kozari Putevi are two interlinked settlements on the edge of the city, a tram ride away from the city centre, in the vicinity of a chemical industrial zone. Most of the estimated 11,000 population are poor, and most of these are of minority origin: Bosniak/Muslims, Roma/Gypsies and a smaller Serbian community. The settlement expanded in the 1960s and 1970s as Zagreb required cheap labour. It still lacks essential infrastructure, with many buildings being built without planning permission. Already living within a settlement on the margins of the capital, Roma/Gypsies live within a kind of sub-ghetto in Kozari Bok/Putevi itself. Numbering some 700 in total, most members of the Roma/Gypsy community are unemployed, with a few seasonal workers. Few Roma/Gypsies attend the primary school, which has not particularly encouraged additional Roma/Gypsy enrolment, since it is already oversubscribed and operates a three-shift system with oversized classes. In recent years, some Roma/Gypsy families in the community have seized the initiative, organising a pioneering preschool programme, with activists supporting parents, especially mothers, to pursue enrolment through obtaining documents and lobbying the school authorities.

We talked with 12 children, aged from 5 to 14:

Girl, nine years old, not enrolled in school

"I do not want to be anything. I know how to make bread and things like that. I think this is enough. I want to be in the house, to clean and to do the washing."

Boy, 12 years old

"I do not like when I am punished and have to go into the corner. But I quite like maths, because this is where I am the best. I would like to be a car mechanic."

Girl, 12 years old

"I am not sure why I am not going to school. It does not matter now."

Girl, ten years old

"My parents enrolled me in school. I do not like it very much because I do not understand Croatian very well and they do not understand me very well. I am not sure that school can be useful for me. Other children sometimes are not friendly."

Girl, nine years old

"I can understand Croatian well. I know what they say to me, but I do not know how to answer back so they would understand me, my words are not clear enough. This is very difficult for me because they think I know nothing. That is not true. It is easier for me to draw then. But I would like to be a policewoman and to be that I have to go to school."

Conclusion

Overall, the picture we have presented in this report is one of cumulative disadvantage and discrimination facing Roma/Gypsy children in Croatia in regard to their relationships with various institutional structures and, in particular, with regard to the educational system. Thus there is a considerable gap between the *de jure* situation regarding minority rights in Croatia and the *de facto* realities on the ground. Whilst there has been a long-standing concern within government with the policy questions of Roma/Gypsies and education, this has been confused and confusing, and there are real problems in terms of co-ordination, and the development of clear and realisable plans of action. Nevertheless, if the issue were to receive greater attention, related to models of good practice both in Croatia and outside, there would seem to be the possibility of real progress being made. In the following section, we make a series of tentative suggestions and recommendations, both in terms of education and more widely, which could be the focus for renewed debate and action.

Recommendations

Given that the Republic of Croatia has ratified, or has deemed to have ratified those treaties already entered into by former Yugoslavia, all relevant international conventions and charters for the protection of human and minority rights, including:

- the UN Convention on the Rights of the Child, 1989
- the International Convention on Combating all Forms of Racial Discrimination, 1965
- the UNESCO Convention Against Discrimination in Education, 1960
- the European Convention on Human Rights Protection and Basic Freedom with 1997 Protocols I, II, III, IV, V, VI, VII, and XI
- the European Convention on Regional and Minority Languages, 1997
- the Framework Convention for the Protection of National Minorities, 1997

and that after the recognition of Croatia as an independent state, the following international conventions were ratified:

- the International Covenant on Economic, Social and Cultural Rights (ratified 1992)
- the International Covenant on Civil and Political Rights (ratified 1992)
- the Optional Protocol to the International Covenant on Civil and Political Rights (ratified 1995)
- the Second Optional Protocol to the International Covenant on Civil and Political Rights (ratified 1995)

- the International Covenant on the Elimination of All Forms of Racial Discrimination (ratified 1992)
- the Convention on the Elimination of All Forms of Discrimination against Women (ratified 1992)
- the Convention against Torture and Other Cruel, Inhuman or Degrading Treatment or Punishment (ratified 1992)
- the Convention on the Rights of the Child (ratified 1992)
- the Convention on the Status of Refugees, 1951 (ratified 1992)
- the Optional Protocol, Protection Non-European Refugees, 1967 (ratified 1992)
- the Convention on the Prevention and Punishment of the Crime of Genocide, 1948 (ratified 1992)
- the Geneva Conventions, 1949 (ratified 1992)
- the Additional Protocol, on Protection of Victims of International Armed Conflicts, 1997 (ratified 1992)
- the Additional Protocol, on Protection of Victims of Non-International Armed Conflicts, 1977 (ratified 1992)
- the Forced Labour Convention (ratified 1991)
- the Freedom of Association and Protection of the Right to Organise Convention, 1991
- the Right to Organise and Collective Bargaining Convention, 1991
- the Equal Remuneration Convention, 1991
- the Abolition of Forced Labour Convention, 1997
- the Discrimination (Employment and Occupation) Convention, 1991
- the Minimum Age Convention, 1991

(all as of July 2000)

Save the Children recommends that:

The Parliament and Government of the Republic of Croatia

- Establish citizenship rights for Roma/Gypsies in Croatia on the basis of long-standing residence, and use a proactive policy of informing Roma/Gypsies of their rights and encouraging Roma/Gypsies to become citizens of Croatia.
- Ensure that all Roma/Gypsies are enrolled in the Croatian educational system regardless of their residence or citizenship, in line with the Convention on the Rights of the Child. This will need a more positive and proactive approach in line with best practice throughout the world on the education of stateless children.
- Ensure that in addition to the 2001 census, a systematic study of the status of Roma/Gypsies in Croatia, including their numbers, regional patterns and social status, is carried out. Such a study could then be used in planning for challenging disadvantage over the next decade. Data must be disaggregated on the basis of ethnicity, age and gender, with particular attention paid to ensuring that data on ethnicity are not misused and are based on self-identification.
- Ensure that Roma/Gypsy children have access to preschool facilities in areas of Roma/Gypsy settlements. This will involve supporting existing state kindergartens in employing Roma/Gypsy teachers and assistants, helping to set up classes in the Romani language and funding private and

NGO initiatives specifically addressing access of Roma/Gypsies to preschool.

- Ensure that Roma/Gypsy children in primary school are integrated into the normal curriculum, with additional classes in the Croatian language where appropriate. Wherever Roma/Gypsy children are present in significant numbers in schools, there should be some teaching in Romani languages for all children in the school, and a part of the curriculum should be devoted to Roma/Gypsy history and culture. Schools should make particular efforts to involve the parents of Roma/Gypsy children in schools and to employ liaison workers, mentors and teaching assistants, preferably Roma/Gypsies or those fluent in Romani languages, to facilitate links between home, the community and the school. Special attention should be paid to Roma/Gypsy children in their final year of primary education, to promote access to secondary education. The practice of segregation of Roma/Gypsy children in schools should be stopped. Campaigns should also focus on the need to educate non-Roma/Gypsy children and their parents on Roma/Gypsy issues and rights.
- Provide scholarships for Roma/Gypsy children to attend and complete secondary education and additional scholarships for those who go on to higher education.
- Implement a clear policy of recruitment of Roma/Gypsies into teacher training, including the establishment of new access programmes for those who do not have the required formal qualifications. Teacher training should include much more attention to cultural awareness and minority-rights issues. This should be based on real, not tokenistic, involvement of Roma/Gypsy communities and organisations in all aspects of such programmes.
- Complete the National Development Programme for Roma/Gypsies as soon as possible, and provide it with adequate funds over a five-year period to implement the action plans.
- Appoint an adviser for Roma/Gypsy education, from the Roma/Gypsy community, within the Ministry of Education. There should also be such advisers at the county and municipal levels in areas of Roma/Gypsy settlement. Roma/Gypsies need to be represented on all governmental and parliamentary committees dealing with minority issues.
- Allocate resources from central government for NGO initiatives on Roma/Gypsy education, based on best practice. These should be channelled through the competition organised by the governmental Office for Co-operation with NGOs, allowing for funding of a wide range of diverse initiatives.
- Ensure that all initiatives for Roma/Gypsies are regularly and systematically evaluated to identify good practice and ensure that lessons learned are integrated into national policy and practice. This evaluation should involve representatives of the Roma/Gypsy community in leading roles.

The international organisations, including the UN Commission on Human Rights, the

Special Rapporteur on the Right to Education and the Special Rapporteur on Contemporary Forms of Racism, Racial Discrimination, Xenophobia and Related Intolerance, and the European Union:

- Closely monitor the international obligations undertaken by the Croatian government in respect of the right to education, paying particular attention to the right to education of Roma/Gypsy children.

Acknowledgements

The report is based on a compilation of the activist experiences of the authors; many policy papers and research documents; and interviews with policy-makers, Roma/Gypsy representatives, and Roma/Gypsy children and young people. The authors, Jasmina Papa and Ramiza Mehmedi wish to thank all those who gave up time for discussions with them.

Croatia: Notes on the text

1 Per capita GDP is now approximately $US4,000, comparing favourably with most other post-Yugoslav countries (that in FRY is approximately $US1,400; in Macedonia $US1,200; in Bosnia Herzegovina $US1,260 and in Slovenia $US9,000).

2 Institute of Statistics – Population Census 1991.

3 Hrvatić and Ivančić, "The Historical and Social Characteristics of Roma in Croatia", *Journal for General Social Issues (Društvena istraživanja)*, 2000, 9:2-3, Table 1a.

4 The are 553 municipalities in Croatia, some of which have the status of towns or cities. Zagreb is a special case, and is itself a county.

5 Dominic, "Roma: People and/or Social Problem?" Undergraduate dissertation, University of Zagreb, School of Social Work, 1997.

6 Hrvatić and Ivančić (See note 3).

7 Bogdan, "Romany National Community in the Republic of Croatia", in *Glas Roma: Education and Upbringing of Romani Children in Croatia*, 1994; ERRC, *Field Report: the ERRC in Croatia*, 1998.

8 Štambuk, "Roma in Croatia in the Nineties", *Journal for General Social Issues (Društvena istraživanja)*, 2000, 9:2-3.

9 Boyashi are one of the groups of Romanian-speaking Gypsies (often with a non-Rom consciousness) that are found throughout Europe. They are also referred to in other contexts as Karavlahs (in BiH, for example)and Rudara/Rudari (in Bulgaria, for example).

10 Štambuk (see note 8), Table 6.

11 Štambuk (see note 8), Table 19.

12 Ringold, *Roma and the Transition in Central and Eastern Europe*, World Bank 2000, p. 10.

13 Štambuk (see note 8), Table 26.

14 Štambuk (see note 8), Table 27. Social assistance is currently 350 Croatian Kuna (HRK) monthly (approximately £GB29), and is claimed by only some 5 per cent of the total population.

15 Centres for Social Work have existed since the early 1970s. They are quasi-governmental institutions staffed by a multidisciplinary team, and responsible for a wide range of legal advice and preventive services for vulnerable families. They continue to have an income support role and a degree of discretion regarding financial and in-kind assistance.

16 Balent, "The experience of the Centre for Social Work in Čakovec", *Roma in Croatia Today (Romi u Hrvatskoj danas)*, Zagreb, Group for the Direct Protection of Human Rights, 1998, p 90.

17 ERRC, *Field Report: the ERRC in Croatia*, 1998.

18 Dominić, "Roma: People and/or Social Problem?" Undergraduate dissertation, University of Zagreb, School of Social Work, 1997.

19 Interview, November 2000; Butković 2000,

20 Štambuk (see note 8), Table 11.

21 Pintarić *et al.*, "Socio-Economic Influence on the Success (or Failure) of Roma Children in School", in *Glas Roma: Education and Upbringing of Romani Children in Croatia*, 1994.

22 Pintarić *et al.* (see note 21), p 89.

23 Pleše, "Education of Roma in the Drnje Primary School", in *Glas Roma: Education and Upbringing of Romani Children in Croatia*, 1994.

24 Viduković-Mukić, Interview, November 2000.

25 Hrvatić, "Towards a Conceptualisation of a Croatian Educational Model for Roma Children", in *Glas Roma: Education and Upbringing of Romani Children in Croatia*, 1994.

26 ERRC, *Field Report: the ERRC in Croatia*, 1998.

27 Croatia Report to CRC, para 384, 1994.

28 Official Gazette 51, 2000.

29 Government Office for National Minorities Report, 1999.

30 Domazet 2000.

31 Domazet 2000.

32 ECRI, Report on Croatia, 9 November 1999.

33 *Glas Roma*, 1995.

34 ERRC, *Field Report: the ERRC in Croatia*, 1998.

35 *Glas Roma*, 1995.

6 Federal Republic of Yugoslavia: an overview

Although the Federal Republic of Yugoslavia (FRY) is formally a single country, formed of two constituent republics, Serbia and Montenegro, three separate entries are covered in this report, namely Serbia, Montenegro and Kosovo.

FRY is the rump successor state of the former Socialist Federal Republic of Yugoslavia, from which other republics broke away in the early 1990s. The break-up was marked by a series of wars which caused hundreds of thousands of deaths, for which the recently deposed former President of FRY Slobodan Milosevic has been blamed as a primary instigator. FRY itself is now subject to pressures towards break-up similar to those which resulted in the end of the old Yugoslavia. Its democratic transition has been delayed by over a decade due to the longevity of the Milosevic regime. His presidency ended only after the October 2000 "democratic revolution", which brought Vojislav Kostunica to power in his place. All public service institutions, including educational institutions, are in need of thorough structural reform. Serbia's infrastructure was badly damaged by the NATO bombing campaign in spring 1999. As Serbia, Montenegro and Kosovo for all practical purposes already have or are acquiring* separate governance arrangements, with separate sources of democratic legitimacy, the shape of the coming structural renovation will differ between the three territories, cementing their divergence.

Kosovo is formally one of two autonomous provinces of Serbia (Vojvodina being the other). However, after the FRY/Serbian authorities unleashed a military campaign of mass expulsion, murder and pillage upon Kosovo's majority ethnic Albanian population, following on from a decade of repression, they were stripped of control over the province in June 1999 by the authority of a UN Security Council Resolution. Governance of Kosovo was placed in the hands of a UN interim administration, backed by a 45,000-strong international military force. Kosovo's 80 per cent plus ethnic Albanian majority clearly has a unanimous wish for full independence, but the UN is mandated to provide "substantial autonomy" within FRY/Serbia only, until a final political settlement is reached.

Under the leadership of President Milo Djukanovic, Montenegro has steered a cautious path in the direction of independence from FRY and parliamentary elections held in April 2001 were widely seen as a referendum on Djukanovic's independence proposals. Although pro-independence parties won, the margin was narrow, suggesting that swift moves to independence may prove destabilising.

From the late 1980s onwards, ethnic nationalism and the stirring of ethnic hatreds have been a prime political currency, creating very adverse conditions for the advancement and realisation

*Kosovan general elections are scheduled for late 2001.

of minority rights. Within FRY, this has had the most devastating results in Kosovo. For nearly a decade in the 1990s, 90 per cent of Kosovo's children were denied their right to education by the FRY/Serbian authorities on ethnic and linguistic grounds, and had to make do with makeshift private provision. For Roma/Gypsies it has been the aftermath of the Kosovan war which has proved most catastrophic. From June 1999, they were the victims of a wave of violence perpetrated by returning ethnic Albanians. The majority have fled, either as IDPs to Serbia and Montenegro, or as refugees to Macedonia, Bosnia and Herzegovina and other countries.

7 Federal Republic of Yugoslavia: Serbia

As in other countries in the region, Roma/Gypsy children are over-represented in special schools for children with disabilities. For example, Roma/Gypsy children make up about 80 per cent of children in Vojvodina's 13 special schools.

"When testing Roma children, I notice that they have problems with abstract concepts... Or, for example, I ask a child what he should do when he sees smoke coming out of a house. The right answer is that he would call the fire brigade or tell an adult that a fire had broken out in the house. Roma children as a rule reply that the stove should be cleaned or the stove pipes fixed to stop the smoke coming out. Then I have to fail the child."

Psychologist, special school

"How can a Roma child do a projection of a comic strip at the test when it has never had a comic book in its hands? But that doesn't mean they are not intelligent. Just a couple of days ago, two workmen were trying to get a cabinet into a classroom and couldn't get it through the door. Then a Roma boy from the eighth grade came along and told them at what angle to hold it to get it into the room."

Psychologist, special school

"They tell me, oh, they tell me,
that I'm just a Gypsy girl
and don't belong in their crowd.
And why that is, I never know,
nor what came over them."

Roma girl, 12 years old

Summary

Context

Serbia's economy and institutions were corroded or ossified by a decade of wars, isolation and sanctions. Much of its infrastructure was destroyed in the NATO bombing campaign of 1999. Due to the longevity of the Milosevic regime, Serbia's post-communist social and economic transition is beginning only now – a full decade after its Eastern European neighbours.

Roma/Gypsy population

Censuses over the last 50 years revealed a wildly fluctuating Roma/Gypsy population. A decline from the 1981 peak figure of 168,000 is attributable to the rise of inter-ethnic intolerance and war, which made Roma/Gypsies even more likely to declare themselves members of the majority community. Estimates of Serbia's true Roma/Gypsy population range between 360,000 and over 500,000. They form a complex mixture of groups. Most live in shanty settlements on town or village peripheries, and suffer from high unemployment, poverty, and high morbidity and mortality rates. Since 1999, between 30,000 and 80,000 displaced Roma/Gypsies from Kosovo (Roma, Ashkali and Egyptians) have added to the population. They received little state support and harsh, arbitrary treatment. Roma/Gypsies do not have the status of a national minority in Serbia.

Roma/Gypsies and education

The flawed 1991 census showed that 62 per cent of Roma/Gypsies had not completed primary education, and over a third had no schooling or virtually none. Only 4.41 per cent of the 15-19-year-old age-group progressed to secondary education. Although primary education is free, most Roma/Gypsy parents cannot afford to buy the necessary books and other school supplies. Their home environment often blocks Roma/Gypsy children's progress in education – overcrowding and lack of electricity prevents children from doing homework, and parents who are themselves poorly educated do not regard education as a priority. Due to poverty, very many Roma/Gypsy children are required to do wage-earning work, and a large number of girls marry at 13-16, prompting school drop-out. Roma/Gypsy IDP children from Kosovo were initially refused enrolment in Serbian schools.

Language provision

In practice, Roma/Gypsy children do not have access to teaching in Romanes, which is for many their native language. Moreover, there is no systematic provision for Roma/Gypsy children to be taught Serbian at the outset of their school career, thus making it very difficult for them to follow the lessons. Because Roma/Gypsies are not recognised as a national minority, they do not enjoy the right to education in their own language.

This in turn prevents the accumulation of any capacity for its introduction, eg, there are no institutions for teacher training in Romanes.

Special schools

There are no overall official data on the number of Roma/Gypsy children attending Serbia's 38 special schools for children with mental disabilities. Where data are available, 70-80 per cent of the attending children are Roma/Gypsies. Failures of language provision cause Roma/Gypsy children quickly to fall behind in regular schools, and a system of assessment that fails to take into account cultural characteristics often results in their transfer to special schools – a process of "pseudo-retardation". Free meals and medical care for children in the special schools act as an incentive for poor families to accede to this, condemning their children to an educational dead end.

Balance of NGO and government activity

International NGOs and domestic Roma/Gypsy organisations have been conducting a range of education projects – kindergarten, school integration and study support, with negligible support from the Ministry of Education. A sustained initiative to introduce "Romani with elements of national culture" as an elective subject in Vojvodina schools is led by the NGO *Matica Romska*.

Serbia report contents

Introduction – The Roma/Gypsy population

Demography

In 1995, Minority Rights Group International estimated that there were between 400,000 and 450,000 Roma/Gypsies in what was then Yugoslavia, of whom over 90 per cent were in Serbia (ie, a minimum of 360,000 Roma/Gypsies in Serbia).[1] The leader of the Roma Congress Party (*Romska kongresna stranka*), Dragoljub Acković, argues that according to research conducted by his party, the real number of Roma/Gypsies in Serbia is much higher – in excess of 500,000.[2] The Roma Cultural Society (*Matica Romska*) gives an estimate that is higher again – between 600,000 and 700,000.[3] According to the OECD, about 40 per cent of the Roma population are under 14 years of age.[4]

The 1991 census is the most recent official count of the population in the former Yugoslavia. A census for March 2001 was planned, but at the time of writing this had been postponed. Provisional estimates of 7,807,000 for the total population were made in 1998. However, no ethnic breakdown was available. Demographers have major reservations about the 1991 census figures, given that it was conducted at a time when national minorities were subject to considerable pressure from Serb nationalists – enough to lead the Kosovo Albanians to boycott the census. However, it does at least give some indication of ethnic composition.

According to this census, there were 140,237 Roma/Gypsies in Serbia (1.4 per cent). For Serbia alone, ie, not including Kosovo, this translated in to 94,492 Roma/Gypsies (1.2 per cent).[5] Other smaller ethnic minorities include Romanians and Slovaks. The largest concentration of Roma/Gypsies was in Belgrade (14,220), followed by 14,162 in the Pirotski District, 8,593 in the Nisavski District and 8,567 in the Jablanički District (all three districts are in southern Serbia). Of the 24,336 Roma/Gypsies registered in Vojvodina, most lived in the North Banat District (6,418) and South Banat District (5,644).

If we look at the numbers of Roma/Gypsies officially recorded in the period 1948 to 1991, we can see a pattern emerging. According to the 1948 census, there were 72,736 Roma/Gypsies in Yugoslavia. In 1961, the number dropped to 31,674. In 1971 it rose again to 78,485 and then again in 1981 to 168,195. In the 1991 census, however, the number fell once more to 140,237. These major fluctuations cannot be ascribed to demographic shifts alone. Instead we have to consider the political context, and how definitions and contexts shifted during this time. It seems that when political, economic and social conditions were more stable, Roma/Gypsies were more inclined to declare their ethnic identity. However, when they felt under threat, such as during the wars in the former Yugoslavia, they felt less inclined to declare their real identity.

The president of *Matica Romska*, Trifun Dimić, believes that the discrepancies between official and estimated figures of Roma/Gypsies in Serbia are due to what he calls "ethnic mimicry," ie, when Roma/Gypsies opt to declare themselves as members of the majority community. He cites as an example his own Slana Bara suburb of Novi Sad, Vojvodina, where the majority of the 1,000 Roma/Gypsy inhabitants declared themselves as Serb, Romanian or Yugoslav. Dimić considers that this kind of "mimicry" is a widespread attempt at avoiding racial prejudice.[6]

Different Roma/Gypsy groups and language

Roma/Gypsies in Serbia form a complex mixture of groups. Generally speaking, religion is not a criterion for group division of Roma/Gypsies in Serbia: significant numbers of contemporary Christians are ex-Muslims, and members of the same group practise different religions in different regions.

The oldest wave of Gypsies, who settled in what is today Serbian land in the fourteenth century, comprises several subdivisions. Some of them lost the Romani language and their mother tongue is now Serbian. These include the so-called *beli Tsigani* (ie, white Gypsies), who are Christians, as well as Muslim Roma/Gypsies, who came from Bosnia and Herzegovina. They also include *Tamari* (a name which comes from *Themeske Roma* – ie, local Gypsies) and *Gjorgjovci* in southern Serbia. *Arlia* groups can be found in eastern and southern Serbia (regions which were incorporated into the Serbian state in the second half of the nineteenth century). This group speaks the so-called Balkan (Non-Vlax) dialects of Romanes; most of them are Muslims. Other groups, which also belong to this dialectal group, include *Bugurdzhia* in southern Serbia.

The most widely distributed groups speaking a common dialect of Romanes in Serbia are those speaking Old Vlax dialects. Their forefathers came from Wallachia and settled in Serbian lands mainly in the seventeenth and eighteenth centuries. So-called *Gurbeti* groups can be seen as falling within this Old Vlax dialectal group. Most Gurbets in Serbia are Christians. Whereas some of them are permanently settled and have been so for many centuries, others are former nomads. Related to them in terms of their dialects are a number of other groups, for example the Serbian *Chergara* (or *Kaniara*), the *Dzhambazi* in southern Serbia, the Bosnian *Chergara* and *Kaloperi* (predominantly Muslims) and so on.

In Serbia (including Vojvodina) there are now only a comparatively few representatives of the New Vlax dialectal group of Romanes. These mainly consist of *Kelderara* and *Lovara* (most of them migrated into Western Europe in the 1960s and 1970s). There are also many Romanian-speaking Roma/Gypsies, mostly with preferred Wallachian identity, the so-called *Karavlasi* (called also *Rudara*, *Koritari*, *Lingurari*, *Vretenari*, *Ursari*, *Beyashi*). In Vojvodina there are also *Rumungri* (Ungrika Roma). Whereas some speak Romanes from Carpathian dialectal groups, others speak only Hungarian.

In contemporary Serbia (including Vojvodina) there are also many Roma/Gypsies who have migrated from Kosovo – some during the 1960s and 1970s, and others during and after the Kosovo crisis. During the war in Kosovo and after the withdrawal of the Yugoslav and Serbian

forces, large numbers of Roma, Egyptians and Ashkali from that region moved to central Serbia and Vojvodina. According to different sources, they number between 30,000 and 80,000 people. Other groups from Kosovo include *Arlia*, *Gurbeti*, *Kovachi* (or *Arabadzhi*), *Bugurdzhii* and *Dzhambazi*. Among these refugees there are also Albanian-speaking Madjups, Albanian-speaking Egyptians and Ashkali, all of whom distinguish themselves from Roma. In addition to these, there are numerous subgroups that cross-cut the groups outlined above, thereby revealing the complexity of these communities.

The socio-economic situation of Roma/Gypsies

Economically and socially, Roma/Gypsies are one of the most disadvantaged population groups in Serbia. As with the rest of FRY and indeed the region as a whole, they suffer from high unemployment, poverty and low levels of education. One study published in 2000 revealed that just 20 per cent of the Roma/Gypsy labour force held regular jobs, and only 5 per cent of these workers were employed in state companies.[7] Those who did have some kind of work held the least desirable and most poorly paid jobs: day labourers and herdsmen in rural areas, and unskilled workers, street cleaners, garbage collectors and grave-diggers in urban areas. Many Roma/Gypsies in Serbia have moved away from their traditional occupations, such as music. It is possible now to find only a few examples of young Roma/Gypsies entering this profession.[8]

The majority of Roma/Gypsies live in settlements on the outskirts of villages and cities. Housing conditions are extremely poor: houses are often built of tin, cardboard, planks and plastic sheeting. These settlements are usually built in zoned areas and hence do not have access to running water, sewers, electricity or waste collection. Public transport stops far short of such settlements. Poor living conditions are compounded by poor health. Poverty means a low-quality diet, at best consisting of just bread, potatoes, corn meal and seasonal fruits and vegetables. As a result, there are high morbidity and mortality rates, especially among young children.

The 1999 war in Kosovo, which displaced over 40,000 Roma/Gypsies, further compounded this situation.[9] Tens of thousands of Roma/Gypsies were forced to find refuge in settlements in central Serbia and Vojvodina. They received little state support, if any. In fact they were subject to harsh treatment from the authorities. The Humanitarian Law Centre (HLC), for example, registered several attempts to force Roma/Gypsies to return to Kosovo in the second half of June 1999. Police turned many back at the border and threatened to deny them humanitarian aid and shelter.

Inter-ethnic relations

There are some examples of attempts at positively promoting Roma/Gypsy culture, such as the Roma Culture Week organised by Belgrade's New Theatre and Dance Centre. This was staged in Belgrade, Novi Sad and Nis from 21 to 26 January 2001. The event presented different aspects of Roma culture in a series of lectures, concerts, exhibitions and performances.[10]

However, as is the case across the region, prejudice against Roma/Gypsies in Serbia is extremely high. Discrimination against Roma/ Gypsies can be found in all areas of public life, including mainstream media, such as the Pink and Palma television stations.[11] For example, after Vojislav Kostunica's election victory in 2000, Milovan Ilić, an entertainment celebrity and host of the *Minimaksovizija* show on Palma TV, made repeated jokes about Roma/Gypsies.[12]

Numerous surveys have revealed a pronounced "ethnic distance" between the majority populations and Roma/Gypsies in Serbia.[13] The prevailing view, especially among poorly educated non-Roma/Gypsy respondents in suburban areas, is that all professional and personal ties with Roma/Gypsies must be avoided. As the educational level of the respondents increases, the ethnic distance steadily decreases. A public opinion poll conducted in April 2000 in Nis is a good illustration.[14] By contrast with inhabitants of suburban areas, significantly more respondents in Nis accepted Roma/Gypsies as their equals. Thus 41 per cent of the Nis respondents said that Roma/Gypsy children should be able to learn their native language in addition to Serbian. In terms of marriage, however, both groups of respondents demonstrated almost the same "ethnic distance": asked whether they would marry a Roma/Gypsy, 80 per cent of respondents in suburban areas and 79 per cent in Nis replied that they would not.

The deep-rooted nature of this prejudice is illustrated further in relation to the question of burials. Although half of the respondents in Nis (50 per cent) had nothing against Roma/Gypsies being buried in the local cemetery, the remainder opted for three other possibilities: a separate section for Roma/Gypsies in the local cemetery (31 per cent), a completely separate cemetery for Roma/Gypsies (23 per cent), and the burial of Roma/Gypsies outside settlements (4 per cent). Respondents in suburban areas were even less tolerant: only 27 per cent said that they had nothing against Roma/Gypsies being buried in their local cemetery, 33 per cent replied that there should be a separate section for them, and 10 per cent held the view that Roma/Gypsies should be buried outside the settlement limits.

Research by HLC revealed that in the period 1992-2000, Roma/Gypsies in Serbia were frequently victims of torture and abuse by the police and subject to physical violence and discrimination by members of the general public. HLC investigated 90 incidents that occurred in this period in which Roma/Gypsies were targets of unlawful police conduct and physical violence and discrimination by private citizens, and registered 26 cases of assaults by "skinheads" and others. The most extreme example is an incident which took place outside a Belgrade elementary school: a group of skinheads inflicted 17 knife wounds on Gordana Jovanovic, a 13-year-old Roma/Gypsy girl.

During this period, HLC also recorded that the homes of several Roma/Gypsies were torched, Roma/Gypsies were beaten up and racist slogans were scrawled on walls. Reacting to these racist slogans, the president of *Matica Romska*, Trifun Dimić, said: "It's not a big problem that some hooligan scrawls these hate messages. The biggest problem is that no one seems to care."[15]

The legal status of Roma/Gypsies

Roma/Gypsies are not granted official national-minority status in Serbia. Over the past decade, many representatives of Romani associations, political parties and cultural organisations have addressed the Serbian parliament and federal authorities on several occasions, requesting that the Roma/Gypsy population be officially granted this status, and thereby enjoy human rights belonging to national minorities in Serbia.
In 1990, Dr Svenka Savic, professor at the Faculty of Philosophy in Novi Sad, advocated for the recognition of the Roma/Gypsy minority as a national minority at a conference entitled "Social status and culture of the Roma in Vojvodina".[16]
The Commission for the Study of the Life and Customs of the Roma at the Serbian Academy of Science and Arts holds that the Roma/Gypsy minority should enjoy the same rights as other ethnic communities in Serbia. At a conference on the standardisation of the Romani language in Yugoslavia, academician Milos Macura expressed the view of the Commission that Roma should be afforded all the rights and possibilities afforded to other communities in Serbia.[17]

Minority rights

The Federal Republic of Yugoslavia and Serbia are bound by all the international instruments in the fields of minority rights, the rights of the child, and the right to education ratified by the former Socialist Republic of Yugoslavia. The new state continues to apply the international acts outlined above on the "basis of Yugoslavia's uninterrupted status as a personality of international law".

Domestic legislation in Serbia does not specifically target national minorities. Instead, the rights and freedoms of members of national minorities are guaranteed by the Constitution of the Federal Republic of Yugoslavia,[18] the Serbian Constitution, legislation on the official use of languages and scripts, and legalisation on elementary, secondary and higher education.

Under the FRY Constitution, all citizens are equal before the law, irrespective of nationality, race, sex, language, faith, political or other beliefs, education, social origin, property or other personal status.[19] National minorities are entitled to preserve, foster and express their ethnic, cultural, linguistic and other peculiarities and to use their national symbols, in accordance with international law.[20] The FRY Constitution also guarantees to national minorities the freedom to express their national culture and to use their mother tongue language and script.[21] It also guarantees the right to:
- access education, information and media in their own language[22]
- establish educational and cultural organisations or associations[23]
- establish and foster unhindered relations with co-nationals in FRY and outside its borders with co-nationals in other states, and to take part in international NGOs provided that these relations are not detrimental to FRY or to a member republic[24]
- use their own language in proceedings before a tribunal or government agency or other authority.[25]

The Serbian Constitution, in conformity with the law, also provides for the use of minority languages and scripts, alongside Serbian, in areas populated by a particular minority.[26] It guarantees to members of national minorities the right to education in their own language, in conformity with the law.[27] Other minority rights are derived from the provisions of the Serbian Constitution regulating the rights and freedoms of *all* citizens, for example, the freedom to express ethnicity and equality before the law.

The right to education

Members of minorities in Serbia have the right to education from preschool to university levels. However, this is not backed up by a system of state-funded pre-schools, and parents must pay fees. Further still, the right to education in a minority language is exercised only by members of the Albanian, Hungarian, Slovak, Romanian and Ruthenian minorities. In practice, Roma/Gypsies do not have access to education in their own language.

Classroom teaching for national minorities is provided in accordance with the Serbian curriculum. Although there is some scope for developing curricula to suit instruction in minority languages, in practice, textbooks used are usually translated from Serbian. In this way, curricula often serve an ideological function rather than being based on any scientific or educational principle.[28] School programmes have to be approved by the Minister of Education. These programmes are drawn up without consultation with relevant experts on multicultural issues and fail to take into account the principles of multicultural education. For example, school programmes rarely, if at all, contain any reference to the history of different ethnic groups, including that of Roma/Gypsies.[29]

Children of refugees from the former Yugoslav republics and internally displaced persons (IDPs) from Kosovo have the right to attend school, on condition that they are registered in the territory of Serbia. However, following the conclusion of the Military-Technical Agreement between the Yugoslav Army and NATO and the deployment of the international forces in Kosovo in June 1999, the Serbian Minister of Education, by way of an internal regulation, forbade the enrolment of children of Kosovo IDPs in Serbian schools other than those in areas adjacent to the administrative line with Kosovo. This interdiction was justified on the grounds that the IDPs would soon be returning to their homes in Kosovo. However, in the face of strong pressure from both the public and the IDPs, the regulation was soon withdrawn, and these children were able to attend schools throughout Serbia on the same terms as all other children, ie, on the presentation of the child's birth certificate and registration of residence.

The Serbian Child Welfare Act envisages the right of children to attend preschool facilities for the year prior to enrolment in elementary school.[30] It sets out that instruction in these institutions is to be provided in Serbian or, where relevant, in minority languages.[31] Since preschool institutions are established and funded by the municipalities, the local authorities decide who should receive instruction in minority languages.

However, there are no fixed criteria for this. Although the curriculum has to be approved by the Minister of Education, the institution itself is free to organise preparatory classes in Serbian for children of minority communities.[32] Preschool is not free, and fees are adjusted to the incomes of the parents. In areas with a negative population growth, there is no charge for the third child.[33]

Elementary school is compulsory and free for eight years. All children who are not diagnosed as disabled enrol in elementary school at seven years of age.[34] All elementary schools are state-run: only ballet and music schools can be established privately.

Classroom teaching in either one minority language or in both a minority and the Serbian language[35] is provided in areas with an ethnically mixed population, although this does not relate to Roma/Gypsy minorities and the use of Romanes.

It is provided when there are at least 15 children from the first grade who wish to receive instruction in a minority language. Classes with fewer children may be organised, but only with the approval of the Minister of Education.[36] For instance, in 1996-97 the Minister of Education approved the forming of a first grade class, which consisted of just five children who wished to receive instruction in Hungarian.[37] The Elementary Schools Act does not allow for the possibility of parents or others financing classes with fewer minority students.

The manner in which curricula are taught in two languages is prescribed by the Minister of Education. If classroom teaching is provided only in a minority language, extra courses in Serbian are compulsory. When non-Serb children receive instruction in Serbian, they are entitled to courses in their native language and national culture.[38]

Regarding the education of minorities, the Secondary Schools Act contains provisions identical to those in the Elementary Schools Act. Broadly, there are three kinds of secondary schools: for students preparing to enter university, art school or vocational school.[39] They provide four years of education, with the exception of some vocational schools, whose courses run for three years. Candidates for secondary schools are required to take a competitive admission exam.

Under the Serbian University Act, universities or university departments may be founded by the state or privately endowed. Generally, students need to complete secondary school before being able to enrol at university. On completion of a first degree, students may continue with postgraduate studies.

The decision on whether to provide instruction in a minority language at university level is taken by the university or department concerned. This is subject to approval from the Serbian government. Previously, universities would be expected to provide instruction in a minority language when at least 30 students pursuing the same field of study requested it. However, this is not guaranteed in the current University Act. Likewise, national minorities are no longer entitled to take university admission exams in the language in which they completed secondary school.[40] Students who wish to study in a foreign or minority language must take a test in the respective language before a committee. Under the law, faculty members must also obtain a certificate from their departments of their ability to teach in a minority language.[41]

In practice

The right to education for Roma/Gypsy children

The Federal Republic of Yugoslavia is the only post-communist country that has not yet embarked on a genuine process of transition. This is naturally reflected in its school system and minorities education policy. Thus far there has been practically no official policy regarding the education of Roma/Gypsies, who have little chance of receiving classroom instruction in their own language. The only gestures have been experimental projects lasting one or more years, implemented in one or two municipalities, and those have been only symbolic contributions to integrating Roma/Gypsies in the school system.

Abandonment and dropping out

According to a recent OECD report, 75,000 Roma/Gypsy children of compulsory school age are not in school. This represents about 10 per cent of total enrolments in grades one to eight in Serbia. The report further notes that most Roma/Gypsy children do not start school at all, start late or drop out after only one or two years.[42] According to an unpublished World Bank paper, only one-third of Roma/Gypsy children who enter school complete primary education.[43]

According to the 1991 census, 62 per cent of Roma/Gypsies had not finished primary education, and 36 per cent were without any schooling or at most had completed just three grades. The census also recorded that 22,591 (26 per cent) of Roma/Gypsies in Serbia were illiterate, with rates ranging from 15 per cent illiteracy in the 15-19-year age-group to 71 per

Table 7.1 Educational structure of the Roma/Gypsy population: Elementary

Age-group	Number	No education or completed only grades 1, 2 or 3	Completed grades 4, 5, 6 or 7	Completed elementary education	Continued to higher levels of education	Unknown level of education	Total
15-19	14,965	28.70%	27.53%	38.40%	4.43%	0.93%	100%
20-24	13,274	22.61%	24.98%	36.68%	14.59%	1.14%	100%
25-29	11,289	25.82%	23.52%	34.63%	14.96%	1.04%	100%
30-34	10,255	29.95%	27.08%	29.69%	12.09%	1.16%	100%
35-39	8,557	33.28%	30.09%	26.51%	9.29%	0.8%	100%
40-44	6,493	35.46%	32.68%	22.67%	8.29%	0.89%	100%
45-49	4,598	44.52%	31.56%	16.09%	6.99%	0.82%	100%
50-54	4,505	51.49%	31.05%	11.58%	4.97%	0.88%	100%
55-59	3,901	65.64%	21.60%	7.51%	4.15%	1.07%	100%
60-64	2,986	74.14%	17.95%	4.35%	2.68%	0.87%	100%
65+	3,637	80.36%	13.85%	3.08%	1.51%	1.18%	100%
Age not known	1,342	40.68%	14.08%	22.05%	5.89%	17.28%	100%
Total numbers	85,802	31,045	22,488	23,405	7,788	1,076	100%
Total %		36.18%	26.21%	27.45%	9.08%	1.25%	100%

cent illiteracy in those aged 65 years and over. For reasons outlined above, together with the fact that data is only collected for those aged 15 years and above, the 1991 census is an unreliable source of data. However, it does provide us with some broad indications. Tables 7.1, 7.2 and 7.3 show the education structure of the Roma/Gypsy population according to school level based on the 1991 census.[44]

The drop-out rate among Roma/Gypsy children is highest in the third and fourth grades. Though elementary education is free, parents have to buy textbooks, notebooks and other school supplies for their children, which most Roma/Gypsy parents cannot afford. Roma/Gypsy families have barely enough for subsistence, especially those displaced from Kosovo, and they cannot afford even second-hand textbooks. Children also find it hard to study and so to keep up at school. For example, when children return home after the afternoon shift in school,[45] ie, after 8pm, Roma/Gypsy children cannot do their homework or study because of the lack of electricity.

Table 7.2 Educational structure of the Roma/Gypsy population: Secondary

Age-group	Number in age group	Total with secondary education*		Trade school for skilled workers	Trade school for highly skilled workers	High school	Secondary technical school	Secondary vocational school
		Number	%					
15-19	14,965	660	4.41%	56	6	17	85	496
20-24	13,274	1,871	14.10%	142	20	50	225	1,434
25-29	11,289	1,566	13.87%	156	28	59	335	988
30-34	10,255	1,070	10.43%	326	29	95	535	85
35-39	8,557	678	7.92%	263	31	52	298	34
40-44	6,493	444	6.83%	187	19	18	197	23
45-49	4,598	261	5.67%	112	21	20	103	5
50-54	4,505	189	4.19%	86	22	9	67	5
55-59	3,901	139	3.56%	76	11	12	38	2
60-64	2,986	65	2.17%	32	2	7	20	4
65+	3,637	48	1.32%	25	2	5	11	5
Unknown	1,342	71	5.29%	12	1	10	29	19
Total	85,802	7,062	8.23%	1,473	192	354	1,943	3,100

Note: * Shows the total who had a secondary education and did not continue to higher or university education.

Due to poverty, many Roma/Gypsy parents feel it necessary to encourage their children to find work and help to contribute to the family income. As a result of this, many children either drop out or do not enrol in school in the first place. A survey in the Mali London settlement in Pančevo, for instance, showed that 69 per cent of school-children were doing some kind of wage-earning work.[46] For some Roma/Gypsy communities, early marriage is another factor which encourages low enrolment and high drop-out rates, especially among girls. Research carried out in Masuric, for example, showed that a large number of girls married at 14 or 15 years. The survey carried out in the Mali London settlement also showed that 42 per cent of Roma/Gypsy women were illiterate, and that 44 per cent had dropped out of school between the ages of 13 and 17 due to marriage.[47] After marriage, Roma/Gypsy women have very little chance of finishing school. Although there are night schools for adults and elementary and secondary schools for students who need only take exams and are not required to attend classes, they do not have crèche facilities.

Table 7.3 Educational structure of the Roma/Gypsy population: University and higher education

Age-group	Number in age group	Higher education		University education	
		Number	%	Number	%
15-19	14,965	4	0.02%		-
20-24	13,274	46	0.35%	19	0.14%
25-29	11,289	67	0.59%	57	0.50%
30-34	10,255	89	0.86%	83	0.80%
35-39	8,557	73	0.85%	45	0.52%
40-44	6,493	61	0.94%	33	0.50%
45-49	4,598	34	0.39%	27	0.58%
50-54	4,505	28	0.62%	7	0.15%
55-59	3,901	12	0.30%	11	0.28%
60-64	2,986	8	0.26%	7	0.23%
65 and over	3,637	4	0.11%	3	0.08%
Unknown	1,342	2	0.14%	6	0.44%
Total	85,802	428	0.50%	298	0.35%

Furthermore, most night schools are designed for those already in some kind of work and require payment of tuition fees.

Discrimination is another factor that underpins high drop-out rates among Roma/Gypsy children. Research carried out by HLC, for example, revealed that Roma/Gypsy children in elementary and secondary schools are frequent targets of abuse from teachers and peers as well as attacks by skinheads. In 2000, HLC officially recorded two cases of Roma/Gypsy children dropping out of school and two cases of transfer to other schools because of violence.[48]

Many see the poor education of Roma/Gypsy parents as one of the main reasons behind high drop-out rates among Roma/Gypsy children. Some argue that for many Roma/Gypsy parents a formal education is not seen as a priority or a precondition for upward mobility.[49] A survey conducted in the Romani village of Masurica in southern Serbia showed that 36 per cent of the respondents wanted their children to finish only

four grades of elementary school and that
18 per cent were undecided as to whether or not
they wanted an education for their children.[50]
The survey in the Mali London settlement in
Pančev asked Roma/Gypsy parents what they
wanted their children to be when they grew up.
As Table 7.4 shows, a high proportion wanted
their sons to be craftsmen and their daughters to
be hairdressers or nurses. Roma/Gypsies in the
settlement who had received an education had
done so only up to elementary level. Of those
over 15 years of age, 80 per cent had not finished
elementary school.[51]

Roma/Gypsies and special schools

There are 38 special schools across Serbia, which
consist of both elementary and secondary
schools. In addition to these, there are 30 regular
schools in Vojvodina that have separate classes for
disabled children. Apart from Vojvodina, there are
no official data on the number of Roma/Gypsies
who attend these schools.

In Vojvodina, there are 13 special schools, and
Roma/Gypsy children make up about 80 per cent
of children in such schools. These schools
provide instruction in Serbian, Hungarian, Slovak
and Ruthenian. According to the province's
Secretariat for Education, Science and Culture, in
1997/1998 there were 440 Roma/Gypsy children
enrolled in these 13 special schools, as well as in
separate classes. Of these, 83 per cent were taught
in Serbian, 16 per cent in Hungarian, 0.5 per cent
in Slovak, and 0.5 per cent in Ruthenian. Tuition
is not provided in Romanes.

The over-representation of Roma/Gypsies in
the special-school system can be ascribed to the

Table 7.4a Parental ambitions: sons

	Number of parents
Mechanic, locksmith, auto mechanic	6
Craftsman (without specifying)	4
Medical doctor	4
Worker (without specifying)	3
Teacher	2
Musician	2
Policeman	2
Director	2
Veterinarian	1
Farmer	1
Soccer player	1
Non-specific answers*	3

Table 7.4b Parental ambitions: daughters

	Number of parents
Hairdresser	7
Nurse	6
Medical doctor	3
Worker	1
Housewife	3
Non-specific answers*	6

* eg, as God wills, anything that would enable her/him to earn her living, a good job, to have an education.

flawed process of evaluation and diagnosis.
Roma/Gypsy children who enter regular schools
often find it hard to master the curriculum given
that instruction is not conducted in their first
language, nor are there mechanisms in place to

support bilingual or multilingual pupils. When no additional tutoring is provided, such pupils tend to fall behind. It is most commonly at this point that the school psychologist recommends their transfer to a special school. In line with the Elementary Schools Act, the medical commission then evaluates the pupil and assesses the type and degree of "mental deficiency".[52] This involves a series of psychological and other similar tests based on majority norms that do not take into account Roma/Gypsy culture specifics. At the proposal of the commission, the relevant municipal administration body assigns the child to an appropriate school.

Teachers in mainstream schools also play a significant part in the referral process. Frustrated by the excessive curriculum, poorly paid and often prejudiced against Roma/Gypsies, teachers frequently recommend the transfer of Roma/Gypsy children to special schools.

Research carried out by HLC reveals that evaluations of healthy Roma/Gypsy children that result in their diagnosis as "mentally retarded" constitute discrimination against Roma/Gypsies. The medical commissions do not take into consideration the fact that these children often do not speak Serbian as their first language and are socially disadvantaged in many ways. Tests are carried out in Serbian and do not allow for different interpretations, according to different cultural backgrounds.

Although parents may appeal against decisions with the Ministry of Education, Roma/Gypsy parents often accept the evaluation of their child as mentally disabled. Some believe that parents

accept such diagnosis as it enables Roma/Gypsy parents access to the various benefits. For example, a child who is diagnosed as moderately or severely disabled attends school for the whole day rather than in shifts and receives free meals and medical care. Humanitarian organisations such as the Red Cross also offer support to such pupils by providing snacks. However, most Roma/Gypsy parents do not complain against the municipal authorities' decision simply because they are not aware that they can and, in particular, are not provided with the information and means to take forward a complaint.

The disproportionate number of Roma/Gypsies in special schools is detrimental to Roma/Gypsy children in a number of ways. First, their high numbers in special schools reinforce existing prejudice and fuel discrimination. Secondly, the level of education they receive in such schools is inferior to that provided in mainstream schools and, thirdly, on completion of special school, Roma/Gypsy children have little possibility of continuing their education and even less chance of finding work.

A psychologist at a Kragujevac school for children with slight mental disabilities says:

"We don't separate Roma children from the others. The procedure whereby children are referred to special schools, their evaluation and educational and general treatment is the same for Roma as for all the other children. The name of the school was this year changed to Dragoljub Božović Žuća Elementary School. This was done so that the children would not be set apart. This is an elementary school for

children with slight mental handicaps. There is no mention of the word "special," not even in the name.

The curriculum for slightly handicapped children in elementary school is the same as that in all elementary schools, only somewhat condensed, and specific educational and other methods are used in working with the children.

There is in the school a centre for moderately and severely disabled children. It is completely separate and not within the elementary school system. We have no record of the ethnic composition of the student body. We do not ask Roma children to declare their ethnicity.

Generally speaking, there is no difference between the results achieved by Roma children and the other children in this school. There is a higher percentage of Roma children compared to the overall Roma population. There are 2 per cent or 3 per cent mentally disabled

children in the general population. Where Roma children are concerned, the percentage is somewhat higher – about 5 per cent on average.

The higher number of Roma children in special schools compared to others is not due to their natural, inherent mental and intellectual inferiority. Roma children grow up under the unfavourable impact of factors such as poor social status, poor education of their parents, unemployment, psychologically and socially disrupted family relations, inadequate housing, and in different cultural and linguistic conditions.

If their intellectual abilities are to be developed optimally in accordance with their inherent, genetic predispositions, they must be stimulated. Mental retardation arises from both genetic and external factors. The specifics of the Roma population are the result of their growing up in specific conditions. These children are pscudo-retarded, which means that their retardation is the result of unfavourable environmental factors.

The prerequisites for the normal mental development of Roma children from specific communities are:
- improvement of the social and economic status of the Roma family
- establishment of preschool facilities for these children
- additional tutoring in regular schools and specific methods of work with these children in elementary school, and development of individualisation."

A psychologist at the Sirogojno Special School in the Zemun district of Belgrade, in which 70 per cent of the 250 children are Roma/Gypsies, told HLC:[53]

"Roma children are educationally neglected. They don't understand the test questions and have no work ethic. It is not a priority of Roma parents to have their children go to school. That educationally neglected Roma children can integrate into regular schools is a fairy tale. We end up with frustrated and neurotic children.

When testing Roma children, I notice that they have problems with abstract concepts. This is because of the rather poor vocabulary of the Romani language. For instance, they do not have the word 'dignity'. A Roma child cannot describe to me the meaning of the word because it has never heard it before. It can't understand it.

Or, for example, I ask a child what he should do when he sees smoke coming out of a house. The right answer is that he would call the fire brigade or tell an adult that a fire had broken out in the house. Roma children as a rule reply that the stove should be cleaned or the stove pipes fixed to stop the smoke coming out. Then I have to fail the child. I ask if they would rather give money to the Red Cross or to a beggar and Roma children say they would give it to the Red Cross, which is the correct answer. But when I ask why, they say because the Red Cross helps them. That is the wrong answer. Or, for instance, I ask what an apple and a pear have in common. Roma children know they are both fruits. However, when we get more abstract and I ask what makes them similar, they say something like, "They both have stems". Wrong answer again.

The parents of many of our children also went to this school and, through inertia, enrol their children here. They know it is easier to finish this school than a regular school where the curriculum is harder. And they know that their children will get free meals and snacks, textbooks and, often, humanitarian aid. It is characteristic of them that they take the line of least resistance."

A psychologist who works at a special school in the Novi Beograd district of Belgrade told the HLC that 80 per cent of the 104 children there were Roma/Gypsies:[54]

"Officially, the Novi Beograd Special Elementary School has no children of average intellect. The problems of the Roma children are the problems of the whole Roma population. The attitude of us "whites" toward the Roma population is also a problem. Amongst ourselves, we psychologists call the results of intelligence tests administered to Roma children "Gypsy IQ", meaning that they show up as retarded when they take our "white" tests. But it also means that the tests are not designed to take into account Roma specifics. The problem is that, like the tests, regular schools are not adapted to the Roma population. We in fact help Roma children because, by referring them to special schools, we get them out of regular schools where they are not able to master the curriculum. It is true that the Roma population has a higher percentage of pseudo-retarded children. The reasons are self-evident: poverty and the parents' lack of education. The curriculum in regular schools is hard even for children of normal intellect. If we had a better education system, there would be fewer Roma in special schools.

Where the IQ of Roma children is concerned, the law backs me up. They are unable to score more than 70 points on the test, which places them in the slightly retarded category. How can a Roma child do a projection of a comic strip at the test when it has never had a comic book in its hands? But that doesn't mean they are not intelligent. Just a couple of days ago, two workmen were trying to get a cabinet into a classroom and couldn't get it through the door. Then a Roma boy from the eighth grade came along and told them at what angle to hold it to get it into the room.

Roma children in this school feel themselves to be superior to white children. They are aware that learning is much easier for them. The slightly retarded white children at our school cannot compare with the far more intelligent Roma children."

When asked by the HLC's researcher if her special school would have to close down if Roma/Gypsy children were not wrongly assigned to it, she replied:

"I can tell you that all the Roma children now in this school are pseudo-retarded. But we do it to get Roma children out of a hopelessly wrong educational system."

A neuropsychiatrist with the Mental Health Institute of the Novi Beograd Medical Centre in Belgrade expresses how she views the educational problems of Roma/Gypsy girls:[55]

"Children belonging to different subcultures are educationally neglected, don't know the language and score poorly in tests. These children not only don't know Serbian, they don't know their own language either. Their parents are usually illiterate and have absolutely no appreciation of education. To the test question "From what is bread obtained?" such children reply "From garbage cans", or when asked "Where does milk come from?" they say "From the store". The biggest problem is a child who starts school at the age of 9, 10 or 12. What to do with such a child? I can't place a physically developed girl of 12, the age when she should already be having children according to their customs, in the first grade together with 7-year-olds. If the child is not too intellectually neglected, I refer it to a school where it does not attend classes and only takes the required exams. If it is, then we try with a special school."

A therapist at the Milan Rakić Elementary School, which runs a preparatory class for Roma/Gypsy children, speaks of her experience:[56]

"The intelligence tests are not adapted for Roma children, primarily because they are educationally neglected. Roma children start school almost completely ignorant. The one group of children who have taken the preparatory class so far are now in a regular school and have fitted in well. We have 12 children in the preparatory class at present.

Children who have finished the preparatory class settle down in school much better than other Roma children, better even than children from Roma families who are better off but refused to put their children in this programme.

Working with Roma children, we have noticed that their main problem is not knowing the language. Our team consists of a therapist, psychologist, teacher and a Roma university student who interprets for us. The children study both Romani and Serbian. We devote major attention to the study of the languages, and work also on psychomotor retraining, stimulating preoperative and operative thinking, the children's socialisation, and take them to cultural events. We take them to the theatre, with performances for children in Romani and Serbian, and to the zoo."

Language provision

For many Roma/Gypsies in Serbia, Romanes is their first language. Although the education system makes it possible for national minorities to be educated in their own language from preschool to university, Roma/Gypsies are the only linguistic minority that does not have a minority-language programme in Serbia. Most Roma/Gypsy children attend schools where the teaching is in either Serbian or a minority language.

A number of attempts have been made in the past to deal with problems of access and relevance, and some basic steps were taken: a Romani grammar, dictionary and primer were published, and Romanes was introduced as an elective subject in several Kosovo municipalities in 1985. Although the project produced solid results, nonetheless it has since ceased to exist. Nine years later, in 1994, the Ministry of Education set up a committee to draft a programme for the study of the Romani language with elements of national culture from the first grade of elementary school. The committee, however, failed to complete its assignment. Elementary schools for Roma/Gypsies were established in some Vojvodina municipalities (Senta, Horgos and Apatin) but yielded poor results.

A former secretary for minority affairs in the Government of the Autonomous Province of Vojvodina commented to HLC on the policies on Roma/Gypsy education in Vojvodina:

"Roma only partially exercise their right to an education in their own language. They may take Romani with elements of national culture as an elective subject in elementary school, but they do not realise their right to classroom instruction in all subjects in Romani.

The Elementary Schools Act requires at least 15 children from a minority group to state their wish to receive instruction in their own language, a request to this effect by their parents to the Minister of Education, and his approval. Where Romani as an elective subject is concerned, the Minister has approved classes with less than 15 children. A precondition for the introduction of instruction in all subjects in a minority language is that the Ministry announce a public competition for textbooks in the respective language. Teachers would also have to be trained to teach all subjects in that language.

Only the Serbian Ministry of Education can announce a public competition for textbooks. Introduction of minority languages in schools also requires the approval of the Minister of Education. The provincial authorities have no competence in the field of education. The Elementary Schools Act is applied uniformly in Serbia and education is in the purview of the Serbian Ministry of Education. The same holds for secondary schools and universities.

It is necessary to provide trained teachers for future Romani language and culture departments at universities. And this requires:
- an institutional framework
- creation of a social climate to ensure systematic education of Roma
- co-operation with the international community and associations focusing on Roma education issues

- establishment of art and cultural societies which would not provide mere entertainment but present the highest cultural achievements. Roma, for example, need a theatre because it is an essential factor in the education of every people, hence Roma too.

Romani is not an official language because there is no regular education in the Romani language. The main criterion for introducing a minority language as an official language is the existence of organised regular classroom instruction in that language. Such instruction is provided in the Hungarian, Romanian, Slovak and Ruthenian languages, but not in Romani. This is why Romani is not an official language. The criteria are laid down by the statute of the Autonomous Province. When I say regular instruction, I mean teaching of all the subjects in the curriculum in a minority language. That is the condition for realising the right to official use of a minority language.[57]

Under the Child Welfare Act,[58] introduction of a minority-language programme in preschool institutions requires that the teachers have completed appropriate courses of study in the respective language, or that they have taken and passed a test in the language at a post-secondary school or university department. There are no post-secondary schools or university departments in Serbia with courses in Romani, hence there are no teachers with the required qualifications.

The Minister of Education has not adopted a programme or curriculum for education in Romani. The Elementary Schools Act, however, envisages the possibility that minorities who do not have schools in their own language could study as an elective subject their language and the basics of their people's history, literature and culture. Thus in December 1998, "Romani with elements of national culture" was introduced as an elective subject for Roma/Gypsy children in nine elementary schools in Vojvodina. The project was launched by *Matica Romska*, and financially supported by the Serbian Ministry of Education and the Vojvodina Secretariat for Education, Science and Culture. The curriculum was drawn up by *Matica Romska* president Trifun Dimić and approved by the Serbian Ministry of Education. The textbooks were also written by Dimić. The non-governmental Open Society Fund financially assisted the printing of a Romani primer and other textbooks. "Romani with elements of national culture" is not taught in a single school in central Serbia, nor is it possible for Roma/Gypsies to acquire a secondary or university education in their own language, the main reason being the lack of qualified teachers.

However, according to the Greek Helsinki Monitor, an elementary school in Obrenovac near Belgrade recently reintroduced elective Romani language classes for Roma/Gypsy children.[59] In October 2000, the school's new board had discontinued Romani classes, but with support from HLC, the Roma Society of Obrenovac, as well as the Ministry of Education, the classes resumed in April 2001. This is one of only a few examples in Serbia.

NGO practice in the area

Over 20 NGOs with projects focusing on the issue of education for Roma/Gypsy children have emerged in Serbia in recent years, some of which have been founded by Roma/Gypsies themselves. However, none of these projects have been implemented in co-operation with the Serbian Ministry of Education. Instead, they are mainly supported by international NGOs and donors.

With the support of international organisations, NGOs in Serbia have established kindergartens, and organised programmes for preschool and additional tutoring in Romanes. A number of organisations founded by Roma/Gypsies have been particularly effective. These include: the Roma Education Centre, Nis; the Democratic Union of Roma, Belgrade; Roma Heart, Belgrade; the 8th April Community Centre, Belgrade; and the Roma Cultural Centre, Subotica. In addition to local initiatives, since 1996 the Open Society Foundation has introduced the international Step-by-Step programme. This has involved projects aimed at the socialisation of deprived Roma/Gypsy children, and has funded kindergartens developed by the Centre for Interactive Pedagogy (CIP), entitled "Kindergarten as a Family Centre". CIP adapted the preschool part of the programme for Roma/Gypsy children and has applied it in the past four years in kindergartens in Nis, Kragujevac, Belgrade, Čantavir, Krusevac and Surdulica. The programme was endorsed by the Serbian Ministry of Education and supported by professors of psychology and pedagogy at Belgrade University's Department of Humanities.

Some 500 children between the ages of four and seven attend these kindergartens each year. In smaller communities, the kindergartens are open to all children, which helps Roma/Gypsy pupils learn Serbian and prepare for elementary school. A survey conducted by CIP and the Open Society Foundation revealed that the children who attended the kindergarten in Nis learned Serbian well enough to pass the tests for elementary school. Out of those children who went on to finish their first year in elementary school in 1998-99, 44 per cent of them passed with a grade average of 4, and 26 per cent with a grade average of 5 (see Table 7.5).[60]

The Belgrade-based Society for Upgrading Roma Settlements has organised a supplementary programme for Roma/Gypsy children from grades one to four with the aim of promoting

their integration into the school system. The programme, which includes additional tutoring and activities to motivate the children and stimulate their intellect and socialisation, is conducted in three elementary schools, each of which has two specially trained teachers. This programme was developed without any assistance from the Ministry of Education.

The Roma Information Centre is collaborating with elementary-school psychologists in Kragujevac on a programme called "Children Without Borders". The objective of this programme is to eliminate ethnic and religious prejudice and foster acceptance of ethnic diversity. The Centre has organised a series of psychological workshops for children from different ethnic and religious communities. Each group comprises five Roma, five Serb and five children displaced from Kosovo between the ages of 11 and 14.

CIP has developed a programme designed specifically for elementary-school teachers. This programme is aimed at overcoming prejudice, developing tolerance and openness, and is scheduled to start in 2001.

The Open Society Foundation provides scholarships for Roma/Gypsy young people engaged in full-time undergraduate and postgraduate education. In 2000, 62 Roma/Gypsy students received such scholarships. The Open Society Foundation also organises English-language courses for Roma/Gypsy students and activists in Novi Sad, Belgrade, Kragujevac, Nis and Subotica. The European Roma Rights Centre is another

Table 7.5 Results achieved in the 1998-99 school year by Roma/Gypsy children who went to the Nis kindergarten, compared to those who did not

Children who did not attend kindergarten	Children who attended kindergarten
Test 67% passed 33% knew Serbian	**Test** 100% passed 97% knew Serbian
School attendance Regular – 47% Occasionally absent – 27% Always absent – 27%	**School attendance** Regular – 99% – –
Results and grade average 40% finished 1st grade Grade average 5 – 0% Grade average 4 – 3% Grade average 3 – 17% Grade average 2 – 20%	**Results and grade average** 100% finished 1st grade Grade average 5 – 26% Grade average 4 – 44% Grade average 3 – 17% Grade average 2 – 13%

organisation that offers scholarships and internship programmes, but specifically for Roma/Gypsy law students.

To inform children about their rights, the HLC has published an illustrated booklet entitled "Children's Rights" in Romani and Serbian, based on the UN Convention on the Rights of the Child. It has been distributed to schools and children across the Federal Republic of Yugoslavia. Editions in Albanian and Turkish are now also being prepared for children in Kosovo. Save the Children UK helped to publish the UN Convention on the Rights of the Child in Romanes, and has financially supported projects for the preparatory, preschool and supplementary education of Roma/Gypsy children.

Norwegian Popular Relief finances a project of supplementary lessons for Roma/Gypsy children entitled "New Knowledge Workshop". The teachers are staff members of the 8th April Roma Community Centre in Belgrade.[61]

Numerous other organisations, including Oxfam, the International Rescue Committee, the International Orthodox Charity and the International Committee of the Red Cross, are involved in various projects to promote the education of Roma/Gypsy children.

UNICEF plans to carry out with the new Serbian government a project entitled "Education for All", with the aim of improving the grades of minority children in special schools. This offers scope for re-evaluating test results of Roma/Gypsy children wrongly diagnosed as "mentally

deficient". Similarly, the Education Forum in Belgrade was established to draw up proposals for the integration of Roma/Gypsy children in the school system. One of its most important goals is to prevent Roma/Gypsy children from being wrongly evaluated as mentally disabled.

Marcel Kortijade, an expert in Romani studies and professor at the Institute for Nation, Language, Civilisation and Oriental Studies in Paris, has proposed the founding of a department at Belgrade University for the study of the Romani language as standardised at the Fourth World Roma Congress in Warsaw in 1990. To support this process, he also suggested that a group of Roma/Gypsy students be sent to study Romani at his Institute.

Finally, as part of its project "Minority Issues in Education," the Novi Sad Centre for Multiculturalism has set up a group of experts, including a Roma/Gypsy representative. The purpose of this group is to draft legislation for regulating minority education in Vojvodina. Two round table discussions are planned for when the draft is ready, to allow for input into the final version from members of minority groups.

Voices of Roma/Gypsy children

LB, 12 years old, Desanka Maksimovic Elementary School, Belgrade

They Tell Me

They tell me, oh, they tell me,
that I'm just a Gypsy girl
and don't belong in their crowd.
And why that is, I never know,
nor what came over them.
Isn't my dress just like hers?
Isn't my smile just like hers?
Don't they know that, deep down,
we Gypsies are sound and true?
Like her, I have a mother too,
and my house is big and clean.
And my eyes, just like hers,
sparkle merrily in the sun.
They tell me, oh, they tell me,
I'm just a little Gypsy girl.
Yet they don't know what this means.
We too keep our patron Saint's Day,
and my heart is full of love.

All of the following contributions from children were given in interviews between September and December 2000.

FJSh, 11 years old, at elementary school in Belgrade
"I came to Belgrade from Gnjilane in Kosovo on June 17, 1999, and enrolled in a school here. I am in the fifth grade now. Back in Gnjilane I went to the Vuk Stefanovic Karadžić School. I had excellent grades there. In Kosovo I had Romani language classes at school, but I don't have any here in this school.

I used to have excellent grades, now I have very good grades. That's because I don't have enough space to study. I live together with six people in a small room. The room is in a Romani settlement which doesn't have water or electricity. Mum and Dad don't have enough money to buy me all the books I need. I wish I could have all the books so I could be excellent in school again. My father has finished elementary school but my mother hasn't."

SB, 15 years old, at elementary school in Belgrade
"The kids in my class say I'm a Gypsy and curse my 'Gypsy mother'. A boy in my class called... sometimes hits me when he curses my 'Gypsy mother'. A lot of kids call me 'Gypsy' in the school yard. When we are in the school yard, the kids sometimes kick me and say I'm a Gypsy. I complained to the teacher several times and she said she would tell them to stop it. But they just keep on doing it.

KS, 11 years old, at elementary school in Belgrade
"When I was in the fourth grade, the kids gave me a hard time. They kept saying 'Fuck your Gypsy mother', and called me 'dirty Gypsy' and other names. One of them would start and then everybody joined in, some of the girls too. There are two Romani boys in my class and they insult them too, just like they insult me. In May this year a boy, AS, kicked me and said 'Get out of here, you Gypsy! Just look at you!' AJ hit me in the face with a ball and said 'Why did you steal my money, Gypsy?' My classmate MP shoved and hit me, calling me 'Gypsy'. I didn't complain to my parents, but I told my teacher. I told her that they kept insulting me because I am a Gypsy. She told

off the kids who insulted me and said we were all children and all the same. But they kept on insulting me. I am in the fifth grade now and the kids don't insult me any more. At our school, Serb children don't want to mix with us Romanis. I hang out with my cousin Jelena and other Roma girls. Only one Serb girl is friendly with us. She has never insulted us or called us 'Gypsies'."

ZM, nine years old, at elementary school in Belgrade
"I am in the second grade. The kids at school shout 'cigu-ligu'[62] at me. They slap me and curse 'my Gypsy mother' nearly every day. I complained to my mother and to my teacher.

He told me to look the other way and keep going if they bothered me again. Several times he saw them hitting me and cursing my 'Gypsy mother' and told them to stop insulting me. A month ago, two older boys hit me and insulted me in the school yard, and cursed my 'Gypsy mother'. One of them held me and the other one punched me in the head. When he said 'Fuck your Gypsy mother' I said back to him, 'Fuck your peasant mother' and tried to get away. But they caught me and made me take it back before letting me go. S and T from the second and fourth grades pick on me a lot, hitting me and saying 'Fuck your Gypsy mother'."

HS, 14 years old, at elementary school in Belgrade
"I'm in the sixth grade. I'm the only Roma in my class. The boys in my class curse my 'Gypsy mother' and tell me not to come to school any more. The girls don't. The boys bonk me on the head. It happens nearly every day. I told my teacher about it and she told me to go to the principal. My teacher told them in class to stop picking on me. I didn't go to the principal. I told my mother, but she didn't go to school to complain to the teacher."

SS, 11 years old, at elementary school in Belgrade
"I'm a fifth-grader. A boy called PŠ keeps giving me a hard time and says 'Fuck your Gypsy mother!' He punched me in the arm once during a gym class. I didn't complain to my teacher. I told my Mum, but my parents didn't do anything and said they didn't want to make things worse."

JV, 14 years old, at elementary school in Kragujevac
"We speak Serbian at home. I don't speak Romani, but I understand it. I heard at school that non-Romani children swear at Romani kids a lot and curse their 'Gypsy mothers'. I have never been insulted at school because I'm a Roma. I invite kids who aren't Romani to my birthday parties and they come. I also go to my Serbian friends' birthday parties.

When I finish elementary school I'm going to go to a school for hairdressers. I am a very good student. My mother and father have finished elementary school. I have a brother who's 16. He dropped out of school when he was in the fifth grade. I think he did it because of his teacher. Our grandfather always told

him not to go to school. He said the same thing to me too. He said all I needed to know was how to write my name. He kept saying schooling was useless if you couldn't get a job afterwards.

The school psychologist told me I could come to the 'Children Without Borders' workshops. She said Romani children should take part in them, and that embarrassed me. I felt silly because I don't want to hear somebody say 'Here come the Roma'."

MD, 14 years old, at elementary school in Kragujevac
"I'm a good student and I'm going to go to a school for hairdressers. I can't speak Romani, but I understand it. I have some friends who are not Roma. They come to my birthday parties and I go to theirs.

When the psychologist told me to come to the 'Children Without Borders' workshops she organises and said Romani children should be there too, it made me feel kind of awkward. That's because there are more Serbs there, some from other schools, and I thought they would look down on me. Later on, I got to like being in the group. When she said 'Romani children' back then, I felt embarrassed because I don't want to be seen as different from everybody else."

AT, 14 years old, at elementary school in Kragujevac
"My father is a Rom and my mother is Serb. I don't know what I am. When our school psychologist, asked me to come to the 'Children Without Borders' workshops and she said she wanted to have Romani children there too, I felt kind of silly. I thought the others

wouldn't like having me there because I'm a Roma. But I got to like being in the group in the workshops."

BJ, 12 years old, at elementary school in Deronje, Vojvodina

"I've heard that kids in other villages have classes in Romani. When Romani classes started in my school, my father said it was interesting. I was curious to see what they would be like and I found them interesting because I can speak Romani. Romani kids were shy at first but later on they all wanted to come. Our teacher helped us a lot. Ever since the Romani classes started, the Serb kids have been telling us that we are going to a Gypsy school to learn how to steal. Some of them are my classmates and some are from other classes. A boy called TL and one from the fourth grade, SJ, keep picking on me. They sometimes slap us and curse our 'Gypsy mothers'. TL once kicked me in the knees, cursed my 'Gypsy mother' and called me a thief. I hit him back and he went and complained to our teacher. She sent us both to the principal and said we had done a bad thing but that she wasn't going to take sides."

DJ, ten years old, at elementary school in Deronje, Vojvodina

"There are three Romani kids in my class. Nobody ever called me bad names or bullied me because I'm a Gypsy. We all play together during the breaks. We never argue, except when we play soccer, but nobody swears or curses even then. I invite only Romani kids to my birthday parties. I don't invite Serbs and they don't invite me either."

TJ, ten years old, at elementary school in Deronje, Vojvodina

"There are 18 of us in my class. Two are Roma. Romani kids hang out together with Serbs. The Serb kids never threw me out of our soccer team, because I'm a good player. Our teacher told us we have to get along and be friends. She said that because of a fight that broke out between Roma and non-Romani kids during a break. A Serb boy cursed a Roma kid's 'Gypsy mother'.

I invite both Roma and Serb kids to my birthday parties. Of the Serb kids, only NS, who is my best friend, invites me to his parties."

BJ, 14 years old, at elementary school in Deronje, Vojvodina

"I am the only Roma of the 14 kids in my class. When we were younger, Romani and Serb children didn't get along. But we don't have any problems now. I have friends who aren't Roma. Our homeroom teacher has always told us that we should get along with each other. I invite Serb kids to my birthday parties too, and they come."

Recommendations

Given that the Federal Republic of Yugoslavia has ratified and must apply in Serbia:

- the International Covenant on Civil and Political Rights (ratified 1971, entered into force 23 March 1976)
- the International Covenant on Economic, Social and Cultural Rights (ratified 1971, entered into force 3 January 1976)
- the International Convention on the Elimination of All Forms of Racial Discrimination (ratified 1967, entered into force 4 January 1969)
- the UN Convention on the Rights of the Child (ratified 1990, entered into force 3 July 1991)
- the UNESCO Convention against Discrimination in Education (ratified 1964)
- the Framework Convention for the Protection of National Minorities (ratified 11 May 2001, entered into force 1 September 2001)

Save the Children recommends that:

The Parliament and Government of the Republic of Serbia

- Enact, in collaboration with representatives of the Roma/Gypsy community in Serbia and consulting experts in minority affairs, a Law on National Minorities that would conform with international standards. The Law should specify which ethnic groups in Serbia have national minority status and, hence, enjoy the appropriate rights.
- Ensure preparatory classes for Roma/Gypsy children in at least one preschool institution in each municipality in Serbia. The classes should be attended by all Roma/Gypsy children, irrespective of the social, cultural and educational backgrounds of their families. Both the Serbian and the Romani languages should be taught in these classes.
- Ensure supplementary classes for Roma/Gypsy children in elementary schools in order to facilitate their integration into the educational system.
- Establish at the Belgrade University Department of Languages a Romani Language Chair in order to train Romani language teachers for elementary and secondary schools.
- Provide incentives and additional resources for Roma/Gypsies entering university. The criteria for the admission of Roma/Gypsies should be milder, and government scholarships should be awarded to all full-time Roma/Gypsy students. These measures would facilitate the creation of a body of university-trained Roma/Gypsies.
- Establish a government team of experts to formulate proposals for the integration of Roma/Gypsy children in regular schools.
- Ensure the presence of a Roma/Gypsy medical doctor on medical commissions evaluating Roma/Gypsy children for admission to elementary school in order to counter-balance the uniform tests, which are not adapted for Roma/Gypsy children, and to avoid the deeply rooted bias and prejudice against Roma/Gypsies having an effect on the placement of children.
- Amend the curricula of elementary and secondary schools. The Ministry of Education should devote special attention to strengthening ties between the ethnic communities in Serbia in order that they could learn more

about each other's history, culture, customs and the like, and thereby promote ethnic and religious tolerance.

- Establish human-rights and ethnic-tolerance workshops designed specifically for teachers.
- Ensure that it works together with children with the aim of eliminating ethnic and religious prejudice, in particular by establishing psychological workshops, publishing the appropriate literature and co-operating with the media in the promotion of ethnic and religious tolerance.

The international organisations, including the UN Commission on Human Rights, the Special Rapporteur on the Right to Education and the Special Rapporteur on Contemporary Forms of Racism, Racial Discrimination, Xenophobia and Related Intolerance, and the European Union:

- Closely monitor the international obligations undertaken by the FRY government in respect of the right to education, with particular attention to the right to education of Roma/ Gypsy children in Serbia.

Serbia: Notes on the text

1 Jean-Pierre Liégeois and Nicolae Gheorghe, *Roma/Gypsies: A European Minority*, Minority Rights Group International, London, 1995.

2 *Romologija 4*, Novi Sad, April 1997.

3 Group of authors, *Minorities in Serbia*, Helsinki Committee for Human Rights in Serbia, Belgrade, 2000.

4 *Thematic Reviews of Education Policy – Serbia*, Pact for Peace and Stability in South-Eastern Europe, Task Force for Education Table 1, June 2001.

5 Population of Serbia according to ethnicity, *1991 census*, Federal Statistics Office, Belgrade, 1993.

6 *Naša Borba*, 5 August 1997.

7 Group of authors, *Manjine u Srbiji* (Minorities in Serbia), Helsinki Committee for Human Rights in Serbia, Belgrade, 2000, p. 96.

8 Ilija Marinković, a Romani boy, entered the Vienna Music Conservatory, at the age of 9.

9 United Nations High Commissioner for Refugees (UNHCR) publication, July 2000. According to the UNHCR, between 40,000 and 50,000 Roma fled Kosovo to Serbia and Montenegro after June 1999.

10 "Vares Aver" (Something Else), *NIN*, 25 January 2001; "Afirmacija manjina" (Affirmation of Minorities), *Danas*, 26 January 2001.

11 The owner of Pink TV is Željko Mitrović, formerly a prominent member of the Yugoslav Left party founded by Mirjana Marković, while Palma TV is owned by Miodrag Vujović, a founder of the Socialist Party of Serbia.

12 Remarks, allusions and jokes of a distinctly discriminatory, nationalistic and racist nature feature all too frequently in Milovan Ilić's show.

13 Ethnic distance, a term used in social psychology, is a measure of the psychological distance between two different ethnic groups expressed in the readiness of the members of one group to accept or reject social relations with members of another group. Social relations are graded from the weakest, such as acquaintance and residing in the same building, to the strongest, such as marriage.

14 Dragoljub Djordjević, *Romi – nase komsije* (Roma – Our Neighbours), sociological-ethnological study of Roma, Niš, April 2000.

15 *Nasa Borba*, 5 August 1997.

16 Organised by *Matica Srpska*, Novi Sad, 25 January 1990.

17 *Romologija 4*, Novi Sad, April 1997.

18 The FR Yugoslavia Constitution was promulgated on 27 April 1992 and Serbia's on 28 September 1990. Autonomous legislative and legal systems were established in the 1990-1992 period and Serbia functioned as an independent state in all but name: government agencies did not apply federal laws and its parliament enacted legislation, decrees and other acts whereby the republic arrogated much of the competence of the federal state. See: Slobodan Vučetić, *Privatizovana država* (A Privatised State), Stubovi kulture, Belgrade, 1996.

19 Art. 20, Federal Constitution.

20 Art. 11, Federal Constitution.

21 Art. 45, Federal Constitution.

22 Art. 46, Federal Constitution.

23 Art. 47, Federal Constitution.

24 Art. 48, Federal Constitution.

25 Art. 49, Federal Constitution.

26 Art. 8 (2), Serbian Constitution.

27 Art. 32 (4), Serbian Constitution.

28 *Ratnistvo, patriotizam, patrijarhalnost* (Martialism, Patriotism, Patriarchalism), Analysis of elementary school textbooks, Dr Ružica Roksandić and Dr Vesna Pesić (eds), Centar za antiratnu akciju, Belgrade, 1994.

29 Miroslav Samardžić, *Položaj manjina u Vojvodina* (Position of Minorities in Vojvodina), Centar za antiratnu akciju, Belgrade, 1998.

30 Art. 32, Child Welfare Act.

31 Art. 44, Child Welfare Act.

32 Art. 25, Elementary Schools Act.

33 Art. 30, Child Welfare Act.

34 Art. 39, Elementary Schools Act.

35 In practice, instruction in two languages is provided in classes made up of children of different ethnic groups. Teaching in such classes is in Serbian and a minority language, and the children respond in their native tongue (schools in Pivnica and Kulpin, Vojvodina, where the children are Serb and Slovak). Goran Basić, *Položaj manjina u SR Jugoslavija* (Position of Minorities in FR Yugoslavia), in Collected papers: *Položaj manjina u Saveznoj Republici Jugoslavija*, Serbian Academy of Sciences and Arts; Conferences, Volume LXXXIV, Department of Social Sciences, Book 19, p. 83.

36 Art. 5, Elementary Schools Act.

37 Group of authors, *Minorities in Serbia*, Helsinki Committee for Human Rights in Serbia, Belgrade, 2000, p. 20.

38 Art. 5, Elementary Schools Act.

39 Secondary Schools Act, *Službeni glasnik RS* (Serbian Official Gazette), Nos. 50/92, 24/96.

40 This provision was contained in several statutes. See, eg, Art. 21, Education Law of the Socialist Autonomous Province of Vojvodina, *Službeni list SAPV* (SAPV Official Gazette), No. 21.

41 Art. 23, University Act.

42 *Thematic Reviews of Education Policy – Serbia*, Pact for Peace and Stability in South-Eastern Europe, Task Force for Education, Table 1, June 2001.

43 M Mertaugh, unpublished report, World Bank, 2001, cited in *Thematic Reviews of Education Policy – Serbia*, Pact for Peace and Stability in South-Eastern Europe, Task Force for Education, Table 1, June 2001.

44 *Osnovni skupovi stanovništva u zemlji i inostranstvu* (Basic Population Groups in the Country and Abroad), Census Book 15, Federal Bureau of Statistics, Belgrade, 1995.

45 Owing to the lack of space, elementary and secondary schools in Serbia operate two shifts: from 7.30am to approximately 2pm, and from 2pm to 8pm.

46 *Mali London, romsko naselje u Pančevu, Problemi i moguća rešenja* (Mali London, Romani settlement in Pančevo, Problems and Possible Solutions, Society for the Promotion of Romani Settlements and Institute of Criminological and Sociological Studies, Belgrade, 1999, p. 48.

47 *Ibid.*, p. 55.

48 See section "Voices of Roma/Gypsy Children."

49 The overall social climate in Serbia over the past ten years was not in favour of formal education. The lifestyles and values promoted by the new rich did not include a formal education, leading to the belief that schooling was not necessary for success.

50 Mitrovic, Aleksandra and Zajic, Gradimir, *Decenija s Romima u Masurici* (A Decade with Masurica Roma), in *Društvene promene i položaj Roma* (Social Changes and the Position of Roma), Serbian Academy of Sciences and Arts, Belgrade, 1993, p. 96.

51 *Mali London, romsko naselje u Pančevu, Problemi i moguća rešenja* (Mali London, Romani settlement in Pančevo, Problems and Possible Solutions), Society for the Promotion of Romani Settlements and Institute of Criminological and Sociological Studies, Belgrade, 1999, p. 52.

52 Art. 85, Elementary Schools Act.

53 HLC interview, 24 February 1999.

54 HLC interview, 18 February 1999.

55 HLC interview, 1 March 1999.

56 HLC interview, 25 February 1999.

57 This is not so. Compare Art. 11 of Serbian Law on Official Use of Languages and Scripts: "(1) Municipalities inhabited by members of national minorities shall determine which minority languages are in official use in their territory. (2) The language and/or minority languages in official use in a municipality shall be determined by the Statute of the municipality. (3) Minority languages in official use in the Assembly of the Autonomous Province shall be determined by its Statute."

58 Art. 59, Child Welfare Act.

59 Greek Helsinki Monitor, 16 April 2001.

60 Elementary school grades in Yugoslavia are expressed in numbers, from 1 (fail) to 5 (excellent).

61 The New Knowledge Workshop takes place in the Belgrade suburb of Mali Mokri Lug. Supplementary lessons in Serbian, English, mathematics, use of computers and the Internet are held for six hours twice a week, or, alternatively, for four hours three times a week. There are also art and music workshops, courses in journalism, a counselling service, lectures for Roma/Gypsy women, a children's choir and band, Romani language courses and field trips for poor Roma/Gypsy children.

62 Allusion to "Ciga" – shortened form of Gypsy in Serbian.

8 Federal Republic of Yugoslavia: Montenegro

It is estimated that an average of just 30 Roma/Gypsies finish elementary school each year (0.25 per cent of the school-age population). At the time of writing, only three Roma/ Gypsy children were attending secondary schools.

"I used to live in Peć. When we came here three years ago, I thought I'd be going to a regular school. But I didn't have my report cards from my old school so I couldn't enrol in any elementary schools."

Roma boy, 14 years old

"Some of the children attended schools in Kosovo where they were taught in Albanian and therefore speak only Albanian. These children were not able to continue their education in Montenegro... We worked with pre-schoolers from the age seven to nine. When the programme was finished, we tested the children, using the official tests. Thanks to these tests and the recommendations of the children's teachers, 50 children were enrolled in the first grade of elementary school in the extension here at the camp."

Principal of an extension school
in an IDP camp

Summary

Context
Montenegro is Serbia's junior partner in the Federal Republic of Yugoslavia. Under President Djukanovic it steered an independent course during the latter years of the Milosevic regime, seeking better relations with the West. The republic may declare formal independence, which would bring the Federal Republic of Yugoslavia to an end.

Roma/Gypsy population
Censuses have always underestimated the Roma/Gypsy population, counting as few as nine in 1953, rising to 1,471 in 1971. One NGO estimates that 20,000 Roma/Gypsies are permanently settled in Montenegro and that 6,500-7,000 Roma/Gypsy IDPs have come from Kosovo since 1999. Most of the IDPs are accommodated in camps. The permanently settled Roma/Gypsies are mainly Muslims and are divided into three main groups, which do not identify with each other. The largest group is the *Kovaci*. They are the most integrated into majority society, with smaller families and proportionally more of their children attending school than the other two groups. *Madjupi* speak Romani or Albanian and are settled in urban areas. *Gabelji* came to Montenegro only in the early twentieth century and are semi-nomadic. Roma/Gypsies are the most disadvantaged population group in Montenegro with high rates of

unemployment, and those who work have the hardest and worst-paid menial jobs. Living conditions, nutrition and health-care provision are poor. Mortality and birth rates are high, and average life expectancy low.

Roma/Gypsies and education

Of the 12,000 children of the settled Roma/Gypsy population who are of school age, fewer than 1,000 are attending primary school, and many of these drop out after a few grades. An average of just 30 complete primary education each year, and currently only three are in secondary education. According to official censuses, 80-90 per cent of adult Roma/Gypsies in Montenegro are illiterate. Their lack of experience of education inevitably impacts upon their children's school attendance and ability to study. Yet poverty, language incompatibility and discrimination are also barriers. In a survey of 14-30-year-old Roma/Gypsies in Kotor, 55 per cent said they discontinued education because they were subjected to verbal and physical violence in school. Illiteracy and school-attendance rates are slightly worse among Kosovan Roma/Gypsy IDPs. Open segregation is practised by the authorities in their education – separate Roma/Gypsy classes were established in an extension built onto the local primary school for children of the Konik II IDP camp.

Language provision

The majority of Roma/Gypsies in Montenegro speak Romanes or Albanian rather than Serbian. A large majority of the Kosovan Roma/Gypsy IDPs speak only Albanian. Although they have been given the possibility of attending Albanian language schools, Montenegrin Albanians have expressed hostility toward them, so Roma/Gypsy IDP children do not in practice attend them. Schools do not provide instruction in Romanes, due to a lack of qualified teachers and textbooks.

Special schools

Two per cent of children in special schools are Roma/Gypsy children – a relatively low proportion. Assessment techniques appear to have been adapted to avoid excessive referrals of Roma/Gypsy children.

Balance of NGO and government activity

Although the Montenegrin Constitution guarantees more education rights to Roma/Gypsies than the FRY Constitution, they are not implemented in practice. UNICEF co-ordinates and contributes to a range of education support projects, particularly for Roma/Gypsy IDPs, in partnership with international NGOs, and is also building the capacity of domestic NGOs for this work.

Montenegro report contents

Introduction – the Roma/Gypsy population

Demography

There are no precise or comprehensive data on Roma/Gypsies in Montenegro.[1] In 1995, Minority Rights Group International estimated that there were between 400,000 and 450,000 Roma/Gypsies in what was then Yugoslavia. Of these they estimated that fewer than ten per cent were in Montenegro, that is, a maximum of 40,000-45,000 (6.5 per cent-7 per cent of the Montenegro population), a figure which far exceeds the official population census figure.[2] According to the 1991 census, Montenegro had a total population of 615,035, of whom 3,282 (0.53 per cent) were Roma/Gypsies. Higher numbers of Roma/Gypsies were found in larger cities. For example, in Podgorica there were 1,676 (1.1 per cent) Roma/Gypsies in 1991, and in Nikšić, 802 (1.1 per cent).[3]

The term "Tsigan", ie, "Gypsy" was used to denote Roma/Gypsies in the population counts conducted from 1948 to 1971. The first census after World War II, in 1948, counted 377,189 people in Montenegro, of whom 162 were Roma/Gypsies. The 1953 census showed a total population of 419,873, among whom only nine Roma/Gypsies were counted, and these were only in the Bar District (six in the Ulcinj and three in the Bar municipality). Since there were no figures for other districts, it may be assumed that Roma/Gypsies were not registered as such in this census. The 1961 census revealed a total population of 471,894, of whom 183 or 0.04 per cent were counted as Roma/Gypsies. The term

"Roma" was first used officially in the 1971 census. Out of a total population of 584,310, 1,471 (0.25 per cent) were registered as Roma/Gypsies.

Trifun Dimić, a distinguished Yugoslav expert, believes that the census figures are erroneous, as they proceed from the assumption that minority populations always declare their real ethnicity. Roma/Gypsies often declare themselves to be members of the majority population group in areas in which they live in order to avoid the racial prejudice, segregation and discrimination to which they are customarily subjected.

As well as settled Roma/Gypsies living in Montenegro, there are also many internally displaced and refugee communities. The Montenegrin Red Cross, for example, registered 17,000 Roma/Gypsy refugees in Montenegro during the period from December 1991 to December 2000. Of this number, 7,500 settled in Podgorica and 2,700 in Nikšić. Some 3,000 were placed in two refugee centres at Konik in Vrela Ribnička near Podgorica.

Table 8.1 Roma/Gypsies in Montenegro, according to Grupa Margo

Region/City	Approximate number of Roma/Gypsies
1. Northern Montenegro	2,400
2. Podgorica	10,000
3. Nikšić	2,900
4. Southern Montenegro	3,700
5. Cetinje	600
Total	19,600

Grupa Margo, an NGO based in Tivat, also estimates a much larger Roma/Gypsy population, made up of both settled and displaced communities. It estimates that at least 20,000 reside permanently in Montenegro, plus between 6,500 and 7,000 who were displaced from Kosovo (see Table 8.1).

Since the break-up of the former Socialist Republic of Yugoslavia, 46,604 displaced persons have found refuge in Montenegro, that is,

7.5 per cent of the total population according to the 1991 census figures.[4] NGOs estimate that between 65,000 and 70,000 refugees and displaced persons from the territory of the former Yugoslavia are currently in Montenegro, that is over ten per cent of the population (1991 census).[5] According to the Office of the Montenegrin Commissioner for Displaced Persons, there are in total 32,120 persons displaced from Kosovo, of whom 6,440 (20 per cent) are Roma/Gypsies and 972 (3 per cent) declare themselves as Egyptians[6] (see Table 8.2).

A brief historical overview

Although a significant proportion of Roma/Gypsies currently living in Montenegro are refugees from Kosovo, most Roma/Gypsies are settled and have been living in Montenegro for many centuries. According to the ethnologist Stana Marušic, unlike in Serbia, Roma/Gypsies settled in Montenegro before the advent of the Ottoman Empire in this part of the Balkans. The first written documents that refer to Roma/Gypsies in Montenegro date from the eighteenth century.[7] According to these documents, they lived mainly in northern Montenegro and in the vicinity of major highways. During the reign of King Nikola in the nineteenth century, Romani groups were delineated by profession. Today, Roma/Gypsies in Montenegro are mainly Muslims and are divided into three main groups, each of which considers itself as having little in common with the others.

The group documented as first arriving in this part of the Balkans was the *Kovači*, named after the blacksmith trade – a trade which was handed down over many generations. They speak mainly Serbian, but for some of them their first language is Albanian. They are the largest Roma/Gypsy group in Montenegro and the most integrated into society. Their families are smaller and their children are more likely than those from other groups to attend formal schooling. Although the rate of illiteracy for this group is lower, according to the 1981 census, it was still recorded as high as 80 per cent.

Madjupi, the second group, came from Kosovo and Macedonia during Ottoman rule and settled in urban areas. Montenegro offered a favourable climate and opportunities for work. They settled in the Vrela Ribnička and Čepurke neighbourhoods of Podgorica. It was not until 1972 that they moved from this area, due to rapid urban growth. Whereas some continue to speak Romani, others speak Albanian as their first language. According to the 1981 census figures, 85 per cent of this group were illiterate.

The third group, *Gabelji*, are semi-nomadic Roma/Gypsies. They came to Montenegro in the early twentieth century and consider themselves a separate entity, disclaiming any relationship with the *Kovači* and *Madjupi*. The 1991 census recorded that 90 per cent of Gabelji were illiterate.

The socio-economic situation of Roma/Gypsies in Montenegro

Roma/Gypsies, both in economic and social terms, are considered the most disadvantaged population group in Montenegro. A number of factors have been identified as contributing to this situation, most significantly, high unemployment

Table 8.2 Displaced persons in Montenegro, according to the Office of the Commissioner for Displaced Persons

Municipality	Montenegrin	Serb	Roma	Muslim	Albanian	Egyptian	Other	Total
Andrijevica	743	551		1	5		6	1,306
Bar	1,817	2,107	737	427	109	54	98	5,349
Berane	2,473	1,543	545	471	16	149	52	5,249
Bijelo Polje	283	198	100	502	36		19	1,198
Budva	484	564	9	81	8		42	1,168
Cetinje	29	18					1	48
Danilovgrad	395	100	4		9		1	509
Herceg Novi	279	348	106	19	6		20	778
Kolašin	162	85		5			4	256
Kotor	98	113	25	33	34	16	7	326
Mojkovac	90	64		1			2	157
Nikšić	209	136	673	31	16	38	40	1,443
Plav	367	198	7	935	214	6	15	1,742
Plužine	3							3
Pljevlja	82	66	3	17	7		1	176
Podgorica	3,362	1,180	3,828	509	238	440	101	9,658
Rožaje	13	42	52	691	113	164	3	1,078
Šavnik	1	1						2
Tivat	220	377	151	121	18	100	17	1,004
Ulcinj	46	154	200	178	344	5	38	965
Žabljak	11							11
Total		7,845	6,440	4,082	1,173	972	404	32,186
%	34.7%	24.4%	20.0%	12.7%	3.7%	3.0%	1.5%	

and low levels of education. Roma/Gypsies who do have work hold the hardest and least-paid jobs, such as street cleaners, manual workers, gravediggers, waste collectors in urban areas, and day labourers and craftsmen in rural areas. A large number of Roma/Gypsies, mostly children, elderly people and disabled people, also engage in begging, whilst others earn a living as street musicians.

Roma/Gypsy settlements tend to be located on the outskirts of cities and villages, in spite of zoning laws, which prohibit building in these areas. As a result, such settlements are not serviced by public transport or waste collection. The dwellings are flimsy structures of cheap and easily found materials such as tin, wood and plastic sheeting, and are without running water, drains or electricity. The dilapidated appearance of these settlements and their physical isolation contributes significantly to Roma/Gypsies feeling alienated. It also fuels racial prejudice on the part of the majority population.

Roma/Gypsies suffer from a high incidence of malnutrition. Poor living conditions are also compounded by inadequate provision of health services. This, combined with the failure of the state to implement effective family planning services, means that Roma/Gypsies have both a high mortality rate, especially among infants, and a high birth rate. One implication of this is that many Roma/Gypsy families are relatively large. For both settled Roma/Gypsies and those displaced from Kosovo, it has been estimated that they have an average of seven members per family (see Table 8.3). As a result, almost one-third of the Roma/Gypsy population in

Montenegro are children under the age of 7 years and about one-quarter are between 7 and 16 years. Of the total number of Roma/Gypsies at the Konik refugee centre, 64 per cent of the 1,432 living there are under 20 years of age. These figures are at least partly explained by the fact that the Roma/Gypsy population has a much shorter life expectancy than other groups.

The position of Roma/Gypsy refugees in Montenegro deteriorated significantly after 1999 when some 7,500 Roma/Gypsies displaced from Kosovo were forced to find refuge in Montenegro.[8] Most of the Kosovan Roma/Gypsies were placed in refugee centres in major Montenegrin cities. The Konik I and Konik II camps in Podgorica are better equipped and organised than other refugee centres. Konik I holds 399 Roma/Gypsy families with 2,290 members. Of these, 38 families live in houses with communal kitchens, and the remainder live in barracks, with four families to each barrack. Conditions in the other refugee facilities in Montenegro are much poorer, especially in Nikšić, where they are located between local iron and steel mills and the Brlja Romani settlement.

Due to high levels of unemployment, poor living conditions and ill health, almost all Roma/Gypsy families in Montenegro are recipients of some kind of social assistance. However, often this is not enough to secure minimum standards of living.

Inter-ethnic relations

As in other countries, there exist many stereotypes about Roma/Gypsies and anti-Roma/Gypsy prejudice prevails among the majority

Table 8.3 Roma/Gypsies and family size in Montenegro, 2000

	Displaced Kosovo Roma/Gypsies	Montenegrin Roma/Gypsies	Overall population
Total number of families	250	100	100
More than 4 members	41 (16.4%)	12	35
5 – 9 members	152 (60.8%)	69	62
Over 10 members	57 (22.8%)	19	3
Total number of members	1,839 (100%)	719 (100%)	529 (100%)
Men	921 (50.08%)	341 (47.50%)	265 (50.09%)
Women	918 (49.92%)	378 (52.50%)	264 (49.91%)
Total number of children	1,072 (58.29%)	355 (49.30%)	131 (24.76%)
Children under 7	563 (30.61%)	189 (26.30%)	84 (15.87%)
Children between 7 and 16	509 (27.68%)	166 (23.00%)	47 (8.88%)
Average number of family members	7.36	7.19	5.29

Source: Dr Božidar Jakšić, *Life of displaced Kosovo Roma in Montenegro (Podgorica and Nikšić) and possibilities for integration*, Belgrade-Podgorica, 2000, p.17.

Montenegrin population. Numerous sociological studies and surveys conducted in recent years in Montenegro indicate a wide social and ethnic distance between the majority population and Roma/Gypsies.[9] Dr Božidar Jakšić recently surveyed displaced Kosovan Roma/Gypsies, Montenegrin Roma/Gypsies and the majority population in order to gauge inter-ethnic relations between the Romani and non-Romani populations.

Of the surveyed Kosovan Roma/Gypsies, 51 per cent were for marriage with Montenegrins and 49 per cent were against it. For 90 per cent of those surveyed, friendship with Montenegrins was desirable and the same number said they would like to work together with them.[10] In terms of the Montenegrin Romani population, 44 per cent of the respondents came out in favour of marriage with Montenegrins; 56 per cent were against it. Almost 100 per cent of those surveyed expressed a positive attitude towards living together with other Montenegrins.

In the same survey, Montenegrins demonstrated a far greater ethnic distance from Roma/Gypsies: 97 per cent rejected marriage with Romani people and 59 per cent did not want to maintain friendly relations with them. Roma/Gypsies were regarded as undesirable neighbours by 57 per cent of respondents, and 61 per cent came out against working with them.

A survey conducted by Živorad Tasić for *Grupa Margo* among the majority Montenegrin population produced somewhat more encouraging results.[11] According to his findings, 50 per cent of respondents would like to have Roma/Gypsy neighbours and 60 per cent said they had nothing against their children attending school together with Romani children. The majority, 78 per cent, accepted Roma/Gypsies as co-citizens and 63 per cent accepted Roma/Gypsies as co-workers. However, although 87 per cent were favourably inclined toward some form of contact with Roma/Gypsies, 85 per cent nonetheless considered that Roma/Gypsies should live in their own separate settlements. Ultimately, the survey indicated that 69 per cent did not want Roma/Gypsies to be fully integrated into Montenegrin society.

The level of hostility revealed in these surveys translates into Roma/Gypsy children often dropping out of school. In a survey by the Kotor-based NGO *Anima*, 55 per cent of the Roma/Gypsy respondents between the ages of 14 and 30 said they had discontinued their education because of the verbal and physical violence they were subjected to in school.[12]

Minority rights

The Federal Republic of Yugoslavia and the Republic of Montenegro[13] are bound by all the international acts in the fields of minority rights, the rights of the child and the right to education ratified by the former Socialist Federal Republic of Yugoslavia. The new state continues to apply the international acts outlined above on the "basis of Yugoslavia's uninterrupted status as a personality of international law":

The rights of national minorities in Montenegro are regulated by the Constitution of FRY, the Constitution of the Republic of Montenegro and Montenegrin republican legislation on the official use of languages and scripts, education, freedom of association, and the electronic and printed media.

The Montenegrin Constitution lays down a broader framework for the protection of minority rights than the FRY Constitution. The latter uses the term "national minorities" to denote members of minority ethnic communities, whereas the Montenegrin Constitution uses the terms "national and ethnic groups."[14] The Montenegrin Constitution states that members of national and ethnic groups enjoy equal rights. However, neither the Constitution nor the republican statutes contain any criteria for differentiating between the two groups. Neither federal nor republican legislation lists the national minorities or ethnic groups to which they refer.

Under both the FRY and the Montenegrin Constitutions, national minorities are entitled to protection of their ethnic, cultural, linguistic and religious identity in accordance with international standards.[15] They have the right to use their language and script, to education and information media in their language, and to use their national symbols, in accordance with the law.[16]

Both Constitutions guarantee to national minorities the right to establish educational, cultural and religious organisations and associations. Whereas the FRY Constitution says only that the state *may* financially assist these organisations, the Montenegrin Constitution makes financial assistance obligatory.[17]

In the field of education, too, the Montenegrin Constitution provides broader rights for minorities, since it requires the Ministry of Education to include the history and culture of national minorities in school curricula.[18] No such provision is contained in the FRY Constitution.

Members of national minorities have the right to use their own language in proceedings before courts or government agencies.[19] In contrast to the FRY Constitution, the Montenegrin Constitution also guarantees proportional representation of minorities in public services, government agencies and local government.[20]

National minorities are entitled to establish and foster contacts with their co-nationals outside of Montenegro with whom they share a cultural and historical heritage and religious beliefs, on condition that these contacts are not detrimental for Montenegro. They also have the right to take part in regional international NGOs, and to address international institutions to protect their constitutionally guaranteed rights and liberties.[21]

They may not, however, exercise their special rights in a manner contrary to the Montenegrin Constitution or to the principles of international law, or to the detriment of the territorial integrity of Montenegro.[22]

The Montenegrin Constitution obliges the government actively to protect and promote the rights of national minorities. A Council for the Protection of the Rights of Members of National Minorities has recently been established. It is chaired by the President of the Republic, and its composition and powers are determined by the Montenegrin parliament.[23] The Council's aim is to foster and protect the national, ethnic, cultural, linguistic and religious identity of national minorities, and ensure that they are able to exercise their constitutionally guaranteed rights.

The other rights of members of national and ethnic groups derive from the provisions of the Montenegrin Constitution treating the rights and liberties of all citizens.

Roma/Gypsies in Montenegro in practice do not exercise most of the rights guaranteed to national minorities and ethnic communities. As an ethnic group, their status is not stipulated in law: they do not exercise the right to education in their own language; the curricula of elementary and secondary schools do not include study of Roma/Gypsy culture and history; the Romani language is not in official use in any of Montenegro's municipalities; and the government does not finance any Romani cultural institutions. Furthermore, Roma/Gypsies are not proportionally represented in public services, government agencies or local government.

The right to education

National minorities and displaced persons in Montenegro are entitled to education from preschool to university. For displaced persons, this is based on the condition that they are officially registered as residing in the republic. The Montenegrin Preschool Education Act states that instruction in these institutions is provided in the Serbian language, but may also be provided in Albanian.[24] The programmes of preschool institutions are determined by the Ministry of Education, and parents choose the language in which their children will receive instruction.[25]

Elementary education is compulsory for all children between the ages of 7 and 15 years.[26] For children aged over 15 years, elementary education is provided in separate classes in elementary schools or in elementary schools for adults.[27] Parents or legal guardians are responsible for enrolling their children in elementary school and ensuring their regular attendance. Elementary schools are obliged to report to the Ministry of Education when a child has not been enrolled or does not attend school regularly.[28] If a parent/ legal guardian fails to enrol a child, or the child does not attend or irregularly attends school, the parent/guardian is liable to pay a fine ranging from one-half of to 20 times the minimum wage.[29] The fine may be levied repeatedly if the parent/guardian continues to disregard his or her responsibility in this regard.

In areas where national minorities constitute a majority, schools or classes are established to provide instruction in the minority language and, conditions permitting, such instruction may be provided also in other schools and classes.[30] The law envisages the possibility of establishing bilingual schools or classes in multi-ethnic communities.[31] When classroom instruction is in a minority language, Serbian-language courses are compulsory.[32] Schools providing classroom instruction in minority languages keep their registers in both Serbian and the relevant minority language.[33] Semi-annual and annual report cards are also issued in both languages.[34]

Under the Montenegrin Secondary School Act, secondary education is provided in general-programme, vocational and art schools.[35] Depending on the composition of the local population, classroom instruction for members of national or ethnic groups may be in the language of the group.[36] Schools or classes in which instruction is provided in both Serbian and Albanian, or only in Albanian, may be established in areas with a mixed population of Serbs, Montenegrins and Albanians. Instruction in Albanian-language schools is in accordance with the uniform programmes and curricula determined by law,[37] and Serbian-language courses are compulsory.

Under the Montenegrin University Act, the university is a public institution based in Podgorica, and has the legal status of an artificial person. The university comprises post-secondary schools, departments, art academies, scientific institutions in fields of study in which higher education is not provided, the Foreign Languages Institute, and the university library.[38] Instruction at the university is in Serbian. The law also envisages the possibility of instruction being provided in a major world language.[39] Those who wish to enter

the university are required to pass competitive admission exams, which are taken three months before enrolment,[40] and must have a secondary education diploma as required by the statute of the unit (department, etc) they wish to attend.[41]

In practice

The right to education of Roma/ Gypsy children

The Montenegrin Ministry of Education does not have data according to ethnic group on the number of children attending elementary and secondary schools. The reason given is that schools do not ask children to declare their ethnicity. Other sources, however, have tried to estimate numbers of Roma/Gypsy children attending schools. According to UNICEF figures for the year 2000, 190 Romani children were enrolled in regular schools, 50 each in Podgorica, Rožaje and Tivat, 11 in Berane and 29 in Bar. Serbian is the official language in Montenegro.[42] In areas with a majority Albanian population, there are preschools, elementary and secondary schools providing instruction in either Albanian alone, or in both Albanian and Serbian. When instruction is only in Albanian, Serbian-language courses are compulsory.

According to official censuses, at least 80 per cent of adult Roma/Gypsies in Montenegro are illiterate. According to research carried out by Živorad Tasić, an activist of *Grupa Margo*, eight per cent have completed elementary school, and those with a secondary-school diploma are few and far between. Only two Roma/Gypsies in Montenegro have university degrees. Almost 45 per cent of the Romani population are children of school age. Of the 12,000 Roma/Gypsy children, under 1,000 attend elementary school (about eight per cent). Most drop out after finishing a few grades and an average of just 30 finish elementary school each year (ie, 0.25 per cent of the school-age population). At the time of writing, only three Roma/Gypsy children were attending secondary schools.[43]

A survey carried out by Božidar Jakšić among Kosovan Roma/Gypsies revealed that 62 per cent of respondents either did not go to school at all or did not finish it, and only 4 per cent had completed secondary education. The situation for Montenegrin Roma/Gypsies seemed slightly better: 80 per cent of Montenegrin Roma/Gypsies either did not go to school at all or did not finish it. Among this group, 27 per cent of children were recorded as currently attending elementary school.[44] InterSOS also carried out a survey at the Konik I camp and found that all the women living there were illiterate.[45]

Some see cultural traditions, such as early marriage (practised by some Roma/Gypsy communities), as important factors to consider when understanding low-level attendance and high drop-out rates. A worker from the Konik II camp argues that we need to look much deeper:

> "Roma are on the margins of society. Here at this camp we live far from everything and it is very hard to get involved in life outside the camp. That's something we want to change. The Roma are a people who function very well among themselves, but they do not like to mix with others. In spite of the very poor living conditions, such as exist in this camp, Roma

manage to survive. A large number of Roma do not know Serbian. A large number speak Albanian and many also Romani. Children live in families in which almost all members are illiterate. Where education is concerned, Roma children do not have role models in their families. The result is that their values system is out of joint and they are unable to acquire habits which would make it possible for them to finish school. Parents do not take proper care of their children, do not supervise them to see if they go to school or monitor their progress, for the simple reason that they did not learn to do so from their own parents."

However, factors such as these do not relate to all Roma/Gypsies and need to be placed alongside other factors of poor economic status, language barriers and high levels of discrimination.

Special schools in Montenegro

Under the Montenegrin Act on Special Education, special education is provided in preschool institutions, special, elementary and secondary schools, as well as in other educational institutions. The education authority, in accordance with a special committee made up of medical specialists, psychologists, counsellors and social workers, established jointly by the Ministries of Education and Public Health, establishes the various criteria for the categorisation of disabled children.[46]

There are six special schools for disabled children in Montenegro, four in Podgorica and one each in Kotor and Bijela. The number of Roma/Gypsy children attending these schools is provided in Table 8.4.

Table 8.4 Special schools for disabled children

Special school	Total children	Romani children
School for deaf and hearing-impaired children, Kotor	150	1
Mladost Home for Children, Bijela	160	Ethnicity unknown
School for Rehabilitation of Disabled Children, Podgorica	80	2
1 June School for Slightly Mentally Retarded Children, Podgorica	130	5
Reform School, Podgorica	30	2
School for Severely Mentally Retarded Children and Youth, Podgorica	140	2 children and 3 adults
Total	690 (100%)	15 (2%)

Instruction in special schools is in the Serbian language only. All those members of the Montenegrin Committee for Evaluation of Children who agreed to be interviewed underlined that the criteria used for determining access were reliable and realistic, citing as proof the proportionate number of Romani children currently attending special schools.

According to a psychologist who serves on the Committee:

"The majority of Roma children show up as pseudo-retarded, or falsely retarded, when they take the intelligence test. This is due in great part to the lack of stimuli in their communities. Roma children who do not know the language in which the test is administered are assigned a Romani-speaking person who translates for them. I have not noticed a significant number of Roma children with symptoms of real mental retardation. Roma children are more frequently than others sent to psychologists for evaluation of their capability to attend regular schools, and they score good results on these tests."

A counsellor at the School for Mentally Retarded Children in Podgorica stated that:

"Children in the fifth category, or slightly mentally retarded, are placed in our school. The school has separate boarding facilities for girls and boys and is considered to be the best-equipped special school. We have 130 children, of whom 70 are boarders and 60 day students. There are five Romani children between the ages of 8 and 15. For two of these children and their parents, the most important thing is that the school provides them with meals, clothes and shoes, because they are from the Konik I camp here in Podgorica. These Roma children attend quite regularly and their school results are satisfactory. They are making especially good progress in learning Serbian."

According to a therapist and director of the School for Severely Mentally Retarded Children and Youth in Podgorica:

"Retarded persons are placed in this school on the basis of decisions taken by the competent Social Welfare Centre, the Ministry of Education and the republican Committee for Categorisation of Retarded Children. The school provides instruction for severely retarded persons, those with an IQ below 20, and aims to capacitate them for work and to educate them. We have five Roma in our school, two children and three adults over 50. Members of other national and ethnic groups also attend this school."

A social worker with the School for Rehabilitation of Disabled Children in Podgorica stated that there were only two Romani children in this school:

"We have 80 children in all, 40 of whom attend elementary school, 35 are in secondary school and 5 are preschoolers. These children are from Serbia, [Federation of] Bosnia and Herzegovina, Republika Srpska and Montenegro. There are only two Romani children in the school."

A social worker at the Reform School in Podgorica, spoke of work with educationally neglected Roma/Gypsy children:

"Juvenile delinquents, who have committed offences and were placed in our school by the competent authorities, attend elementary and secondary school. They are trained to become auto mechanics, locksmiths and carpenters. There used to be more Romani children here a few years ago. Here they had food, clothes, shoes and a warm place. We tried to get them into classes, but their attendance became irregular and then they stopped coming at all. We had a programme together with InterSOS, which was to last four months. It was intended for Romani children from the Konik I and II camps in Podgorica, and we were to teach them to be auto mechanics. They came in the first two months, although not very often, and later stopped showing up, so that the programme had to be discontinued."

Language provision

The majority of Roma/Gypsies in Montenegro, especially those displaced from Kosovo, speak either Albanian or Romanes, not Serbian. Data gathered by *Grupa Margo* indicates that 90 per cent of Roma/Gypsies from Kosovo currently living in Montenegro speak Albanian. A survey conducted by Božidar Jakšić also with Roma/Gypsies from Kosovo revealed a higher proportion who spoke Romanes: 58 per cent declared that Albanian was their native language while 36 per cent declared that it was Romanes. Only a small number of Roma/Gypsies stated that Serbian was their native language.[47]

Although there are some differences in exact figures, it is still recognised that a large majority of Kosovan Roma/Gypsy children speak Albanian and are therefore given the possibility of attending Albanian-language schools in Podgorica and Ulcinj. However, Montenegrin Albanians express hostile attitudes to Kosovan Roma/Gypsies, and thus, fearing possible incidents,

Roma/Gypsy children tend to keep away from such schools.

Despite the high proportion of Roma/Gypsies speaking Romanes, schools in Montenegro do not provide instruction in Romanes. This is seen as being due to a lack of qualified teachers and textbooks.[48] In light of this, the NGO *Crnogorska Romska Inicijativa* (Montenegrin Roma Initiative) has requested that the Ministry of Education approve the publication of a Romani primer for use in the first grade of elementary school. At the time of writing, the Ministry was still considering this proposal.

NGO practice in the area

There have been various attempts by NGOs to support Roma/Gypsy children in education. UNICEF, COOPI, InterSOS, NPA, and *Enfants du Monde – Droits de l'Homme* maintain a series of different projects for the education of Romani children. These organisations work in co-operation with domestic NGOs, for example, in setting up workshops, informal education programmes and kindergartens for Roma/Gypsy children.

UNICEF actively directs informal education programmes in Montenegro, preparing Romani children to enter regular elementary schools. For example, it sponsors a programme of "informal education" for Romani children aged between 6-18 years who have been displaced from Kosovo. There are 37 teachers employed and 1,000 children enrolled on the programme. The programme lasts for one year and aims to facilitate the integration of the children into the education system. The curriculum consists of six standard subjects: Serbian language, mathematics, natural and social studies, music, physical education and art, with additional classes in hygiene. Three classes are held each week, each session lasting 45 minutes. On completion of the course, the children are expected to enrol in regular schools.[49]

In addition to this, regular classroom instruction in Serbian, together with computer courses, have been organised at the 25 Maj Elementary School in Rožaje for 2000/2001. This is targeted at Romani schoolchildren from Kosovo as part of a joint project of the Montenegrin Ministry of Education, UNICEF and the Mercy Corps humanitarian organisation.

Enfants du Monde – Droits de l'Homme and UNICEF work together on organising supplementary classes in some elementary school subjects and literacy courses for children who are not in school. The programmes are designed for refugee and displaced children.

InterSOS, UNICEF and WorldVision conduct informal education programmes for 250 Romani children at the Konik I camp in Podgorica. As part of this initiative, they have established a kindergarten with 2 teachers for 25 children who do not live in the camp, and plan to increase the number of children who can attend.

UNICEF plans to strengthen and affirm local NGOs focusing on Roma/Gypsy education issues, and to organise seminars and workshops on the rights of the child.

InterSOS plans to launch two programmes to supplement the existing programmes for preschool children. The aim is to increase the number of children in kindergartens. One of the programmes will be carried out in conjunction with UNICEF.

Božidar Vuković Podgoričanin Elementary School recently built an extension to accommodate two classes for Kosovan Roma/Gypsy children from the Konik II camp. They follow the same curriculum, yet their classes remain separate. The educational authorities assert that this is necessary because of the lack of space in the school building itself. However, the establishment of classes solely for Roma/Gypsies is an indication of open segregation, which precludes the integration of Roma/Gypsy children in the Montenegrin education system and constitutes a drastic departure from international standards in this field. In addition to these classrooms, a programme of informal education has also been organised at the camp itself, with a view to helping children prepare for regular schooling.

The principal of the Konik II extension sees the classes held in the camp and, in turn, the principles of informal education as very important:

> "We realised it was necessary to create any kind of conditions for the education of Roma children, even an extension, because the most important thing was to continue making progress with Roma children. We launched the programme for the education of Romani children, both from Kosovo and those of Montenegrin Roma, on 11 January 2000.

The programme is sponsored by UNICEF, InterSOS and WorldVision and is the first of its kind in the world. Five hundred children are in the programme, though the number varies because the families move. It's an informal school. Not all the children attend regularly. I speak with the parents in the camp every day, trying to convince them that their children should continue their education. Some of the children attended schools in Kosovo, where they were taught in Albanian and therefore speak only Albanian. These children were not able to continue their education in Montenegro. The goals of the programme are to teach the Roma children the language in which instruction is given, to include them in the formal system, their socialisation and their integration in the local society. Another goal is the training of teachers.

The first stage of the programme was from January to August 2000. We worked with preschoolers from the age seven to nine. When the programme was finished, we tested the children, using the official tests. Thanks to these tests and the recommendations of the children's teachers, 50 children were enrolled in the first grade of elementary school in the extension here at the camp.

Besides the crafts workshop, we have supplementary classes for children who find it hard to keep up with their schoolwork, an art club for gifted children and a carpentry shop where they do artistic woodwork.

The *Vrela*[50] newspaper gives a big contribution to education with its reports on the daily life of Roma in their own language."

Before its scaling down in Montenegro, Save the Children USA was also involved with this camp. It established two kindergartens for 120 children at the Konik II camp. Five Romani teachers, who attended a nine-day training seminar, implement active methods of working with the children to prepare them for school. Two of the teachers speak Serbian, Albanian and Romani. In Berane, Save the Children USA also set up a kindergarten for displaced children at the Petnica refugee centre.

Humanitarac (Humanitarian), a Montenegrin NGO based in Nikšić, has been successful in preparing Roma/Gypsy children to enter elementary school. In the course of 2000, *Humanitarac* organised Serbian-language classes and psychosocial work with children between the ages of six and nine. As a result of this, 40 Romani children enrolled in regular elementary school in the 2000-01 school year. In order to include older children aged from 9 to 18, the organisation had to seek assistance from the Ministry of Education, since the law does not allow education of this age-group according to programmes designed for adults. The Ministry was responsive and in 2000-01, 62 Roma/Gypsy children attended classes at the Adult Education Centre. In such centres, instruction lasts 45 days in the first four grades and 90 days in grades five to eight. Many Roma/Gypsies take advantage of this and complete two grades in one year.

The *Početak* (Beginning) Roma Association was founded in Nikšić in October 2000. Its goals are the education of Roma/Gypsy children and youth, and the realisation of their right to learn about and foster their culture and traditions.

Početak receives financial assistance from the Open Society Institute in Podgorica and Save the Children UK.[51]

The Ksenija Centre for Girls, a Podgorica NGO, and the Reform School in Podgorica carried out a joint six-month project to promote social ties between inmates of the Reform School and their peers from outside, in order to challenge isolation and prejudice. Workshops were held four times a month at the Reform School and once a month at the Centre for Girls.

Romski Centar, an NGO in Nikšić, is financed by UNICEF and is working on a number of programmes. These include supplementary classes for Roma/Gypsy children enrolled in the Adult Education Centre, classes to prepare Romani children for entry into elementary school, literacy courses for Roma/Gypsy women, sewing, knitting and needlework and similar workshops for Roma/Gypsy children and adults, and psychological, legal and medical counselling. Children attend classes every day. A total of 143 Romani children are involved in some kind of activity at *Romski Centar*.

The international organisation Norwegian People's Aid runs programmes for Roma/Gypsies, which are typical of many interventions, based on hygiene, creative and music workshops. Fifteen elementary and secondary schools are involved in its Model-Making programme. In December 2000, it launched a programme entitled "With education to a better life". This involves 39 Romani children aged from 9 to 15 in the third grade and another 30 who are attending first grade at the Adult Education Centre,

18 attending local elementary schools and 3 attending secondary schools. The secondary-school students finished the 1999-2000 school year with good results, as did 93 per cent of the third-graders at the Adult Education Centre. Of the first-graders, 78 per cent completed the year without failing in any of the subjects. The children who did best were rewarded with a one-week winter vacation on Mt Lovćen.

The Open Society Institute in Podgorica and the NGO *Početak* are preparing a project designed for children displaced from Kosovo who live in three Roma/Gypsy settlements in Nikšić – Brlja, Trebjesa and Željezara. There will be three workshops in the framework of this project to prepare children to enter regular schools. Instruction will be in Serbian and partly in the Romani language, and only experts in specific fields will work with the children. A collection of poems in Romani and the Humanitarian Law Centre's bilingual Serbian/Romani publication on the UN Convention on the Rights of the Child, called "Children's Rights", will be used. As no schools in Nikšić provide instruction in Albanian, the only language most of these children know, the project will give them an opportunity to learn enough Serbian to be able to attend regular schools, and to learn some Romani. The Open Society Institute also plans to start the Step-by-Step project for children of pre-school age next year.

A number of humanitarian organisations have also been concerned with helping Roma/Gypsies to improve their economic and social status, in some cases by securing permanent jobs. Italy's COOPI, for example, financed the construction of a recycling facility at Vrela Ribnička, next to the city waste dump and junkyard, and handed it over to the Podgorica Sanitation Department. The precondition for the realisation of the project was that the Sanitation Department would employ Roma/Gypsies in the facility. Two metal presses have been installed so far and six Roma/Gypsies employed. Once two more presses have been installed, more Roma/Gypsies will be employed.[52]

Norwegian People's Aid has organised employment training seminars for Roma/Gypsies and other Montenegrin citizens in Herceg Novi, Tivat, Budva, Podgorica, Nikšić, Plav and Berane. Many of the participants, one-third of whom were Roma/Gypsies, went on to find employment as "eco-rangers".

Voices of Roma/Gypsy children

All of the following contributions from children and young people were given in interviews held in December 2000.

IB, boy, ten years old, in grade three, elementary school in Nikšić

"I'm always fighting with the kids at school. They all pick on me so I hit them. Then we all get into trouble with the teacher who shouts at us. I don't have my birthday parties at school. Other kids bring cakes and stuff for everyone in the class and celebrate their birthdays. I can't bring anything so I don't tell anyone it's my birthday.

A friend called Jelena told me they scare other kids by saying Gypsies will do something bad to them. That's nasty. I don't hassle anyone who doesn't hassle me.

I'd like to be a pilot when I grow up. I hope people won't mind having a Roma driving the plane."

IZ, boy, ten years old, attends informal education classes at the Konik II refugee camp

"I didn't go to school in Djakovica from where I came here. I'm going to the school at the camp now.

Once, about a year ago, me and my brothers went to the elementary school a few kilometres from the Konik II camp where I live. We went there to play with other kids in the school yard. When we got near the school, six boys closed in on me and asked 'What do you want here, you little Shiptar?' They said I was a mafioso. One of them punched me in the face. I turned round and ran all the way home. My parents were scared and said I wasn't to go near that school again. I went again a few months later and something like it happened again. They chased me but I got away. It wasn't the same boys. I never went to play near the school again."

MN, girl, 13 years old, in elementary school in Nikšić

"I moved to Nikšić with my parents and brother from Kosovska Mitrovica in 1998. I was excellent in school in Kosovska Mitrovica. It was summer when we came to Nikšić and my parents and I were deciding on which school I would go to. There are a lot of elementary schools here in Nikšić but we chose this one because the teachers are stricter.

My Mum is a seamstress and she finished elementary school, like my Dad too. Dad learned the bricklayer's trade from his father and works for a private business. We rent a small house not far from my school. It has two big rooms and a small bathroom. My best friend lives in a building on the other side of the street."

AN, boy, 15 years old, in grade two, Adult Education Centre in Nikšić

"I came from Peć three years ago. My Mum and Dad work hard. My big brother can't go to school because he works. He's helping some people to put up and paint a fence. I'm always arguing with boys who aren't Romani. We fight almost every day. I don't have sports shoes like theirs. I wear the same pair when it rains, when it's sunny and when I play soccer. They make fun of me and keep calling me a Gypsy. I like the teacher at the Romski Centar where we have supplementary classes, a lot. We play, sing and learn to count there, and I always get the best marks."

CB, boy, 14 years old, in grade three at the Adult Education Centre in Nikšić

"I used to live in Peć. When we came here three years ago, I thought I'd be going to a regular school. But I didn't have my report cards from my old school so I couldn't enrol in any elementary schools. I work in the city-mortuary chapel. Me and my kid brother went around begging this summer. I don't fight with other kids. I can feel that they don't like me so I don't play with them."

BU, eight years old, in grade one at the Olga Golović Elementary School in Nikšić

"I'm in the first grade and I sit at a desk at the back of the class. When we play marbles during the breaks, we fight about who's going to be first. Sometimes I'm first and sometimes I'm last.

When I don't have enough time to learn things at school, I go to the Romski Centar, where the teacher explains it to me. I tell her what I know and get the best marks.

We're doing a play at the Romski Centar. I'm the lion and my lines are the longest of anyone's."

UH, young woman, 22 years old, InterSOS activist, brings Roma/Gypsy children in settlements near Nikšić to the Romski Centar

"I bring the first-graders from the settlements, children who come to regular and supplementary classes here. In the beginning I had to interpret because a lot of the children spoke only Albanian. I come to the Centar to learn to sew.

I'm sorry I never went to school. I couldn't because I was the oldest child in my family and I had to clean house and cook. It's too late now. It's high time I was married. My folks are afraid I'm too old and will never get married. I don't go to town. I've never been on the Nikšić promenade. My folks don't like me to go out. Maybe they are scared. Boys make passes at me when I go down the street to the Romski Centar."

DH, boy, 12 years old, in grade three at the Adult Education Centre in Nikšić

"I'm in the third grade at the Adult Education Centre. I used to go to the Olga Golović Elementary School but they threw me out because I made three mistakes. The first mistake was hitting a boy in my class because of a blonde girl I liked. The second was when I set off a loud firecracker in school. And then I got into a fight with a boy who cursed my Gypsy mother while the teacher was on her coffee break. I don't know if I would go back to elementary school. I like maths and counting German marks. I have brothers older than me who don't go to school because they work. When there's counting to be done, especially money, they call me to add it up."

MH, young man, 16 years old, does not go to school

"I don't go to school because I work. Me and my father are helping to build a house. I carry stuff and help the builders with anything they need. Two years ago, I collected old bottles and newspapers. My parents work too. I'm learning to read and write at the Romski Centar and go there when I can. I'm the best at the Montenegrin kolo in the folk dance group."

DjK, 13 years old, in grade three at the Adult Education Centre in Nikšić

"I want to be a singer when I grow up. I don't keep company a lot with Serb kids, and spend more time with Romani kids. For my last birthday, I had a party at the Romski Centar. We sang and danced.

I don't have any brothers or sisters. My Mum comes to the Romski Centar to learn sewing.

We don't see a lot of Dad because he goes to the villages around here to gather and cut wood. My mother comes to most of the PTA meetings at the Adult Education Centre."

GA, young man, 17 years old, student at the Secondary Mechanical Engineering School in Nikšić
"I finished the regular elementary school. I'm now in the third grade of the Secondary Mechanical Engineering School. I chose the auto-mechanics section because I'd like to fix cars one day. I don't have any problems in school. I don't think anyone minds that I'm Romani."

NB, girl, 11 years old, in grade four, elementary school in Nikšić
"I'm in the fourth grade of elementary school. I have two brothers and a sister. They go to school too. My sister is in the third and my brothers in the sixth grade of elementary school. I help them with their homework a lot of times because I'm a good student. No one

bothers us at school. Boys hang round me a lot and quarrel over me. We're all good friends in the class. One time I got into an argument with a girl and she said I was a Gypsy. Our teacher said that wasn't nice, that she should apologise and that we should be good friends."

Recommendations

Given that the Federal Republic of Yugoslavia has ratified and must apply in Montengro:
- the International Covenant on Civil and Political Rights (ratified 1971, entered into force 23 March 1976)
- the International Covenant on Economic, Social and Cultural Rights (ratified 1971, entered into force 3 January 1976)
- the International Convention on the Elimination of All Forms of Racial Discrimination (ratified 1967, entered into force 4 January 1969)

- the UN Convention on the Rights of the Child (ratified 1990, entered into force 3 July 1991)
- the UNESCO Convention against Discrimination in Education (ratified 1964)
- the Framework Convention for the Protection of National Minorities (ratified 11 May 2001, entered into force 1 September 2001)

Save the Children recommends that:

The Parliament and Government of the Republic of Montenegro

- Enacts, in collaboration with representatives of national minorities in Montenegro, including representatives of the Romani community, a Law on National Minorities. The Law should specify which ethnic communities in Montenegro have the status of a minority and, hence, the rights enjoyed by minorities.
- Co-ordinates the activities of republican and local government bodies, schools and NGOs on joint projects to eliminate ethnic and religious intolerance. Special attention should be devoted to co-ordination with teachers and children, organising human-rights workshops in schools, bringing out appropriate publications and co-operation with the media in eliminating ethnic intolerance.

The Ministry of Education of Montenegro

- Proposes amendments to school programmes and curricula in order to expand in history, geography, sociology and other textbooks for elementary schools sections on the history and culture of Roma/Gypsies. This would be in keeping with Article 71 of the Montenegrin Constitution, which states that the programmes of educational institutions shall include the history and culture of national and ethnic groups.
- Introduces educational records on children who declare themselves as Roma/Gypsies and are attending elementary and secondary schools in Montenegro. These records would be used to draw up separate programmes for children belonging to the Romani ethnic group.
- Opens extensions of Adult Education Centres near large Romani settlements to provide elementary education.
- Re-examines the justification of maintaining the two separate extension classes of the Božidar Vuković Podgoričanin Elementary School exclusively for Roma/Gypsy children at the Konik II refugee camp.
- Organises the training of qualified teachers to provide instruction in the Romani language in regular schools and informal education programmes.
- Organises preparatory classes in pre-school facilities for all Romani children in municipalities where Roma/Gypsies live.
- Organises supplementary classes for Roma/Gypsy children in elementary schools in order to facilitate their integration in the process of education.
- Examines the effects over the long term of the application of the punitive provisions of the Elementary School Act under which parents/legal guardians are bound to enrol their children in elementary school, and elementary schools are bound to notify the Ministry of Education of children who have not been enrolled or do not attend school regularly.[53]

The international organisations, including the UN Commission on Human Rights, the Special Rapporteur on the Right to Education and the Special Rapporteur on Contemporary Forms of Racism, Racial Discrimination, Xenophobia and Related Intolerance, and the European Union

- Closely monitor the international obligations undertaken by the government of the Republic of Montenegro in respect of the right to education with particular attention to the right to education of Roma/Gypsy children in Montenegro.

Montenegro: Notes on the text

1 The Federal Republic of Yugoslavia comprises two republics: Serbia and Montenegro. This report focuses on Montenegro, while the education of Roma children in Serbia is the subject of a separate report.

2 Jean-Pierre Liegéois and Nicolae Gheorghe, *Roma/Gypsies, A European Minority*, Minority Rights Group International, London, 1995.

3 Ethnic composition of Montenegrin population according to 1991 census, Bureau of Statistics, *Statistical Yearbook of the Republic of Montenegro*, Podgorica, 2000.

4 Office of the Montenegrin Commissioner for Displaced Persons, 2000.

5 The findings of Živorad Tasić, an activist of *Grupa Margo*, were published in *Republika*, Belgrade, 2000 and *Matica Crnogorska*, Podgorica, 2001. His paper *Romi u Crnoj Gori – status i perspektive* (Roma in Montenegro – Status and Prospects) was not published in its entirety.

6 This minority is from Kosovo and its members speak Albanian. They define themselves as "Egyptians" rather than Roma/Gypsies.

7 Momčilo Lutovac, *Romi u Crnoj Gori* (Roma in Montenegro), Društvo prijatelja knjige, Ivangrad, 1987.

8 Figures of the Office of the Montenegrin Commissioner for Displaced Persons, Podgorica, 2000.

9 Ethnic distance, a term used in social psychology, is a measure of the psychological distance between two different ethnic groups expressed in the readiness of the members of one group to accept or reject social relations with members of another group. Social relations are graded from the weakest, such as acquaintance and residing in the same building, to the strongest, such as marriage.

10 Dr Božidar Jakšić, *Life of Displaced Kosovo Roma in Montenegro (Podgorica and Nikšić) and Possibilities for Integration*, Belgrade-Podgorica, 2000, p. 38.

11 Tasić (see note 4).

12 Tasić (see note 4).

13 The Federal Republic of Yugoslavia comprises two republics: Serbia and Montenegro. This report focuses on Montenegro, while the education of Roma children in Serbia is the subject of a separate report.

14 Chapter 5, *Special Rights of Members of National and Ethnic Groups*, Montenegrin Constitution, *Službeni list RCG*, No. 48/92.

15 Art. 11, Yugoslav Constitution; Art. 67, Montenegrin Constitution.

16 Art. 45, Yugoslav Constitution; Articles 68 and 69, Montenegrin Constitution.

17 Compare Art. 47, Yugoslav Constitution and Art. 70, Montenegrin Constitution.

18 Art. 71, Montenegrin Constitution.

19 Compare Art. 49, Yugoslav Constitution and Art. 72, Montenegrin Constitution.

20 Art. 73, Montenegrin Constitution.

21 Art. 48, Yugoslav Constitution; Art. 74, Montenegrin Constitution.

22 Art. 75, Montenegrin Constitution.

23 Art. 76, Montenegrin Constitution.

24 Ethnic Albanians are the only minority community in Montenegro who in practice exercise most of the rights guaranteed to national minorities, eg, the rights to education and information media in their language, and the right to use their own language in proceedings before courts and other bodies.

25 Art. 6, Pre-school Education Act.

26 Art. 3 and 4, Elementary School Act.

27 Art. 5, Elementary School Act.

28 Art. 59, Elementary School Act.

29 Art. 131, Elementary School Act.

30 Art. 11, Elementary School Act.

31 Art. 12, Elementary School Act.

32 Art. 13, Elementary School Act.

33 Art. 24, Elementary School Act.

34 Art. 26 (5), Elementary School Act.

35 Art. 3, Secondary School Act.

36 Art. 14, Secondary School Act.

37 Art. 14, Secondary School Act.

38 Art. 4, University Act.

39 Art. 6, University Act.

40 Art. 52, University Act.

41 Art. 53, University Act.

42 Art. 9 (1), Montenegrin Constitution.

43 Tasić (see note 4).

44 Jakšić (see note 13).

45 Jakšić (see note 13).

46 Articles 2, 3, 6, 11 and 13, Act on Special Education.

47 Jakšić (see note 13), p. 19.

48 Jakšić (see note 13), p. 19.

49 Statement by Branka Kovačević, assistant programme officer with UNICEF, Podgorica.

50 Newspaper for refugees and displaced persons in Montenegro.

51 *Blic*, 20 October 2000.

52 *Vrela* (newspaper for refugees and displaced persons in Montenegro), July-December 2000 edition.

53 Art. 59, Elementary School Act.

9 Federal Republic of Yugoslavia: Kosovo[1]

During the 1990s, the majority-Albanian population, excluded from state schools, set up an underresourced parallel system. Many Roma/Gypsy children and young people were effectively denied schooling, creating a ten-year education gap for many and undermining a belief in the role of education for today's Roma/Gypsy children.

"Most of the parents are illiterate, have never been to school and often do not understand why it is important for their children to go to school and that it could be a way to grant them a better future."

> Manager of a programme to provide education to displaced Roma children

"The day when I started going to school again I was the happiest child in the world. After we were expelled from my village, Zatriq, after the war and came to the Colonia settlement in Gjakova I was feeling very bad. I knew that other children were going to school."

> Roma boy, 13 years old, in a catch-up class

Summary

Context

Kosovo was Socialist Yugoslavia's poorest, least developed and most alienated territory. A decade of repression of Kosovo's Albanian majority by the Serbian authorities culminated in war and NATO intervention in 1999. Kosovo's marginalised Roma/Gypsy population was caught in the middle of the Serb-Albanian conflict, and has faced a violent backlash from Albanians since the end of the war. The new authorities, UNMIK and KFOR, have been slow to recognise and address Roma/Gypsy security, livelihood and social-inclusion needs.

Roma/Gypsy population

Of Kosovo's 2 million population, between 100,000 and 150,000 are Roma/Gypsies. The aftermath of the conflict has added extra layers of danger and hardship to the discrimination, social exclusion and poverty they faced prior to the war. After the UN takeover in mid-1999, Albanians launched attacks on Roma/Gypsies, blaming them for siding with the Serbs. Up to 100,000 Roma/Gypsies fled to neighbouring republics. Many of those who remain face grave security problems – continuing revenge attacks or predation which take advantage of their social vulnerability. Restricted freedom of movement limits their access to services and employment. Many remaining communities are sustained only by humanitarian assistance and the presence of KFOR. The conflict has sharpened three distinct Gypsy identities: Roma, Ashkali and Egyptians. Roma lived all over Kosovo and tended to ally themselves with the Serbs. Ashkali and Egyptians, respectively inhabiting east and west Kosovo, only speak Albanian and do not claim any links with the Roma.

Roma/Gypsies and education

Few Roma/Gypsies complete primary school, with many dropping out at an early stage, or not attending at all. This means that very few enter secondary education, let alone higher education. Displacement and lack of physical security have constituted the overriding barriers to education access since summer 1999. Many Ashkali and Egyptian communities in particular suffered a ten-year gap in education provision in the 1990s – caught in the crevice between the official Serbian and parallel Albanian education systems. This has increased illiteracy rates and leaves very few qualified for non-menial jobs. This legacy, together with decades of discrimination against Roma/Gypsies in employment, has created a corrosive intergenerational cycle of low-education and employment ambitions and attainment. With many parents viewing education as a low priority luxury, family poverty impacts immediately upon children's school attendance. Children can be required to work to supplement family income or to help at home instead of going to school. Lack of

adequate clothes and shoes, especially in winter, and of money for exercise and textbooks, often prevents attendance or provides humiliations at the hands of teachers or peers, which prompt drop-out. Indifference on the part of teachers and bullying and name-calling by children from majority communities have made many schools into hostile environments for Roma/Gypsy children, particularly since the 1999 war.

Balance of NGO and government activity

Government policy to ensure access to employment and education for Roma/Gypsies has to date been more declarative than real. Only in spring 2001 did UNMIK conduct comprehensive surveys of Roma/Gypsy children's school attendance. Both UNMIK and NGOs are internationally funded. UNMIK governance is particularly inclusive of NGOs, eg, UNMIK's minorities school-bus project is deployed in support of NGO education projects. The current crop of NGO catch-up class projects, school integration, pre-school and socio-educative projects for Roma/Gypsy children provides pilot experience to UNMIK as it begins to formulate focused policy for Roma/Gypsy education. Although UNMIK itself has failed to provide employment opportunities for Roma/Gypsies, its institution of Local Community Officers, whose brief is to foster social inclusion of Roma/Gypsy communities, has potential.

Kosovo report contents

Introduction

The legacy of Kosovo's recent conflict has important implications for the education and life chances of the children of its three Roma/Gypsy[2] communities – the Roma, the Ashkali and the Egyptians. For Kosovan Roma/Gypsies the conflict has added a further dimension of difficulty and danger to the interlocking web of discrimination, poverty and social exclusion which typically confronts Roma/Gypsy communities in Central and Eastern European countries. It has opened up a fault-line between the different Roma/Gypsy communities, with the Roma on one side of a divide, and the Ashkali and Egyptians on the other.

Kosovo's intercommunal conflict became manifest in the late 1980s and degenerated into war from February 1998. Due to its immense impact both on the position of Roma/Gypsy communities in Kosovan society and on education arrangements, many references will be made to it in this report. The structures of administration, rule of law and security provision which have operated in Kosovo under United Nations auspices since summer 1999 are very particular and still evolving. These are also described where necessary to provide a context within which developments can be understood.

Kosovo is currently governed by the United Nations Interim Administration Mission in Kosovo (UNMIK) under the authority of UN Security Council Resolution 1244 of 10 June 1999. The administration is backed by KFOR – a 45,000-strong NATO-led military security force, which was deployed in the province in

June 1999 in accordance with a military-technical agreement reached with Serbia as a result of the NATO bombing campaign. UNMIK's mandate is to build peace, democracy, stability and self-government in Kosovo on a multi-ethnic basis. It organised municipal elections in October 2000, and plans to hold a general election on 17 November 2001 in order to provide Kosovo with a measure of democratically mandated self-government.

Kosovo's future status is yet to be clarified. It presently remains a province of Serbia. The majority ethnic Albanian population clearly wants full independence, and at a practical level has severed all ties and connections with Serbia.

The lead-up to war and international intervention

Under Yugoslavia's 1974 Constitution, Kosovo was granted the status of an autonomous province of Serbia, with its own parliament and institutions, and rights broadly equivalent to those of a Yugoslav republic. It was the poorest, least developed area of Yugoslavia.

Albanians and Serbs form the two main ethnic communities in Kosovo. Their demographic position relative to each other has been the subject of dispute, propaganda, manipulation, resettlement schemes and episodes of mass expulsion. Other smaller ethnic groups in Kosovo such as Roma/Gypsies have faced difficult dilemmas of loyalty and sometimes "double marginalisation" (ie, from both sides) in trying to find a niche for themselves in a fractured society dominated by the Albanian-Serb divide.

Albanians have formed a growing majority of Kosovo's population throughout the post-World War II period of the existence of the Socialist Republic of Yugoslavia and its subsequent disintegration. This is despite periodic government schemes and pressure to encourage Albanian emigration and Serbian and Montenegrin immigration. Although the Albanians boycotted the 1991 census after the Serbian authorities' mass sacking of 120,000-160,000 Albanian public-sector workers, including staff of the Kosovan statistics bureau, the estimate made by the Federal Statistical Office is not reportedly disputed by the leading Kosovar-Albanian demographer Dr Hivzi Islami.[3] There were an estimated 1,596,440 Albanians (81.6 per cent), 194,190 Serbs and 20,365 Montenegrins (together nearly 11 per cent). Other smaller ethnic groups include Turks, Slavic Muslims (Bosniaks), Goranis and Roma/Gypsies. Kosovo's current total population is estimated at about 2.2 million.

In 1988-89, Kosovo's autonomous status was revoked by Serbian President Slobodan Milosevic. Serbian direct rule over Kosovo discriminated against the Albanian majority and Serbian security forces enforced their control by means of human-rights violations. During the 1990s, up to half a million of the Kosovan population, mainly young Albanian adults, migrated to Western Europe and North America to seek asylum.

After eight years of civil resistance, in which the Albanian population of Kosovo created and maintained parallel political and social structures, including an alternative education system, armed resistance to Serbian direct rule began in the form of the Kosovo Liberation Army (KLA), a small guerrilla organisation. Fighting broke out in Kosovo's central Drenica region in early 1998, and spread into other rural areas as the KLA quickly grew into a mass, yet loose, military organisation. Massacres of civilians by Serbian forces and a major internal displacement of population provoked international outrage. Under a threat of possible NATO bombing, in autumn 1998 Serbia agreed to the deployment in Kosovo of the unarmed OSCE Kosovo Verification Mission, which monitored a ceasefire, partial withdrawal of troops and human-rights compliance. Amid a renewed deterioration of the security situation in early 1999, the Contact Group of five major powers called the Kosovar-Albanian and Serbian sides to talks in Rambouillet, France, to reach a political settlement, which was to be guaranteed an international military force. The Kosovar-Albanian delegation eventually accepted the terms, which did not explicitly offer them their goal of independence; but the Serbian side refused them, instead stepping up its military forces and operations in Kosovo. The Kosovo Verification Mission was withdrawn and NATO launched its bombing campaign on 24 March 1999. Serbian forces began orchestrating mass expulsion of the ethnic Albanian population: 850,000 became refugees in Macedonia, Albania and Montenegro, and a further 500,000 were internally displaced. During the 78-day bombing campaign, an estimated 6,000 – 10,000 Kosovar-Albanian civilians were killed by Serb forces.

Roma/Gypsies and the Serb-Albanian conflict

Roma/Gypsies have long been regarded as second-class citizens by Serbs and Albanians alike. Opportunism and short-term alliances of convenience have governed the two main ethnic communities' relations and exchanges with Roma/Gypsies. With most Roma/Gypsies living in extreme poverty and enduring a day-to-day struggle for subsistence, they were not in a position to adopt and maintain a consistent long-term strategy with regard to the Albanian-Serb conflict, and proved vulnerable to manipulation. From 1989 onwards, Kosovan Roma tended to side with the Serbs, although in a dependent relationship. In some Roma communities, many joined Milosevic's Socialist Party of Serbia (SPS). Roma children attended Serbian schools, from which Albanians were excluded. During the war a significant number of Roma men were mobilised into Serbian paramilitary forces. After the Serbian withdrawal, Roma/Gypsy communities reaped the whirlwind for the Roma community leaders' strategic miscalculation.

The legacy of summer 1999

The ethnic Albanian refugees returned swiftly *en masse* in the days and weeks following the initial deployment of KFOR into Kosovo. Many of Kosovo's Serb population departed in the wake of the retreating Serb army. Others moved to areas in Kosovo that still had majority Serb populations. Since June 1999, UNHCR has registered 222,800 internally displaced persons (IDPs) from Kosovo in Serbia and Montenegro. The majority of these post-war IDPs are Serbs and Montenegrins, whose numbers inside Kosovo are estimated to have now shrunk to 100,000 or less. A significant minority of these IDPs are Roma/Gypsies, whose numbers are harder to quantify. The net effect of outward migration and displacement during the 1990s and since the war has been to reduce the population actually residing inside Kosovo to 1.5 – 1.7 million.

While UNMIK was establishing itself during summer and autumn 1999, ethnic Albanians embarked on a wave of revenge attacks, targeting Serbs and other minorities perceived to have taken their side in the war. Roma were particularly targeted in these attacks, together with other Gypsy communities – the Ashkalija and Egyptians. Many Roma/Gypsies fled the territory, to Serbia, Montenegro and other countries.

The European Roma Rights Centre has described this massive wave of anti-Roma/Gypsy violence as: "the single biggest catastrophe to befall the Romani community since the Romani holocaust in World War II".[4] Roma and their property were the prime targets for the attacks of vengeful Kosovar Albanians. Ashkalija and, to a lesser extent, Egyptians were targeted too. Like the Roma, some Ashkalija were seen as having collaborated with the Serbian side in the war. The similar dark-skinned appearance of most Roma, Ashkalija and Egyptians marked them out for indiscriminate attacks.[5] In the initial weeks of KFOR's deployment, with attention focused on Kosovar Albanians, and with KFOR's understanding of local situations refracted

through its mainly Kosovar-Albanian interpreters, there was little awareness of the existence, location and vulnerability of Roma/Gypsy communities. KFOR was therefore ill-prepared to counter the wave of violence that was visited upon them.

Some Roma neighbourhoods and communities were totally purged. The Roma neighbourhood in southern Mitrovica was razed to the ground. Of a pre-war population of several thousand, only three Roma families now remain in Prishtina. The majority of the remaining Roma, Ashkali and Egyptian communities are depleted, some to the point where a few more departures will render them unviable. Nonetheless, the situation across Kosovo is not uniform. The attacks and ongoing tensions have been harsher in central and eastern Kosovo, with several remaining Roma communities living virtually in siege conditions. Ashkalija also face restricted freedom of movement due to ongoing security concerns, and some communities continue to endure grenade attacks, arson and stone-throwing. The situation in western Kosovo has been somewhat calmer. For example, the large urban Roma and Egyptian populations respectively of Prizren and Gjakova faced a lower level of attacks, remain relatively stable and have local freedom of movement.

Roma/Gypsies have continued to be victimised by elements of the majority Kosovar-Albanian population, but to a lesser degree than in the latter half of 1999. The occurrence of some violent incidents in Serbian areas indicates that Kosovar Albanians are not the only perpetrators of attacks against Roma/Gypsy communities. Motivations for ongoing attacks on Roma/Gypsies or their property vary. Revenge-motivated attacks occur in some locations where the majority Albanian community blames its Roma/Gypsy neighbours for involvement or complicity in atrocities committed against them by Serbian forces during the war. In other areas, the social vulnerability and outcast status of a Roma/Gypsy community makes it prey to opportunistic attacks and abuses. These are often linked to attempts to seize or execute a forced sale of assets, particularly real estate. Until a few months before the writing of this report, Ashkalija tended to believe that, as only Roma were identified locally as former Serb allies, Ashkalija would not be targeted. However, this was to misunderstand the motivation and the factors facilitating the attacks, which have now spread to affect Ashkalija too.

Attacks and abuses against Roma/Gypsies have continued, yet very few arrests or convictions have been secured. UNMIK police, now numbering roughly 4,200 throughout Kosovo, crucially lack an information-gathering network within the Kosovan civilian population. Working through translators drawn mainly from the majority Kosovar-Albanian population, accompanying mainly Kosovar-Albanian police officers of the nascent Kosovo Police Service, and faced with the internal solidarity of the Kosovar-Albanian majority society, it is difficult for UNMIK police to gain the trust of Roma/Gypsies. Many Roma/Gypsies feel intimidated about approaching the police, afraid that their complaints will be leaked through Kosovar-Albanian networks and provoke further abuses. Bias in favour of ethnic kin and against minorities such as Serbs and Roma/Gypsies is also often alleged against prosecutors and judges drawn from the majority Albanian community.

An illustration of the primacy of social networks over institutions (and the latter's dysfunction) in the matter of security was given by a sports teacher, whose neighbourhood has recently begun to suffer from attacks. Some of his sports pupils are members of the Kosovo Protection Corps (KPC), and he requested four of them to stay in the neighbourhood to deter night-time attacks. In other areas of Kosovo, members of the KPC have been implicated in beatings and abductions of Roma/Gypsies. His pupils agreed and their presence did indeed deter further attacks in the neighbourhood, something which KFOR patrols had been unable to do. However, they had to give up their vigil for fear of being arrested by KFOR, as such "policing" activities are outside the KPC's mandate. When they did so, the attacks resumed.

The Roma/Gypsy population

Before the Serb-Albanian conflict became manifest in 1988-89, Serbs and Albanians did not differentiate between the different Roma/Gypsy communities, referring to them all as *Tsigani* or *Maxhupët*. Among the Roma/Gypsies themselves, the three distinct group identities – Roma, Ashkalija and Egyptians – were also less developed than they are today. In census statistics they were all grouped together as Roma/Gypsies. Calculating the true number of Kosovo's Roma/ Gypsy population has been difficult, as many have identified themselves in censuses as Albanians,

or as other ethnic groups such as Serbs. In the 1961 census their number was reported to be as low as 3,202. Yet in the 1981 census 34,126 (2.2 per cent of Kosovo's total population) were counted. The flawed 1991 census recorded 45,745 Roma/Gypsies (2.3 per cent of the total population). Estimates of the true number of all Roma/Gypsies living in Kosovo prior to 1999, including Ashkalija, Egyptians and Roma, ranged from 100,000 to 150,000.[6] Up to 100,000 are believed to have fled Kosovo in the wake of the war, and 30,000 are estimated to remain in Kosovo at present, although these figures should be treated with caution.

It is also possible, to a limited degree, to estimate separate numbers for the three groups. Before the summer of 1999, Roma communities could be found across Kosovo. One estimate of their numbers was as high as 97,000.[7] However the real figure is generally regarded as being considerably lower. Kosovan Roma identify themselves with the broader Roma community found in most European countries. Their first language is Romani and for most their second language is Serbo-Croat/Serbian, although some also speak Albanian.

Ashkali and Egyptians acknowledge themselves to be essentially one and the same people, yet each group disputes the legitimacy of the other's identity. Egyptians believe that Ashkali are really Egyptians, and vice versa. There is a geographic divide between them, with those in eastern and central Kosovo identifying themselves as Ashkalija and those in western Kosovo identifying themselves as Egyptians. Ashkalija and Egyptians

differ from the Roma in that they speak Albanian
as their mother tongue and have traditionally been
more integrated with the Albanian community.
Many Ashkalija can also speak Serbo-Croat as a
second language. Most Egyptians speak only
Albanian. Neither group aspires to Romani
identity, nor has any discernible interest in
learning the Romani language. Ashkalija only
really began vigorously to promote a separate
identity for themselves after the war, to
distinguish themselves from the Roma, with
whom they have lived in mingled communities in
several areas. Ashkalija found a need to distance
themselves from Roma because the latter were
perceived to have taken the side of the Serbs
in the war (as had a minority of Ashkalija).
The Egyptian community identity is more
long-standing, and moves to achieve its
recognition in Kosovo began over a decade ago.

Ashkalija and Egyptians found themselves
grouped together with Albanians by Serbian
policy measures from the late 1980s. Most had
Albanian names and many (particularly Egyptians)
could speak only Albanian, so that they had very
little contact with Serbs. A number of intellectuals
came together in 1990 to define their separateness
from the Roma and to promote an identity
distinct from them.[8] A push by Egyptians for
recognition in the early 1990s became a subject
of Serbian political manoeuvring. The FRY
authorities issued new ethnic classifications, which
recognised Egyptians as a distinct ethnic group
in the FRY for the first time (although Egyptian
communities already existed in Albania and
elsewhere). Egyptians themselves celebrated it
as a liberating move – the *de jure* recognition of a
de facto community.[9] However, it was seen by

Albanians as part of a Serbian government
strategy to build up other ethnic groups in
Kosovo as a counterweight to themselves.[10]
This debate reached its sharpest definition at
the Rambouillet talks in January 1999, where
the Serbian/FRY-government delegation
demonstratively included representatives of
different Kosovan ethnic groups "loyal" to the
regime, which included both a Roma and an
Egyptian representative. In the post-war period,
many Egyptians have voiced a concern that their
inclusion in this delegation compromised the
image and legitimacy of their community.

The socio-economic status of Roma/Gypsies in Kosovo

Unemployment in Roma/Gypsy communities is
extremely high, and near universal in some
communities. Roma have more of a trading
tradition than Ashkalija and Egyptians, who tend
to rely on selling their physical labour. Limited
freedom of movement and the hostility of the
majority population have severely restricted
Roma trading opportunities. Children often
work to supplement the family income. In some
communities, such as the Egyptian neighbourhood of Colonia in Gjakova, they join in such
marginal livelihood activities as scavenging for
scrap metal, salvaging objects on rubbish dumps
or looking for discarded food. Portering in
markets and odd labouring jobs are characteristic
tasks that Roma/Gypsy teenage boys are
engaged in.

In urban settings the biggest employer of
Roma/Gypsies is usually the municipal garbage
collection and cleaning company. In the mainly
Ashkali village of Dubrava outside Ferizaj/

Urosevac, which has no particular security problems, only one in ten of the 156 families has an employed breadwinner. In more beleaguered communities the employment situation is even more desperate. An illustration of the failure of UNMIK to provide employment to Roma/ Gypsies is that two Ferizaj/Urosevac Roma teachers were not re-hired after the war, despite there being 15 Roma children who used to go to the town's Serbian school. The children have remained at home with no schooling for two years.

While extremely high Roma/Gypsy unemployment occurs against a background of high unemployment among all Kosovo's communities, including the majority Albanians, there is a perceived failure on the part of UNMIK structures and international organisations to ensure employment opportunities for Roma/ Gypsies. When the international security forces and civil administration were recruiting their establishment of local staff, people from Roma/Gypsy communities were too afraid for their safety or too uninformed to put themselves forward for these opportunities. As a result, there is negligible Roma/Gypsy representation in the interim administration at all levels, except in the municipal cleaning and rubbish-disposal companies. International contractors carrying out projects for UNMIK or KFOR also appear to employ very few or no Roma/Gypsies. According to a local Ashkali representative, of the hundreds of jobs created near Ferizaj/Urosevac in the construction and running of Camp Bondsteel for the United States army, not one has gone to an Ashkali or Roma. One international NGO reports that it received threats from local Serbs for having hired Roma/Gypsy camp residents as guards and cleaners for one of its projects rather than Serbs living nearby.[11]

With generally low attainment in education, particularly in the wake of what was for many Ashkali and Egyptian communities a ten year education gap in the 1990s, relatively few Roma/ Gypsies are able to take advantage of the few employment opportunities that do arise. But discrimination against Roma/Gypsies in employment predates both the UNMIK period and the decade of Serbian direct rule that preceded it. Older Roma/Gypsies who attended school in the 1970s and 1980s recall that even those who completed secondary education and received vocational qualifications found it difficult to get jobs for which they were qualified, with other candidates almost always being preferred to Roma/Gypsies. One interviewee born in 1965 recounted that to secure jobs, some Roma/ Gypsies would offer the director of an organisation or enterprise their first six months' wages in return for being hired – only to be dismissed after six months. Decades of discrimination in employment have had a demoralising effect, resulting in a culture of very limited employment ambitions, which affects parents' attitudes towards the value of education for their children.

Access to property, amenities and services

Of the minority of Roma/Gypsies who have managed to remain in their own homes, a significant number continue to face threats to their security that effectively "imprison" them within their own micro-communities, unable to access public services and amenities, including shops. In autumn 1999, researcher Paul Polansky found more than 30 Roma families in Prishtina who had reportedly not left their homes in several months for fear of being kidnapped or killed. Most of their houses had a walled-in patio where they kept goats and chickens. For months on end they survived on goats' milk and eggs alone.[12] In some areas shops are reported to have refused to serve Roma/Gypsies. Denial of access to amenities and services, harassment and threats continue to cause more displacement.

The social vulnerability of Roma/Gypsies or their physical absence, during a period when Kosovo's property system has effectively collapsed into a free-for-all, threatens to leave many permanently deprived of their property. Occupation of property belonging to Roma is widespread. Even more threatening is the growing phenomenon of Kosovar Albanians clearing land of the remains of burned and abandoned Roma homes to make way for new house building. The removal of all physical trace of what was there before and its replacement with a new building will make it extremely difficult for Roma/Gypsies to reclaim their property in the future.

Lacking a tradition of literacy, and alienated from authority and officialdom during the periods of Albanian and Serbian domination alike, Roma/Gypsies are the least likely of all the ethnic communities to have acquired or retained documentary proof of ownership of their homes. Their adverse security situation and inexperience in dealing with bureaucracy leave them badly placed to lobby for the restitution of their rights. Many Roma/Gypsy settlements were in any case built on the periphery of towns, outside the

planning and zoning regulations of their time, and therefore lack any official documentation. As a result, many Roma/Gypsy neighbourhoods lack essential amenities such as water supply, sewerage systems and properly surfaced roads. Their exclusion from town plans inhibited the development of electricity supply, telephone links and postal coverage. Repair and maintenance of essential infrastructure has allegedly been given a lower priority by new municipal authorities in Roma/Gypsy neighbourhoods than in neighbourhoods housing members of the majority community. Some Roma/Gypsy communities also claim that they have been disproportionately subject to water, electricity and telephone disconnections.

As external funding for emergency assistance winds down, budgets for social and humanitarian assistance have become increasingly restricted. More means-testing and targeting of benefits to elderly and disabled beneficiaries threatens to sideline the "category II" clients of the UNMIK Department for Health and Social Welfare – the able-bodied unemployed. This will disproportionately impact upon Roma/Gypsy communities, whose inability to gain employment, due to discrimination, and a lack of security, freedom of movement and qualifications, makes many families almost wholly reliant on government and NGO assistance.

As institutions and assistance programmes have evolved in the two years since the war, discrimination against Roma/Gypsies and other minorities has become institutionalised in mechanisms for allocating assistance. For example, the task of identifying beneficiary

villages and families in the official reconstruction-assistance programme was taken over in 2000 by municipal housing commissions. These have minimal minority participation, and this has led to allegations of discrimination and unfair distribution of resources. Under the official guidelines five to ten per cent of the funds were to be made available to minority communities, yet by the end of 2000 the actual figure stood at two per cent. A combination of failure to provide security and adequate reconstruction assistance continues to inhibit returns of Roma/Gypsy families and communities.

Community leadership and representation

Factors limiting or hindering Roma/Gypsies' political participation and representation include restricted freedom of movement, low literacy levels and inexperience in dealing with officialdom. These lead to lost votes through failure to be registered and the inadvertent

spoiling of ballot papers. The Ashkali Albanian Democratic Party of Kosovo had a candidate directly elected in Fushë Kosovë/Kosovo Polje in the October 2000 municipal elections, and subsequently had additional candidates co-opted onto municipal assemblies. While the party has given Ashkali communities a political voice, there have been complaints that in some locations it has attempted to assume a monopoly role as a conduit for aid distributions to Ashkalija. A political party representing Egyptians contested the elections in Gjakova, and in April 2001 a community leader in the Plementina IDP camp, formed another Ashkali party. Roma, Ashkalija and Egyptians have not sought a unified political voice. At a Kosovo-wide level, the latter two communities have distanced themselves from Roma and argued about which of the two should have the one place reserved by UNMIK to represent both Ashkali and Egyptians on the Kosovo Transitional Council. At a local level, Ashkalija and Roma communities have initiated contacts with each other in Ferizaj/Urosevac in recognition of the fact that they face common problems.

The social isolation, low levels of education and patriarchal tradition of Roma/Gypsy communities do not lend themselves easily to high-quality community leadership. At a political level, UNMIK's guarantee of representation to the ethnic minority communities in municipal and Kosovo-wide assemblies and government, without, for instance, further stipulating guaranteed levels of women's representation, risks entrenching a patriarchal and isolationist leadership culture.

However, several Roma/Gypsy community leaders are breaking the mould in positive ways. A small number of NGOs such as the Ashkali NGO Democratic Hope in Podjeve/Podujevo and Democratic Hope of Dubrava are making notable efforts to improve the image of their communities and integrate them with the surrounding majority population. Some Roma/Gypsy community activists have made excellent contributions to education. A few have frustrated and blocked sound education initiatives, and some – intentionally or otherwise – have done both.

The establishment of Roma/Gypsy NGOs offers an opportunity to create frameworks for community action, plurality and multi-polarity of leadership, and the building of leadership capacity. The OSCE has encouraged and assisted the establishment of several Roma/Gypsy NGOs. It reports that several Roma NGOs currently exist, or are in the process of registration, in Prizren, Gjilan/Gnjilane, Kamenica, Rahovec/Orahovac (a women's NGO), Gracanica, Strpce and Mitrovica. Several Ashkali local-community NGOs also exist, such as the two mentioned above and organisations in Fushë Kosovë/Kosovo Polje. There are also Egyptian associations in western Kosovo. Despite the opportunities, in some locations a plurality of NGOs has not been matched by a pluralistic outlook, and they have instead been employed as vehicles by rival leaders vying for, or defending against the prospect of, monopoly influence. This has particularly been the case in the post-war urban or IDP communities. Leadership of Roma/Gypsy communities in villages tends to be more stable and of a longer vintage.

Obligations assumed by UNMIK

The general legal framework
The UN Security Council Resolution 1244 (1999)[13] of 10 June 1999 established the framework for the removal of FRY and Serbian police, military and paramilitary formations from Kosovo, and the deployment in their place of an effective international civil and security presence. This was tasked with the demilitarization of the KLA and the establishment of a secure environment. The Resolution authorised the UN Secretary General to create an interim administration to establish and oversee the building of provisional democratic self-governing institutions through which Kosovo could enjoy substantial autonomy within the FRY, pending a final political settlement of Kosovo's status.

The duties envisaged for the interim administration (UNMIK) included:

- supporting the reconstruction of key infrastructure and other economic reconstruction
- supporting, in co-ordination with international humanitarian organisations, humanitarian and disaster relief aid
- maintaining civil law and order, including establishing local police forces, and in the immediate term deploying international police personnel to serve in Kosovo
- protecting and promoting human rights
- assuring the safe and unimpeded return of all refugees and displaced persons to their homes in Kosovo.

Although detached from the Constitution of the Federal Republic of Yugoslavia, Kosovo is unable to develop a full Constitution of its own.[14] The applicable law in Kosovo is decided by decrees (UNMIK Regulations) handed down by the Special Representative of the Secretary General (SRSG) in Kosovo, currently Hans Haekkerup. UNMIK Regulations remain in force until repealed by UNMIK or superseded by laws and regulations subsequently issued by future institutions established under a political settlement of Kosovo's status.

Kosovo's present body of law is a patchwork of decrees derived from the authority of Security Council Resolution 1244 combined with elements of domestic law resurrected from Kosovo's pre-1990 autonomy era. An early UNMIK Regulation stipulated that the laws applicable in Kosovo prior to 24 March 1999 would continue to apply in so far as they did not conflict with the fulfilment of UNMIK's mandate or any UNMIK Regulation. However, this attempt by UNMIK to apply laws passed by Serbia and FRY during the period of Milosevic's direct rule over Kosovo in the 1990s met with such resistance that the SRSG issued new UNMIK Regulations (1999/24 and 25) on 12 December 1999. These changed the applicable law to that which had been in force in Kosovo on 22 March 1989, except where superseded by UNMIK Regulations.

Kosovo's constitutional status is unlikely to be decided for some time to come. The bridging mechanism is the Constitutional Framework for Provisional Self-Government in Kosovo, decreed on 15 May 2001 by Hans Haekkerup.[15]

The institutional framework

The UN administration in Kosovo has been constructed with four "Pillars" of government, under overall UN leadership. The post-conflict emergency humanitarian operation was entrusted to UNHCR as Pillar 1, and was phased out in June 2000. The UN took direct responsibility for civil administration, forming Pillar 2. Pillar 3, democratisation and institution-building, has been entrusted to the OSCE, building on the experience of its earlier Kosovo Verification Mission. The European Union is managing Pillar 4: reconstruction and economic development. In practice, these structures (especially Pillars 2 and 4) took several months to establish, during which the administration gap at local level was filled by KLA-controlled bodies.[16] A new replacement Pillar 1 – Police and Justice – was devolved from Pillar 2 on 18 May 2001 "to provide greater focus, centrality and co-ordination" to UNMIK's efforts in that sphere.[17]

The military deployment implemented by NATO divided Kosovo into five Areas of Responsibility (AORs), each containing several of Kosovo's 30 municipalities.[18] The five AORs have since served as supra-municipal units for the structuring of civilian policing and civil administration functions. Administration at central, AOR and municipality levels is guided by international staff, who work alongside Kosovan counterparts. Since the October 2000 municipal elections, Kosovan co-heads at municipal level comprise a mix of appointed and elected officials. At central level, the national co-heads have been appointed under a temporary power-sharing arrangement agreed by UNMIK in January 2000 with the main Kosovar Albanian political parties and the on/off involvement of Kosovan Serb representatives. As part of this, the Albanian parties agreed to dissolve their rival self-declared "governments" and assemblies. After the scheduled November 2001 general election, all of the national co-heads will be elected officials.

International judges, prosecutors and police were brought in by UNMIK while Kosovan counterparts were selected and trained to work alongside them, with the ultimate aim of handing over justice and law enforcement to Kosovans. UNMIK also maintains a several-thousand-strong Kosovo Protection Corps (KPC), mainly consisting of ex-KLA fighters. Its role is an ongoing source of contention. It sees itself as the nucleus of a future Kosovan army, but UNMIK insists that it must confine itself to civil-defence duties. There are reports of the KPC assuming policing roles for which it has no official mandate. Human-rights abuses committed by uniformed KPC personnel, including beatings and

abductions of Roma/Gypsies, have also been reported.[19]

Minority rights

UNMIK policy and constraints

UNMIK Regulation 1999/1 of 25 July 1999 "On the authority of the interim administration in Kosovo"[20] stipulated that:

> "All persons undertaking public duties or holding public office in Kosovo shall observe internationally recognised human-rights standards and shall not discriminate against any person on any ground such as sex, race, colour, language, religion, political or other opinion, national, ethnic or social origin, association with a national community, property, birth or other status."

UNMIK is engaged in a difficult balancing act of building democratic institutions accountable to the majority, while trying also to guarantee the rights of minorities in a territory where a "zero sum" perception of ethnic politics has become ingrained. The Albanian and Serb communities remain highly polarised. Their mutual animosity also influences relations between majority Albanians and other minorities, and in many locations members of minority communities are often denied their basic human rights. At a day-to-day level UNMIK and KFOR operate a stopgap policy of containment, with KFOR maintaining a permanent security presence or mounting frequent patrols in threatened communities. To aid the provision of security to minority communities UNMIK found it necessary to issue a number of regulations. These include:

- "On the prohibition against inciting to national, racial, religious or ethnic hatred, discord or intolerance" (2000/4 of 1 February 2000), stipulating fines and/or prison sentences of up to five, eight or ten years for violators, and
- "On the exclusion of persons for a limited duration to secure public peace, safety and order" (2000/62 of 30 November 2000), giving the authorities power to serve orders of temporary exclusion from a specified area on persons they suspect of preparing acts of violence.

Chapter 3, Paragraph 4 of the Constitutional Framework of May 2001 reiterates and codifies an ongoing UNMIK commitment to the over 200,000 members of Kosovo's minority communities who have fled from Kosovo or been displaced within its borders. It states:

> "All refugees and displaced persons from Kosovo shall have the right to return to their homes, and to recover their property and personal possessions. The competent institutions and organs in Kosovo shall take all measures necessary to facilitate the safe return of refugees and displaced persons to Kosovo, and shall co-operate fully with all efforts by the United Nations High Commissioner for Refugees and other international and non-governmental organisations concerning the return of refugees and displaced persons."

UNMIK attempts to square the circle of respecting the will of the majority and guaranteeing rights to the minorities in a number of ways. These include, for example, co-opting minority-community representatives, closely supervising elected officials and retaining certain areas of responsibility within UNMIK's central departments, which are dominated by international staff.

A mechanism which UNMIK attempts to use is the allocation of posts to members of each of Kosovo's ethnic communities, whether in the administration, courts, police or KPC, in proportion to their share of Kosovo's total population. In practice, it has proved difficult to recruit Serbs and other minorities such as Roma/Gypsies to serve on bodies that are dominated by Kosovar Albanians.

Minority rights stipulated in municipal regulations

UNMIK Regulation 2000/45 "On Self-Government of Municipalities in Kosovo" (which preceded the Constitutional Framework by a year) "takes into account" some European regional standards on the rights of minorities: the European Charter for Regional or Minority Languages and the Council of Europe's Framework Convention for the Protection of National Minorities. Section 9 of the Regulation stipulates that:

> "Members of communities shall have the right to communicate in their own language with municipal bodies and all municipal civil servants."

This guarantees, in theory, that all municipal assembly meetings and all official documents are translated into both Albanian and Serbian.

In municipalities where the community's language is neither Albanian nor Serbian, translations are to be made into the language of that community.

Section 47 of Regulation 2000/45 authorises the SRSG to set aside any municipality decision which: "does not take sufficiently into account the rights and interests of the communities which are not in the majority in the territory of the municipality". This power acts as a back-stop to arrangements made by the Communities Committee and the Mediation Committee.[21] The SRSG is also given the power to augment the results of municipal elections by co-opting "additional members to the Municipal Assembly if he considers it necessary to do so in order to ensure representation of all communities pursuant to United Nations Security Council resolution 1244". Only one Roma/Gypsy candidate in Kosovo was elected to a municipal assembly in the October 2000 elections (in Fushë Kosovë/ Kosovo Polje), and the SRSG has been using this power extensively to co-opt representatives of minority communities to municipal assemblies. In the 27 municipalities where the election results were certified as of 1 March 2001, there were a total of 869 elected representatives and 123 appointees. The latter included ten Ashkalija, four Egyptians and nine Roma.[22] While this achieves representation for vulnerable Roma/Gypsy communities in an adverse social climate, its short-circuiting of the democratic process also imposes a cost – there is no mechanism for ensuring that co-opted representatives have the genuine support of their communities. As a result, they may be regarded as less legitimate than their elected counterparts (there is anecdotal evidence of Roma/Gypsy

members being sidelined). The practice may also cement ethnic boundaries and divisions, inhibiting the development of an inclusive politics that cuts across ethnic boundaries.

Rights of minorities in the Constitutional Framework

The structure of the Constitutional Framework guarantees representation for minority communities in the assembly and government of Kosovo (due to be elected in November 2001), building on structures already piloted at municipal level. Of 120 seats in the assembly, 20 are to be reserved for parties, coalitions, citizens' initiatives and independent candidates representing non-Albanian Kosovo communities. Their share of the seats will then be calculated in proportion to the number of valid votes received in the election to the assembly. Four of these seats are to be allocated to the Roma, Ashkali and Egyptian communities.[23] There are also quotas for inclusion of Serb minority and non-Serb minority members in the presidency of the assembly and in the government.[24] Sections 9.1.39-42 of the Framework set out an obligatory mediation procedure in the event of any assembly member objecting to the adoption of a law on the grounds that its provisions:
• discriminate against his community[25]
• adversely affect rights guaranteed to it under the Framework
• seriously interfere with the ability of the community to preserve, protect or express its ethnic, cultural, religious or linguistic identity.

Additionally, a Committee on Rights and Interests of Communities, composed of two members from each of Kosovo's communities elected to

the assembly, may at its own initiative propose laws or other measures to address the concerns of communities, and makes recommendations on any proposed law referred to it by a member of the presidency of the assembly.[26]

Chapter 4 of the Framework – "Rights of Communities and Their Members" – tabulates a list of rights pertaining to communities for the purpose of preserving, protecting and expressing their ethnic, cultural, religious and linguistic identities. It further mandates the Provisional Institutions of Self-Government both to create appropriate conditions for these rights and to implement them. The list includes the rights to:

- use their language and alphabets freely, including before the courts, agencies, and other public bodies in Kosovo
- enjoy access to information in their own language
- enjoy equal opportunity with respect to employment in public bodies at all levels and with respect to access to public services at all levels

- enjoy unhindered contacts among themselves and with members of their respective communities within and outside of Kosovo
- use and display community symbols, subject to the law
- establish associations to promote the interests of their community
- enjoy unhindered contacts with, and participate in, local, regional and international non-governmental organisations in accordance with the procedures of such organisations
- provide information in the language and alphabet of their community, including by establishing and maintaining their own media
- promote respect for community traditions
- preserve sites of religious, historical or cultural importance to the community, in co-operation with relevant public authorities
- receive and provide public health and social services, on a non-discriminatory basis, in accordance with applicable standards
- operate religious institutions
- be guaranteed access to, and representation in, public broadcast media, as well as programming in relevant languages, and

• finance their activities by collecting voluntary contributions from their members or from organisations outside Kosovo, or by receiving such funding as may be provided by the Provisional Institutions of Self-Government or by local public authorities, so long as such financing is conducted in a fully transparent manner.

Promotion of Roma/Gypsy rights

One difficulty with the guarantees of minority rights contained in the Constitutional Framework and UNMIK Regulations is that they are decrees handed down over the last two years by international administrators. That is, they are not positions that have evolved and accumulated over time through processes led by the democratically expressed will of Kosovo's population. UNMIK is making various efforts to fill this gap, for example, by promoting the integration and acceptance of Roma/Gypsy communities, and observing their rights at ground level, both through institutional innovation and endorsement of a framework agreement between Kosovar Albanian and Roma/Gypsy leaders.

On 30 June 2000, UNMIK established the institution of the Ombudsperson (UNMIK Regulation 2000/38) to receive and act upon complaints of human-rights violations or actions constituting abuse of authority. The Constitutional Framework states that:

"The Ombudsperson shall give particular priority to allegations of especially severe or systematic violations, allegations founded on discrimination, including discrimination against Communities and their members,

and allegations of violations of rights of Communities and their members."[27]

Since 2000, the UNMIK Department of Local Administration has been appointing international Local Community Officers (LCOs) in municipalities where there are significant minority communities. There are currently 28 LCOs. Their primary purpose is to facilitate an improvement of security and freedom of movement for minority communities and to aid the creation of conditions for fulfilment of the right to return. In order that they can achieve this, LCOs enjoy a unique status in the UNMIK structure in that they have the right to liaise with and co-ordinate action with all agencies, including KFOR, at all levels of authority. Their specific delegated tasks include assisting the establishment of the Municipal Assembly Communities Committees and Mediation Committees stipulated by UNMIK Regulation 2000/45, and the establishment of minority Community Offices.[28] The intended function of the Community Offices, which seven municipalities had established by 7 March 2001, is to enhance the protection of community rights and ensure equal access for minority communities to municipal services such as health care and education.[29]

The *Platform for Joint Action Regarding Kosovar Roma, Ashkalija and Egyptian Communities* resulted from a declaration agreed by Kosovar Albanian leaders with the leaders of Roma, Ashkalija and Egyptian communities following a Humanitarian Roundtable organised by UNHCR in Prishtina on 12 April 2000. It was subsequently endorsed at a special joint session of the Kosovo Transition Council and the Interim Administrative Council on 28 April 2000, during the visit of representatives of the UN Security Council to Kosovo. The Platform document set objectives to be met in co-operation between Kosovan leaders from all communities and UNMIK, which has also assumed specific obligations set out in the Platform document.[30] The community leaders signed up to the goal of: "bring[ing] an end to discrimination, harassment and persecution of members of the Kosovar Roma, Ashkalija and Egyptian communities", with the longer-term objective to "achieve the emancipation of these communities, and to ensure that they fully participate as free and equal members in Kosovo society".

In the preamble to the Platform document, responsibility for implementation of its provisions is placed upon the leadership of Kosovar Albanians and on the leaders of Kosovan Roma/Gypsy communities, with UNMIK, international organisations and the international community as a whole to provide institutional assistance and support as necessary. The document also places several direct obligations upon UNMIK. The duties of the Kosovar Albanian leaders are to:
- disseminate the agreement and urge support for it
- publicly condemn all acts of violence and harassment
- publicly reject the notion of collective guilt for individual crimes
- make visits to Roma/Gypsy communities to demonstrate support for them and obtain better understanding of their situation
- use influence to promote, and participate in, positive media portrayal of Roma/Gypsies.

Roma/Gypsy leaders are also to work in close consultation with UNHCR towards achieving the return to their homes of displaced and refugee Roma/Gypsies. This includes promptly deciding on their participation in the Kosovo Transition Council, and presenting proposals to UNMIK and the OSCE for establishment of radio and print media devoted to their respective communities.

Provisions under the rubric of "Promoting the rule of law" stipulate shared responsibility for ending impunity:
- "The leaders of [the Kosovar Albanian and Roma/Gypsy] communities will call for their constituents to co-operate fully with legal and judicial processes so that all crimes can be prosecuted and punished according to the rule of law.
- The Department of Justice will see to it that individuals who have committed major crimes during and after the conflict of 1999 are prosecuted and punished according to law."

The Platform document obliges UNMIK departments to take specific steps to guarantee to Roma/Gypsies their access to assistance and rights, for example:
- "The Department of Social Welfare and the Centres for Social Work will ensure that members of the Kosovar Roma, Ashkalija and Egyptian communities are not discriminated against in the allocation of social welfare, food assistance and other humanitarian aid. The Department and the Centres will take a proactive approach to ensuring that the welfare needs of these communities are met.
- The Department of Reconstruction and the Municipal Housing Committees will

ensure that returnees will have access to reconstruction assistance in accordance with existing criteria and procedures, and on a non-discriminatory basis.

- The Departments of Public Services and Local Administration will actively promote the recruitment of members of the Kosovar Roma, Ashkalija and Egyptian communities into public functions in accordance with existing criteria.
- The OSCE and the Department of Civil Society and Democratic Governance will take active steps to encourage, develop and support the creation of civil society institutions among the Kosovar Roma, Ashkalija and Egyptian communities."

UNMIK is obliged to report both on Roma/Gypsy representation in local government and on progress in implementation of all the relevant action points. There are also specific provisions on access to education, which are covered in the following section.

The right to education

Educational rights of minorities set out in UNMIK documents

Chapter 4 of the Constitutional Framework, which lists the rights of communities, includes two provisions guaranteeing specific rights on education. Communities and their members shall have the right to:

- receive education in their own language, and
- provide for education and establish educational institutions, in particular for schooling in their own language and alphabet and in community

culture and history, for which financial assistance may be provided, including from public funds in accordance with applicable law; provided that curricula respect the applicable law and reflect a spirit of tolerance among communities and respect for human rights and the cultural traditions of all communities.

The *Platform for Joint Action Regarding Kosovar Roma, Ashkalija and Egyptian Communities* elaborates the following UNMIK obligations with regard to access to education:

- "The Department of Education, in co-operation with the local administrations, will develop a special programme to ensure that all Kosovar Roma, Ashkalija and Egyptian children have access to education, particularly at the primary level. This programme will include efforts to promote Kosovar Roma, Ashkalija and Egyptian enrolment in secondary and tertiary institutions and to enhance the communities' awareness of the benefits of formal education.
- The Department of Education, local administrations and UNMIK will promote the introduction of optional non-Albanian language classes in the regular curriculum, and financially support educational institutions that provide instruction in non-Albanian languages.
- In primary and secondary schools throughout Kosovo, civic education classes will be designed to strengthen respect for human rights and fundamental freedoms, and to promote understanding and tolerance of all ethnic and religious groups. Lessons will be introduced on the history, culture and traditions of all ethnic communities."

Kosovo's education system – a legacy of conflict

The history of education in Kosovo in recent decades, particularly the 1990s, is unique to the region. The following summary, charting developments over the last 30 years, aims to provide a context to the challenges facing Roma/Gypsy children and a "lost generation" of Roma/Gypsy young adults today in their educational and life chances.

The period of autonomy, late 1960s – 1989

With Kosovo's acquisition of autonomous status in the late 1960s, formalised by the 1974 Yugoslav Constitution, the province's Albanian majority embarked on a course of cultural emancipation, after several decades of repression. The University of Prishtina was opened in 1970 and educational provision in Albanian was expanded at all levels. Serbian children continued to receive education in their own language, and study of the Albanian language was introduced as a compulsory subject. Albanian children studied Serbo-Croat as a second language. By the late 1970s about 95 per cent of children in Kosovo received elementary education. Illiteracy was reduced from 94 per cent before 1950 to 30 per cent by the 1970s. However, there were gender disparities: in 1981, 26 per cent of women and 9 per cent of men in Kosovo were illiterate.[31] Subordination of women and high birth rates are features of both Kosovan Albanian and Kosovan Roma/Gypsy communities, particularly in rural locations. According to one Albanian scholar:[32]

"Women [in rural Kosovo] are kept secluded at home when they do not work in the fields, get minimal education, and are totally subordinate to male authority ... A community denying half of its members access to a full education can never be a civilised community."

Ashkalija and Egyptians also benefited from the expansion of Albanian-language education. Literacy and formal education had not traditionally been given particular importance in many Roma/Gypsy communities, because parents often saw these attributes as irrelevant to Roma/Gypsy livelihood strategies – which were mainly small-trading and labouring. Nevertheless, there was a significant take-up of education by all three Roma/Gypsy communities during this period, though regular school attendance was lower among Roma/Gypsies than among Albanians. Fines were levied against parents who failed to send their children to school. Mefail Mustafa, an Ashkali education activist, commented that in the period before 1990 it was virtually impossible to find any Ashkali without primary education, barring a few girls in rural areas, although some girls would be taken out of primary school a year or two before completion, at the age of 12 or 13. It was during this period that additional classes in Romanes were introduced for Roma children in at least one town where there was a large Roma community (Gjilan/Gnjilane).

Conflict and the parallel systems, 1989–1999

From 1989 to 1992, the Serbian authorities introduced an escalating series of measures intended to reverse the gains in Albanian-language provision of the autonomy years. In September 1989, ethnic segregation of Serbian and Albanian pupils was introduced into schools in the form of physical partitions, separate floors or different shifts, with facilities allocated to the advantage of the relatively small number of Serbian pupils and teachers. In 1990, all of Kosovo's education legislation of the autonomy era was repealed by the Serbian parliament and a uniform curriculum in the Serbian language was imposed. Albanian teachers attempted to work on as before, rejecting the new curriculum. In 1991, the Serbian authorities ceased paying them and announced a plan to close many secondary schools, leaving places only for 28 per cent of the Albanian pupils finishing primary school. In September 1991, Serbian armed police enforced the exclusion of Albanian pupils from all Kosovo's schools. Protests met with police beatings and detentions. In 1992, Albanian teachers and pupils were able to re-enter most primary school buildings, albeit without pay, heating or any other provision, but many high school buildings were confiscated, their inventories removed, and Albanian books destroyed. Albanians' access to libraries and museums was also curtailed. The University of Prishtina, which acted as the intellectual engine of the Kosovar-Albanian cultural renaissance and new national self-awareness in the 1970s and 1980s, received a Serbian rector in 1991, who regarded it as "a factory of evil" and set about purging its entire Albanian staff.[33]

In 1992, high-school classes began to be reconvened by Albanian teachers in residual buildings and private homes. In February 1992, the sacked Albanian staff of Prishtina University reopened a version of it spread across 250 private buildings throughout the city. In 1996, an Italian religious order brokered an agreement with the FRY/Serbian authorities for the return of some university buildings to the Kosovar Albanians. Albanian students staged large demonstrations in 1997 to demand its implementation, but they were violently dispersed by Serbian police and security forces. The agreement was not implemented until spring 1998, after international pressure. Overcrowding and lack of chairs, desks, textbooks and winter heating dogged the emerging Kosovar-Albanian parallel education system. Teachers initially taught for no pay, expecting this to be a short-lived situation. For the first two to three years there was considerable police harassment – seizures of school documents, beatings and detentions of teachers. From 1993, the new shadow state structures of "the Republic of Kosova", established by the Kosovar Albanians as a competing reality to the Serbian takeover, began to pay token wages to the 18,000 teachers, reaching about DM150 per month in 1997. The money was collected as a voluntary tax, paid by virtually all Kosovar Albanian families and businesses and supplemented by funds from Kosovar Albanian exiles. Nevertheless, wages often went unpaid for many months, and maintaining morale and motivation was difficult for teachers and pupils alike. Pupil drop-out rates rose. By 1997, about 25 per cent were failing to finish primary school. Girls, especially in rural areas, were the most likely to drop out or not to progress to high school.

As state education provision now excluded about 90 per cent of the province's children, Serb pupils and teachers worked in conditions of extreme over-capacity, while their Albanian counterparts struggled nearby with overcrowded unheated facilities. Howard Clark, in his book on the Kosovar Albanian civil resistance, cites a village school where eight Serb pupils had at their disposal nine classrooms, a gym, a science laboratory and two offices. Serb and Albanian children no longer learned each other's language at school and had virtually no social contact.

This drastic ethnic polarisation of education presented the smaller ethnic minorities with difficult choices. In many cases, the Ashkalija and Egyptians were effectively left with no options at all. Turks tended to opt for the Albanian parallel system, while Serbo-Croat-speaking Slavic Moslems (Bosniaks) of linguistic necessity had to opt for Serbian schools. The situation with the three Roma/Gypsy communities was fragmented. Choosing to ally themselves with the now dominant nationality, most Roma opted for the Serbian system.[34] Linguistic incompatibility meant that Ashkalija and Egyptians could not do so, but neither were they always able to access the Albanian parallel system. As Albanians struggled to maintain the system, completely reliant on the reserves and resources of their kin and clan networks, Ashkalija and Egyptians "outsiders" were not always welcomed. In Ferizaj/Urosevac it is reported that Ashkalija children who looked white enough could go to the Albanian schools, while the darker-complexioned children had to stay at home. In Gjakova the situation was reportedly easier, with a number of Egyptian children attending Albanian primary schools. In Fushë Kosovë/Kosovo Polje, Ashkalija and Roma lived in a mixed community. The latter's close relationship with the Serbian authorities reportedly made it awkward for Ashkalija to be seen using the town's Albanian parallel primary school. Some went there initially, but soon dropped out. Thus, for many Roma/Gypsies in

Fushë Kosovë/Kosovo Polje, as was the case all over Kosovo, the years of the parallel systems entailed a lost decade, offering no accessible education at all.

War, disruption and subsequent re-establishment of education

By autumn 1998, a sustained offensive by Serbian security forces against the Kosovo Liberation Army caused damage and dislocation across rural Kosovo, driving about half a million people from their homes. In places like Gjakova and Peja/Pec, there was a large influx of children from the devastated surrounding villages into urban Albanian parallel schools. From the beginning of the NATO bombing in March 1999, education in Kosovo effectively ceased as most Kosovans were driven from their homes by Serbian forces. The 850,000-plus refugees and IDPs who poured into Macedonia, Albania and Montenegro included a very high proportion of school-age children. Catch-up classes were organised for refugee and IDP children with the support of UNICEF and other international agencies. UNICEF estimates that 85 per cent of children of primary-school age in camps and host communities attended school outside Kosovo.[35] Many Roma/Gypsies who fled to Macedonia registered as Albanians, so it is difficult to gauge what proportion of these children attended school.

By early August 1999, 90 per cent of Kosovar Albanian refugees had returned to the territory. Initial assessment of Kosovo's stock of 1,000 school buildings showed that nearly 40 per cent were destroyed or severely damaged, nearly 25 per cent moderately damaged, and virtually all needed new furniture and equipment. Many children and indeed teachers were traumatised by their war experiences. The embryonic UN administration (UNMIK) was able to call upon the experienced personnel of the Kosovar-Albanian parallel education network to open catch-up classes in hundreds of schools from summer 1999, some temporarily housed in tents. UNICEF loosely co-ordinated the array of international NGOs and KFOR units which carried out school-repair projects over the following 18 months. Mine and UXO (unexploded ordnance)-awareness classes were introduced into the curriculum by specialist international NGOs, although 130-170 casualties, many of them children, occurred in the first month alone (June-July 1999).

The admirable efforts quickly to reinstate education by and for the returning ethnic Albanian majority were nevertheless occurring while Roma/Gypsies were being terrorised. Many fled Kosovo, while others sought refuge in temporary camps inside Kosovo or hid in their homes. A very low proportion of Roma/Gypsy children dared to attend the re-opening schools at this time, and therefore, the majority missed not only education, but also mine and UXO-awareness classes, vaccination programmes and other health care that was being delivered through schools at that time. In late October 1999, most of Kosovo's 1,000 schools opened, slightly late, for the start of a new school year. UNMIK took responsibility for the payment of 28,000 teachers and education staff. In Serb-dominated areas,

teachers were encouraged by the FRY/Serbian authorities not to get involved with UNMIK. They continued to work to their contracts with the Serbian Ministry of Education, receiving their wages from Belgrade.

The inherited education system and proposed reforms

In their essential structures and practices, both the education systems bequeathed to the new Kosovo in summer 1999 – the Albanian parallel system and the Serbian "official" system – were un-reformed from the period of the Socialist Federal Republic of Yugoslavia. The system as a whole had been isolated from new trends and advances in pedagogy, methodology and education management.[36] Ethnic nationalism, conservatism and, especially in the case of the Albanian parallel system, degradation of buildings, equipment, teaching staff and skills all signified the extent of the regression from the position that had been achieved by the 1980s. Financing of the Albanian parallel system is estimated to have run at only 10-20 per cent of pre-1989 levels.[37] By 1997, 20 per cent of the teachers working in the Albanian parallel system were unqualified.[38] Even before 1989, pedagogy had a lowly status as an academic discipline, and it was felt that thorough knowledge of a subject was sufficient qualification for teaching it.[39] As a result, teaching by rote remains the norm and there is little in the way of child-centred or interactive teaching methods, and coherent learning evaluation.[40]

The legacy of the parallel system is a subject of ongoing debate. Does it provide a solid foundation for a new education system or is it essentially a barrier to progress, requiring

demolition before a modern system, catering to a multi-ethnic Kosovo, can be built in its place? Howard Clark concludes that the parallel system existed "more to strengthen national conscious-ness than to open minds".[41] While it provided UNMIK with a viable means of getting the majority of Kosovo's school-age population back into education after the war, that parallel system's ethnic particularity also complicated UNMIK's task of educating the children of Kosovo's non-Albanian minorities. The curriculum of the Albanian parallel system continues to be used by UNMIK, pending reform. Likewise, UNMIK has had existing textbooks reprinted, pending the development of new ones.

In a discussion paper circulated in January 2001, Michael Daxner, the international co-head of the UNMIK Department of Education and Science (DES), sketches out a vision for educational reform in Kosovo. He envisages that a depoliticised education system will play a key role in nurturing a durable civil society. An overhaul of teacher training is central to the projected reforms. The culture of education should change from a normative and teacher-oriented system to provision of a child-centred learning environment. The focus of education will shift from the building of a particular national identity towards the development of individual personality, to allow young Kosovans to be accepted as well-educated and qualified mature Europeans. The particular importance of this is that the new education system will be partly geared to preparing many graduates for temporary labour migration to Western Europe and North America. Education performance and assessment standards, therefore, are being modelled with the

European labour market in mind. European standards and expectations are intended also to provide a context within which pressure can be brought to bear for the introduction of integrated multi-ethnic education in Kosovo.

The DES was created under UNMIK Regulation 2000/11 of 3 March 2000. It succeeded the earlier Inter-agency Co-ordination Group on Education, chaired by UNICEF. The functions of the DES are to formulate education policy and strategy, with specialist tasks contracted out to "lead agencies" and day-to-day management of schools devolved to municipalities. One of the DES's responsibilities, defined by the Regulation, is:

> "the promotion of a single, unified, non-discriminatory and inclusive education system so that each person's right to education is respected and quality learning opportunities are available to all, irrespective of their ethnic or social origin, race or gender, disability, religion, political or other opinion".

The Regulation also requires the DES to "implement non-discriminatory personnel policies designed to ensure that the composition of the staff of the Department reflects the multi-ethnic character of Kosovo". On behalf of the DES, the Council of Europe is drafting a new law on general and vocational education and school organisation for Kosovo, scheduled for the end of 2001, and a new law to regulate the University of Prishtina. In the meantime, the DES continues to function within the legal framework of the period of the Socialist Autonomous Province of Kosovo, such as the 1979 Law on Primary Education (28/79). The 1979 law guarantees education in the pupil's mother tongue, yet lists only Albanian, Serbo-Croat and Turkish as applicable languages, with no mention of Romanes (Articles 12 & 13).

The DES has had to issue a myriad of departmental regulations and instructions to address issues and problems as they arise. It plans to have these temporary regulations assembled into an organised volume by July 2001.[42]

Specialist reform tasks have been delegated to different international agencies. It is envisaged that their functions will evolve into autonomous state agencies during Kosovo's transition process. The designated lead agencies and their tasks are:

- UNICEF, which is working on curriculum development, early childhood education and psycho-social projects
- the Canadian International Development Agency, which has contracted consultants to develop teacher training
- GTZ, which is taking responsibility for overhauling vocational education, and
- NORAD, which is dealing with education for children with disabilities.

At the time of writing, all of these agencies are still in the early stages of planning their work. The participation of the UNICEF curriculum-development consultant in a meeting with Roma, Ashkalija and Egyptian education activists in April 2001 is an encouraging sign.

The relationship between the DES, education officers in the five AOR regions and the 30 municipal authorities is still evolving. Michael Daxner envisages that the future organisation of education will be a quadrangle of: pupil – teacher – municipal environment – local community.[43] UNMIK Regulation 45/2000 "On Self-Government of Municipalities in Kosovo" sets the framework for local officials elected in the October 2000 municipal elections to assume responsibility for education. However, this presents the DES with a problem as:

> "It is the policy of UNMIK that no political party or assembly shall have any direct influence on education in Kosovo".[44]

The DES's solution has been to limit the responsibilities of the elected directors of the Municipal Education Directorates to the "hardware" of education – maintenance of school buildings and of the learning environment. The DES has in parallel appointed two education administrators in each municipality, who report direct to the DES and are responsible for the "software" of education, ie, management, personnel, curricula, textbooks and teaching methods. In some municipalities, this has resulted in a situation whereby the losing candidates in the October 2000 municipal elections have been appointed by the DES as education administrators, and now hold more effective power than their elected former rivals.

Prior to the Albanian parallel education system, a decentralised system of management of education had been introduced with the 1974 Yugoslav Constitution, which retained locally generated revenue at the municipal level for funding education.[45] Currently, education and other functions of government continue to be financed in the main by international contributions to the UNMIK budget – contributions that will inevitably diminish. Teachers' salaries are now pegged only a little

above the level set by the Albanian parallel system, at DM265 per month for primary-school teachers, DM285 for secondary-school teachers, and DM325 for university teachers, far short of their relative pre-1989 rates.[46] This inevitably affects morale. In one municipality, at least 40 per cent of teachers are estimated to supplement their income with a second job.[47]

The World Bank advocates reforming education funding to institute the allocation of block grants to municipalities on the basis of pupil numbers rather than on the current basis of teachers and buildings. The Bank is already piloting this approach in the framework of its Kosovo Education and Health Finance Project. This could bring about improved provision for Roma, Ashkali and Egyptian communities, which were bypassed or given insufficient consideration in pre-UNMIK education planning. It poses a challenge, however, in that estimation and registration of the Roma/Gypsy population is unreliable. Rigidly applied, it may ultimately disadvantage isolated and minority communities, requiring additional teaching inputs, such as classes in Romanes. Although failing to specify compensatory mechanisms to address the particular needs of Roma/Gypsy communities, the Bank accepts that: "The formula can be modified over time to target public resources on disadvantaged groups or areas which are not performing up to established standards."[48] For his part, Michael Daxner states that:[49]

> "We are strongly committed to a policy of equity in schooling for all Kosovar children and to bridging the gap in educational opportunities between minorities and

majority ethnic groups... (some minorities will be given additional aid, input and resources to encourage their children to return to school so that they can attain the same academic levels of their grade peers)."

Stages of education and Roma/Gypsy participation in them

Community and family poverty and social disadvantage have both immediate and long-term impacts on the participation of Roma/Gypsy children in education. Discrimination and hostility faced by Roma/Gypsy children inside schools from children of other communities or from teachers can also take its toll.

Parents' inability to clothe their children presentably is frequently cited as a reason for children missing school. A lack of suitable winter clothing and boots increases drop-out rates in cold or wet weather. Roma/Gypsy parents sensibly reason that keeping children at home in bad weather if they do not have warm clothes and shoes reduces the risk of illness. Often, a lack of family funds to buy textbooks and exercise books limits Roma/Gypsy children's participation in the classroom, and makes them stand out among their peers, causing teachers to become frustrated with them. Families' immediate income or care needs often claim priority over their children's education – school attendance is regularly disrupted by withdrawals to care for younger brothers or sisters or to earn some vital extra family income.

Social exclusion, discrimination, chronic patterns of marginal employment and unemployment have instituted a cycle of low educational motivation and attainment from one generation to the next in many Roma/Gypsy families. Having had few benefits from education themselves, many parents see it as an irrelevant luxury with a high "opportunity cost" that they can ill afford for their children. A corrosive culture of low ambition has been reinforced in many locations by the ten-year education gap of the 1990s. As a result, many Roma/Gypsy communities and families have not embraced educational opportunity even in places where the most obvious external impediments to their children's participation have been removed. The situation in Podjeve/Podujevo offers an interesting example. The Ashkali community there is well integrated with the Kosovar Albanian population and has few security problems. The local economy holds some of the best prospects in Kosovo for Roma/Gypsies to find employment. Nevertheless, out of a total Ashkali population of 900, from which one could expect up to 300 to be of school age (although community leaders have said that there are 150 such children), only ten children are in regular school attendance.[50]

A tendency of many Roma/Gypsy parents not to view school as a priority for their children is often met by an equally indifferent attitude to Roma/Gypsy pupils on the part of Kosovar Albanian or Serb teachers. There are numerous accounts of teachers placing Roma/Gypsy children at the back of the class. Given the possible security and inter-ethnic problems that could result, many Kosovar Albanian and Serb teachers are reluctant to take responsibility for dealing with the needs of Roma/Gypsy children. Teachers become impatient with children's irregular attendance, their poor state of preparedness for education in comparison with other children and their lower standards of personal presentation and hygiene. As a result, they often deal out humiliations that eventually make school a barely tolerable experience for Roma/Gypsy children. The very small number of teachers drawn from Roma/Gypsy communities, and the current lack of training for the majority of Kosovo's teachers to sensitize them to the needs of Roma/Gypsy children, means that, for the time being, there is little to counter a prevailing culture among teachers that dismisses and discriminates against Roma/Gypsy children.

The attitude towards Roma/Gypsy children of Kosovar Albanian peers has been corroded by the war. Children have emulated the heightened hostility of adults towards Roma/Gypsies in the post-war period. Some of the Roma/Gypsy children interviewed for this report had stopped attending school after being attacked on their journey to school by Kosovar Albanian children, or subjected to name-calling in school. There are also reports of bullying of Roma/Gypsy children by their Serbian peers. In summer 2000, there was a dramatic drop in school attendance of Roma children from the IDP camp in northern Mitrovica (from 75 to 10). This was attributed to bullying by Serb children.[51]

The war and its aftermath cut Roma/Gypsy IDP communities off from education facilities. Yet, at least within Kosovo, UNHCR, UNICEF, UNMIK and NGO implementing partners gradually instituted or supported schooling arrangements for each of the IDP camps. For several remaining Roma communities however, the war has changed the social and institutional landscape around them to such an extent that their children are totally isolated from educational opportunity – for example, Roma teenagers in Ferizaj/Urosevac do not speak the language used in any local school.

Preschool education

Preschool education for three to six year olds is neither compulsory nor free in Kosovo, and provision is sparse. Only a very small number of Roma/Gypsy children are recorded as participating in preschool education. A handful of NGO projects are now providing preschool education opportunities for Roma/Gypsy children in a few selected communities: *Solidarites'* project in Gjakova's Colonia neighbourhood; kindergartens run by *Enfants du Monde* in the IDP camps of Leposavic and Plementina; International Rescue Committee's kindergarten projects in *Rufci i Ri*'s Migjeni School in Lipjan/Lipljan municipality, and in Gjilan/Gnjilane.

Just over two per cent of the pre-school child population attend preschool. The Kosovo Education Centre recorded that only 4,821 children attended preschool in 1999-2000, including kindergartens and primary-school preparatory classes (for six year olds).[52] According to the Kosovo Education Centre, there are Serbian-language preschool institutions in Serb-dominated municipalities, as well as three additional preschools in municipalities with an ethnic Albanian majority.

Primary education

Although primary education is compulsory and free for all children, textbooks and exercise books are not. These need to be purchased by parents (although donations and aid projects have assisted some families to do this in some areas over the last two years). Poverty, in some cases accompanied by a parental reluctance to devote scarce family resources to non-essentials, means that many Roma/Gypsy children lack the most basic equipment to participate in classes. This is both a practical barrier and a powerful disincentive for children who would prefer not to have their families' poverty exposed on a daily basis.[53] Registration of children at a primary school can generally be done only at the beginning of a new school year, and requires presentation of the child's birth certificate and domicile registration. In many cases this acts as a barrier to Roma/Gypsy parents. UNMIK Regulation 2000/51 stipulates that parental failure to enrol a child in a school is punishable by a DM300 fine. But it does not specify penalties for failure to ensure the child's attendance in practice. In addition, there have been cases of teachers citing irregular attendance or failure to have the necessary books as reasons for excluding Roma/Gypsy children from school.[54] Reliable figures do not yet exist on the proportion of Roma/Gypsy children who complete primary school and thereby qualify for secondary education, but it is a small minority. Many of the Roma/Gypsy children interviewed for this report had completed just one or two years of primary school before dropping out.

Previously, under the 1979 law, primary schooling lasted eight years, from the ages of 7 to 15 years. UNMIK Regulation 2000/51 "On the Age of Compulsory School Attendance in Kosovo", issued on 30 August 2000, extended the period of primary education to nine years, now from the ages of 6 to 15 years. Primary education takes place in two cycles. In some rural areas there is a central primary school teaching both cycles, with satellite feeder schools in surrounding villages teaching only the lower cycle. In the lower cycle, which takes in the first four grades, children are taught mainly by one teacher. For lower-cycle primary school teachers, the qualifications required are either a higher school degree in teaching or a university degree in education. The upper cycle (grades five to eight) is sometimes referred to as "subject teaching", and is taught by different specialist teachers, who are required to have a higher school or university degree in the relevant subject.[55] On successful completion of all grades, primary school pupils receive a certificate, which is essential for their access to further education and to many types of employment. Of a total of 534 recognised primary schools in Kosovo, 456 are Albanian language only, 57 Serbian language only, 7 Bosniak only, and 14 mixed consisting of Albanian, Bosniak and Turkish.[56]

Secondary education

Secondary education is not compulsory, but is free and lasts for four years, from age 15 to 19 years. As such a small minority of Roma/Gypsy children complete primary education, the number of Roma/Gypsy high-school and vocational-school students is small. This pool is further undermined by the demands and constraints of poverty, and by a culture of low expectations, in that many Roma/Gypsy adults have little or no evidence of the supposed benefits to be derived from secondary education. Interviews with Roma/Gypsy teenagers conducted for this report, together with enthusiastic take-up of vocational training projects provided by NGOs, demonstrate that many would like to train for a profession. However, lack of literacy and/or a primary-education completion certificate prevents them from accessing the secondary vocational-education system.

Secondary-school teachers are expected to hold a university degree in the subject that they teach. As with primary education, secondary education is managed at municipal level. Children who progress to this level choose between attending a high school or a vocational school, where they learn a particular trade or profession. There are general high schools, usually in areas of dispersed population. More common are two-branch high schools, which are usually in urban areas. These offer alternative streams in social sciences and linguistics or science and mathematics. There are also philological and pedagogical high schools. Currently, 52 per cent of high school pupils study science and mathematics, 30 per cent social sciences and linguistics, 9 per cent "general", 7 per cent pedagogy and 2 per cent philology.[57] During the years of the parallel education systems in the 1990s, a majority of secondary-school pupils opted for high schools. One reason for this was that vocational-school buildings and their specialist equipment were denied to the majority Albanians by the FRY/Serbian authorities, as were the state-sector jobs that the vocational schools prepared students for. As a result, many vocational schools fell into disuse. Large numbers of young Albanians migrated to Western Europe

after finishing their secondary education to escape inevitable unemployment and/or conscription into the FRY/Serbian army, and to earn vital remittance income for their families. High-school education was more useful for this than a narrow vocational education. There is a reversal of this trend in the new Kosovo. In 1999-2000, 60 per cent of secondary school pupils opted for vocational schools, and just 40 per cent for general high schools. The World Bank estimates that 70 per cent of secondary students are now enrolled in vocational schools or programmes.[58]

The vocational schools offer 16 different fields of study, with between five and seven different career paths available within each of them. Currently, the most popular fields of study in the vocational schools are health and social welfare (26 per cent of vocational students), electrical engineering (20 per cent), economics, law and administration (19 per cent) and machinery and metal processing (17 per cent).[59] Nevertheless, the inherited vocational school system is a long way from meeting Kosovo's current and future labour-market needs – where broad-based skills, flexibility and continuous learning are required. The World Bank has argued that there should not be a rush to re-establish and re-equip the secondary-education system along its traditional lines, but that a thorough reform agenda should be shaped.[60]

Higher education and teacher training
There are only a handful of Ashkali and Egyptian students at the University of Prishtina. Aside from the fact that virtually all Roma/Gypsy families would be unable to afford to support a child to study away from home, Prishtina does not provide a comfortable or particularly secure study environment for Roma/Gypsies. In the initial months after the war, Prishtina was very dangerous for them and all but a few families from the city's Roma population fled at that time. The situation has calmed since then and some Ashkali are occasionally seen on the streets, but security remains a concern for any Roma/Gypsy in Prishtina. Six higher schools in other Kosovan towns, and one in Prishtina, come under the umbrella of the university. Four of the higher schools – in Prishtina, Prizren, Gjilan and Gjakova – are pedagogical. Many high-school graduates from outside Prishtina who have no means to support themselves away from home turn to the pedagogical higher schools for a chance of higher education. Prizren and Gjakova, respectively, still have quite large and relatively secure Roma and Egyptian communities, so the higher schools in those two towns offer a possibility of higher education and teacher training to those young Roma/Gypsy adults who have completed high school there.

The University of Prishtina is centrally funded. Although UNMIK intends it to be multi-ethnic, in practice it currently serves the majority ethnic Albanian community, a reversal of the situation that prevailed until June 1999, when the university facilities were the preserve of the Serbian community and denied to the Albanians. The university has 14 faculties, including the Teachers' Faculty. University professors and lecturers are arguably worse off now that they receive their salary from the UNMIK budget rather than from students' contributions, as was the case during the parallel system.

Adult education

The primary-education system in theory provides education to illiterate adults aged over 15.[61] Institutions of adult education – "night schools" – existed in the former Yugoslavia, but have disappeared over the last decade.[62] Given the high proportion of illiterate adults in Roma/Gypsy communities, there are many who could benefit from adult-literacy programmes if these were organised in accessible locations at accessible times and were affordable. This would improve employment prospects and, in turn, improve the educational chances of children or younger siblings.

Although no permanent adult education institutions have yet been established, some project and programme initiatives do provide opportunities for adult-literacy training to Roma/Gypsy communities in a few areas. The Forum for Democratisation (FID), a Gjakova NGO, hopes to gain funding for a literacy and catch-up class project for Roma/Gypsy adults. In addition, a large-scale literacy project for women and girls recently started, funded by UNICEF, co-ordinated by the Kosovo Foundation for Open Society and implemented by the Kosovo Education Centre and an umbrella of 21 local women's NGOs. Its aim is to educate illiterate adults throughout Kosovo. In its first phase it will focus on illiterate women and girls in rural areas. Three of the implementing women's NGOs are Roma/Ashkalija groups, working with Roma/ Ashkalija women.[63]

The World Bank advocates the development of adult training in business management, technical and engineering skills needed to ensure the effective operation of public-sector resources and utilities. It envisages the development of a network of public, private and NGO/non-profit training providers, funded partly by government funds and partly by cost recovery from clients.[64] However, currently the World Bank's vision does not appear to include adult-literacy education, nor does the Department of Education and Science give any signs of prioritising the creation of sustained institutions of adult learning.

Government practice

While it is still too early to speak with confidence about good government practice in relation to Roma/Gypsy education, there are signs of positive practices that could be augmented and scaled up.

Holistic practice – creating conditions for education

A multifaceted approach fostering social inclusion is required to identify and eliminate the multiple constraints on Roma/Gypsy access to education both at a local and at a Kosovo-wide level. The most fundamental task is to secure the viability of Roma/Gypsy communities in the new Kosovo – their physical security and opportunities to earn a living. Communities that cannot secure these essentials will inevitably follow the tens of thousands of Roma/Gypsies who have already left Kosovo.

At local level

UNMIK Local Community Officers (LCOs), whose function has been described earlier, could provide a linchpin for a comprehensive social-inclusion approach. Their ability to collaborate with all agencies at all levels should allow them to identify impediments to community well-being in general and to educational access in particular. They could also bring to bear the necessary combination of institutional authority, expertise and resources to resolve them. The potential for LCOs to develop a presence in Roma/Gypsy communities should enable them to identify specific measures to address local problems.

In some areas, it is still necessary for KFOR to provide escorts for Roma/Gypsy children making the journey to and from school. The presence of security checkpoints or escorts can reinforce isolation and stigmatisation in the long term, but their premature removal can expose children to unacceptable risks. LCOs will be well placed to give advice regarding the timely reduction of security measures as the level of threat to the community reduces.

The local community office arrangements made by the Ferizaj/Urosevac LCO since December 2000 are notable for the level of direct access and interaction they provide to the municipality's Ashkali and Roma communities. Importantly, they employ Ashkali and Roma as staff. From his arrival in October 2000, the LCO has built upon existing community capacity, developing premises that were already being used by Ashkali as community meeting points into "advice centres", where people can get information or raise concerns about access to social services, welfare assistance, health care and education. More ambitiously, it is also hoped that the local community offices will provide an organisational focus for community development projects. The LCO has engaged six local staff to work in the central local community office and its three satellites – four Ashkali, one Roma, and one Bosniak/Gorani. They are paid local salary rates, with the intention that the positions should be sustained and ultimately paid for by the municipal budget.

Being able to generate a reasonable and regular income will remove a key impediment to Roma/Gypsy families' ability to ensure their children's full participation in education. The Ferizaj/Urosevac LCO is also working with Ashkali community representatives on a two- to four-year development plan that includes specific income-generation schemes for the community.

At Kosovo-wide level

Detailed, regular monitoring and reporting of the human-rights situation of ethnic minority communities, including Roma, Ashkali and Egyptians, has been instituted jointly by UNHCR and the OSCE, collated through the Ad Hoc Task Force on Minorities. Beginning with a preliminary assessment published in July 1999, the Task Force has been issuing reports at two- to five-month intervals. These *Joint Assessments of the Situation of Ethnic Minorities in Kosovo* provide a valuable information and reference resource for policy-makers, NGOs or any interested observer – chronicling attacks on minorities and analysing patterns of discrimination and human-rights abuses. Each report now devotes attention and analysis to particular sectors in which the different ethnic minority communities face barriers in realising their rights. The *6th Joint Assessment*, covering October 2000 to February 2001, devoted particular attention to the issues of security and return, access to health services, employment, and political structures, and property rights. A particular emphasis on education is planned for the *Joint Assessment* due to be issued in about July 2001.

From late 2000, an encouraging development in several UNMIK departments has been the establishment of specialist Minority Officer positions, which will result in more attention, policy focus and sustained programming for minorities across a range of sectors. In December 2000, the Department of Health and Social Welfare appointed an international Officer for Minorities. This officer has initiated the survey of vaccination coverage of Roma/Gypsy children which is being implemented through the LCOs. Thus two new posts, created respectively at local and Kosovo-wide level, have started working together. The Department of Education and Science has followed suit with a dedicated officer.

As security and sustainability of Roma/Gypsy communities can only be guaranteed in the long term by their acceptance by the majority population, UNMIK has been implementing a range of activities at different levels to promote inter-ethnic dialogue and agreement. UNHCR's organisation of humanitarian roundtables, with the participation of the political leaders of the Kosovar-Albanian community and Roma,

Ashkalija and Egyptian community leaders, resulted firstly in an agreed declaration of principles and then the UNMIK-endorsed *Platform for Joint Action Regarding Kosovar Roma, Ashkalija and Egyptian Communities*. The latter document led to the organisation of two technical consultation meetings, in September 2000 and January 2001, to review its implementation. This had been followed by a process of breaking down consultation on the Platform document into its constituent parts, such as Access to Education, Access to Social Welfare and Humanitarian Assistance. Fulfilling an obligation entered into under the Platform document, the leaders of the main Kosovar Albanian political parties made a series of high-profile visits to Roma/Gypsy communities, meeting communities in Prizren and Ferizaj/Urosevac in June 2000, and in Peja/Pec in September 2000. Kosovo-wide intercommunity dialogue was augmented by the participation of municipal assembly members from a wide diversity of ethnic communities, including Roma, Ashkalija and Egyptians, in the Airlie House II conference in the USA in February-March 2001, which provided training to mayors and municipal officials.[65]

Education policy

UNMIK has been slow in implementing the education-access obligations it assumed in the Platform document in April 2000. Until early 2001, a scattering of NGO projects substituted for a coherent UNMIK strategy in this regard. For clear political reasons, policy-making and provision for the Serbian community has taken precedence over consideration of the other smaller, non-Serbian minority communities.

Roma/Gypsy communities' lack of a strong international political lobby and their marginalisation at local level have rendered them particularly prone to invisibility as far as policy-makers are concerned. A position articulated by the DES is that minority-community problems cannot be solved without resolving the problems of the majority community first. At one level this is practical and correct, but it is also an approach which places Roma/Gypsies firmly in their usual position at the back of the queue. Nevertheless, at the time of writing (May 2001), there does appear to be a new UNMIK focus on the issue of Roma/Gypsy access to education. Dedicated personnel, surveys, consultations and policy-drafting have been instituted. It is hoped that the experience gained over the previous year by the various NGO projects run in loose co-ordination with the DES will now be mobilised and scaled up, resulting in an informed and holistic approach to the issue.

The scope for more NGO minority education projects may be increasing. As overall aid funds for Kosovo fall, the share being allocated for development of minority communities in this post-emergency phase is rising as a proportion of the whole. More NGOs are therefore likely to be attracted to working in this area. It is therefore important that the DES grasps this opportunity for co-ordination, for dissemination and replication of approaches found to have been successful, and for learning from those which were not successful.

Focused Department of Education personnel and policy

In February 2001, the DES appointed an international staff member to the newly created post of Minorities Officer, providing for the first time a consistent point of contact for minority education issues. This officer has responsibility for developing a comprehensive Policy Development and Action Plan for non-Serb Minorities. At the time of writing the Action Plan is still at a draft stage.[66] It is intended to address not only all major issues pertaining to non-Serb minority children and students, but also the ethnic composition of the educational teaching and administrative staff at all levels, and of the DES staff. The intention is to integrate the Action Plan with all the reforms in education which are being planned: the new education law; the vocational education system, teacher training and curriculum development. The latter three reforms are being developed outside the DES by lead agencies. In relation to these three reforms, the DES role will be to outline the policy framework and political intentions and to provide co-ordination.

A range of possible projects has been suggested for implementation within the framework of the Action Plan. Replication is proposed of projects which have already been implemented in one or two locations, such as:

- catch-up courses for students who have been out of school for a significant period of time or who have never attended school, such as the Emin Duraku school pilot project in Gjakova, and
- integration programmes, where appropriate, such as the work of the International Rescue

Committee (IRC) on integrating Ashkali children into the Salman Reza School in Fushë Kosovë/Kosovo Polje.

A wider range of possible proactive measures is suggested, all still at a hypothetical stage:

- "assistant teachers" in selected schools to assist with language problems and students who have fallen behind the regular curriculum
- non-formal adult education including literacy and numeracy
- equivalency courses and certification for adults who would like to have a secondary diploma
- special programmes for minorities entering vocational schools
- programmes to promote attendance in school in general, and in secondary school and university in particular, including public-awareness programmes aimed at parents
- programmes for minorities with disabilities
- scholarships for university, including teacher training.

Education surveys of Roma/Gypsy communities

In spring 2001, the Department of Education and Science began the process of undertaking a Kosovo-wide survey of the numbers of non-Serb minority children both attending and not attending school. Prior to this survey, no comprehensive reliable data were available to UNMIK to enable it to begin formulating policies and programmes for the education of Roma/Gypsy children. The DES survey is designed to provide "a baseline from which priorities, policy and plans can be developed".[67]

In the DES survey questionnaire, children or their parents are asked to provide a range of information, including their nationality, their mother tongue, and whether they have been displaced from their permanent place of habitation. They are asked to identify the school attended, the language of instruction used and the language of instruction the children or their parents would prefer. Children who do not attend school are asked which year they stopped attending or if they never went at all, and to give reasons. A large field is provided for comments.

The survey is being routed through the LCOs in nearly all municipalities, who can delegate the task of conducting the survey to a competent local agency. In some areas, implementation of the survey has been the responsibility of NGOs doing educational work with minorities (for example, *Solidarites* and Bethany Christian Services in Gjakova).[68] A possible problem with this approach is a potential for uneven implementation of the survey, with the best coverage in areas already served by NGO programmes, and weak or patchy coverage in areas or communities where such capacity is currently lacking. In at least one respect the design of the questionnaire may lead to misleading results, since it does not sufficiently differentiate between enrolment in a school and actual or regular attendance. An example of this misunderstanding is research carried out by IRC on school attendance of Roma and Ashkali children in Podjeve/Podujevo. Although it was plain that hundreds of children were not attending school, only 20 or so children were revealed by the survey as not attending school, since "attendance" was understood to be the same as "enrolment".[69]

The DES survey will not be the exclusive source of information on Roma/Gypsy communities' access to and attitudes towards education. It is being conducted at a time when several other arms of the UNMIK and collaborating agencies are likewise planning research on Roma/Gypsy education. UNICEF intends to perform research on children not attending school.[70] After consultation with the DES, in May 2001 the OSCE Human Rights Department carried out a detailed sample survey of the attitudes to education of roughly 20 Roma/Gypsy families in each of the five Kosovo regions/AORs (ie, 100 questionnaires in all). The questionnaire asked for details of children in school, children out of school and parental plans for their preschool-age children. It solicited comments on such themes as the quality of education provided, the state of relations with non-Roma/Gypsy co-pupils, the benefits and difficulties of the language of instruction. It included questions such as:

- What has the children's experience been in school?
- What would help the children have a better experience in school?
- How do you think school should best prepare your children for life and work in Kosovo?
- How would you like to see your culture represented in school?
- Do you think it is necessary for children to have an education to succeed here?
- What can be done to encourage your children to attend school?

This depth of questioning will serve as a useful supplement to the DES research. With the appointment of the Minorities Officer in the DES, information can be collated, pooled and made available to policy-makers more efficiently than it has been in the past. The previous lack of a "fixed abode" in UNMIK for Roma/Gypsy education complicated the collation, distribution and analysis of pilot surveys undertaken in some locations during 2000 by a variety of NGO and OSCE actors, despite efforts to distribute them through inter-agency working groups.

A local survey conducted in summer 2000 by an OSCE Human Rights Officer in Ferizaj/Urosevac offers a positive example of how a research exercise can itself draw attention to education at local level with tangible results, even in the absence of resources for a sustained follow-up programme or project. The idea for the survey arose from the discussions of two local working groups. An inter-agency education group sought different initiatives to increase the enrolment of Roma and Ashkali children in schools, including the arrangement of meetings between local school directors and representatives of the Roma and Ashkali communities. A weekly Ashkali/Roma roundtable, held at the OSCE field office, brings together Ashkali and Roma community leaders, UNMIK, UNICEF, UNHCR, UNMIK police, the International Organisation for Migration (IOM) and NGOs such as ADRA and the Norwegian Refugee Council. It was within this framework that the education survey was agreed upon, implemented and followed up.

A "Day of Education" event was organised in each of the municipality's four Roma/Ashkalija neighbourhoods. There were organised games for children. Volunteers interviewed children who approached them, using a highly structured

one-page questionnaire.[71] The questions focused particularly on what was preventing children attending school. According to the UNHCR/OSCE:[72]

"There was a very limited response from the Roma community. The Ashkaelia, however, did respond, and the information collected by OSCE with respect to the educational needs of the children of primary-school age revealed the following: of 398 children interviewed, 237 (60 per cent) were not attending school; 133 (56 per cent) of those who were illiterate or excluded from education were females, and 142 (60 per cent) of this category were aged seven to nine and potential candidates for enrolment in the current educational cycle 2000-2001. The results of this survey serve to underline the kind of intensive efforts that need to be made to address the educational needs of minority communities. As follow-up,

OSCE has engaged the community representatives and the educational authorities in order to promote school attendance, particularly for the seven to nine year olds. On 23 September the Council of the Mahalla of the Roma/Ashkaelia stated that 324 Ashkaelia children attend primary schools (first to eighth year) in Urosevac/Ferizaj municipality. Only eight Roma children attend primary school. However, 56 out of 139 illiterate children (40 per cent) have successfully enrolled in the school year 2000-2001. This still left approximately 35 per cent of Ashkaelia children who were not enrolled."

Consultation of community representatives in education design

Two technical consultation meetings were held by UNMIK, in September 2000 and January 2001, to follow up on the *Platform for Joint Action Regarding Kosovar Roma, Ashkalija and Egyptian*

Communities. Both meetings included consideration of education. Roma/Gypsy political leaders were able to discuss the subject with department officials of the Joint Interim Administrative Structure. Subsequently, because the DES felt it was important to focus community consultation on education at a different level, to avoid its undue politicisation, in April 2001, it organised the first of what is intended to be an ongoing series of meetings specifically with Roma/Gypsy education activists. The meeting was attended by seven or eight Roma/Gypsy activists (most of them Ashkali, with one or two Roma), three Kosovar Albanian education activists and seven "internationals" – from the DES, UNICEF and the OSCE. Thus, Roma/Gypsy representation was uneven and in the minority. There were no Egyptian representatives or Serbian-speaking Roma and all of the Roma/Gypsy activists were men. Nevertheless, a foundation for future meetings was laid, and there is scope for the DES to work proactively to expand and vary Roma/Gypsy representation at future meetings to include, for example, representatives of Roma/Gypsy women's groups and the parent committees being developed by some NGO education projects. Discussion at the April 2001 meeting focused on curriculum development. This initial dialogue was only partially successful. The meeting demonstrated tensions and misunderstandings, with some Roma/Gypsy activists suspecting that the "internationals" were seeking to impose a separate, socially isolating curriculum on their communities. There was a clearly expressed wish for a curriculum that enabled integration into Kosovan society, yet with the possibility of add-on classes for Roma children in subjects such as Romani language

and culture. Some of the Roma/Gypsy activists pointed to the education arrangements of Kosovo's autonomy era in the 1970s and 1980s as an excellent model for successful multi-ethnic education.[73]

UNICEF Pilot Schools

UNICEF has designated two pilot schools in each of the five Kosovan regions/AORs for the development of best practice to be replicated in other schools. Of the ten schools, one is Serbian and four have mixed Albanian and minority pupils. The pilots are intended as a testing ground for building an inclusive, multi-ethnic system of education with increased school-community interaction as a driving force. The schools are thus at the first stage of attempting to realise an ambitious, and still largely theoretical, vision.[74] Community outreach activity will include proactive work to bring in out-of-school children and to help children make the transition from primary to secondary school – particularly targeting girls and children from minorities, who are most prone to dropping out at this stage. Retraining of teachers will emphasise promotion of psychosocial sensitivity, enabling them to adopt alternative approaches, promoting the acceptance of diversity and the piloting of human-rights-based elements in curricula.[75]

DES School Bus Project

The DES Minority Bus Project intends to provide 20 school buses for minority communities throughout Kosovo, both Serb and non-Serb. The depletion and/or displacement of many minority communities throughout Kosovo since June 1999 has left several of them effectively cut off from education facilities, due to a combination of practical transportation difficulties and security concerns. While most of the buses scheduled for introduction in April 2001 are designated for Serb communities, two of the ten buses designated for the central Prishtina region/AOR are likely to be allocated to Roma/Gypsy communities. One will be for Roma and Ashkalija children of the Plementina IDP camp, to take them to local Serbian and Albanian schools respectively. The other will be for Ashkalija children of villages in Lipjan/Lipljan municipality, where security concerns and long travelling distances to schools have combined to severely limit Roma/Gypsy education opportunities.[76]

NGO practice in the area

In Kosovo, NGO work is not as clearly differentiated from government work as in most other European countries. In Central and Eastern Europe in particular, internationally funded NGO programmes often attempt to plug large gaps in Roma/Gypsy education provision that are the result of governments' reluctance to devote national revenue to it. In Kosovo, the work of both government and NGOs is currently funded from international donations. The question of the sustainability of individual NGO projects and/or their outputs is a constant. The acid test of financial and political sustainability will come when the DES budget makes the transition from international subventions to domestically generated revenue, and when international administrators fade into the background to be almost wholly replaced by national staff and leadership.

Various international and local NGOs are, or have been, implementing projects for Roma/Gypsy education in several locations. Typical projects include the organisation of:

- **Temporary catch-up classes**: for children whose education was disrupted by the war or earlier, as a result of social, economic and cultural factors. Catch-up classes are designed to ease children's integration into regular schools. Many Roma/Gypsy children have missed several years of schooling and are much older than other children in the grade they would be expected to join at their current literacy level. UNICEF has worked with Ashkali community representatives to organise attendance at a catch-up school it provided in Fushë Kosovë/Kosovo Polje in 2000, followed by integration of the children into local schools where IRC has been working. IRC is planning more catch-up classes in 2001. In Gjakova, two local NGOs have managed a six-month catch-up class project, which ended in May 2001, for up to 120 Egyptian children and young adults at the town's Emin Duraku Primary School.

- **New community schools**: within isolated or displaced Roma/Gypsy community enclaves, where security concerns have prevented children from attending schools outside. ICS, IRC and *Enfants du Monde* have been supporting the Jeta e Re School at the Plementina camp for Ashkali and Roma IDPs, established by the initiative of camp residents. In Gjilan/Gnjilane, a school was created within the beleaguered Roma community by the joint efforts of the community and UNMIK.

- **Preschool orientation, kindergartens, facilities for socio-educative adaptation**: to increase Roma/Gypsy children's chances of attending school and of their success once there. Examples are in Gjakova, where *Solidarites* is establishing a socio-educative centre for the children of the Egyptian shanty neighbourhood of Colonia. IRC has organised a kindergarten in Rufc i Ri/Rufcini village school in Lipjan/Lipljan municipality where one of the purposes is preschool integration of Albanian and Ashkali children.

- **Psychosocial activities**: organised leisure activity, such as arts, games, sport, artistic workshops, summer camps and expeditions are often used as a means of integrating Roma/Gypsy children with those from majority communities, through playing and creating together.

- **Vocational and apprenticeship programmes**: to increase Roma/Gypsy teenagers' and young adults' employability. In the case of computer and English-language courses, a particular aim is to increase their prospects of employment with international agencies present in Kosovo and to enable them to negotiate with those agencies. In Gjilan/Gnjilane, IRC has organised hairdressing and computer courses in a youth centre open to all communities – it is located close to the Roma neighbourhood. Currently, three Roma girls and seven Albanian girls are doing the course (three more Roma girls intend to join), and Roma boys are attending the computer course. In Fushë Kosovë/Kosovo Polje, premises owned by Ashkali community NGO leaders within the Roma/Gypsy neighbourhood are being used for internationally funded vocational courses – computers, hairdressing and dressmaking. In at least one case, vocational classes have been offered as a stopgap to children for whom no regular education is currently available. Computer classes organised by the World Assembly of Muslim Youth in Ferizaj/Urosevac have been offered to 14 non-Albanian-speaking Roma and Gorani/Bosniak 14-18 year olds, for whom no Serbian-language school is now available or accessible (they have expressed a wish to learn English too, if such classes can be organised).

- **Adult-literacy programmes**: to empower Roma/Gypsy adults, increasing their employability, parenting skills, and enabling them to provide a more supportive home environment for their children's education. A Kosovo-wide phased programme has recently started, to be implemented by 21 women's NGOs. The programme is not exclusively targeted at Roma/Gypsies, yet the inclusion of three Roma/Gypsy women's NGOs and the profile of the programme's intended beneficiaries indicate that many of them will be Roma/Gypsies.

- **Integration programmes**: either as a follow-through of catch-up class projects, to manage the integration into regular schools of Roma/Gypsy children who have been attending catch-up classes, or as stand-alone projects to integrate Roma/Gypsy children into local schools. From September 2000 the local Ashkali NGO "Future for All" and IRC worked together in Fushë Kosovë/Kosovo Polje to integrate Ashkali children who had completed the UNICEF catch-up school into the Selman Reza primary school. Seventy of the 200 children aged seven to ten years old made the transition. The two NGOs met parents every two or three days and escorted children to school in order to achieve this result. Integration projects require sustained work with both Roma/Gypsy and majority communities and a commitment to monitoring and follow-up. In 2000, a Save the Children integration project in Decani/Decan municipality illustrated the problem of attempting such a task as a short-term intervention. A mix of community work and transport provision was applied to bring Roma/Gypsy children from the village of Hereq, where there was no school, to the school in the neighbouring Kosovar-Albanian village. The project initially delivered results. However, the closure of Save the Children's branch office in Gjakova, which managed the project, meant that no monitoring took place for several months. In June 2001, it was reported that the children were no longer attending the school.

Case studies

Not by bricks and mortar alone

With funding from the Arabic Humanitarian Association, British KFOR mounted a project in late 1999/early 2000 to build a new school in the mixed Albanian-Ashkali village of Hallaq i Vogel/Mali Alas, in Lipjan/Lipljan municipality. A narrow focus on creation of the school building, a lack of understanding of the history and depth of intercommunity tensions and a failure to consult, both at community and UNMIK level, resulted in the project's failure.

During the NATO bombing campaign in 1999, Serbian paramilitaries killed 21 Kosovar-Albanian men in the village.[77] The Kosovar-Albanian population of the village was compelled to leave, returning after the arrival of international forces in summer 1999. The Serbs allowed the Ashkali population to remain. Allegedly, members of some Ashkali families had assisted the Serbian paramilitaries by identifying the Kosovar-Albanian men who were subsequently killed. After the war, tensions between the returning Albanian villagers and the 220-250 Ashkali inhabitants were extremely high. British KFOR established a permanent security presence in the village. Nevertheless, there was a wave of grenade attacks against Ashkali homes from August to October 1999, and further incidents in 2000, which resulted in the death of three Ashkalija.

Hallaq i Vogel/Mali Alas did not have its own school. Children travelled to the Migjeni Primary School in the neighbouring Kosovar-Albanian village of Rufci i Ri/Rufcini, 3km away. Without undertaking any community work or consulting any other UNMIK bodies, British KFOR began to construct a new school building next to the site of the mass grave in Hallaq i Vogel/Mali Alas.

The building was completed in early spring 2000 and the invitation of UNMIK representatives to its opening provided the latter with their first knowledge of the project's existence. At the opening ceremony, Albanian children immediately attacked Ashkali children with stones. The school was abandoned and remains locked and unused at the time of writing. Albanian children continue to travel to the school in Rufci i Ri/Rufcini, and Ashkali children stay at home.

Keeping education in communities – providing a safe education or reinforcing isolation?

Some Roma/Gypsy communities, such as the mixed communities of the IDP camps at Plementina and Leposavic, and the diminished urban Roma community of Gjilan/Gnjilane, reacted to security risks by creating schools within their own safe but narrow confines. The opening of these schools had a morale-raising impact in the communities and provided an education where none would otherwise be available. However, the continuation and consolidation of these schools poses difficult strategic questions. Should they be further developed as valuable education incubators for these communities, or does this risk ultimately cementing their social and educational isolation?

The Jeta e Re ("New Life") School was created in August 1999 from the initiative of members of an Ashkali/Roma IDP camp based in Plementina. *Conzorzio Italiano di Solidarietà* (ICS), the camp's managing NGO, and UNHCR assisted in establishing the school, and IRC has been involved in its further development, with some inputs from *Enfants du Monde*. Camp residents took on the teaching roles themselves. None of the six teachers were qualified, having had other jobs before the war. However, they were enthusiastic and dedicated. IRC secured some training for them and they are now reportedly employing methods recommended in teacher-training programmes. They teach only the lower cycle of primary education (years one to four). Because the school and its teachers are not certified as a part of Kosovo's official education system, UNMIK pays the teachers as notional support staff of a nearby village school. Until

May 2000 only one room was available, and teaching was conducted in three daily shifts. Three more classrooms have since been built. From a total camp contingent of 250-300 children aged 6-18, about 80-100 children aged 6-14 attended the school in 1999 and 2000. Most of the attending children are Ashkalija, with about 28 Roma. Many of the children had not been to school before, or had dropped out at an early stage, so the camp teachers interviewed and tested the children who wanted to attend and placed them in multi-age classes according to their academic level. Six classes were taught, five of them in Albanian, and one in Serbian for the Roma children.

The teacher-activists of Jeta e Re School are pressing for its formalisation. However, it has not proved possible to recruit qualified teachers from outside the camp to come into the school, either to teach subjects of the upper-primary cycle or to augment the teaching of the lower cycle. IRC has focused its efforts on negotiating with the directors of nearby Albanian- and Serbian-language schools to accept, respectively, Ashkali and Roma children from the camp who are ready for the upper cycle. The DES minority school bus project will be engaged, and it is hoped that 20-30 children from the camp will go to these schools from September 2001. It is reported that in 2001 attendance at the Jeta e Re School has dropped from a peak of 107 in 2000 to about 60-80 children. The IDP camp is meant to be a temporary arrangement. A mixture of returns and emigration has seen its population drop from a total of 900 in December 1999 to approximately 700-750 at the time of writing. None of the camp's residents is reported to be in employment outside the camp, and all are dependent on humanitarian food assistance, which is gradually being reduced. This is therefore not a stable population upon which to plan a formal school. Extending teaching to the upper cycle of primary education at the camp school could contribute to perpetuating the camp's isolation, and lose the opportunities for integration that could result from camp children attending local village schools with children from the surrounding community.

In Gjilan/Gnjilane the remaining Roma community, down to about 320 from its pre-war population of several thousand, lives compactly on two streets in the centre of the town, with a KFOR security checkpoint, surrounded by a mainly hostile Kosovar-Albanian population. With their freedom of movement curtailed since summer 1999, the Roma community has been physically cut off from the Serbian-language education provision. Since UNMIK took over, Serbian-language education has been re-established in a catch-up school elsewhere in the town and a school in a nearby village. In January 2000, a catch-up school was therefore established within the Roma community as a temporary measure. Under the agreement signed between UNMIK and the Roma community leader, two to three Serbian teachers would be paid by UNMIK to teach catch-up lessons, which would enable Roma children to integrate into Serbian or Albanian schools by September 2000. The school, housed in a private home in the community, was renovated and equipped with the help of international organisations and NGOs.

Subsequent developments at the temporary Roma catch-up school diverged substantially from UNMIK's intentions. Instead of integrating children into regular Serbian- or (in the case of younger children) Albanian-language schools, the Roma school grew and consolidated. Its complement of two to three UNMIK-paid teachers has been reinforced by another ten Serbian teachers, who also teach at the catch-up school in the town and are being paid by the Serbian Ministry of Education. The school provides both the lower and upper cycles of primary education. Apart from Serbian, languages taught in the upper cycle include English and Russian, but not Albanian. Attempts to find a suitably qualified teacher to teach some classes in Romanes have proved unsuccessful. Attendance at the school has been relatively low. Of roughly 100 school-age Roma children, teachers have reported 38 in regular attendance, while children themselves estimate the number to be 25. The security risk for Roma children living outside the quarter has been cited as the reason for irregular attendance. Teachers explained that KFOR stopped providing these children with escorts. KFOR responded that the escorts stopped because the children stopped going to school.

Although the availability of KFOR security escorts and an easing of the security situation offer opportunities for educational integration of the children of the Gjilan/Gnjilane Roma community (three of them do in fact attend a Serbian secondary school), the "temporary" school as it is presently structured risks solidifying the Roma community's isolation.

Catch-up classes – the Gjakova Emin Duraku School pilot project

A six-month project of primary school catch-up classes for up to 120 Roma/Gypsy children (and some adults who missed out on education) commenced at Gjakova's Emin Duraku School in autumn 2000, and finished in May 2001. It was organised and implemented jointly between three local Gjakovar NGOs, and funded through the Kosovo Foundation for an Open Society, with the encouragement of the DES.

The catch-up classes were organised for three hours per day, in the afternoons. Four grades of classes were established, each to cram in the learning equivalent of two years of primary school, from class one to eight. Demand for classes one and two was high, so two parallel classes were laid on for this level, making a total of five classes, each with a register of roughly 22-25 pupils. Usual regular attendance of 18-19 per class was reported. Upon completion of the project, pupils of the first three levels received certificates respectively attesting to their completion of the second, fourth and sixth classes of primary school, which will allow those who are still of school age to join a regular primary school from September 2001. Those in the project's most senior class group, covering years seven to eight of primary school, received primary-education completion certificates. Applications for entry into regular school are made in June for the start of the school year in September. With DES support, the managing NGO has been negotiating with the directors of Gjakova secondary schools to try also to secure

some places on an affirmative-action basis for graduates of the Emin Duraku project who have not passed the school entrance exam. The project manager has said that even if only 5 of the 20 in the project's senior class register at a secondary school, he will consider it a good result.

Two Gjakovar Kosovar-Albanian NGOs, the Forum for Democratisation (FID) and *Elita*, have had responsibility for the project's implementation and its financial management. The Albanian-Egyptian Association surveyed and mobilised Egyptian families and communities to provide lists of out-of-school children for the project, and to encourage and maintain their participation. FID has provided project management, including negotiation with the Emin Duraku School and the hiring of eight teachers. Elita has provided minibus transport for some of the children, and a school lunch every day. The project has been resource-intensive. The teachers were hired at a premium DM500-per-month wage. Additional incentives have included distributions of clothes to attending children. In setting up the project, its leaders placed little emphasis upon exploration of why so many Egyptian children have not been attending school. The project manager expresses confidence that the reasons are to be found exclusively in Roma/Gypsy cultural tradition.[78] Before embarking on this project, he visited NGOs in Bulgaria to learn from their experiences.

Beyond incentives, a monthly meeting of teachers and parents was instituted to bind communities to the project. Avdullah Qafani, who is its deputy director, a leading member of the Albanian-Egyptian Association, a co-opted vice-president of the Gjakova Municipal Assembly and a hospital doctor, also helped to sustain the project. The project's opening day featured an incident that could have damaged its viability from the outset. On seeing the Egyptian children arrive at the school, Kosovar-Albanian construction workers on a building site nearby incited some of the Albanian children to demonstrate against the Egyptian pupils. In front of the audience of officials, journalists and NGO representatives assembled for the opening, the children shouted slogans such as "Blacks, out of our school!" The then president of the Gjakova Municipal Administrative Board and prominent ex-KLA member, Mazllom Kumnova, made a helpful speech, emphasising that "We can never have freedom if we are against somebody". Avdullah Qafani went from class to class to try to reassure the pupils, telling them that what they had experienced was a normal reaction from children who had suffered in the war.[79]

FID reports that it already has some funding to replicate the project in Peja/Pec, where collaboration with the Albanian-Egyptian Association and Roma representatives has produced a list of 120 Roma/Gypsy children who could benefit from catch-up classes. Some live in outlying villages, and FID hopes that the DES minorities school bus project will provide transportation for them and an additional 20 children from Klina municipality to the planned classes. FID is also considering a more intensive version of the project for Egyptians in Gjakova who are above school age. The DES has scrutinised the Emin Duraku project as a guide for the implementation of further projects throughout Kosovo. IRC has also examined it for its replication possibilities in the IRC Program for Roma and Ashkalia Education, which is being implemented in the central Prishtina region/AOR. IRC is adopting elements of the teaching methodology, including the deployment of the Emin Duraku project teachers to help train teachers for its own programme. However, IRC is understood to have concerns about the viability of replicating project incentives such as high teacher salaries and the provision of school lunches.

Implanting education orientation into a community – the Colonia socio-educative project

In April/May 2001 the French NGO, *Solidarités*, set up a preschool/back-to-school orientation facility in the Egyptian neighbourhood of Colonia on the periphery of Gjakova, the poorest, most run-down Roma/Gypsy neighbourhood in the town. Initially accommodated in two large tents on open ground beside the neighbourhood, the facility will eventually be housed in a building to be specially constructed for it in Colonia. *Solidarités* has hired a multi-ethnic team consisting of a Kosovar-Albanian full-time educator and three part-time faciliators (one Albanian, two Egyptians) to conduct the orientation activities. Children will be organised into different morning and afternoon groups, one for those aged three to seven years, the other for those aged 7-14 years. (At the time of writing, while the project is housed in tents, only morning activities are undertaken, since it is too hot under the tents in the afternoons.) Different programmes of organised play, drawing, singing, reading and writing classes, are organised for the two groups.

It is hoped that the presence of the facility in the neighbourhood will establish and build a school/educational culture within the community. While children's readiness to accept and adopt that culture is readily apparent, the facility also has an important role to play in nurturing its acceptance by all parents. The project's educators and animators act as advocates for children's educational rights on two fronts – with their parents and with their teachers. One of the animators interviewed for this report had immediate plans to intercede personally with the director of Emin Duraku School to allow a boy from Colonia back into regular classes – his teacher had refused to allow him back after his parents had withdrawn him for a week to do some labouring work. Sustained functioning of the facility holds out a prospect of gradually changing the social climate in Colonia until it becomes socially unacceptable for parents not to send their children regularly to school. The question of sustainability continues to exercise *Solidarités*. They are attempting to establish the facility in a way which will lend itself to a hand-over in future to the municipal education authorities.[80]

Seeking integration – Enfants du Monde's programme for displaced children in Leposavic
Since January 2000, the NGO *Enfants du Monde – Droits de l'Homme* has been working on the provision of education to both Roma/Gypsy and Serbian children living in the nine collective centres and one camp that accommodate 700 IDPs in Leposavic, a Serbian-dominated municipality in northern Kosovo. The camp, located in a warehouse and managed by Caritas Belgium, houses 180 Roma/Gypsies. Most are Roma displaced from southern Mitrovica. There

are also some Egyptians and Ashkali from other areas of Kosovo. They do not face particular security problems, being generally accepted by the local Serb population.

When *Enfants du Monde* began its work, none of the children in the Roma camp were attending school. The NGO's goal has been to get as many as possible of them integrated into regular schools. Moreover, it has provided a supporting framework for Roma/Gypsy children's education to compensate for their poor living conditions. Given a general lack of parental engagement, *Enfants du Monde* has been trying to improve the prospects of children attending school beyond the life of the programme by attempting to stimulate and nurture parents' sense of responsibility for supporting children's education.

As a first step, the NGO assessed the children's educational level. They were allocated into groups according to their age and attainment, and catch-up classes were instituted. Those who were too old to be enrolled in regular schools and had not attended school before were taught basic literacy, while school-age children were prepared for integration into regular schools from September 2000. As most of the children were more accustomed to speaking Albanian than Serbian, one of the main tasks was to improve their grasp of Serbian language.

By September 2000 it had still not been possible for *Enfants du Monde* to gain the agreement of the director of the primary school in Leposavic to admit the Roma children. He was dubious about their grasp of Serbian and not particularly sympathetic to their needs. A solution was found by transporting 20 children who were ready for regular school, ranging from grades one to eight, to the Branko Radicevic Primary School in northern Mitrovica, where the director was welcoming. Transport has been provided every day by Caritas Belgium, and attendance is generally good. *Enfants du Monde* has continued to run catch-up classes at the camp for 36 other children aged from 7 to 16 years old. The NGO has tested the children every term to measure their progress, and presently estimates that a further 20 of these children will be ready to attend school in the following school year. Continued effort by *Enfants du Monde* in developing a dialogue with the director of the Leposavic Primary School has resulted in his agreement to admit Roma IDP children from September 2001. Thus 17 of the 20 currently being bussed to Mitrovica will transfer to the Leposavic Primary School, where they will be joined by a new group of children from the catch-up classes. Three children currently in the eighth grade in the Branko Radicevic Primary School will enrol in secondary schools in Leposavic or Mitrovica. However, there is likely to be no provision at all for 16 children who are either too old for primary-school enrolment or whose educational attainment is too low.

Enfants du Monde provides a range of support to the children's education and development that is missing from their home and social environment. The NGO offers homework-support sessions to all school-going children, whether studying in the catch-up classes or regular school, in the mornings and afternoons. It has taken over the running of the camp kindergarten from ICS, and in September 2000 transferred it from tents inside the camp to larger premises with better facilities next to the camp. About 25 children attend, aged from three to six years old. A range of activities is organised for the three to five year olds in monthly project cycles – games, arts, stories and shows. Children of six years old undergo preparation for primary school in a separate classroom. They are taught Latin and Cyrillic letters, numbers and Serbian language, enlivened by poems, songs and play. *Enfants du Monde* also uses the kindergarten facilities to teach children about cleanliness and personal presentation to reduce their chances of being taunted by other pupils. The NGO sees these classes as vital in assisting Roma/Gypsy children's integration into mainstream education, as local Serbs often cite poor personal hygiene as a ground for discrimination against Roma/Gypsies. According to Roma/Gypsy parents, poor sanitary facilities at the camp make it difficult for them to maintain their children's personal hygiene. Children's enthusiasm for the kindergarten is manifest, yet the *Enfants du Monde* programme manager has commented:

> "As with school, the lack of interest of the parents is blatant. Indeed, they do not care that much about the implemented activities and if the animators do not go into the camp to take the children, the parents will not take the initiative to bring them to the kindergarten."

For psychosocial stimulation of the children, and to aid their cultural and social integration with the surrounding Serb population, *Enfants du Monde* organises a range of activities. These include daily workshops in premises it has rented next to the camp, open to camp children and local

Serb children alike, in theatre, plastic arts and photography. Children themselves choose which workshops to participate in and must commit themselves to attending on a regular basis. There has been a good level of participation in the workshops by local Serb children, and of socialisation between the Roma and Serb children. Nevertheless, Serb children recently refused to participate any more if Roma children were there. This appears to have been prompted by Serb parents. In March 2001, *Enfants du Monde* invited a French stilt-walking troupe to perform in the Roma IDP camp and local schools. They held workshops for Roma and local and IDP Serb children in stilt-walking, as a result of which the children worked together on a show, which they performed in Leposavic's Primary School and cultural centre, and then on the streets of the town.

Although both regular schools and *Enfants du Monde*'s catch-up classes break for the summer in June, the NGO plans to continue study-support activity over the summer, particularly targeted on the children earmarked for enrolment in primary school from September 2001. With the prospect of the programme being wound up by late summer 2001, its manager has commented on this and the general prospects of the sustainability of the Roma children's education:

"Thus, September will be a deciding period and will tell if we reached our objective regarding schooling. This success not only depends on the children and their capacity of learning, but mainly on the involvement of the adults. Indeed, the parents from the Roma community do not care a lot about the scholarship of their children and are not a strong support in this process. Most of the parents are illiterate, have never been to school and often do not understand why it is important for their children to go to school and that it could be a way to grant them a better future. We have been trying for several months to make the parents feel more responsible for the education of their children, through regular meetings and the appointment of delegates for the class meetings, but this is a long and hard road. Moreover, if the director of the school of Mitrovica was understanding towards absences of the children and the lack of involvement of parents, it will not be the same with the director of the school of Leposavic, who is more rigid and less understanding towards the Roma issue."

Enfants du Monde also has concerns for the future sustainability and profile of the kindergarten it has established next to the Roma camp. The NGO does not want kindergarten provision for the Roma children to end when it has to pull out from late summer 2001, nor does it want the kindergarten to have a future as a socially isolating parallel structure for Roma children only. The regular kindergarten of Leposavic has limited space and its director is reluctant to admit Roma children, knowing that the parents of Serbian children would be likely to protest or withdraw their children. The best compromise *Enfants du Monde* is currently hoping for is for the Roma kindergarten to be adopted as a branch of the regular kindergarten of Leposavic, with frequent exchanges and joint activities between the two.[81]

Intensive community work for educational integration – the IRC programme

The International Rescue Committee's approach to Roma/Gypsy education projects emphasises community capacity-building, promoting intercommunity dialogue and educational integration of Roma/Gypsy children with the majority community. It is an approach with a long-term perspective, requiring intensive and sustained input from IRC staff, without the use of incentives and inputs that could produce immediate results, but which would be unlikely to be sustained beyond the short term. IRC is implementing its Program for Roma and Ashkalia Education in several locations in the central Prishtina region/AOR: Fushë Kosovë/Kosovo Polje, villages of Lipjan/Lipljan municipality, Plementina IDP camp and its surroundings in Obilic municipality, and also in Gnjilane/Gjilan.

The IRC programme manager commented: "If you do the community work at the outset, it has knock-on benefits for the whole programme later." IRC attempted to pick up the pieces in Hallaq i Vogel/Mali Alas after the failed school-opening described above. Forty Ashkali children of school age were not attending school, while the village's Albanian children continued to travel to the Migjeni primary school in neighbouring Rufci i Ri/Rufcini. IRC and UNICEF visited in April 2000 and consulted with teachers, parents and Albanian and Ashkali community leaders to seek out ways of reintegrating the Ashkali children into education. But neither community was ready for this. Four months later IRC returned, having been informed by UNMIK that some tentative intercommunity communication had restarted in the village. IRC embarked on an intensive process of community work – supporting parents' groups in both communities, initially organising separate meetings for them with teachers, and then eventually bringing the groups together, persuading them to find common ground at least in the sphere of the education of their children. IRC carried out educational assessments of the Ashkali children and, using teachers from the UNICEF catch-up school in Fushë Kosovë/Kosovo Polje as trainers, gave teachers of the Migjeni School orientation in the programme's teaching approaches and their own experiences. IRC worked together with the director and staff of Migjeni School to plan the integration of Ashkali children.

IRC distributed clothes and shoes to the Ashkali children and UNMIK co-ordinated a KFOR security escort for the 3km walk to the school. The Ashkali parents' group nominated one of their members to accompany the children with KFOR. However, on the first day of the planned integration in October 2000, a grenade attack was launched on an Ashkali household. Ashkali parents reacted by refusing to send their children to school. Nevertheless, at the time of writing the younger children, studying at class one level, have been largely able to integrate into the school. However, there has been resistance from their Albanian peers to the idea of accepting older Ashkali children, and they do not attend.

Many of the Ashkali parents have had no education and some appear to seek out reasons to avoid sending their children to school. To keep the grade one pupils attending school has required sustained, intensive efforts from IRC, working with a core group of parents of both

communities and arranging and managing a large number of community meetings. IRC has also held regular meetings with a teachers' council at the school, discussing integration issues and monitoring security – which could include threats and fights between children of the different communities. Building this capacity will enable the school staff to take over responsibility for calling joint Ashkali-Albanian parent meetings, approaching UNMIK police and KFOR for security support, and contacting DES staff when they perceive action to be needed on the part of policy-makers to support and promote progress. IRC is seeking to increase the numbers of Ashkali parents willing to escort their children to and from school, to build routines which can be continued when the KFOR security escorts

can be dispensed with – routines which will themselves contribute to the creation of a climate that will allow the downgrading of the security measures.

In addition to supporting Roma/Gypsy children's integration into existing educational institutions, the IRC programme has created additional institutions for preschool and vocational education, which contribute to the social integration of Roma/Gypsy and majority-community children. IRC supported the establishment of a kindergarten at Migjeni School in order to integrate Ashkali and Albanian children from the age of five, and give them an educational head start. The NGO has established youth centres in some of the programme's locations, sited where youth of both Roma/ Gypsy and majority communities can use them. Organised youth groups, from the ages of 15 to 24, are used as a focus for raising awareness of education and the delivery of apprenticeship and vocational courses.

In Hallaq i Vogel/Mali Alas, a room in a disused private house has been renovated for use as a youth centre. Its owner has made it available rent-free for the next ten years. IRC has declined to pay rent for and equip existing youth centres, as it is determined that the facilities it establishes are seen as being "of" the community rather than "provided" by IRC. It has also avoided perpetuating Roma/Gypsy communities' social isolation by locating youth centres where they are accessible only to Roma/Gypsy youth. IRC declined offers to establish facilities in premises belonging to the families of Roma/ Gypsy community leaders, fearing that this could make relationships difficult in the longer term. IRC's emphasis on building a broad base of community support and involvement in education through the creation and sustenance of parents' groups has clashed on occasion with the desire of some individuals to have status by being the sole interlocutors in dialogue with "internationals". The formation of parents' groups to support education integration proved difficult in neighbourhoods where two or more community leaders have established separate community initiatives and are competing for funding and loyalties. On occasion, IRC has had to deal with this by bypassing leaders and establishing dialogue directly with families, slowly and laboriously establishing a group of parents' representatives.[82]

Voices of Roma/Gypsy children

Ashkali, Egyptian and Roma children were interviewed for this report in different settings, including conversations in their homes, an impromptu meeting in an urban Ashkali/Roma neighbourhood, and in the context of organised education activities – Egyptian and Ashkali pupils who were attending preschool classes arranged respectively in a peri-urban and a village community, and Egyptian children attending catch-up classes in an urban school. Children's voices reported by other sources have also been included.

A high proportion of the children interviewed expressed considerable enthusiasm about the idea of receiving education. Yet their accounts reveal how so many factors beyond their control make their attendance at school fragile and conditional, causing so many to drop out at an early stage, and to be adrift from their peers in the majority community by many years. Pressures from parents were cited – to work or to look after younger children. A particular factor that emerged, blighting Roma/Gypsy children's experience of education, was their experience of suffering humiliations at school, due to their poverty, difficulties in turning themselves out smartly, and bullying or intolerant behaviour by children of the majority community, or by teachers.

Lots of the children interviewed exhibited an air of fatalism about their future and were vague about what they would do in their adult life. Many of those who did express a career aspiration appeared to lack any kind of plan of how they would achieve it. Quite a few expressed interest in becoming doctors or teachers, yet this will be an uphill task for children who have already missed several years of education. The social isolation of Roma/Gypsy communities and a paucity of role models within them limited the range of careers to which the children aspire.

Some children said they were hungry most of the time. The majority of the children interviewed were short for their ages, indicating long-term undernourishment.

L, Roma boy, 13 years old, has become fluent in Italian by fraternising with Italian KFOR troops. Attending the first/second class in the Emin Duraku School catch-up class project in Gjakova, he was interviewed by Avdullah Qafani around February/March 2001

"The day when I started going to school again I was the happiest child in the world. After we were expelled from my village, Zatriq, after the war and came to the Colonia settlement in Gjakova I was feeling very bad. I knew that other children were going to school. They were learning and playing. My only joy was my friendship with the Italian soldiers. Next year I will go to a regular school. I want to become a pilot."

Interviewed for this report in May 2001
"Before I went to school in Vranice village. I completed two classes there. I used to want to be a pilot, but I've changed my mind. Now I want to be a teacher."
Question: "Why no longer a pilot?"
Answer: "Because I can't fly a plane."
Q: "But you know how to teach?"
A: "No, but I can learn."

Q: "And you can't learn to fly?"
A: "It's better to be a teacher."

B, Roma boy, nine years old, completed the first class in a Serbian school in Ferizaj/Urosevac, but with its disappearance has been unable to continue his education for the last two years, spoke haltingly in Albanian, a language in which he is not fluent

"I enjoyed school. I liked maths. I am not going any more. I've just been playing for the last two years. When I grow up I want to work in a factory."
Q: "If you had a choice, which language would you like to study in – Romanes, Serbian, Albanian?"
A: (with trepidation and hesitation) "Serbian. I'll go to any school, even if it's in Albanian."

H, Roma girl, 12 years old, in the sixth class of primary school, Prizren, interviewed by Avdullah Qafani, around February 2001

"I am one of the best pupils in my class. I am now doing an English course. I can't do the computer course though, because my father doesn't have money for both. I hope to be a nurse. Later, if we can afford it, why not even a doctor? I don't have the complex that I am worth less than the others."

Four Roma and Ashkali children interviewed at Plementina IDP camp by IRC 83

"I don't want to go to school with Albanian or Serbian children because the teacher will put me at the back of the class."

"We lived with Albanians, played with them, and they were our friends. But they told us to leave because we were Gypsies."

"They burned our houses. I don't want to learn with them."

"We've heard that there might be Albanians coming to teach, but I don't agree. I'll throw my bag away and never come back to school."

D, Ashkali boy, 12 years old, in preschool orientation classes in Dubrava village, near Ferizaj/Urosevac, preparing to try again attending the primary school in a neighbouring Albanian village. Albanian children reportedly took against D because of his poor clothes. His family is particularly poor. He is one of six children, whose father will not send them all to school

"I never went to school before. I was scared. I tried once, two years ago. But it lasted two weeks. When I walked to school and back the Albanian kids attacked us – all of us. I'll start school again now, and I'll take it to the end. I want to be a doctor."

Q, Ashkali boy, 13 years old, Dubrava village

"Of course I have Albanian friends. Lots of them. I visit their homes and they come to see me too. I've been at Zaskok School for six years. I'll finish in two years time. I've kept going to school all the time, except during the war. We hid at home. We wanted to go abroad, but it was impossible. Maths is my favourite subject. I am excellent at it. My family didn't have money to buy the books I need, but the school gave them. I want to go to high school in Saudi Arabia and be a doctor there."

A and D, two deaf Ashkali boys, 13 and 3 years old, with their mother, southern Kosovo

Mother: "A has never been to school. When he was seven I sent him to a school for deaf children in Prizren, but he came back after a month. I can't send him there now. I know that we are poor, but at least we could have education. My husband is sick and paralysed. He gets DM120 government assistance per month. We have five children. The money is not enough."

A: (in sign language interpreted by his mother) "I want to finish school and work. I want to be someone."

D: (with gestures, to his elder brother) "Go and wash your face first."

N, Ashkali girl, 16 years old, Ferizaj/Urosevac (with her elder brother)

N: "I started school when I was nine, but I left after three months because my brothers were jealous and the teacher was bad and used to beat us."

Brother: "Tell the truth. You didn't have exercise books or shoes."

N: "I'd love to go to school now. If there was an intensive school to learn Albanian and other things. I can't go back with the little kids now. I want to be an interpreter. If people here offer us a course I am willing to learn English." (To the translator indicating the author) "Tell him to find us shoes."

L and B, Ashkali sisters, 14 and 10 years old, Ferizaj/Urosevac. L was "married" at the age of 12 and now has a 7-month-old baby.

L: "I never went to school. We have a tradition that if we get married we don't go to school any more."

B: "I just started the 1st class in primary school. I'm enjoying it. I like Albanian literature the most. I want to be a teacher, to teach the others. But we always feel hungry – all the time. Including in school."

H, Ashkali girl, 11 years old, Ferizaj/Urosevac. She and her 12-year-old brother stand out in their local Ashkali community as the only children of their age to have kept going to school from the age of 7

"I'm in the fourth class now. I can read and write. My brother is very good and we go to school together. I want to carry on with school. After I finish university I'll learn English and use it to translate and help others. I won't get married before then."

B, Ashkali young man, 19 years old, Ferizaj/Urosevac

"I started school when I was eight and went for two years. I stopped because I didn't have any of the things I needed. No books, clothes, shoes. My father was not working. But I'm studying karate now. If I have a chance to finish my education I'd like to be a karate champion. If I had money I'd study karate abroad. Money is stopping us from going to school."

M, Egyptian boy, seven years old, in first class of a regular primary school, Gjakova

"At school when Albanian boys argue with each other they fight one to one. But if one of us Egyptians gets in a fight with an Albanian boy, all the other Albanians gang up on you. They surround you in a circle and beat you."

P, Egyptian girl, 13 years old, Colonia neighbourhood, Gjakova, attending both the Solidarités preschool centre and the second class in the Emin Duraku School catch-up class project

"I'll go to a regular school after this, then maybe secondary school. Emin Duraku School is a good place. The teacher is nice. I like mathematics. My parents didn't have money to buy all the things I need for school, but they've got some money now – my two brothers are working in Qabrati." (She shrugged when asked what she thought she would do when she grows up.)

E, Egyptian boy, 14 years old, Colonia neighbourhood, Gjakova, attending the Solidarités preschool centre

"I was in regular school. I was in the first class in the Emin Duraku School. I was one of the best in my classroom. I sat in the first row and I had Albanian friends. I had good relations with all my class. But I stopped a month ago. I worked one week for money and the teachers told me I couldn't come back. But the school director said I do have the right to come back. I was loading and unloading cement. My family needed the money."

"At school I like mathematics and reading and writing. I'd like to learn the computer, and to work as a surveyor. I want that job because I'll learn everything and be smarter and happier. It's very hard for me to study. It's difficult at home. Only my father works and all he gets is DM100 per month."

R, Egyptian girl, 11 years old, in first/second class of the Emin Duraku School catch-up class project in Gjakova

"I used to go to Mustafa Bakija School [a Gjakova primary school]. I finished the third class there. I went back there for one week after the war, but I couldn't continue because of the name-calling. All the other children called me a *maxhup* and I couldn't take that. They didn't do it before the war. I'll go back to a regular school after this."

Question: "Which one?"

A: (Hesitation)

Q: " Mustafa Bakija?"

A: "Oh well, I suppose so. Let it be Mustafa Bakija."

Q: "What do you want to do when you grow up?"

A: "I want to do dressmaking."

Q: (from teacher) "You wanted to be a doctor. Why did you change your mind?"

A: "Oh well, let it be a doctor then."

Q: "Where do you want to live when you grow up?"

A: "Germany. It's a better life in Germany than here."

S, Egyptian boy, 14 years old, in first/second class of the Emin Duraku School catch-up class project in Gjakova

"I'm worried that I'm too old for regular school now. I got to the third class before, but I didn't finish it. I was in Germany and I went to school there, but we were sent back to Kosovo, and I couldn't go back to a regular school here. I want to go to Germany and live there forever. To Munster."

V, Egyptian girl, 15 years old, in first/second class of the Emin Duraku School catch-up class project in Gjakova

"I'd like to continue school, but I know it's impossible because I'm too old. I went to [a] primary school in Piskota village. I had lots of friends there and I went for four years. I stopped because we couldn't afford the books. That was the only reason. I made the decision – it was five years ago. My mother found a job after that. I wanted to go back to school, but I was too old by then. I'd like to continue in a secondary school, but I don't know how. I enjoy hairdressing – I cut my friends' hair."

R and E, Egyptian sisters, 16 and 14 years old, from Colonia settlement, in fifth/sixth class of the Emin Duraku School catch-up class project in Gjakova

"Until the war our neighbours were Serbs and with their dogs they made it uncomfortable for us to go to school. They called us *Tsigani*."

F, Egyptian young man, 18 years old, in fifth/sixth class of the Emin Duraku School catch-up class project in Gjakova

"I decided to come here to finish primary school and find a good job as a car mechanic. I hope to continue in a vocational school."

P and S, Egyptian young women, 21 years old, from a village near Gjakova, in fifth/sixth class of the Emin Duraku School catch-up class project in Gjakova

S: "I had a younger brother and both my parents were working, so there was no-one to take care of him. I didn't go to school regularly so I stopped altogether."

P: "I had the same problem. I had to look after my younger sister. I completed six classes back then and I left six years ago. I hope this project will be prolonged."

S: "I regret that I can't go to a regular school now. I wish we could have an opportunity to go to a secondary school, and then get good jobs."

P., Egyptian young man, 25 years old, in seventh/eighth class of the Emin Duraku School catch-up class project in Gjakova

"I am working in the municipal cleaning company Qabrati. If it's possible it would be a good idea to find another job – I only get DM150 per month. The certificate from here will help. I'd like to be a driver."

Recommendations

Provision 3.2 of the Constitutional Framework for Provisional Self-Government in Kosovo, promulgated on 15 May 2001, stipulates that the Provisional Institutions of Self-Government shall observe and ensure internationally recognised human rights and fundamental freedoms, including the rights and freedoms set forth in:
- the Universal Declaration of Human Rights
- the European Convention for the Protection of Human Rights and Fundamental Freedoms and the Protocols thereto
- the International Covenant on Civil and Political Rights and the Protocols thereto
- the International Covenant on Economic, Social and Cultural Rights
- the Convention on the Elimination of All Forms of Racial Discrimination
- the Convention on the Elimination of All Forms of Discrimination Against Women

- the Convention Against Torture and Other Cruel, Inhumane or Degrading Treatment or Punishment
- the International Convention on the Rights of the Child
- the European Charter for Regional or Minority Languages
- the Council of Europe's Framework Convention for the Protection of National Minorities.

The Secretary General of the United Nations has highlighted the responsibility of UNMIK to place human rights at the core of its mission and its special responsibility to uphold the human-rights standards that it has created.

Given that Provision 3.2 states that: "The provisions on rights and freedoms set forth in these instruments shall be directly applicable in Kosovo as part of this Constitutional Framework"[84]

Save the Children recommends that:

The United Nations Interim Administration Mission in Kosovo (UNMIK)
- Intensifies efforts to promote and support the implementation of the objectives set out in the "Platform for Joint Action Regarding Kosovar Roma, Ashkalija and Egyptian Communities" and ensures that these efforts are maintained and supported by the Provisional Institutions of Self-Government, including the new Assembly and Government due to be elected in November 2001.

- Implements the commitments it has itself entered into under the Joint Platform guaranteeing Roma/Gypsies' access to education, social welfare and assistance, and employment.
- Commissions participatory surveys in Roma/Gypsy communities on the impact of poverty, poor health and nutritional status and other socio-economic barriers to Roma/Gypsy access to education, in order to provide an informed basis for actions which will address these.

The UNMIK Department of Education and Science (DES)

- Prioritises, without further delay, the development of its policy on Non-Serb Minorities (Roma/Gypsies and others) and measures for its implementation including costings, schedules and the identification of designated personnel responsible for implementation.
- Consolidates and expands consultation on education with Roma/Gypsy representatives, ensuring that all communities are represented and that plural voices from within communities are heard, including those of women, parents and children.
- Establishes adult education and training institutions accessible to Roma/Gypsy communities in which both adult-literacy courses and the skills training are available, thus providing a bridge into education, the Kosovan economy and wider society for motivated Roma/Gypsy adults.

- Institutes measures to bring about a classroom culture that is supportive to Roma/Gypsy children, including training for teachers, school directors and municipal education administrators in human rights, and sensitisation to Roma/Gypsy culture. Efforts should be made to train and employ more teachers of Roma/Gypsy ethnicity.
- In furtherance of the above, considers the introduction into schools of Roma/Gypsy teacher assistants or animators.
- Ensures that resources are available to allow for the teaching of Romani culture, history and language, where communities and parents have requested it, and for the provision of teaching assistants, animators, or catch-up classes as necessary.
- Provides incentives and additional resources for Roma/Gypsies wishing to enter further or higher education and gives consideration to affirmative-action measures to increase the numbers of Roma/Gypsies represented in further and higher education.
- Ensures the restructuring of Kosovo's education system in a way that affords the greatest prestige to schools and other education institutions which feature and promote an intake of mixed ethnicity, have a multicultural ethic, and where teaching is conducted in the different languages of Kosovo *and* international languages.

The international organisations, including
the UN Commission on Human Rights, the
Special Rapporteur on the Right to Education
and the Special Rapporteur on Contemporary
Forms of Racism, Racial Discrimination,
Xenophobia and Related Intolerance, and the
European Union
• Closely monitor developments in Kosovo with
  respect to the right to education of Roma/
  Gypsy children.

Kosovo: notes on the text

1 It should be noted that continuing instability in Kosovo has
impacted upon the gathering of information for this report.
Security considerations made it difficult to conduct research in the
Serbian-dominated municipalities of the north and also resulted
in more first-hand research being conducted among the Ashkali
and Egyptians, to the disadvantage of the Roma.

2 In Kosovo only one of the three Gypsy communities self-
identifies as "Roma" or "Romani", and the other two (Ashkali and
Egyptians) reject such description of themselves. In this report we
will use the term "Roma/Gypsies" to refer to the three
communities collectively, the term "Roma" to refer to the Roma
alone, and the term "Gypsies" to refer to the Ashkali and
Egyptians collectively.

3 Conversation of Dr Islami with his University of Prishtina
colleague Dukagjin Pupovci, Director of the Kosovo Education
Centre, 2001, reported to the author. Dr Islami's booklet
Demographic Reality in Kosova was published by the Kosovo
Information Centre in 1994. His more detailed study *Evolucioni dhe
Transicioni Demografik* was published in Albanian by Dukagjini press,
Peja/Pec, 1999.

4 Tatjana Peric, "Kosovo Roma today: violence, insecurity,
enclaves and displacement" in *Roma Rights* No. 1, 2000,
http://errc.org/rr_nr1_2000/kosovo.shtml

5 The anti-Roma/Gypsy "pogroms" of summer and autumn 1999
have been documented by several organisations and individuals.
The ERRC has compiled its writings on the situation of Roma/
Gypsies in Kosovo into a publication entitled *Roma in the Kosovo
Crisis*, available online at http://errc.org/publications/indices/
kosovo.shtml. Human Rights Watch published a report in August
1999, documenting *Abuses against Serbs and Roma in the New Kosovo*,
available at www.hrw.org/hrw/reports/1999/kosov2/. Nicolaus v.
Holtey, *Zwei Reisen zur Erkundung der Lage der Ashkali und Roma im
Kosovo*, 22 February 2000, available online at: www.bndlg.de/
~wplarre/na000302.htm, details the attacks in the form of a
diary – in German.

6 See the OSCE report: *Kosovo/Kosova As Seen, As Told, Part IV: The Impact of the Conflict on Communities and Groups in Kosovo Society: Kosovo "Gypsies" (Maxhupet) – Roma*, available online at www.osce.org/kosovo/reports/hr/part1/ch20.htm, and Paul Polansky, *The Gypsies of Kosova: A Survey of their Communities after the War*, available online at www.decani.yunet.com/gypsies.html

7 Z Andjelkovic, S Scepanovic and G Prlincevic *Days of Terror (in the Presence of the Internal Forces)*, Centre for Peace and Tolerance, Belgrade, 2000.

8 Mefail Mustafa, Ashkali education activist, Fushë Kosovë/ Kosovo Polje, interviewed by the author May 2001.

9 *Identity formation among minorities in the Balkans: The cases of Roma, Egyptians and Ashkali in Kosovo*, Minority Studies Society Studii Romani, Sofia, 2001, p. 33.

10 For example, some believe that many were inclined to over-estimate the numbers of Roma who were generally aligned on the Serb side of the Albanian-Serb conflict in the 1990s, such as in the case of Z Andjelkovic, S Scepanovic and G Prlincevic *Days of Terror (in the Presence of the Internal Forces)*, Centre for Peace and Tolerance, Belgrade, 2000. The authors in this case are closely linked to the former FRY/Serbian authorities in Kosovo.

11 Ana Simic, *Assistance Programme to the Displaced Children of Leposavic and Plementina*, report from *Enfants du Monde*.

12 Paul Polansky, *The Gypsies of Kosova: A survey of their communities after the war*, 31 October 1999, available online at www.decani.yunet.com/gypsies.html

13 The full text of the resolution can be accessed at www.un.org/Docs/scres/1999/99sc1244.htm

14 During the period of its political autonomy within Socialist Yugoslavia, Kosovo did have a Constitution of its own.

15 This was born out of the failure to reach a negotiated formula that satisfied all the four Kosovan members of the Interim Administration Council – a consultative body representing Kosovo's main political factors: three Albanian parties and a Serb representative.

16 This period, in summer, autumn and winter 1999, when UNMIK had not fully established its control on the ground and municipal administrations were run by the KLA, is documented in the International Crisis Group's Balkans report No. 79 of 18 October 1999: *Waiting for UNMIK: Local Administration in Kosovo*, available online at www.crisisweb.org.

17 Gary Matthews, Principal Deputy SRSG, UNMIK press conference, 21 May 2001.

18 British KFOR was allocated the central AOR, based on Prishtina; US KFOR – the south-east, based on Gjilan/Gnjilane; German KFOR – the south-west, based on Prizren; Italian KFOR – the west, based on Peja/Pec; and French KFOR – the north, where the now-divided city of Mitrovica is the largest population centre.

19 Nicolaus v. Holtey, *Zwei Reisen zur Erkundung der Lage der Ashkali und Roma im Kosovo*, 22 February 2000, available online at: www.bndlg.de/~wplarre/na000302.htm, page 18 – abduction on 13 October 1999 of Xhemajl Qizmolli, an Ashkali man from Vushtri/Vucitrn who has reportedly not been seen again; Emily Shaw: "Unprotected: attacks continue against Kosovo's Romani minorities", in *Roma Rights*, Newsletter of the European Roma Rights Centre, No. 3, 2000, p. 66-67 – alleged beatings of Ashkali by KPC in Mitrovica in summer 1999 and September 2000.

20 All the UNMIK regulations are available online at www.un.org/peace/kosovo/pages/regulations/

21 Described and analysed in some detail in the UNHCR/OSCE *7th Joint Assessment of the Situation of Ethnic Minorities in Kosovo (period covering October 2000 to February 2001)*, pp. 23-24. Available online, together with previous such reports, at: www.osce.org/kosovo/publications

22 Ibid, p. 22.

23 Section 9.1.3 of the Constitutional Framework.

24 Respectively 9.1.7.(e) and 9.3.5.(a) & (b) of the Framework.

25 "His" as given in the Framework. For all the attention given to mechanisms for ensuring representation of ethnic minority communities, the Framework is notably gender-blind – making no provisions to promote the participation of women, and using the male personal pronoun throughout.

26 Provisions 9.1.12-17 of the Framework.

27 Provision 10.3.

28 Jim Adams, Gjakova LCO, author's telephone interview, May 2001.

29 UNHCR/OSCE *7th Joint Assessment of the Situation of Ethnic Minorities in Kosovo (period covering October 2000 through February 2001)*, p. 24.

30 UNHCR/OSCE *6th Joint Assessment of the Situation of Ethnic Minorities in Kosovo (period covering June through September 2000)*, p. 17.

31 Hivzi Islami, *Demographic Reality in Kosova*, p. 48.

32 A Pipa, "The other Albania: A Balkan perspective", in A Pipa and S Repishti (eds), *Studies on Kosova*, Columbia University Press, New York, 1984. p. 250.

33 See Howard Clark, *Civil Resistance in Kosovo*, Pluto Press, London, 2000, for a fuller description of the Serbian authorities' measures and the Kosovar Albanians' response to them.

34 Ibid.

35 UNICEF – *Education Situation Report No. 1: Bringing Children Back to School in Kosovo*, Prishtina, 27 July 1999.

36 World Bank, "Education" chapter in *Kosovo, Federal Republic of Yugoslavia: Economic and Social Reforms for Peace and Reconciliation*, 1 February 2001, p. 109. Available online at: http://www.seerecon.org/Kosovo/KosovoDonorPrograms/WBEconReport/wb-kosovo-econreport.htm

37 Ibid, p. 109.

38 Clark (see note 33), p. 100.

39 Dukagjin Pupovci, Director of the Kosovo Education Centre, author's interview, May 2001.

40 World Bank, "Education" (see note 36), p. 116.

41 Clark (see note 33), p. 104.

42 John Holmes, DES legal officer, author's interview by telephone, April 2001.

43 Michael Daxner (international co-head of the UNMIK Department of Education and Science), discussion paper, unpublished, circulated by email in January 2001, p. 7.

44 UNMIK Press Release 528, Department of Education & Science, to advance decentralisation with introduction of education administration on municipal level, 9 March 2001.

45 World Bank, "Education" (see note 36), p. 113.

46 World Bank, "Education" (see note 36), p. 117-118.

47 Zef Osmani, Director of Gjakova Municipal Education Directorate, author's interview, April 2001.

48 World Bank, "Education" (see note 36), p. 121.

49 Daxner (see note 43), p. 13.

50 Prachi Srivastava, UNMIK regional education officer (Prishtina – central region/AOR), author's interview, May 2001.

51 UNHCR/OSCE *6th Joint Assessment of the Situation of Ethnic Minorities in Kosovo (period covering June through September 2000)*, p. 45.

52 Kosovo Education Centre, *Education in Kosova: Figures and Facts*, Prishtina, November 2000.

53 Author's field research, Ferizaj/Urosevac, April 2001.

54 In Gjakova an enthusiastic 14-year-old Egyptian pupil was refused readmittance to a primary school in May 2001 after his parents removed him for a week to do some paid labouring work – author's field research. In Ferizaj/Urosevac, an Ashkali parent described how one of his two children was told by the teacher to leave after he could only muster enough money for one child's contribution to a DM18-per-pupil levy charged by the school to finance a new winter-heating system. Both these individual cases were resolved after NGO or parental lobbying of the respective schools' directors, yet they illustrate a tendency which has probably resulted in many Roma/Gypsy pupils dropping out.

55 Michael Daxner has suggested using the new ninth grade as an intermediary phase to aid orientation in children's transition either to general or vocational high schools or to employment. Daxner (see note 43), p. 3-4

56 Kosovo Education Centre (see note 52), p. 16-17.

57 Kosovo Education Centre (see note 52), p. 26. The Kosovo Education Centre's data on Serbian schools are less precise than its data on education in the Albanian-dominated areas.

58 World Bank, "Education" (see note 36), p. 116.

59 Kosovo Education Centre (see note 52), p. 26.

60 World Bank, "Education" (see note 36), p. 116.

61 Kosovo Education Centre (see note 52), p. 16.

62 Dukagjin Pupovci, Director of the Kosovo Education Centre, author's interview, May 2001.

63 Dukagjin Pupovci, email communication with the author, June 2001.

64 World Bank, "Education" (see note 36), p. 116.

65 US Institute of Peace press release, *Kosovo Mayors Offer Bold Vision for Future*, 6 March 2001. Available online at http://www.usip.org/oc/newsroom/pr20010306.html

66 UNMIK DES draft paper *Preliminary Policy Development and Action Plan for Non-Serb Minorities*, 11 December 2000.

67 Ibid, p. 1.

68 Jim Adams, Gjakova LCO, author's telephone interview, May 2001.

69 Anna Lucia D'Emilio, UNICEF Head of Education in Kosovo, author's interview, April 2001.

70 Ibid.

71 Information on the Ferizaj/Urosevac survey was provided by the former regional OSCE Human Rights Officer who implemented it (now transferred to the Prishtina Region), interviewed by the author in April 2001, and an emailed statement from the Human Rights Division of the OSCE Mission in Kosovo.

72 UNHCR/OSCE *6th Joint Assessment of the Situation of Ethnic Minorities in Kosovo (period covering June through September 2000)*, p. 21.

73 Christina Davis, OSCE Minority Adviser, Human Rights Dept; Katharina Ochse, DES Minorities Officer; Anna Lucia D'Emilio, UNICEF Head of Education, Kosovo; Mefail Mustafa, Ashkali education activist – author's interviews, April and May 2001.

74 *Building a Vision for Pilot Schools in Kosovo: The conceptual framework*, UNICEF Kosovo discussion paper, 2001.

75 UNHCR/OSCE *6th Joint Assessment of the Situation of Ethnic Minorities in Kosovo (period covering June through September 2000)*, p. 20.

76 Prachi Srivastava, UNMIK Regional Education Officer, Prishtina, author's interview, May 2001.

77 OSCE, *Kosovo/Kosova As Seen, As Told*, p. 13, available at www.osce.org/kosovo/reports/hr/part1/p5lip.htm

78 Bashkim Rrahmani, author's interview, May 2001.

79 Information on the Emin Duraku school catch-up class project was provided by the author's April and May 2001 interviews with Avdullah Qafani and Bashkim Rrahmani, and a visit to the project in May 2001.

80 Information on the *Solidarités* project was provided by the author's visit to it in May 2001, discussions with project staff and subsequent email communication with its manager Yael Aberdam.

81 Information about the *Enfants du Monde* programme, and quotations, are sourced from an *Enfants du Monde* document, *Assistance Programme to the Displaced Children of Leposavic and Plementina*, emailed to the author in June 2001 by its author, the programme's manager, Ana Simic.

82 Information on the IRC Program for Roma and Ashkalia Education was provided by the author's April and May 2001 interviews with Manjola Kola, the present programme manager, Prachi Srivastava, the former programme manager and two IRC documents written by Prachi Srivastava: the *Program for Roma and Ashkalia Education (PRAE) Final Program Report*, January 2001, and a *Discussion Paper on the Results of Phase 1 of the Roma/Ashkalia Education Program and Implications for Future Program Design*, 24 May 2000.

83 Prachi Srivastava, *Discussion Paper on the Results of Phase 1 of the Roma/Ashkalia Education Program and Implications for Future Program Design*, IRC, 24 May 2000, p. 17.

84 At a technical level, the applicability and line of responsibility for the implementation of these instruments is rather confused. The United Nations Interim Administration Mission in Kosovo (UNMIK) has adopted these standards, but is not bound to these treaties in the usual manner of a State Party. As Kosovo is still notionally a part of FRY/Serbia, the FRY government continues to bear responsibility for reporting to the relevant international monitoring bodies on the implementation in Kosovo of those of the above instruments to which it is a State Party (all bar the Second Protocol to the International Covenant on Civil and Political Rights and the European Charter for Regional or Minority Languages. Although not yet a full member of the Council of Europe, FRY acceded to the Framework Convention for the Protection of National Minorities on 11 May 2001, to take effect from 1 September 2001), although it ceded control of Kosovo to NATO and UNMIK in June 1999.

10 Former Yugoslav Republic of Macedonia

"Do you know, I was once in another school where my friend goes to?! And that is very nice because they have everything there... and do you know that all the children talk in Romanes, but in my school I cannot talk in Romanes because there are other children who do not understand me... I really would like more to go to that school than mine. Ohh... but you know, also the teacher speaks Romanes but not in my school."

Roma/Gypsy boy, seven years old

"I also have some *Gigani* [Gypsies] in my school but they are always quiet, and they do not talk as much as we and the others do. They never play with us and we never play with them. When the teacher asks them something, they are always quiet and then they get bad marks. I do not know why they do not want to learn in the school or why they don't answer when the teacher is asking them questions."

Non-Roma/Gypsy boy, seven years old

Summary

Context

Macedonia is a small country of two million people, which achieved independence in 1991. Throughout the 1990s, the country kept more or less the same educational structure as during the previous regime, with a comprehensive overview initiated only in 2000.

Roma/Gypsy population

Roma/Gypsies are recognised as a national minority. Estimates of the size of the Roma/Gypsy population diverge widely, from the official figure of 48,000 up to the quarter of a million claimed by Roma/Gypsy organisations. The population is made up of a large number of diverse groups. Most speak a dialect of Romani, though there are some native speakers of Turkish or Albanian. Most of the population is considered Muslim. Roma/Gypsies usually live on the outskirts of urban areas, often in very large numbers. Most Roma/Gypsy settlements are very poor and lack basic infrastructure. The Roma/Gypsy population suffers from very high levels of unemployment. Despite low social status and undoubted instances of discrimination, the human rights situation of Roma/Gypsies in

Macedonia has been considered relatively good. School buildings in Roma areas are often of poor quality, and many teachers consider working in them as detrimental to their career. Educational disadvantage is generational, with over 20 per cent of adult Roma considered illiterate, and there can also be cultural obstacles to children (especially girls) staying in school.

Roma/Gypsies and education

There are no official data on preschool attendance but it is widely believed that very few Roma/Gypsy children attend. Small-scale surveys indicate that up 20 per cent of Roma/Gypsy children do not attend compulsory primary school and that their drop-out rate is far higher than the national average. Few Roma/Gypsies complete secondary school and the percentage of Roma/Gypsies in tertiary education is minimal.

Language provision

Lack of preschooling means many Roma/Gypsies are not familiar with the Macedonian language when beginning school. Recognised minorities are entitled to education in their native language at all levels, though this is effectively confined to Albanian, Serbian and Turkish communities. Most Roma pupils learn in schools where Macedonian is the language of instruction. In 1996, provision was made for Romani-language education. However enrolment has actually declined in the four schools offering this service. There are few materials or trained teachers for Romani education.

Special schools

Roma appear to be over-represented amongst children in special schools. They are often placed there for socio-economic rather than educational reasons.

Balance of NGO and government activity

Specific Roma educational initiatives have been almost exclusively developed by NGOs and operate in areas with large Roma populations, aiming to improve preschool attendance and increase familiarity with wider educational requirements. NGOs have also supported projects designed to improve Roma representation in higher education and in helping Roma refugees.

Federal Republic of Macedonia report contents

Since March 2001, after this report was completed, the situation in FYR of Macedonia[1] has changed considerably. A new round of conflict involving ethnic Albanian armed groups and government security forces broke out in early 2001 and has since rumbled on. Centred on mountainous villages around the towns of Tetovo and Kumanovo, continuing government offensives aimed at dislodging the rebels have proved inconclusive, while around 25,000 people have fled to neighbouring Kosovo. Smaller numbers have crossed into the Preshevo valley in southern Serbia, itself subject to tensions with the return of Yugoslav government forces to the ground buffer zone, which had been imposed by NATO following the Kosovo crisis in 1999. As well as cross-border movements, some 15,000 people have been displaced internally within FYR of Macedonia itself. At the time of writing, access for humanitarian organisations to the affected villages remains extremely limited. It is thought that several thousand villagers have so far not left and continue to be exposed to death, injury and deteriorating living conditions. As this report was written prior to the conflict, its implications for the Roma minority and their access to education were not discussed in this report.[2]

Introduction

The establishment of the parliamentary democracy in FYR of Macedonia was based on the Amendments to the Constitution of the Socialist Republic of Macedonia, adopted by the Assembly at the end of 1990. Against the backdrop of the collapse of the former Yugoslavia, these amendments created an institutional framework for the development of a federal unit into an independent state. Following the amendments, the Assembly adopted a number of laws creating the necessary conditions for the first multi-party parliamentary elections in FYR of Macedonia. After elections in November 1990, the first multi-party Assembly of FYR of Macedonia was constituted.

On 8 September 1991, a referendum was held aimed at gauging public opinion on the establishment of Macedonia as a sovereign and independent state. Based on the results of the referendum, the Assembly adopted a Declaration which confirmed the referendum results and established the basic principles of the international capacity of the state. The process of gaining independence of the state and the establishment of the political system of parliamentary democracy was rounded off with the adoption of the new Constitution of the Republic of Macedonia on 17 November 1991.

The Roma/Gypsy population

Demography

Although Roma/Gypsies are recognised as a national minority in FYR of Macedonia, there are no reliable data on this group. According to official statistics, in 1994, out of a total population of just over 2 million, the number of Roma/Gypsies living in FYR of Macedonia was 47,408, that is 2.3 per cent of the population. However, in reality this figure is probably much higher. Roma/Gypsy leaders are said to have estimated a number as high as 250,000, that is 12.5 per cent of the population.[3]

Many Roma/Gypsies live in settlements on the outskirts of towns and cities. The biggest concentrations are found in Skopje, Prilep, Tetovo and Kumanovo. Shuto Orizari-Shutka, for example, is one of the biggest Roma/Gypsy communities in FYR of Macedonia. Three years ago, this community was declared a municipality by the Macedonian government and now has a Romani mayor.

Different Roma/Gypsy groups

In terms of their history, it is generally argued that the origin of Roma/Gypsies in what is present-day FYR of Macedonia can be traced back to the first arrival of Roma/Gypsy groups into Europe. Those Roma/Gypsy groups that stayed tended to settle in rural areas and then later also in towns. As Roma/Gypsy communities came into increasing contact with the population as a whole, problems of prejudice and discrimination increased.

As with other countries in Europe, Roma/Gypsies in FYR of Macedonia do not form one homogeneous group, but a complex mixture of groups. The most significant are *Arlie* or *Erlie*, *Dzambazi* or *Gurbeti*, *Kovaci* or *Arabadjie*, *Maljoci*, *Gavutne* and many others. The majority of Roma/Gypsies in FYR of Macedonia are Muslim (92 per cent).[4]

Language

Most Roma/Gypsies in FYR of Macedonia speak Romanes as their first language. However, there are communities for whom Romanes is not their first language. For example, Roma/Gypsy communities living in the western part of FYR of Macedonia, such as Tetovo, Gostivar and Debar, speak only Albanian and Turkish. In the eastern part of FYR of Macedonia, there are Roma/Gypsy communities who speak both Turkish and Romanes. In the same area, especially in the towns of Stip and Kocani, there are also groups of

Table 10.1 FYR of Macedonia's Roma/Gypsy population

	1953	1981	1994
Total population	1,304,514	1,909,136	2,075,196
Roma/Gypsies	20,462 (1.6%)	43,125 (2.3%)	47,408 (2.3%)

Source: Statistics Centre of Macedonia

Roma/Gypsies who speak only Turkish and identify themselves as Turks. In south-western FYR of Macedonia there are communities living there that identify themselves as Egyptians.[5]

Socio-economic status

Most Roma/Gypsy settlements face problems typically associated with poverty. Very often there is no water-supply system, and most of the houses are unfit for minimum standards of living. A large proportion of Roma/Gypsies living throughout FYR of Macedonia are unemployed. Research conducted by the European Roma Rights Centre (ERRC) found that "Roma are afflicted by a level of massive chronic unemployment which far outstrips official statistics."[6] Many Roma thus rely on state social-welfare programmes. These welfare programmes are limited to a per-capita monthly allowance and rarely allow for a minimum standard of living. As a result, those on social welfare are compelled to search for informal means of income, such as selling various articles, food and clothing in public markets. Some also find work in public institutions, such as those responsible for waste disposal.

Inter-ethnic relations

The human-rights situation in FYR of Macedonia has been subject to less criticism than most other countries in the region. The majority of findings of international researchers and non-governmental organisations seem to agree that the situation of Roma/Gypsies in FYR of Macedonia is marginally better than in most other countries in South-Eastern Europe, most notably in terms of discrimination. For example, Human Rights Watch, Helsinki stated:

"Comparatively speaking, the Roma community in Macedonia is better off than in other countries of the region."[7]

The Minority Rights Group has also said:

"Insofar as group rights and societal status are concerned, the Roma of Macedonia appear to enjoy a far more advantageous situation than do their counterparts in Greece, Bulgaria or Romania."[8]

Still, the picture is complicated. A number of national and international organisations dealing with human-rights issues have observed cases where the fundamental human rights of members of the Roma/Gypsy community have been violated. For example, the ERRC has systematically monitored the situation of Roma/Gypsies in FYR of Macedonia. As identified in its 1998 report, *Pleasant Fiction*, the biggest concerns in terms of the violation of human rights among Roma/Gypsy communities are:[9]

- discrimination against Roma/Gypsies in public places, eg, on the streets, in clubs
- discrimination in terms of gaining employment, eg, numerous examples of Roma/Gypsies unable to gain employment because of their identity
- difficulties in obtaining Macedonian citizenship – there have been numerous cases in which Roma/Gypsies have been unable to obtain citizenship, as the procedure discriminates against those defined as "stateless"
- police brutality again Roma/Gypsies – many cases have been reported by local human-rights organisations.

Minority rights

The new Constitution of FYR of Macedonia confirmed the character and organisation of the state. FYR of Macedonia is defined as a sovereign, independent, democratic and social state, in which the sovereignty originates from the citizens and belongs to the citizens. The Constitution laid down the constitutional basis for a new organisation of the state authority and for developing parliamentary democracy, in which citizens' freedoms and rights and their protection form the basis of the system. The Constitution established the rule of law, the division of state power, political pluralism and free general and democratic elections, free expression of ethnic affiliation, the legal protection of ownership, freedom of the market and entrepreneurship, local self-government and respect of generally accepted provisions of international law.[10]

According to the Constitution, all citizens have equal freedoms and rights regardless of sex, race, colour, national or social origin, political or religious beliefs, property or social status (Art. 9/1). Ultimately, all citizens are equal before the Constitution and the law (Art. 9/2).

The Constitution in particular stipulates that minorities have the right to freedom of expression, to the preservation and development of their identity and the preservation of their national characteristics (Art. 48/1). It further guarantees the protection of the ethnic, cultural, linguistic and religious identities of its minorities (Art. 48/2). Those belonging to national minorities have the right to found cultural and artistic institutions, scientific and other associations for the expression, preservation and development of their identity (Art. 48/3). This article also proclaims the right of minorities to study in their own language during primary and secondary education, under the terms of the law. This does not preclude the learning of the Macedonian language (Art. 48/4).

The right to education

Education is dealt with by the Constitution in the section entitled Economic, Social and Cultural Rights. It stipulates that all citizens have a right to education (Art. 44/1/2) and that primary education is compulsory and free (Art. 44/3). Citizens are declared as having a right, under the terms of the law, to establish private educational institutions at all levels of education, with the exception of primary education (Art. 45). Finally, universities enjoy guaranteed autonomy (Art. 46/1), although the terms of establishment, work and termination of universities are regulated by law (Art. 46/2).

Preschool education
Preschool education in FYR of Macedonia is regulated by a special law for preschool education.[11] After Macedonian liberation in 1945, more of a focus was placed on preschool education and serious efforts were made to include it as part of the general educational system, although maintaining a non-obligatory status. However, it was not until after the school reforms in 1958 that the first law for pre-educational institutions was introduced (NRM 23/59). This law was an attempt to

regulate all significant and relevant issues concerning preschool education. This triggered the subsequent expansion of the preschool network and thus opened up new opportunities for the equal treatment of all children regardless of origin.

In 1974, a new law for the education of children of preschool age (45/74) was drawn up, formalising the place of preschool education in the general system of education. This law covered children aged one to seven years attending kindergartens. For the first time, the education of children in preschool was subject to formal recognition and regulation.

At the beginning of the 1980s, the area of preschool education was further regulated by two laws: the Law for the Social Protection of Children (1981, 6/81) and the Law for Preschool and Primary Education (1983, 19/83), both of which now underpin current preschool education provision.

At this time, pre-education was provided through two types of institutions:

- **Kindergartens/preschool institutions** – state institutions founded by the government, based on proposals made by the Ministry for Employment and Social Policy. The curricula in these institutions are carried out in the appropriate mother-tongue languages: Macedonian, Albanian, Turkish and Serbian.
- *Zabavishta* for ages five to seven – entities which are not legally independent and which operate within existing primary schools. Each school may establish a *zabavishta* once certain criteria outlined by law have been fulfilled and the Ministry of Education has granted

consent. The curriculum in these institutions is also taught in the relevant mother-tongue languages: Macedonian, Albanian, Turkish and Serbian.

Primary education

The first important regulation developed for primary education in what is now FYR of Macedonia was the Constitution of 1946. It stipulated that primary schools would become separated from the church and that primary education would be compulsory and free for all (Art. 37)(NRM Art. 1/47). The first legal document on primary education in the state was introduced in 1948. According to this law, primary schooling is for seven years and is obligatory for all children aged 7-15. Schooling would be carried out for three years in a gymnasium and then four years in an elementary school (NRM 38/48). In 1958, with the new General Law for Schooling, the duration of compulsory schooling was extended to eight years, and it was further stipulated that all schooling take place in one institution. This forms the basis for the current education system.

A new Law for Primary Education was introduced in September 1995 (RM 44/95).[12] It follows the constitutional framework, ensuring that primary education is obligatory for all children aged 7-15 years (Art. 3). Institutions delivering primary education are categorised as follows:

- **Primary schools**. The state and social community are required to provide the terms and conditions to ensure that all children attend school, to provide conditions for the implementation of education and to design and provide the curriculum content.

- **Special schools** and **classes within primary schools** provided for children with disabilities, both in terms of physical and learning difficulties.
- Institutions for the **primary education of adults**.
- Primary schools and other institutions for **musical and dance (ballet) education**.
- **Other institutions**, such as children's houses and pupil/student houses.

It also sets out the following principles:
- Teaching is delivered in the Macedonian language using the Cyrillic alphabet.
- Political and religious groups and activities are forbidden in primary schools, as is religious education.
- Primary schools are public (state) institutions and the establishment of private schools for primary education is not allowed.

While compulsory education is free of charge, schooling requires additional financial resources, for example, for school lunches and the purchase of school materials and books. To ease the difficulties associated with such costs, the Ministry of Education in 1998 guaranteed that all pupils in primary schools receive textbooks free of charge.[13]

Secondary education

After finishing primary school at the age of 15, students have the option of continuing their education in secondary school. Although not compulsory, all citizens have the right to a secondary education regardless of sex, race, skin colour, national or social origin, political or religious belief, property and social status (Art. 3/1/2).

Art. 2/2 of the Law for Secondary Education, 1995 (44/95)[14] stipulates that secondary education is provided in high schools. These can either be run as public schools (state, local and city schools) or as private schools. Whereas it is the government that founds state schools, private schools can be established by domestic or foreign legal entities, or indeed individuals, as specified under the terms of the law. Private schools require a licence issued by the government. This licence details the profile of the school, the number of students and teachers, the equipment and space used, the language that will be used during classes and the curriculum. The government can, under the terms of the law, withdraw a licence at the request of the ministry. The local government can establish either local schools or city schools only in the case of special (vocational) high schools. (City schools apply only to Skopje, as it is considered a special local unit.)

Within this provision, secondary education is organised into the following types of school:
- **Gymnasiums**. These are open to regular students who have finished primary school.
- **Vocational high schools**. Students who have finished primary school can enrol at these schools on either a full-time or a part-time basis. The course lasts for three to four years, with additional specialist training. Those who have not completed primary school can still enrol at vocational schools, but only for up to two years, and this would be in parallel with their professional education. The curricula for vocational schools can also be taught in other institutions, such as those for adults.
- **Art schools**. These are open to students who have completed primary education, with the consent of the Minister.

- **Special schools for disabled students**. Students follow a curriculum for specific jobs or work. Here, the students are categorised according to the type and level of their difficulties.

Students have to undergo a process of open competition in order to enter secondary education. Students must be under 17 years old to be eligible; for disabled people, the upper age limit is 25. Registration is terminated for a student if s/he: finishes, does not register appropriately, signs out, is in prison longer than six months, or repeats the same year of study twice.

Higher education

After much discussion and controversy, a new Law on Higher Education was drawn up on 25 July 2000.[15] The main focus of discussion was on the ethnic dimension of higher education. The law attempts to incorporate European principles whilst at the same time making reasonable decisions to satisfy all interested parties in the country. During the preparation of this law, many EU experts from this field were consulted and their views were considered.

As a result of this law, all citizens of FYR of Macedonia are guaranteed the right to education in higher education institutions (Art. 6/1). The autonomy of the higher education institutions is guaranteed by the Constitution, as well as by the law. This autonomy allows higher education institutions to perform their activities under the principles of intellectual freedom. It also gives them freedom of management.

Higher education institutions in FYR of Macedonia consist of universities, faculties and higher expert schools. There is also an Academy of Arts, which is treated as a faculty by the law. According to the law, the higher education institutions may be institutions established by the state, or private institutions founded by national or foreign persons and legal entities under certain legal conditions. In the case of private universities, the founder must guarantee that s/he will be in a position to refund the money of the students if the institution ceases to function and to cover their costs of transferring to another university. Once all conditions are fulfilled, the founder can start the process of establishing the institution. The founder has to prepare a plan and has to appoint a Founding Commission.

Recent educational initiatives[16]

In June 2000, the government released its *Draft Strategy for Development of Education*, which is a result of an agreement between the World Bank, the Royal Dutch Embassy in Skopje and the Ministry of Education of FYR of Macedonia. A Special Commission of 24 Macedonian and 4 Hungarian experts in the field of education drafted the national strategy, which provides a framework for future reforms with a view to improving the overall system. In the initial draft, Roma/Gypsies are not explicitly referred to, nor are needs associated with bilingualism and/or multilingualism dealt with. The proposed timescale for the implementation of these initiatives is also unclear.

Key intervention areas and corresponding activities outlined in the Draft Strategy include:

- **Development of educational institutions** (4.1.1.), especially infrastructure and equipment. Among other things, this includes:
  - the definition of minimum standards and norms for the infrastructure
  - opening up means of using private financing for education
  - adaptation of the infrastructure for the education of adults
  - the establishment of educational resource centres to support educational institutions
  - addressing the educational needs of the population through formal/informal education.
- **Educational process** (4.1.2.), especially the introduction of changes in the predominant pedagogical culture, so that it is more interactive, participatory, and provides for better development of skills. Possible activities include:
  - the establishment of an independent "Innovation Fund"
  - the development of mechanisms and procedures for increased student participation
  - the development of systems for accreditation of textbooks and teaching tools
  - training programmes for teachers.
- **Teaching staff** (4.1.3.), with activities such as:
  - the establishment of standards for evaluation of the quality of teachers
  - redefining curricula and syllabuses for initial education of teachers
  - creation of a national system for mandatory training of teachers
  - development of a system for expert and pedagogical upgrading of teachers

- creation of conditions for part-time employment
- training of teachers for education of adults.

- **Structural adjustment** (4.1.4.) in preschool, secondary, post-secondary and university levels, in the areas of curricula, programmes and management of schools. Included here, among others things, are:
  - the introduction of a "zero year" in primary school
  - creation of alternative, flexible and economical solutions for preschooling, such as NGO resource centres
  - introduction of post-secondary education
  - introduction of vocational secondary education for adults
  - implementation of short programmes oriented toward the labour-market needs of people without qualifications and certificates.

- **Curricula and syllabuses** (4.2), especially with a view to addressing the problem of an overemphasis on theoretical learning and lack of emphasis on functional skills. Therefore, some of the activities foreseen include:
  - the preparation and development of standards (at global, national and institutional levels) for the development of curricula and syllabuses
  - development of educational and professional standards
  - redefinition of the ratio between general and professional education, theory and practice
  - prioritising the native and the official language, foreign languages, maths, computer science and social sciences in the preparation of the curricula and syllabuses for primary and secondary education
  - adding content and approaches that support multicultural awareness (in different subjects and at all levels of education).

- **Quality evaluation and assessment** (4.3), with a view to improving the quality of the educational system, the transparency of educational standards and the criteria for evaluation and grading, and more adequate monitoring of results at the end of each level of education, amongst other things. Activities are to include:
  - definition of standards of achievement for students
  - preparation of concepts for final exams and graduation for all high schools
  - eventual replacement of entrance exams for the next level of education with the results of the graduation exam
  - standardisation of the final exams in secondary and post-secondary education
  - introduction of national assessment of students
  - provision of autonomy for the Assessment Unit
  - the reorganisation and introduction of institutions with a view to creating the capacity for monitoring, assessing and evaluating education.

There are also aspects of the strategy that deal with the legal framework, management and financing, information collection, and research and development. The Draft Strategy is an open document offering guidelines for the implementation of activities to improve the educational system. Although issues relating to

Roma/Gypsies have yet to be considered, according to discussions at the Ministry of Education a special working group on Romani issues is to be set up. Some key areas that may be considered are those related to different forms of preschooling, including the proposed "zero year"; curricula development for teacher training; criteria and standards for assessment and evaluation of students' achievements; the development of multicultural curricula; and adult education and professional training.

Education in minority languages

According to the Law on Primary School Education (1995), and the Law on Secondary Education (1995), national minorities have the right to carry out education in their mother tongue, while the study of Macedonian language is compulsory. Indeed, it is noted that, along with the Macedonian language, primary and secondary education have been carried out in Albanian, Turkish and Serbian languages for the last 54 years.[17] Kindergartens and preschools are also carried out in the minority languages of Albanian, Turkish and Serbian.[18] Through its curriculum content, primary education, as the basis of education for all children and adults, also provides opportunities for the acknowledgement and development of ethnic and cultural identities of minority nationalities. In schools where there is likely to be the need to teach in minority languages, teachers are required to be familiar with and able to teach in the relevant language(s) (Art. 67/2). A primary school is obliged to test the teacher's knowledge of the appropriate language(s) (Art. 67/4). Minorities in primary schools who receive education in their mother-

tongue language are to be provided with textbooks in that language (Art. 80/3).

Secondary education is conducted in the Macedonian language using the Cyrillic alphabet (Art. 4/1). For members of minority groups education in public schools can be carried out in the language and alphabet of the minority, in a manner and under the terms provided by this law (Art. 4/2). The students covered by Section 2 of this article are obliged also to learn the Macedonian language. Classes in foreign languages are also available, for example, in English, German, French, Italian, and Spanish.

In practice

The right to education of Roma/Gypsy children

In FYR of Macedonia efforts have been made towards incorporating new models of education in the preschool and primary phases to improve education for all, including Roma/Gypsies. One example of this was in 1994, when a number of preschool institutions began implementing the Step-by-Step model. Initially, it was designed to be experimental, but has since become the working model in many preschools and primary schools across FYR of Macedonia. Another model, "Active studying – Interactive learning", has also been in place in primary schools since 1994-95. From 1997-98, this has been translated to *zabavishta* institutions. In addition to these models, a number of others were also explored during the course of the 1990s. For example, "Step Further", "Mozaik" and "Subject Planning". All these had significant implications for traditional ways of learning and working in preschool education and primary schools.

In FYR of Macedonia, most experts from the educational sector agree that one of the most important issues for educational development is the question of how best to incorporate preschool and primary education to form a basis for the educational system as a whole. In light of this, the new models mentioned above are welcomed as helping in this process. Various ideas and methods for linking the preschool and primary education systems are already underway, most notably in the case of the *zabavishta* institutions, which have purposely been made an organic part of primary schools.

In spite of such efforts, it has been noted in various reports that problems persist. For example, the Committee on the Elimination of Racial Discrimination stated:[19]

> "Concern is expressed at the low levels of participation, in particular in secondary and higher education, of certain minorities, notably of Roma children and Albanian girl children in rural areas."

Likewise, the *Report of the European Commission against Racism and Intolerance* of 1999 states that, despite considerable efforts on the part of the government, considerably lower numbers of students from certain minority groups, namely Albanians and Roma/Gypsies, receive secondary and higher education.

Educational problems for Roma/Gypsy children

Mr Sejdo Jasarov, a Romani teacher in several schools where the majority of children are Roma/Gypsies[20] describes what he sees as the main deficiencies of the education system in relation to Roma/Gypsy children, especially in their first two years of schooling:

> "In my opinion the reason why the Roma receive a poor quality education is because nobody has paid attention to the early stages of their education until now. To begin with, when a 7 year old starts primary school, for many Roma children this is their first experience of school. Very few Roma children go to pre-school. Let's take one Roma settlement, Shutka, as an example. As far as I know, nobody from Shutka sends their children to pre-school – there is no pre-school in Shutka, so how can a Roma child living in Shutka be compared with his non-Roma brother or sister? At the stage where a non-Roma child is learning and knows how a computer works, our Roma child is only thinking and knows how to sing and dance. Don't get me wrong, I'm happy that our kids have these talents – and to an extent, these could be a starting point. You know what I mean? Take the music – the rhythm and numbers – of mathematics, we can combine these things to give children the basic educational knowledge they need to prepare them for schooling.
>
> I think that there are some Roma NGOs which are taking such an approach, and then we can get results. With this kind of preparation the Roma children will use the Macedonian

language, which is a large factor in their difficulties for most of the Roma children from the ghettos. Yes, while I was a teacher I had children in my class who were coming without any basic knowledge of Macedonian. And then I had to speak and explain things in Romani".

A Romani director of a school in which nearly all of the pupils are Roma/Gypsy children explains some of the issues he has faced since working there.

"When I started managing the school I was shocked and confused at the situation in the school, because the school did not have windows, many of the classroom doors were broken, there was not enough school equipment and many of the tables and chairs were broken. I did not know where to start. Then I asked the Ministry of Education several times, and some other foundations, to rebuild the school. As always the Ministry did not have much money to give for the rebuilding of the school, but luckily in that period there were some foundations that were interested in giving help to the Roma and they invested some money here. But the process of rebuilding the school has not finished and we are still looking for some donors who would like to help make the situation for the Roma kids more comfortable.

I have a lot of problems with the non-Roma teachers and their thinking about their positions here. Many of them think that they are being punished by the Ministry of Education because of the fact that they have been posted here and have to work in a Roma community.

I had one very interesting case where a teacher was punishing the kids by giving them very bad marks. There was a case when the kids, after the school celebrations of the New Year took some small things from the classroom because they wanted to decorate their houses/rooms in the same way as it was in their school for the New Year. The teacher saw this and immediately wrote a bad mark for those kids.

Our school is faced with various problems, one being capacity. The school is built for 800 students but we have 2,000 here. In this situation, I am forced to have larger groups of students in the classrooms. Recently, there have been a lot of people who want to send their kids to the school, but that will be an extra problem for the existing ones.

The sanitary conditions in the school are very alarming. This is quite an unclean area and we have to clean the school more often than in other schools.

The school has 103 members of staff, 80 are teachers, out of whom just four are Roma. The school needs the most basic essentials to give the kids normal schooling. Other directors are "fighting" to have computers in their schools and here I have to fight about tolerance, basic conditions, getting understanding from the government and the capacity of the school to receive more students."

School abandonment

Overall attendance in primary and secondary schools has varied over recent years. In 1989, official statistics showed that attendance for primary schools had reached 93 per cent. However, by 1993 this had fallen to 85 per cent. Since then there seems to be some evidence that this figure is rising: according to an official report published in 2000, 95 per cent of the relevant age-group is included in primary school.[21] The levels of non-attendance are much higher for minority pupils, and in particular Roma/Gypsy Turkish and Albanian children, as well as those from rural areas. The same report stated that "the largest part of the children that are not attending elementary school are of Roma nationality" [sic]. A survey of Roma/Gypsy families carried out in the context of the UNICEF document[22] gives some indication of this: out of the 2,632 children of primary-school age (7-14 years) included in the survey, about 20 per cent were not in school. This figure is actually an improvement on recent years,

and many attribute it to NGO-related efforts aimed at creating conditions for increased school attendance and sustainable learning.[23] However, for older Roma/Gypsy children the figure is much higher: out of the 1,143 children aged 15-18 years included in the survey, about 65 per cent were not attending secondary school.

According to the Ministry of Education, in the 1999-2000 school year there were just 8,279 Roma/Gypsy pupils in primary school out of a total population of 247,898.[24] According to the Open Society Institute (OSI), and based on the study of Shuto Orizari, the number of Roma/Gypsy children who should be in compulsory primary school is 9,378, if we use official census figures, and 27,000 according to the unofficial figures. This helps give some indication of the numbers of Roma/Gypsies who fall outside the education system. The primary reason given by many parents for the failure to enrol Roma/Gypsy children in kindergarten and primary school is the lack of family income, and conditions which lead the families to be more concerned with survival than educational development.[25]

The official figure for the drop-out rate from primary schools is less than one per cent.[26] However, according to the Ministry of Education, eight per cent of enrolled Roma/Gypsy students dropped out of school in 1998-1999.[27] As children are generally not held back from the first to the fourth grade, it may be assumed that the majority of these drop-outs occur in the upper primary grades, from the fifth- to eighth-grade levels.[28]

In a discussion with the local NGO *Nadez* and the director of the Brothers Ramiz and Hamid School, where Roma/Gypsy students make up 99 per cent of the student population, the author of the OSI report found that general trends point to a situation in which 380 students start the first grade, yet only 100 finish the eighth grade. OSI also heard from a school in Veles that among Roma/Gypsy families who often travel for agricultural-related work, only one or two children finish the eighth grade for every 20 who start school. According to a school director in the town of Stip, out of 16 Roma/Gypsy children who started the first grade, just four are due to finish the eighth grade.[29]

According to an official report for 1995/96, Albanian and Turkish minorities were more likely to drop out of secondary school than their Macedonian peers; no mention was made of Roma/Gypsies. In the 1998-99 school year, the Ministry of Education registered just 478 Roma in secondary education. A UNICEF study carried out in the settlement of Shuto Orizari in Skopje[30] also gives some indication of the number of Roma/Gypsy students in secondary schools. Just 2,107 Roma/Gypsy children attend primary school in this settlement, while 459 do not attend and 66 attend occasionally. At the secondary level, the figures are even starker. There were just 406 students registered, with 712 not attending at all and 25 attending only occasionally. There are a number of possible reasons for the over-representation of minority groups among those who drop out, which according to Kamberski, an expert from the Institute for Pedagogy in Skopje, include:[31]

- poverty which, for example, leads to temporary emigration of parents and thus children abroad, early involvement of children in work, and lack of means for the child to be supplied with the necessary equipment for school, such as textbooks and clothes
- traditional and religious beliefs in certain areas, especially among rural settlements with Albanian and Turkish nationalities, such as not letting girl children attend school after the fifth grade
- inefficiency of state bodies and schools, such as insufficient documentation, inefficient monitoring of parents and tutors, and lack of follow-up with non-attending children
- low motivation to stay at school, due to poor performance, bullying, and discrimination in the classroom
- physical distance from school and the lack of free transport.

At the university level, in the 1998-99 school year, there were 41 registered Roma/Gypsy students, that is 0.3 per cent of the total student population. In 1999/2000, this increased to about 50 students. Although the proportion of Roma/Gypsies in university is still extremely low, it is still an increase on the number of Roma/Gypsy students who were registered initially in 1994, when revised affirmative-action measures were introduced.[32]

In terms of achievement levels among Roma/Gypsy adults, out of the 5,743 parents included in the survey of Shuto Orizari, 18 per cent were illiterate; 22 per cent had not completed primary school education; 43 per cent had completed primary school, 2 per cent had not completed secondary school and less than 1 per cent had completed higher education. The remaining 13 per cent had completed secondary education.[33] Overall achievement levels are lower amongst Roma/Gypsy girls and women. From the fifth grade, there are higher drop-out rates amongst girls. In Shuto Orizari 28 per cent of the women surveyed were illiterate; 27 per cent had not completed primary school; 37 per cent had completed primary school; 6 per cent had not completed secondary school; less than 1 per cent had completed higher education.[34] Figures provided by a Romani women's community organisation located in the largest Romani settlement, in the town of Kumanovo, reflect this pattern: 23 per cent of the women were illiterate; 62 per cent were semi-literate; 13 per cent had a primary education; and just 2 per cent had a secondary education.[35]

Language provision

The language of instruction in preschools, primary schools and some secondary schools in FYR of Macedonia differs, depending on the ethnic make-up of the student body, preference of the parents and availability of human and material resources for carrying out lessons in languages other than Macedonian.[36]

In the 1998-99 school year, 67 per cent of all pupils were in classes where Macedonian language was the language of instruction; 30 per cent were in classes held in the Albanian language; 2 per cent were in Turkish language classes and less than 1 per cent were in classes held in Serbian language. At the secondary school level, 84 per cent were in classes held in Macedonian language; 15 per cent in classes with Albanian language; and less than 1 per cent in Turkish language.[37]

While the number of students in primary schools studying in Macedonian and Serbian is decreasing, the number studying in Albanian and Turkish is increasing. According to the State Office for Statistics, in the school year 1990-91, 71 per cent of all students attended schools in which only the Macedonian language was the medium of instruction, and 27 per cent were in schools where Albanian was also the medium of instruction.[38] However, by the school year of 1997-98, the percentage of students studying in just Macedonian language had decreased to 69 per cent, and the percentage of those studying in Albanian had increased to 29 per cent. This trend is explained as being mainly a result of demographic movements and is expected to continue. It could also be an indication of an increase in access to teaching in Albanian and Turkish.

In primary school classes held in the Macedonian language, pupils registered as "Roma" represented five per cent of the total student population in both 1998-99 and 1999-2000. In Albanian-language classes, Roma represented 0.24 per cent of the total student population in 1998-99 and 0.25 per cent in 1999-2000.[39] The ethnic affiliation of students is determined on the basis of self-identification, and is recorded in the process of registering the child in primary school, when the child and parent(s) meet with the school psychologist and pedagogue.[40]

Most Roma thus attend classes which are taught in the Macedonian language. In practice, this is either in the context of a school where all classes are held in Macedonian, and Roma are therefore in ethnically mixed classroom settings, or in schools where both Albanian- and Macedonian-language classes are held. In the latter case, Roma may be in ethnically mixed classes, or form the large majority of students in the classes carried out in Macedonian, or with some small representation in Albanian language classes.[41] The Ministry of Education noted that:[42]

> "in primary and secondary schools there are no incentives for activities in which students from different nationalities would take part. The lack of school and off-school communication is creating a base for development of prejudice and negative stereotypes toward members of different ethnic background."

Predominantly Roma/Gypsy-student classes, or even mixed classes, are relatively common in primary schools. However, by the secondary level, the number of Romani students has been drastically reduced. Some Romani students state that moving into an environment with fewer Romani classmates and friends was a difficult transition.[43]

It was not until 1996 that optional educational programmes were provided in the Romani language. However, enrolment in these courses has been declining.[44] The practice was implemented in four primary schools. It involved the publication of a textbook and a standardised grammar of the Romani language. These formed the basis of training for a number of Romani teachers who subsequently became teachers of the Romani language. However, this was only for a short period of time; currently no schools deliver lessons in the Romani language. Overall, only 0.1 per cent of teachers in FYR of Macedonia belong to the Roma/Gypsy minority.

In 1997, the Macedonian parliament passed a Law on Languages (Official Gazette no. 5/97), which allows for education at the Pedagogical Faculty in Skopje to be carried out in minority languages.[45] However, although Roma/Gypsies are recognised as a national minority in FYR of Macedonia and thus have the right to carry out education in their mother tongue, no schools deliver lessons in the Romani language, nor are there national textbooks available in Romani. Most Roma/Gypsy students attend schools teaching in the Macedonian language, whilst others attend schools teaching in Albanian or Turkish languages.[46]

The only known schools offering extracurricular primary-school "facultative" courses on Romani language, songs and folk tales are two schools in the Shuto Orizari municipality of Skopje.
The reason often given by state officials for the lack of further implementation of more courses is the lack of qualified teachers and the low-level interest of Romani parents and students.
They also note the "lack of codification" (standardisation) of the Romani language.[47]

In April 2001, the European Commission against Racism and Intolerance (ECRI) was told during its preparation of the *Second Report on the Former Yugoslav Republic of Macedonia* that the Macedonian government is making efforts to improve the quality of Romani language teaching through the preparation of new curricula and courses in the Romani language in order to train teaching staff.[48]
In its report, ECRI encouraged the government to further expand and develop such positive initiatives.

School curricula

According to the 1996 document *Primary Education – Content and Organisation of the Educational Process*, published by the Council of Teachers, a body of the Ministry of Education and Physical Culture, the main goals of primary education in FYR of Macedonia overall are:

- to provide students with individual development in accordance with their level of ability and their age
- to allow students to gain knowledge and skills about nature, society and mankind
- to enable them to use these skills in their lives and further education

- to develop their sense of responsibility, truth, and the meaning of work
- to develop a sense of aesthetics, cultural traditions and national consciousness
- to enable them to respect and fulfil their civil rights and duties.

Progress of primary schools is measured according to these goals. These goals are monitored in two ways: first, by pedagogical experts and, second, by inspectors. The Pedagogical Bureau of Macedonia, a department of the Ministry of Education and Physical Culture, looks at whether the goals and objectives of primary education are realised and how curricular plans and programmes are implemented. The Educational Inspectorate performs the inspection of legal provisions in schools. Inspectors are nominated by the Minister, on the advice of the chief republic educational inspector, and with consent from the government. In addition to these bodies, there is internal supervision in schools, with the director of the school usually being responsible for monitoring internal work.

Secondary-school curricula are set by the government according to Article 9 of the Constitution. The Pedagogical Bureau of Macedonia prepares the curricula and plans for secondary schools. These are then implemented by the Minister for Education and Physical Culture, who is responsible for deciding in which public schools new and experimental educational programmes are to be tested, the nature of provision and ways of issuing and using of new books.

"Special schools" and the education of children with special education needs

Currently, there is no governmental body to maintain statistics on the schooling of children with special educational needs.[49] The Ministry of Education's *Education for All Report – 2000* notes that such data would not really be valid in the current state, as "many children with special education needs live with their families and are not included in any service offering help".[50] Though not considered valid, a figure of 18,000 adults and children defined as "retarded" is registered in the Book of Rules.[51]

At the preschool level, only 60 children were participating in special institutions for children with hearing or visual impairments, or learning disabilities. All such institutions at this level are in Skopje. In general, the integration or acceptance of children with special education needs in regular kindergartens is not an institutionalised norm. In a 1997 survey of kindergartens, only 27 out of 50 kindergartens responded to the questionnaire. From amongst the respondents, 20 kindergartens reported that they had accepted a total of 77 children with special educational needs, 60 of whom were reported to have come from poor families. The other seven kindergartens stated that they never accepted children with special education needs "because their kindergartens are only for healthy children".[52]

While primary education is compulsory for all children, the integration of children with special needs in the educational system of FYR of Macedonia is noted as a current weakness.[53] At most, some 15 per cent of the children with special needs are included in primary education.

The only known figures for children with special education needs integrated into regular primary schools are in Skopje, where 3,000 students are registered, and in Tetovo, where 110 are registered.[54]

The right to an education in the place where you live is meant to be realised in local schools, in special classes in local schools, or in special schools or special institutions. However, it is stated that "Many children with special education needs do not have this right."[55] There are ten special institutions and schools for primary education: six are located in Skopje, two in Trumica, one in Bitola and one in Veles. These institutions fall under the administration of the Ministry of Health and Ministry of Labour and Social Protection. Twenty-eight primary schools with "special classes" are distributed throughout 25 municipalities of the country.[56]

Children believed to have developmental difficulties are referred to a "commission on categorisation", formed of "a pedagogue, psychiatrist, psychologist, social worker and an expert dealing with handicapped defectives".[57] If the evaluation of a child results in the "diagnosis and categorisation" of him/her being mentally retarded, or having a hearing, speech or sight defect, a chronic disease or combined defects, then the child can be admitted into a special school or institution.

However, a report by OSI states that in the city of Veles, where one of these schools is located, a local primary-school director and a local Romani NGO reported that Romani children without special needs attend the school for children with mental or physical disabilities.[58] The president of the Romani NGO *Romani Baht* allegedly reported that most of the 67 students are Roma, and that only 5 to 10 have real problems, while the others attend for social and economic reasons. Likewise, he stated that he had spoken with some of the parents of the children, and found that some also go to the special secondary schools in Skopje, and that there is an arrangement with a local factory to provide low-paying jobs to the "graduates" of these schools. The school was said to have a lot of support from charities, and the students receive books, materials, clothes and meals.

In interviews conducted by the author of the OSI report, the director of one of the local schools stated that five children had transferred to the special school in the 1999-2000 school year, though in her opinion only one had real problems. The transfer was initiated by the parents, without the required testing for "categorisation" by the teacher and psychologist. Having consulted the Pedagogical Institute, she stated that she was informed that the certificate of categorisation should be accorded. In discussing the issue with the director of the special school, she was told that all of the children tested below the appropriate line of intelligence.[59] The OSI report comments:[60]

> "In this case, there seems to be a social-economic motivation of parents for placing their Romani children into the school for children with special needs in Veles, and it was reported that some also continue in the "special" secondary schools in Skopje. It is unknown whether this is an isolated case, and the situation should be further investigated,

both here and in other schools in the country. Such an inquiry should include the roles and responsibilities of each actor/institution implicated in the transfer and acceptance of children who should otherwise be in normal primary schools."

NGO practice in the area

Centre for Social Initiatives Nadez

The Centre for Social Initiatives (CSI) *Nadez* was created in 1997 and is based in Shuto Orizari. The organisation runs a number of projects, two of which are Roma-focused:

- a self-help programme on the education of Roma/Gypsy children in Shuto Orizari, supported by the Ministry of Foreign Work, Netherlands
- a project aimed at promoting the education of Roma/Gypsy children and youth in the municipality of Shuto Orizari, supported by OSI-Macedonia.

The latter project began in October 1998 and was due to finish in June 2001. It started as a model project aimed at demonstrating to government that Roma/Gypsy children are no different from their peers, apart from the fact that Macedonian is not their first language. It is ultimately designed to help prepare young Roma/Gypsy children (preschool age) for their first grade in primary school, and thus support the education of Roma/Gypsy children in primary and secondary schools. Other aims of the project are:

- to encourage Roma/Gypsy children to attend school

- to initiate opportunities and provide practical assistance for school and after-school activities for pupils from primary and secondary schools
- to provide advice and assistance, as well as professional help and support
- to encourage and improve positive relations between parents and other members of the family, for the sake of the children
- to organise optional educational activities
- to raise public awareness and promote public participation, while stressing the specific needs of Roma/Gypsy children.

The project is based around the running of a centre which Roma/Gypsy children are encouraged to attend. It runs a number of programmes, such as:

- **Preschool children's programme.** 100 children aged five to seven years participate. The goal is to teach children the Macedonian language and thus help them prepare for school.
- **Summer programme to prepare for the first grade of school.** 70 children who are registered in primary school for the first grade participate. It takes place in the summer and aims to prepare children for a better start in the first grade.

- **Programme for practical assistance in performing school tasks**. 150 children aged 7 to 16 years participate. The centre gives help to children with their homework and helps them to understand the subjects in school.
- **Programme for acquiring elementary knowledge**. 30 children from primary school participate. Children who attend require extra support in mathematics and the Macedonian language.
- **Co-operation with the families of the pupils**. There are contact meetings with all the parents of the children who come to the centre. These include visits to the parents' homes as well as inviting parents to visit the centre.

The Macedonian Centre for International Co-operation, Operation Days Work and Dan Church Aid

The Macedonian Centre for International Co-operation was founded in 1993 as a non-governmental and non-profit organisation. It works in the area of sustainable development, rehabilitation and humanitarian assistance. Operation Days Work (ODW) is a solidarity organisation of Danish high-school students formed in 1985. Dan Church Aid (DCA) was founded in 1922 and is a Danish church-related, non-missionary relief and development agency working with partners in five continents.

In 2000, DCA and ODW carried out an information and fundraising campaign called "Roma 2000". The campaign was aimed at raising general public awareness, in particular among Danish high school students, about the situation of Roma in Central and Eastern Europe, with the aim of raising money for an education programme for young Roma/Gypsies in Macedonia. As a result of this, a programme was developed by the Macedonian Centre for International Co-operation entitled "Applied education for young Roma in Macedonia". It began in January 2001 and will run until December 2003.

The programme, in its own words, aims to:
- raise awareness of the importance of education among the Roma communities
- raise awareness among the non-Roma communities to encourage the involvement of Roma in the country's school system.
- raise awareness among the government and other institutions of the importance of educating Roma young people
- raise the number of Roma young people completing primary school
- provide vocational training courses for Roma young people
- increase opportunities for employment and self-employment of Roma young people
- assist teachers and schools that work with Roma pupils/students.

The target group is Roma/Gypsy young people aged from 12 to 25 years and in particular, those who have dropped out and those who only attended primary school. This does not preclude working with the Roma/Gypsy population as a whole, as well as with teachers working with Roma/Gypsies and non-Roma/Gypsy pupils. The main aim of the project is to increase the involvement of Roma in education and try to raise their employment possibilities.

The Foundation for an Open Society in Macedonia

The Open Society Foundation in FYR of Macedonia has specific programmes targeting Roma/Gypsies and education.[61] In 2000-01, the OSF "Roma Program" continued to operate a number of programmes related to the schooling and the education of Roma/Gypsies. The programmes include continuing support for:

- Roma/Gypsy high-school and university students with mentoring and scholarships
- launching of the "Romaversitas" programme
- new community learning centres providing support and services with a view to creating equitable educational opportunities for Roma/Gypsy children, young people and parents
- English-language training for Roma/Gypsy students and professionals.

In co-operation with other NGOs, such as the Italian Consortium of Solidarity, the Open Society Institute Roma Participation Program, and the King Baudouin Foundation, assistance has also been afforded to Roma/Gypsy refugee students and their families. In the past, the FOSIM Roma Program has also provided support for the purchase of textbooks and school materials, and support for Roma/Gypsy children from low-income families to participate in Step-by-Step kindergartens.

Other Civil Society Actors[62]

Many Romani communities, NGOs and individuals have been involved in giving humanitarian assistance to Romani communities in Macedonia, including refugees arriving during the height of the Kosovo crisis. The type of assistance afforded has included clothing, food packets and, in some cases, school textbooks and materials for refugee students.

Some Romani and non-Roma NGOs carry out community-development activities, including those related to education, with support from US and European private foundations, embassy support schemes, and in bilateral partnerships.[63] However, it has been noted that "co-operation amongst different donors is very limited [and] there is no mechanism established for sharing information and joining resources".[64]

The Macedonian UNICEF office has generated some activities, especially the commissioning of reports concerning Roma/Gypsies, namely the *Situation Analysis on Roma Women and Children*, published in 1999, and the forthcoming *Vulnerability of Roma children in the Municipality of Shuto Orizari*. Other activities mentioned were support for local preschool and catch-up courses, along with a project working with street children in Bitola. These include in-service teacher training which covers the use of interactive methods and "mentoring". Mentoring and scholarships for Romani university students, accompanied by affirmative-action measures for universities, has meant an increase in the numbers of Roma/Gypsies attending universities.

Voices of Roma/Gypsy children

These interviews were conducted in October 2000 in Kumanovo.

JS, Roma/Gypsy, seven years old
"When I have to go in the school in the morning, I have to wake up at 6.15am, as I have to be in the school by 6.50 because my class starts at 7.00. I do not like that, I hate that. But I like school in the afternoon, the second period... Before the classes start in the afternoon, I have some time to play with my friends. But sometimes I do not like to go to school because I do not have the same toys and other things like my friend does when he goes to school."

"Do you know, I was once in another school where my friend goes to?! And that is very nice because they have everything there. I like that school more than mine. They play together... and do you know that all the children talk in Romanes, but in my school I cannot talk in Romanes because there are other children who do not understand me. I do not know why, but I understand when they are talking between themselves. I really would like more to go to that school than mine. Ohh... but you know, also the teacher speaks Romanes but not in my school."

"Also when I was in the school where my friend goes, I saw a movie there... they had a class when they watched a movie or a video. They also have a lot of pens and for the whole day, they are painting. Also when they paint, the teacher is playing music, which children can choose... the teacher asks you what cassette you want to hear, and then she plays the cassette."

"I do not know why they sit in a circle... their tables are in a circle. But in my classroom, I sit behind everybody else and sometimes I cannot see properly what the teacher is writing on the blackboard."

EE, Roma/Gypsy, fifth grade, Kumanovo
"I like going to school. I have some Roma friends there, but they do not want to learn very much. I am also Roma and I do not know why they do not want learn. I have good marks in school."

"You know, my *Gadje* [non-Roma] friends very often are saying: 'Look at those *Gigani* [Roma], they are so untidy and they do not want to learn in school'. But they then say to me: 'Sorry E, I do not think of you like that even though you are Roma. You are different from them.'"

"Sometimes I do not want to go into school because my class teacher beats us. He beats girls with his hand on their heads, and boys are beaten with slaps."

A number of other short interviews were conducted with Roma/Gypsy and non-Roma/Gypsy children from other areas in Macedonia:

RS, Roma/Gypsy boy, eight years old, Kriva Palanka
"You know when I go to the school, my teacher always wants me to sing for her, saying that all Roma know how to sing and that must know how to sing. And I sing songs of Tose Proevski... I like to sing his songs. Then my

teacher tells me: 'No, I want some *Giganski* [Gypsy] songs because they sound good. Why are you singing Tose Proevski?'"

IS, Non-Roma/Gypsy, second grade, Toli Zordumis School, Kumanovo

"We once visited a real class where just *Gigani* [Gypsies] go. My teacher said: 'OK children, because Easter is coming soon we will go and visit some *Gigani* who really do not look like you. They do not learn the same things that you learn here. They are from Sredorek.'"

DT, Non-Roma/Gypsy boy, seven years old, Stip

"I also have some *Gigani* [Gypsies] in my school but they are always quiet, and they do not talk as much as we and the others do. They never play with us and we never play with them. When the teacher asks them something they are always quiet and then they get bad marks. I do not know why they do not want to learn in the school or why they don't answer when the teacher is asking them questions."

Recommendations

Given that FRY of Macedonia has ratified:

- the Universal Declaration of Human Rights (ratified 1993)
- the International Covenant on Civil and Political Rights (ratified 1993, entered into force 18 January 1994)
- the International Covenant on Economic, Social and Cultural Rights (ratified 1993, entered into force 18 January 1994)
- the International Convention on the Elimination of all Forms of Racial Discrimination (ratified 20 March 1999, entered into force 26 May 1999)
- the Convention on the Rights of the Child (ratified 1992, entered into force 2 December 1993)
- the UNESCO Convention Against Discrimination in Education (1993), as part of the Law for acceptance of all international documents previously ratified by the Socialist Federal Republic of Yugoslavia (1991)
- the European Convention for the Protection of Human Rights and Fundamental Freedoms (ratified 9 November 1995, entered into force 10 April 1997)
- the First Protocol to the European Convention on Human Rights and Fundamental Freedoms (ratified 10 April 1997, entered into force 10 April 1997)
- the Framework Convention for the Protection of National Minorities (ratified 10 April 1997, entered into force February 1998, with the Law for Ratification of the Framework Convention for the Protection of National Minorities (1997))

and that it has signed, but not yet ratified:

- the European Chapter for Regional or Minority Languages (signed 25 July 1996)
- the European Convention on Nationality (signed 6 November 1997)

Save the Children recommends that:

The Government of the Republic of Macedonia

- Ratifies the European Social Charter, the European Charter for Regional or Minority Languages and the European Convention on Nationality.

- Invites the UN Special Rapporteur on the Right to Education to conduct a field visit in order to assess the implementation by the Macedonian government of its obligations in relation to the right to education in general, and in particular the right to education of Roma children, with reference to special schools.
- Produces accurate and comprehensive statistics on Roma/Gypsies, including educational data on access of Roma/Gypsy children to school and on their attainment.
- Extensively consults with Roma/Gypsy communities when devising national policy plans for implementing the right to education of Roma/Gypsy children.
- Integrates Roma/Gypsy representatives in all the areas of policy formulation, structural planning and service provision.
- Addresses related problems, such as unemployment and poverty, which inevitably affect the equal access of Roma/Gypsy children to education.

The international organisations, including the UN Commission on Human Rights, the Special Rapporteur on the Right to Education and the Special Rapporteur on Contemporary Forms of Racism, Racial Discrimination, Xenophobia and Related Intolerance, and the European Union

- Closely monitor the international obligations undertaken by the Macedonian government in respect of the right to education, paying particular attention to the right to education of Roma/Gypsy children in Macedonia.

FYR Macedonia: Notes on the text

1 For ease of reading, FYROM will be referred throughout this report as FYR of Macedonia.

2 Data on refugee and IDP movements are approximate and are for early June 2001.

3 European Roma Rights Centre (ERRC), *Pleasant Fiction: the Human Rights Situation of Roma in Macedonia*, Country Report Series, No.7, Budapest, 1998, p. 34.

4 ADI, *Report on the Implementation of the Framework Convention for the Protection of National Minorities in Macedonia*.

5 For more information, see: Elena Marushiakova *et al.*, *Identity Formation among Minorities in the Balkans: The cases of Roma, Egyptians and Ashkali in Kosovo*, Minority Studies Society Studii Romani, Sofia, 2001.

6 ERRC, *Written Comments of the European Roma Rights Centre (ERRC) Concerning the Former Yugoslav Republic of Macedonia, For Consideration by the European Commission against Racism and Intolerance in Strasbourg in June 1998*, 1998, p. 11.

7 Human Rights Watch/Helsinki, *A Threat to Stability: Human Rights Violations in Macedonia*, Human Rights Watch, New York, 1996, p. 56.

8 Hugh, Poulton, *The Roma in Macedonia: A Balkan Success Story?*, RFE/RL Research Report, Vol. 2, 1993, p. 42.

9 ERRC, *Pleasant Fiction: the Human Rights Situation of Roma in Macedonia*, Country Report Series, No.7, Budapest, 1998.

10 Details of the Constitution are available from the Ministry of Information of the Government of Macedonia website: http://www.sinf.gov.mk/Macedonia/EN/Political.htm.

11 Law on Preschool and Primary Education, 1983, Official Gazette of SRM 19/83.

12 Law on Primary School, 1995, Official Gazette of RM 44/95.

13 Open Society Institute, the Institute for Educational Policy, *Roma in the Education System of Macedonia: A Problem Analysis*, IEP OSI Budapest, 2000 (forthcoming), p. 5.

14 Law on High Education, 1995, Official Gazette of RM 44/95.

15 Law on Higher Education, 2000, Official Gazette of RM 64/00.

16 Open Society Institute, *Roma in the Education System of Macedonia* (see note 13), pp. 25-27

17 Ministry of Education, *Information about the Current Condition in the Education of Minorities In the Republic of Macedonia*, 1999, pp. 6, 20.

18 Ministry of Education, UNESCO *Education for All Report – 2000*, August 1999, p. 2.

19 Committee on the Elimination of Racial Discrimination, *Concluding Observations on the former Yugoslav Republic of Macedonia* (CERD/C/304/Add. 38).

20 Sejdo Jasarov was previously a Roma adviser for the Roma Programme at the Open Society Institute in Macedonia and before that worked for the Roma Participation Programme at the Open Society Institute in Budapest. He is also the author of several books on Romanes for children and the editor of the first Roma news magazine in Macedonia, *Phurt*.

21 Ministry of Education, *Draft Strategy for Development of Education in the Republic of Macedonia*, 2000, p. 11.

22 Divina Lakinska-Popovska, *Vulnerability of Roma children in the Municipality of Shuto Orizari*, UNICEF, United Nations Children's Fund and the World Bank, 2000, unpublished, quoted in Open Society Institute, the Institute for Educational Policy, *Roma in the Education System of Macedonia: A Problem Analysis*, IEP OSI Budapest, 2000 (forthcoming), p. 16.

23 Divina Lakinska-Popovska (see note 22).

24 Divina Lakinska-Popovska (see note 22), p. 6.

25 Open Society Institute, *Roma in the Education System of Macedonia* (see note 13), p. 17.

26 Ministry of Education, *Draft Strategy for Development of Education in the Republic of Macedonia*, 2000, p. 11.

27 Divina Lakinska-Popovska (see note 22), p. 4.

28 Open Society Institute, *Roma in the Education System of Macedonia* (see note 13), p. 17.

29 Open Society Institute, *Roma in the Education System of Macedonia* (see note 13), p. 17.

30 Divina Lakinska-Popovska (see note 22).

31 Kiro Kamberski, *Preschool and Primary Education in the Republic of Macedonia*, Institute for Pedagogy, University "St. Cyril and Methodius", Faculty for Philosophy, Skopje, 2000.

32 Open Society Institute, *Roma in the Education System of Macedonia* (see note 13), p. 18.

33 Divina Lakinska-Popovska (see note 22).

34 Divina Lakinska-Popovska (see note 22).

35 Interview with Romani women's NGO *Kham* in Sredorek settlement, with about 450 Romani families totalling 29,750 members, Kumanovo, June 2000, quoted in Open Society Institute, *Roma in the Education System of Macedonia* (see note 13).

36 Open Society Institute, *Roma in the Education System of Macedonia* (see note 13), p. 12.

37 Ministry of Education, *Information about the Current Condition in the Education of Minorities in the Republic of Macedonia*, 1999, pp. 4, 8, 20.

38 Annual reports of the State Office for Statistics of the Republic of Macedonia.

39 Divina Lakinska-Popovska Divina (see note 22), p. 6.

40 Open Society Institute, *Roma in the Education System of Macedonia* (see note 13), p. 12.

41 Open Society Institute, *Roma in the Education System of Macedonia* (see note 13), p. 13.

42 Ministry of Education, *Draft Strategy for Development of Education in the Republic of Macedonia*, 2000.

43 Discussion with Romani youth in Kumanovo and Veles, quoted in Open Society Institute, *Roma in the Education System of Macedonia* (see note 13), p. 13.

44 Project on Ethnic Relations (2000), *State Policies Toward the Roma in Macedonia, Oct. 13-14, 2000, Skopje, Macedonia*, PER Publications, New Jersey, p. 10.

45 Open Society Institute, *Roma in the Education System of Macedonia* (see note 13), p. 6.

46 Open Society Institute, *Roma in the Education System of Macedonia* (see note 13), p. 6.

47 Open Society Institute, *Roma in the Education System of Macedonia* (see note 13), p. 6.

48 European Commission against Racism and Intolerance (ECRI) (2001), *Second Report on The Former Yugoslav Republic of Macedonia*, adopted on 16 June 2000, Strasbourg, p. 12.

49 Open Society Institute, *Roma in the Education System of Macedonia* (see note 13), p. 9.

50 Ministry of Education, UNESCO *Education for All Report – 2000*, August 1999, p. 58.

51 Ministry of Education, UNESCO *Education for All Report – 2000*, August 1999, p. 58.

52 Ministry of Education, UNESCO *Education for All Report – 2000*, August 1999, p. 60.

53 Ministry of Education, UNESCO *Education for All Report – 2000*, August 1999, p. 60.

54 Ministry of Education, UNESCO *Education for All Report – 2000*, August 1999, p. 62.

55 Ministry of Education, UNESCO *Education for All Report – 2000*, August 1999, p. 62.

56 Ministry of Education, UNESCO *Education for All Report – 2000*, August 1999, p. 62-3.

57 Ministry of Education, UNESCO *Education for All Report – 2000*, August 1999, p. 58.

58 Open Society Institute, *Roma in the Education System of Macedonia* (see note 13), pp. 13-14.

59 Discussions with *Romani Baht* and School Director of 'Blagoja Kirkov' in Veles, June 2000, quoted in Open Society Institute, *Roma in the Education System of Macedonia* (see note 13), p. 14.

60 Open Society Institute, *Roma in the Education System of Macedonia* (see note 13), p. 14.

61 Open Society Institute, *Roma in the Education System of Macedonia* (see note 13), p. 28.

62 Open Society Institute, *Roma in the Education System of Macedonia* (see note 13), p. 28.

63 Some of the organisations mentioned include: EC Phare, UNICEF, CRS, USAID, Save the Children, Search for Common Ground, and bilateral partnerships with the French Embassy, Dutch Embassy, Swiss Bureau for International Co-operation.

64 Foundation Open Society Institute Macedonia, *Draft Strategy for 2001*, extract, version May 2000, p. 7.

11 Romania

A study found that only 17 per cent of Roma/Gypsy children aged between three and six years old participated in preschool in 1997-98, compared with 60 per cent for the population as a whole in 1996-97. A study in 1997-98 showed that for children aged between seven and ten years, school participation was 94 per cent for the entire population of Romania, but only 70 per cent among Roma/Gypsies. Part of the discrepancy can be explained by poverty. According to the 1997 Romania Integrated Household Survey, the poverty rate among Roma/Gypsies was 79 per cent, compared to a national poverty rate of 31 per cent.

"I pick cherries. My mother washes them and in the evening after school, I go and sell them."
"Where?"
"Here, in Mangalia."
"But, why do you sell cherries?"
"To buy notebooks, shoes, clothes..."

Interview with a Roma/Gypsy pupil

Summary

Context

Following the violent overthrow of the Ceaucescu regime in 1989, and as a result of concerns respecting the large and articulate Hungarian minority, the first post-communist government was not enthusiastic about minority issues. From the mid-1990s, a number of initiatives were taken and structures put in place for negotiating and addressing minority concerns, including those of the Roma/Gypsy population. The Constitution provides minorities freedom to develop their culture and languages, but does not define or officially recognise any specific minority community. During the 1990s, education reform sought to rid the system of the ideological baggage of the previous regime, encouraging private schools and decentralising authority and financial support. This has had the effect of greatly increasing the cost to families of education. Recently, the receipt of child allowances has been linked to school attendance.

Roma/Gypsy population

Roma/Gypsies have been a notable feature in the lands that form Romania for many hundreds of years. Estimates of the size of the Roma/Gypsy minority range from 500,000 to 2.5 million (a little over 1 million is a realistic figure). The population is highly diverse and known by a wide variety of names.

Only a small proportion is partially nomadic. Most Roma/Gypsies speak one dialect or other of Romani, though many are native Romanian- or Hungarian-speakers and bilingualism/multilingualism is common. Though geographically widely dispersed, Roma/Gypsy communities are concentrated within certain regions of the country. Historically, Roma/Gypsies have had low social status and many thousands became victims of genocidal policies during WWII. Communist assimilation measures led to significant economic integration and urbanisation, but also to increasing hostility during the later years. Roma/Gypsies have been particularly hard hit by the change of system, especially the large numbers who live in deprived rural areas. They experience high levels of unemployment and impoverishment. Increased social tensions have led to numerous instances of human-rights abuses and the (attempted) migration of tens of thousands.

Roma and education

Lack of monitoring of Roma/Gypsy educational conditions, or even of initiatives specifically targeting Roma/Gypsy pupils, means that there are few reliable data on school success. Surveys indicate that Roma/Gypsy school attendance is significantly lower than the national average and that Roma/Gypsy participation in secondary and higher education is very low. Few Roma/Gypsies attend preschool, though opinion is divided on whether this affects subsequent educational success. Special provision for nomadic Roma/Gypsies allows them to register in school without a permanent address. In addition to government initiatives to encourage Roma/Gypsies into school and to stay there, Romani school inspectors have been appointed in 16 counties. The state also endorses positive discrimination, allocating a number of school and university places, as well as scholarships, specifically to Roma/Gypsy students and allowing vocational schools to have quotas for Roma/Gypsy pupils.

Language provision

Mother-tongue education is allowed at all levels and Romani has been an option in school since 1990. Romani teachers are trained in three colleges and in 2000, over 4,000 pupils learned in the language. Romani language and literature is taught at the University of Bucharest, which attracts a number of Roma/Gypsy students.

Special schools

Data on pupils in special schools are not disaggregated by ethnicity, though Roma/Gypsy children form a very large percentage of the 100,000 children in orphanages.

continued overleaf

continued from previous page

Balance of NGO and government activity

During the 1990s, many Roma/Gypsy organisations and political parties were formed. They have representation in the advisory Council of Nationalities, and over 100 Roma/Gypsies have been elected to local government. Though the heightened political profile of Roma/Gypsies has contributed to notable actions by the state, many specific Roma/Gypsy-related education initiatives are the product of voluntary or NGO efforts or have been developed with the support of international institutions. NGO activities include curriculum development, projects designed to familiarise Roma/Gypsy communities with educational requirements, Romani-language classes and preschool facilities. NGOs have also sought to co-ordinate the activities of various agencies in order to tackle the multiplicity of issues in a holistic way. The state appears to consider NGO activity as complementary to its own and a means of attracting additional resources into the field. There are also instances of co-operation between NGOs and the state, notably in the area of developing Roma/Gypsy-oriented textbooks.

Romania report contents

Introduction – the Roma/Gypsy population

Demography

According to the official 1992 census, the largest minority in Romania is the Hungarian minority, officially referred to as Magyar, standing at about seven per cent of the population. Estimates on the numbers of Roma/Gypsies[1] in Romania vary considerably, from under half a million (the official 1992 census) to up to 2.5 million (The Gypsy Research Centre, Paris). With a population of some 23 million, these figures translate into a proportion of between 2 per cent and 10 per cent. Other minority groups are shown in Table 11. 1.

There are a number of difficulties associated with self-determined ethnic recording. First, some persons of Roma/Gypsy origin perceive themselves as being Romanian citizens, albeit also members of an ethnic minority. Second, there are those who prefer not to identify themselves as Roma/Gypsies because of the fear of discrimination. Finally, births are not always registered, especially for those Roma communities which adopt an itinerant lifestyle. Research undertaken in 1992, independent of the census, gives at least some indication of some of these shortfalls. On the basis of the number of individuals identified by others as Roma/Gypsies, it suggests that the population of Roma/Gypsies, at 1,010,646, that is, 4.4 per cent of the population, is much higher than the 1992 census figure.[3]

Figures on the distribution and composition of Roma/Gypsies throughout Romania are also

Table 11.1 Romania: Population census, 7 January 1992

Ethnic origin*	Number	%
Romanian	20,350,980	89.4
Magyar & Szekel	1,620,199	7.1
Gypsy[2]	409,723	1.8
German, Saxon	119,436	0.5
Ukrainian	66,833	0.3
Russian – Lipoveni	38,688	0.2
Turkish	29,533	0.1
Serbian	29,080	0.1
Tatar	24,649	0.1
Slovakian	20,672	0.1
Bulgarian	9,935	
Jewish	9,107	
Croatian	4,180	
Czech	5,800	
Polish	4,247	
Greek	3,897	
Armenian	2,023	
Other	8,420	
Not stated	1,047	
Total	22,760,449	100.0

*Ethnic identity was based on the free consent of persons to disclose their ethnic origin.

problematic. However, a number of general observations can be made. First, the majority of Roma/Gypsies in Romania are settled. The process of Roma/Gypsy sedentarisation began much earlier in South-Eastern Europe than it did in Western Europe. For Romania, cases of

enforced sedentarisation can be traced back to the fourteenth century, during the period of slavery.[4] Only a small number of Roma/Gypsy communities, such as the *Kalderash* group, still preserve their semi-nomadic life.

Secondly, it is generally understood that Roma/Gypsies are not spread evenly throughout Romania, but are concentrated in certain areas. According to unpublished research by Romani CRISS, large numbers of Roma/Gypsies can be found in counties across Transylvania, as well as in the central and north-eastern parts of Romania, including "Wallachia" and Crisana and the Intra-Carpathian counties.[5] According to the official census, most Roma/Gypsies seem to be in Mures county, where Roma/Gypsies represent 5.7 per cent of the entire population; Sibiu (4.1 per cent); Bihor (3.6 per cent); Arad (2.8 per cent) and Bistrita-Nasaud (2.8 per cent). Other concentrated areas of Roma/Gypsy communities are in the south, in the counties of Giurgiu (3.5 per cent); Calarasi (3.3 per cent) and Ialomita (3.2 per cent). In Bucharest, though Roma/Gypsies number 32,984, they represent only 1.4 per cent of the entire population.

Different Roma/Gypsy groups

It is possible to identify different Roma/Gypsy groups according to how they were categorised during the period of slavery. Roma/Gypsies were subject to collective and hereditary enslavement in the Danubian principalities of Moldavia and Wallachia – many parts of what is today Romania. Roma/Gypsies were divided into categories and subsequently enslaved by the crown, the monasteries or the aristocracy (Boyars). For many this meant domestic, settled slavery. Over time,

the ancestors of the *Vatrashi* category (from "vatra" – fireplace, ie, settled, domestic slaves), also called *kherutno* (ie, those who live in houses), lost their group distinctions and came to form the largest community group, retaining some partially preserved regional and occupational characteristics.

Other groups, mostly descendants of the *Leyasha* category (nomadic), have preserved their identity and traditions. Many Roma/Gypsy slaves during this time were able to continue nomadism and practise traditional occupations, subject, that is, to the payment of an annual tax. These latter groups became a source of migration and many emigrated to the Ottoman Empire in the seventeenth and eighteenth centuries. This migration peaked in the nineteenth century, after the abolition of slavery in 1865, and shifted in direction towards Central and Western Europe and Russia. These relatively well-preserved groups and subgroups in Romania (located in Wallachia, Moldova, and then later the annexed territories of Transylvania, Banat, Maramuresh and Dobrudzha) include *Căldărarsi* (or *Kaldarari*), *Zlatara*, *Kolari*, *Gabori*, *Kazandzhi*, *Pletoshi*, *Korbeni*, *Modorani*, *Tismanari*, *Lautari*, *Ursari*, *Spoitori* and others (the last two communities are linguistically closer to the Balkan dialect group). Roma *Căldărarsi* (or *Kaldarari*) live throughout Romania and speak their own Romanes dialect.

Generally speaking, the mosaic of Roma/Gypsy communities in Romania is extremely complex and has not yet been subjected to any in-depth research. Whilst it is possible to distinguish between Roma/Gypsy communities according to the region where they live, their profession or the language they speak, it is important to be aware of the complex divisions and overlaps that exist among different groups, meta-groups and sub-groups. In terms of occupation, for example, although there are *Ursari* (bear-trainers), *Căldărarsi* (or *Kaldarari*) (tinsmiths/coppersmiths), *Grastari* (horse-dealers) and *Rudari*[6] (woodworkers), multiple groups may practise such occupations. Likewise, it is not possible to distinguish nomadic groups from those which are settled; some groups may be partially nomadic and partially settled.

Language

A large proportion of Roma/Gypsies in Romania, such as the *Căldărarsi* (or *Kaldarari*), *Spoitoari*, *Corbeni*, *Gabori*, *Ursari* and others, continue to speak Romanes as their first language. There are also many groups, such as the *Vatrashi*, who are primarily Romanian-speakers, only a small number having preserved Romanes as an additional language. There is also a significant number of Hungarian-speaking Roma/Gypsies in Transylvania with a preferred Hungarian identity.[7] Finally, there are many groups who are multilingual. For example, Roma *Gabori*, who mainly live in Transylvania (most of them in the Tèrgu-Mures county) and who trade in clothes and kitchenware, are mainly trilingual, speaking Romani, Romanian and Hungarian.

A brief history of Roma/Gypsies in Romania

In spite of the diversity and disparities in numbers, Roma/Gypsies do form a large minority and do maintain a visible presence in Romanian society. While this high visibility is clearly related to their numerical size, it is also a product of their particular history, ie, enslavement during the fourteenth and fifteenth centuries. Over the centuries after the period of slavery, a process of sedentarisation and integration began, partly evident in the census data for 1893 and 1930. According to the 1930 census, 84.5 per cent of self-declared Roma/Gypsies lived in villages and 15.5 per cent in towns, with 37.2 per cent declaring Romanes as their mother tongue. The village population at this time became closely engaged in agriculture, and public opinion was such that Roma/Gypsies were perceived as being well on their way to integration.

In the 1930s, a Roma/Gypsy intellectual elite began to evolve. In 1933, two organisations were formed that aimed to emancipate Roma/Gypsies and improve overall conditions. Attempts were made to assert the term "Roma" as opposed to "Ţigan". Such organisations helped to inform public opinion about the social problems facing Roma/Gypsies. The idea of there being "a Gypsy Question" was a product of the Antonescu regime. At first, there was a secret debate about genetic cleansing. However, this was soon placed on the public agenda under the Antonescu regime, when Romania adopted as state policy political and ideological measures directly taken from Nazi Germany. In 1942, more than 35,000 Roma/Gypsies were transported to Transdneister in advance of German occupation, of whom about half died of cold or starvation.

During the communist period, further pressure was exerted on the Roma/Gypsy minority to settle and work in agricultural co-operatives or as manual labourers in industry. Their living standards improved, as they were included within the country's medical, educational, housing and compulsory-employment systems. At the same time, however, those Roma/Gypsies who were unemployed or employed in traditional trades or crafts were open to the threat of prosecution.

Roma/Gypsies became subject to overt discrimination, particularly during Ceaucescu's dictatorship. References simply were not made to Roma/Gypsies in official documents. Following the census of 1977, which revealed the existence of a high number of Roma/Gypsies, there were renewed attempts at their assimilation. By the 1980s, it was officially declared that Roma/Gypsies had given up their "parasitic way of life". With continuing economic decline in the 1980s, however, Roma/Gypsies were to become the indirect targets of Ceaucescu's "systemisation" programme. Although aimed at the Hungarian minority, entire Roma/Gypsy communities were relocated *en masse* in regions with a large Hungarian minority. Many of these communities were settled in modern high-rise apartments. In addition to this, urban Roma/Gypsy settlements across Romania were subject to liquidation, forcing Roma/Gypsy communities into unofficial ghettos and high-rise apartments. The resulting "urban ghettos" still exist today.

Socio-economic status

Following the collapse of the communist regime, we have seen an overall increase in the rate of poverty for the population as a whole, in both absolute and relative terms. The majority of Romanians consider themselves significantly worse off than during the communist era. While in 1989, the number of those living under the national poverty line in Romania was estimated to be at around one million, by 1998 this had grown to almost eight million people, that is,

a third of the total population. By 1999, the proportion living below the national poverty line had increased further, to 41 per cent.[8] However, estimates markedly shift depending on what measure of poverty line is used. For example, according to the absolute poverty line for the Europe and Central Asia Region ($US2 per day), just 7 per cent of all Romanians were living in poverty in 1998.

Growing poverty has been underpinned by delays in legislative and economic reform, or incomplete reform. Romania experimented with gradual reforms for almost a decade, a combination of stop-and-go policies. These proved to be very costly, so that by 1998 GDP was still at 76 per cent of its pre-transition level, with further declines in 1999 and 2000. A decline in living standards mirrored the decline in economic activity, notably in the level of current consumption per capita. Poverty was aggravated by an increase in inequality, due partly to new occupational risks, like unemployment, and partly to new opportunities, such as the freedom of entrepreneurship, albeit limited.

Since 1989/90, the Roma/Gypsy minority has continued to face harsh economic and social conditions and is subject to pervasive discrimination, both direct and indirect. Rising levels of anti-Roma/Gypsy discrimination and violence have been well documented by human-rights organisations such as the European Roma Rights Centre (ERRC), and by international bodies such as the European Commission. In the first years following the overthrow of the Ceaucescu regime, Romania was the site of approximately 30 anti-Roma/Gypsy pogroms, the outcome of which included killings and the expulsion of entire Roma/Gypsy communities from villages. A report by the ERRC dated September 1996 suggests that anti-Roma/Gypsy community violence continued and was at its peak between 1990 and 1994.[9] However, further examples of anti-Roma racism have since been recorded. For example, in March 2000 the ERRC expressed concern about a recent accusation of police thuggery against several Roma/Gypsies, including women and children who were allegedly beaten. Tear gas was apparently used in the streets to scatter a group of children, and the police used racist epithets.

In addition to such reports, the European Commission reported in 2000 that continued high levels of discrimination are a serious concern in the case of the Roma/Gypsy minority, and that the government's commitment to addressing this situation still remains low. The European Commission reiterated its position that elaborating a national Roma/Gypsy strategy and providing adequate financial support to minority programmes are still priorities within the protection of the rights of Roma/Gypsies, and that progress has been limited to programmes aimed at improving access to education.[10]

As a result of such systematic discrimination together with extremely poor living conditions, many Roma/Gypsies were among the Romanians who emigrated to Germany and Austria in the early years of transition. However, in September 1992, having agreed to provide financial assistance for their resettlement, Germany repatriated 43,000 Romanian refugees, of whom over half were reported to have been from the Roma/ Gypsy community. Such repatriations continued during 1993 and 1994 and subsequently thereafter. These repatriations directly affect the right to education of returnee children, and in particular Roma/Gypsy returnees, as they have to undergo stringent bureaucratic procedures in order to register and thus gain access to formal schooling.

Romania has also seen a growth of internal migration. The rural population of Romania stands at 45 per cent, but increasing numbers, including Roma/Gypsies, are migrating to towns and cities in the hope of finding work. For Roma, this has resulted in the further growth of ghetto-like settlements on the edges of cities and towns. In some of these locations, it has led to an informal system of supplementary social security, where rents go unpaid but evictions are not acted upon. Likewise, gas and electricity bills remain outstanding, but supplies are not disconnected. In advance of the November 2000 election, the government announced that it would meet the costs of unpaid utility bills for 1,300,000 low-income families. Whether this would be directed to Roma/Gypsy families, and whether or not it has been implemented, remains to be seen.

A recent study by the International Management Foundation noted that the only ethnic group whose poverty incidence departed significantly from the average was the Roma/Gypsy minority.[11] Unlike among other minority groups, such as the Hungarian or German minorities, in 1997 the incidence of poverty among Roma/Gypsies was 3.5 times higher than the average poverty rate and their consumption 40 per cent lower than the average consumption per equivalent adult. According to the 1997 Romania Integrated

Household Survey the poverty rate among Roma/Gypsies was 79 per cent compared to a national poverty rate of 31 per cent.[12] Research into the reasons for such disproportionate levels of poverty is limited. The factors cited most often include the unequal distribution of incomes and resources, barriers to welfare support, and discrimination.

Poverty and discrimination are inextricably linked within a cycle of deprivation, which in turn impacts on access to formal education. Increased poverty can contribute to school abandonment, and a lack of education can reduce economic functionality, thereby fuelling poverty. Young people with low levels of educational attainment are one of the social groups at greatest risk of severe poverty.

According to one source, whereas the unemployment rate of the general population was 6 per cent in 1993, for Roma/Gypsies it was 50 per cent.[13] The restructuring and closure of state enterprises has significantly contributed to steep rises in unemployment. The effects have been particularly devastating in mono-industrial areas where entire communities are decimated. Traditional skills and training have become redundant in many places and training for new technologies and industries is not necessarily accessible.

The unemployment rate amongst young people is two to three times higher than the average. In 1998, the 15-24 age group accounted for approximately 45 per cent of those registered as unemployed by the International Labour Office; of these almost 40 per cent lived in the rural areas. Therefore, even for those young people who complete their education through to graduate and postgraduate level, jobs are scarce and wages low.[14] The taking up of a second job, to supplement a professional job, is a common survival strategy and serves to increase competition for part-time semi-skilled and unskilled employment. This places further pressure on those with low educational attainment to derive income from self-employed and marginal activity.

In addition, Romania has a significant unofficial economy and suffers from corruption at all levels of public and private life. Some of these burdens can be linked to aspects of the former communist regime, for example, lack of sufficient management training and skills necessary to

Table 11.2 Registered unemployment rate (annual average % of labour force)

Country	1989	1990	1991	1992	1993	1994	1995	1996	1997	1998
Albania	7.0	10.0	9.0	27.0	22.0	18.0	12.9	12.7	13.9	17.8
Bulgaria				13.2	15.8	14.0	11.4	11.1	14.0	12.2
Romania			3.0	8.2	10.4	10.9	9.5	6.6	8.9	10.3

Source: UNICEF TransMONEE Report, Romania, UNICEF Innocenti Research Centre, Italy, 2000.

transfer to a market economy, but others have arisen out of the process of liberalisation itself.

Taking into account all the above, it is the rural-based economy of Romania that is most often cited as the main barrier to education for all. In 1998, 45 per cent of the population lived in rural areas. A labour-force participation survey carried out in 1997 revealed that 28 per cent of the working population in rural areas had only primary education or no formal education at all, compared with 3 per cent of the urban population. Rural schools were identified as being in worse physical condition, and most rural schools lacked basic teaching materials.[15] Basic problems of transport also persist, whereby

children from some villages are simply unable to reach schools situated far away.

Roma/Gypsy civic and political representation

As in many countries in Central and Eastern Europe, there has been an emerging NGO sector in which Roma/Gypsy organisations, such as Romani CRISS and many others, play a key part. Among the Roma/Gypsy communities in Romania, representation, consultation and participation present a complex and problematic process in both social and political terms. Numerous Roma/Gypsy political organisations have been created, many reflecting group or occupational interests most of which are male dominated. Over 100 are registered as NGOs,

but it is estimated that only about 30 of those are active. The activities of these NGOs can be seen to fall broadly into three types: political activism, representation of specific interest groups and service provision. Supplementing, if not dominating, these Roma/Gypsy NGOs are the large number of NGOs which are not ethnic-specific, but work within the fields of human rights, education, poverty alleviation and community development.

The issues of representation and accountability for all NGOs are complicated by the fact that 90 per cent of all NGOs are concentrated in urban areas, despite the large rural population in Romania. According to one survey, most rural young people (more than 60 per cent) think that NGOs tend not to address rural needs, and 45 per cent feel that they are badly informed as to the actual existence of NGOs.[16] However, some Roma/Gypsy NGOs, even if based in urban areas, are grassroots organisations and thus claim to develop extended programmes in Roma/Gypsy rural communities.[17]

Roma political parties have also emerged, and although they have had little impact at the national level, they have achieved some success at local levels. Minority participation in parliament is guaranteed by Article 59 of the Constitution, which provides for seats for those organisations of citizens belonging to national minorities which fail to obtain the electoral threshold of five per cent. In 1996 and again in 2000, the Roma Party obtained parliamentary representation under this provision. A number of Roma/Gypsies have also been elected to parliament as members of non-ethnic political parties, and Roma/Gypsy

votes were split between several different parties for the 2000 presidential campaign.[18]

In addition to this, some Roma/Gypsy representatives have been included in formal government structures. In 1993, a Roma Party member was elected to the Council of National Minorities. In 1997, officers on Roma issues were appointed in the Ministry of Culture and the Ministry of Education. At a local level, 147 local councillors were elected on the Roma party list and two Roma/Gypsy mayors were elected. The Inter-Ministerial Sub Commission for Roma provides for the participation of Roma/Gypsy delegates as well as of governmental officials from eight ministries. However, it is not clear how representative these appointed government staff are, nor indeed to what extent they are accountable to Roma/Gypsies in general. The involvement of Roma/Gypsies in Romanian politics has been primarily a top-down process restricted to a small number of individuals. Where Roma/Gypsy organisations have attempted to tackle the government directly, their efforts have been largely ineffective. For example, when an official distinction was drawn between Romania and Roma by using the term "Rroma" (ie, with a double "Rr"), many organisations, such as Romani CRISS, welcomed this as an important breakthrough in terms of recognising and promoting Roma identity. However, in 1999, the Ministry of Foreign Affairs, the Prime Minister and parliament made a decision to replace this term "Rom/Rrom" with "Ţigan". The decision was made without consulting Romani organisations or indeed the population as a whole. Organisations such as Romani CRISS are still advocating on this issue.[19]

Whilst it is important to observe that a number of Roma/Gypsies play leading and successful roles in political, economic, social and cultural spheres, a significant and disproportionate majority of Roma/Gypsies remain out of reach of positions of power.

Minority rights

It seems that there is no definition of "national minority" in Romanian law, nor is there any specific legislation on the right to be recognised as a distinct minority group. In practice, the concept of national minority is understood to refer to the "historical minorities" that have lived in Romania for hundreds of years. This usage of the term is reflected not only in the 1992 census, which records the existence of 16 national minorities, but also in the national minority representation of the Council of National Minorities and in parliament.

Article 4(2) of the Constitution states that Romania is the common and indivisible homeland of all its citizens, irrespective of race, nationality, ethnic origin, mother tongue, religion, sex, opinion, political affiliation, fortune or origin.

Article 6 addresses the right to identity and equal opportunities. It provides that:

1   *The state recognises and guarantees the right of persons belonging to national minorities to the preservation, development and expression of their ethnic, cultural, linguistic and religious identity.*

2   *The protecting measures taken by the Romanian state for the preservation, development and expression of identity of the persons belonging to national minorities shall conform to the principles of equality and non-discrimination in relation to other Romanian citizens.*

Equality of rights between all citizens of the country, as specified in the Constitution, guarantees equality of opportunities for all citizens. While recognising and guaranteeing the right to identity and non-discrimination for those belonging to ethnic minorities when implementing measures for preserving, developing and expressing their ethnic, cultural, linguistic and religious identity, the state must *take into consideration* the principles of equality and non-discrimination in relation to Romanian citizens other than the ethnic minority concerned.

On 31 August 2000, the Romanian government published an ordinance entitled "On Preventing and Punishing All Forms of Discrimination", which prohibits all forms of discrimination in various fields. In relation to education, the ordinance provides for the prohibition of discrimination on any grounds in the access to the public and private education systems and in all stages and levels of schooling. The ordinance also provides for affirmative action in favour of minorities when they do not enjoy equal opportunities. When an offence is proved against an individual, sanctions remain relatively weak, with the imposition of fines ranging from 563,751 Romanian lei to 11,353,331 Romanian lei, that is, $US20-400.[20] At the time of writing the average monthly income in Romania was between $US80 and $US100.

The ordinance gained the approval of parliament in November 2000 in advance of the general election. However, the government's consensus and the Prime Minister's signature are needed for the ordinance to enter fully into force. Since the former Prime Minister did not sign the ordinance, it has therefore only partially been enforced. The current Prime Minister has postponed signing the ordinance; it has so far got through the first chamber and is waiting to go through the second. It is expected that the main principles of the ordinance will remain in place, but that small changes will be made.

Article 32(3) of the Constitution stipulates that people belonging to national minorities have the right to receive education in their mother tongue, as well as have lessons on the language itself. The means for exercising such rights are settled by law.

The Department for the Protection of National Minorities (DPNM) was set up in January 1997. The department replaced the Consultative Council for National Minorities, which had been established in 1993 to monitor the specific problems of people belonging to minorities. Until recently, the DPNM reported directly to the Prime Minister. However, it now sits within the Ministry of Public Information and reports to two sub-state secretaries. This has clearly impeded its ability to have a direct impact on government policy. It is organised into three sections: the central executive, the local section and the consultative section. It also maintains a National Office for the Social Reintegration of Roma and has permanent contacts with the Council for National Minorities, an advisory board to the government consisting of representatives of all national minorities living in Romania. The DPNM performs a variety of functions. These include preparing draft legislation in its sphere of competence, preparing opinions on legislation and other legal acts concerning the rights and obligations of national minorities, monitoring internal and international legal standards concerning the protection of national minorities, and providing financial support to minority organisations.[21]

An Inter-Ministerial Committee for National Minorities has been established and has contributed to strengthening the mechanism for Roma/Gypsy participation and the decision-making process on Roma/Gypsy issues. A Working Group of Roma Associations was also set up to facilitate liaison with public authorities. An agreement on elaboration of a strategy for the protection of the Roma/Gypsy minority has been signed between the DPNM and the Working Group. In June 1999, an Inter-Ministerial Subcommission for Roma was established as a subsidiary body of the Inter-Ministerial Committee. It comprises Roma/Gypsy delegates and government representatives.[22] The Subcommission is mandated to assist the Inter-Ministerial Committee in the development of strategies for the implementation stage of the national strategy. However, given that it is made up of relatively low-ranking officials, progress remains slow and it appears that relations between the two bodies have so far been ambiguous.[23]

Notwithstanding this progress in establishing the institutional framework for the improvement of the conditions of Roma/Gypsies, the European Commission, in its 1999 regular report on

"Progress towards Accession", notes that there has been no evidence of similar practice taking place at the ground level.[24] The European Commission emphasises that it is very important for both the government and Roma/Gypsy communities to remain committed to the elaboration and implementation of a strategy for the protection of Roma/Gypsies. In its report, the Commission states that particular attention must be paid to ensuring that all initiatives are properly budgeted for at regional and local levels.

As a result of the general elections in November 2000, Romania has a new president and government, namely Ion Iliescu and the Party of Social Democracy in Romania, which won nearly 50 per cent of the total mandate.[25] It is a relatively straightforward task for ordinances to be annulled, and as of January 2001 the new government has suspended or abolished more than 20 ordinances passed by the former government.[26] Government structures and their personnel will be subject to continual change over forthcoming months. At the time of writing, however, the aforementioned Committee and Working Group were still operational.

On 19 January 2001, the Romanian parliament's lower house adopted the law on public language use, which was then promulgated on 21 April 2001. The Local Public Administration Law not only decentralises public administration, but also gives minorities the right to appeal to local authorities and related bodies in their own languages in areas where they represent at least 20 per cent of the population. Signs will be written in minority languages and local government decisions will be announced in minority languages as well. Some 11,000 towns and villages are estimated to fall into this category. However, as the senate approved a slightly different version of the law, a mediation commission will decide on the final text to be approved by a joint parliamentary session.[27] This law, in theory, provides an instrument for the recognition of the right to an identity and to participation in decision-making at a local level on the part of minorities, thus potentially benefiting Roma/Gypsy minority groups. However, in light of claims made by the mayor of Cluj-Napoca, that the Hungarian minority in Cluj Napoca does not exceed 20 per cent (contradicting official figures) and is therefore not eligible for rights under this provision, it is not clear how effective the law will be in practice.[28]

Mechanisms for addressing human rights violations

Articles 55-57 of the Constitution provide for the creation of an ombudsperson, "the Advocate of the People". The senate appoints the ombudsperson, for a term of office of four years, to defend citizens' rights and freedoms. Article 57 provides that the ombudsperson shall report before the two parliamentary chambers, annually or on their request. The reports may contain recommendations on legislation or measures of any other nature for the defence of the citizens' rights and freedoms. The first ombudsperson was appointed in May 1997 by virtue of the enactment of Law No. 35 and Senate Decision No. 17 of that year. The ombudsperson's role is to examine individual communications alleging human rights violations. Although the ombudsperson's office initially had a section devoted to minority issues, this has since closed;

minority issues now fall within the competence of the section dealing with public order, military issues and other matters.[29]

The ordinance on discrimination, as detailed above, provides for the establishment of the National Council for the Prevention of Discrimination 60 days after its initial drawing up. However, funds have yet to be provided for setting it up. Further still, the ordinance does not mention the nature of this mechanism and the tasks that this body will be mandated to undertake for combating discrimination. At the time of writing, this Council had not yet been established.

Minority rights and international law

Romania is currently a party to a total of 52 legal instruments of the Council of Europe. Romania plays an active part in intergovernmental co-operation within the Council of Europe in connection with the rights of people belonging to national minorities. Upon acceding to the Council of Europe, Romania accepted the jurisdiction of the Commission to receive complaints and also the jurisdiction of the European Court of Human Rights. There is a Council of Europe Information and Documentation Centre in Bucharest.

Romania has agreed to all the documents of the OSCE adopted by that organisation since the Helsinki Final Act signed on 1 August 1975. As a member of the OSCE, Romania participates in the mechanisms of the OSCE: the Ministerial Council, the Committee of Senior Officials and the Office for Democratic Institutions and Human Rights. It also participates in meetings relating to the human dimension of the OSCE. Romania co-operates with the OSCE High

Commissioner for National Minorities. As of 2001, Romania will chair the OSCE.

Romania participates in specialist United Nations forums concerned with human rights, including the rights of people belonging to national minorities. There are offices of the International Labour Organisation, the United Nations Children Fund (UNICEF), the High Commissioner for Refugees and the International Organisation for Migration in Bucharest.

The current Constitution of Romania was adopted on 8 December 1991, after approval by referendum. Article 20(1) of the Constitution declares that the constitutional provisions concerning citizens' rights and freedoms will be interpreted and applied in conformity with the Universal Declaration of Human Rights and with covenants and other treaties to which Romania is a party. Article 20(2) continues by asserting that where any inconsistencies exist between domestic legislation and covenants and treaties on fundamental human rights to which Romania is a party, international regulations shall take precedence. It must be emphasised that this priority is extended to international regulations *only* in the sphere of human rights.

The right to education[30]

Article 5(1) of the Education Law of July 1995 states that Romanian citizens have the right to equal access to all levels and forms of education, irrespective of social and material conditions, sex, race, nationality, and political or religious affiliation.

In relation to minority rights, Article 8(2) states that peoples belonging to national minorities have the right to learn and be educated in their mother-tongue language. Article 118 also declares that persons belonging to national minorities have the right to study and to be trained in their mother tongue at all levels, in all forms of education, according to this law. Article 119(1) gives the possibility, according to local needs, for national minorities to request and organise on a legal basis, groups, classes, sections or schools in the mother tongue of national minorities.

As far as curricula are concerned, Article 120(3) affirms that curricula and manuals of universal and Romanian history will reflect the history and traditions of national minorities in Romania. Furthermore, Article 120(4) states that at the secondary level national minorities can request lessons in history and culture, as appropriate, that are taught in their mother tongue. The Ministry of Education, though, has to approve all curricula and manuals used in such lessons.

Article 121 declares that pupils belonging to national minorities who learn in the Romanian language have, at their request and according to the law, the possibility of studying the mother tongue, literature, history and traditions of the respective national minority.

Finally, Article 180 states that it is the parent (or legal tutor) who ultimately bears responsibility for deciding upon the child's right to learn in the Romanian language, or in the language of a national minority.

In addition to the general Education Law, the Minister of National Education adopted various instructions related to the issue of education and national minorities. Instruction No. 3533 of 31 March 1999 concerns the study of their mother tongue in schools by pupils belonging to national minorities. Article I(1) states that the study of the mother tongue begins in the first grade of primary school. Article III(1) states that from the 1st to the 12th grade, lessons in their mother tongue shall be of three or four hours duration per week.

There are some additional provisions, which aim at facilitating the education of Roma/Gypsy children and young people. For example, for families who often travel, children may begin school at any time, without being subject to the condition of a stable place to live. It is also stated that school management and teachers have no right to influence children's and parents' options concerning the study of the Romani language.

Order No. 3577 of 15 April 1998 promotes access to education for Roma/Gypsy students by establishing positive-discrimination measures for admission into some universities. One hundred and fifty places have been allocated for candidates belonging to Roma/Gypsy communities in different subjects and in different universities throughout the country: Bucharest, Iasi, Sibiu, Craiova and Timisoara. This was repeated in 1999 with the enactment of Order No. 5083 of 26 May 1999.

Order No. 3316 of 24 February 1998 provided measures aimed at the nominal registration of illiterate pupils and their integration into school classrooms. This included an initiative based on the provision of "school caravans", which has yet

to become fully operational. However, it is important to note that nomadism in the Balkans, including Romania, is very different from that practised in Western Europe. All nomadic Roma/Gypsies have permanent winter homes and travel seasonally with periodic breaks. This makes the translation of models from Western Europe, such as caravan schools, at best problematic.

Order No. 3363 of 1 March 1999 regulates the nomination of school inspectors in relation to the education of Roma/Gypsies. As a result of this order, school inspectors of Roma/Gypsy origin have been nominated in 16 counties of Romania. In the remaining counties Roma/Gypsy educational professionals apparently were not available, so non-Roma/Gypsy inspectors were appointed.

Order No. 4281 of 18 August 1999 introduced a programme for combating the marginalisation and social and professional exclusion of young people who have abandoned compulsory education. This is mainly targeted towards young Roma/Gypsies.

Order No. 4542 of 18 September 2000 deals with access of young Roma/Gypsies to vocational schools, high schools, colleges and faculties. From the academic year 2000-01, Roma/Gypsy communities will be able to request local authorities to establish quotas for Roma/Gypsy students. Local education authorities will then be in a position to determine which institutions need quotas and how many.[31]

The amendments to the 1999 Law on Education also made it possible for universities to establish teaching in minority languages. Programmes refer to the provision of education in national minority languages, and aim to reflect each minority's history and culture not only in the framework of the teaching itself, but also in the provision of textbooks and necessary material support, as well as in the training of educational personnel.

According to the government, education is by law a national priority.[32] After 1989, educational provision in Romania went through a thorough process of deconstruction which principally removed ideological indoctrination from education and other restraints imposed by communist educational policy in areas such as languages, history and social sciences. The huge scale of this process cannot be underestimated, nor can the pace of change. Secondary education was diversified and conditions for developing private higher educational institutions were introduced. Areas of study, such as social work, which were banned under the communist regime, were established. Between 1991 and 1992 a period of consolidation prevailed, allowing these extreme changes to bed in.

Between 1993 and 1999 significant restructuring occurred, marked by the development of a coherent educational policy, the diversification of higher education and a revision of the education system that reflected new economic, social and cultural requirements. Changes were made to the Education Law in 1995, 1997 and 1999, in addition to which several other associated legislative provisions were introduced. For example, the Education Law adopted in 1995, is a piece of legislation of special significance, drafted along innovative lines with a view to ensuring the development of the Romanian education system on the basis of humanistic traditions and the values of democracy. It aims to enable individuals to develop freely, fully and harmoniously.

In Romania, education is free and compulsory between the ages of 6 and 16 years. According to UNICEF's TransMONEE report, Romania secured an improved basic gross enrolment rate for children of compulsory school age, from 93.6 per cent in 1989 to 97.0 per cent in 1999.[33]

In principle, education receives a fixed quota of four per cent of GDP within the annual budget. Conditions of economic austerity, however, have undermined this figure. According to the OECD, the budget allocation for education amounted to only 2.5 per cent to 3.5 per cent between 1990 and 1995.[34]

Some of the measures introduced in 1999 by the Ministry of National Education, which aimed to modify further the education system in Romania and bring about greater harmonisation with European norms, may put the notion of free education in doubt. Fiscal crises have threatened funding for education, particularly at preschool and primary levels, reducing subsidies and devolving responsibilities to local governments and families, which often lack the necessary resources. Therefore, the transfer of a series of educational costs to the population may diminish the possibility of equal access to preschool, primary, secondary and higher education. For example, as ownership and administration of preschools have been transferred to municipalities, churches and the private sector, local governments and families have assumed a growing share of the financial responsibility. Therefore access to preschool education is now dependent on the family's ability to support additional costs, such as lunches, textbooks and other educational materials that were previously subsidised by the state. The same trend has been happening in primary education. Furthermore, several taxes have been introduced which must be covered by pupils. These include applications to admission examinations at high schools, vocational schools and universities, delivery of study certificates and voluntary contributions.

This has deterred the poorest families, many of which belong to Roma/Gypsy communities, from sending their children to school.[35]

Children under the age of six years may attend crèches and kindergartens.[36] Preschool education for the very young is intended to provide both nursery and daycare, with an increasing emphasis on preparation for formal schooling for slightly older children. The main curricular objectives of preschool education include learning in and using the Romanian language as well as other minority and foreign languages.[37] This level of education is provided in both public and private institutions, although the large majority of institutions are at present under public management. Private preschool institutions are located predominantly in urban areas.[38] According to the OECD, the availability of preschool education for children aged 3-6/7 years of age has improved from 55.2 per cent in 1994-95 to 65.5 per cent in 1996-97.[39] However, the data available on preschool enrolment are not all concurrent. The World Bank, for example, states that preschool enrolment in 1994 was much higher, at 85.7 per cent, and that between 1989 and 1994 the pupil/teacher ratio improved slightly from 20.3 to 10.01.[40]

Between the ages of 6 and 16 years children attend general education school which is compulsory for nine years. General secondary schools, for which there is an entrance exam, provide education suitable for entering college or university. There are also specialised secondary schools where the emphasis is on industry, agriculture, teacher training and art.

According to the OECD, primary education attendance (grades one to four) increased from 93.8 per cent in 1992-93 to 99.4 per cent in 1994-95 and then slipped to 96.7 per cent in 1996-97.[41] Again this does not match the figures provided by the World Bank, which show a constant decline in enrolment rates from 98.3 per cent in 1990 to 94.6 per cent in 1994.[42] Also, at this stage of schooling there has been an improvement in the pupil/teacher ratio, which decreased from 21.1 to 15.4.[43]

Secondary education includes attendance at *lycées*, for which the numbers have increased significantly. It also includes vocational schools and apprentice schools, where numbers of students have declined, although the numbers of schools and teachers have increased. Such fluctuations reflect the difficulties encountered in predicting the employment trends in an economy that is both in transition and in decline. Secondary education accounted for the most severe fall in the enrolment rate: it was 90.7 per cent in 1990 and fell to 67.8 per cent in 1998. According to the European Steering Committee for Youth, the causes of this dramatic drop are: families' financial incapacity to keep children in school, a lower value being placed on the role of education in public opinion, and high unemployment among secondary-school graduates, which affects decisions on whether to continue with further education.[44]

Secondary-school studies are concluded by undertaking a baccalaurcate examination which opens up the option of higher education. For students who have attended a vocational *lycée* a certificate of vocational competence is issued.

For those not wishing to go to higher education, there is the option of post-secondary education, which provides for specialisation in areas such as agriculture, telecommunications and health; entrance is competitive. There are also "foreman schools" for older students who have practical work experience, but require a technical qualification or retraining. The number of post-secondary schools has more than doubled between 1989 and 1998. The numbers of students and teaching staff trebled during this period.

According to UNICEF, higher education attendance has increased significantly from 6.9 per cent in 1990 to 16.3 per cent in 1994.[45] Participation in both long- and short-term undergraduate and postgraduate courses now requires that students pass entrance exams. Progression within the framework is dependent upon assessment of ability. The sector has been characterised by the extension of private universities (94 per cent of private university students study economic, legal or pedagogic subjects), where fees are somewhat higher than in state provision. The quality of private higher education is generally considered to be better in all fields other than in medicine.

Equality of access has traditionally been affected by access to "coaching". Coaching is a private supplement to education, usually consisting of individual tuition, and is most common for specific subjects such as mathematics and languages, but also in the run-up to exams before entry into, and beyond, higher education. The reforms of 1999 were an attempt to move away from a reliance on individual coaching. However, both the push and the pull factors that maintain this coaching system remain. First, many Romanians recognise the importance of formal education and see it as a passport to economic security. Secondly, teachers receive very low salaries, which are insufficient to meet their basic living costs, so that providing private tuition offers teachers a necessary means of economic survival. All these factors combined affect both directly and indirectly the equality of access to formal education on the part of Roma/Gypsies.

In practice

The right to education of Roma/Gypsy children

As already emphasised, there are few data available on Roma/Gypsies in Romania. This is also the case regarding their participation in formal education. No national figures exist on how many Roma/Gypsy children attend school. In spite of this, over the past five to six years, the Romanian government has introduced various pieces of legislation and policies in the field of education, particularly aimed at improving the educational situation of Roma/Gypsy children. For example, post-secondary school distance-learning mechanisms were established in autumn 2000 in the Faculties of Languages (Romani language and literature) and of Political Studies at the University of Bucharest. Around 60 Roma/Gypsy students enrolled, some of whom were required to apply for scholarships.

At the request of Roma/Gypsy parents in several high schools throughout the country, the government further intended to open additional classrooms within existing schools. Although in theory these classes are not only for Roma/Gypsy

children, but also for all those who are illiterate, Roma/Gypsy children tend to constitute the majority of children attending such classes.
In addition, this raises the question of whether segregated education is the right approach.
For example, in Coltau segregated schooling has been identified as a specific problem: a two-tier system has given rise to a situation in which the material conditions, overall quality and number of teachers in Roma/Gypsy schools is markedly lower than in the neighbouring school for the Hungarian minority.[46] Some argue that, in order to teach the Romani language in some mainstream schools, separate groups need to be organised for this specific subject. However, there have been attempts, mainly on the part of some local school authorities, to use the Romani language-teaching issue as a justification to organise segregated so-called Roma classes. This practice has resulted in discrediting the teaching of Romanes itself. However, some sources claim that this practice is to be discontinued.[47]

Officially, "Roma schools" do not exist, in the sense that schools have not been created specifically for Roma/Gypsy children. Neither are there schools where the curriculum is exclusively Roma-specific. However, unofficially there are schools where all, or nearly all, the pupils are Roma/Gypsy children and where provision is of an inferior quality to mainstream schooling. These schools are located in villages and urban districts where the majority population is Roma/Gypsy, which is then reflected in the composition of the school population.

Further initiatives were announced in March 1999. As discussed previously, the Ministry of Education adopted a decision to appoint a Roma/Gypsy inspector in each of Romania's 41 counties, as a result of which school inspectors of Roma/Gypsy origin have been nominated in 16 counties. One role of the Roma Inspectorate is to make specific recommendations and/or suggest initiatives. For example, in a school in Iasi which caters for 1,200 pupils (50 per cent of whom are Roma/Gypsies), the school inspector helped to initiate a project for one year that aimed to give 30 Roma/Gypsy children the opportunity to graduate to fourth grade. Likewise, in Tamna-Mehedinti, the inspector strongly encouraged the establishment of Romanes language classes. However, the extent of their powers when identifying bad practice remains unclear.
The Roma Inspectors' network seems to be still quite weak in terms of logistics and the level of support received from local educational authorities. This lack of support and infrastructure prevents them from accomplishing a systemic evaluation of education provision for Roma/Gypsy children. Although they are able to contribute to monitoring processes in terms of design and making recommendations, they often cannot act upon or implement their recommendations.[48]

The Minister of Education also announced that the authorities were to introduce a mechanism of positive discrimination favouring Roma/Gypsies in state education institutions. Over 500 places are now reserved on a fees-paid basis for Roma/Gypsies. For example, the "Second Chance" programme established in a secondary school in Cluj Napoca aims to encourage students to continue their education beyond the compulsory age.[49] Although restricted to just

30 places, the emphasis is on the participation of Roma/Gypsy students. Another example is the quota admission to some universities reserved for members of Roma/Gypsy communities. The Romanian government reports that in the academic year 2000-01, 25 scholarships for young Roma/Gypsy students have been allocated to five university colleges.[50] Other universities offered 162 places for Roma/Gypsy students in this year.[51] However, with a focus on vocational as well as academic skills (unlike for other students) this attempt at positive discrimination could still be seen as limited.

Despite this increasing level of apparent support on the part of the Romanian government regarding the issue of Roma/Gypsies and education, there are obvious problems associated with the lack of any monitoring and evaluation. It also contrasts sharply with their treatment of Roma/Gypsies in other spheres of policy. The Romanian government continues to attract criticism from various international bodies for its treatment of the Roma/Gypsy population. For example, the UN Committee on the Rights of the Child, in its Concluding Observations of 7 February 1994, expressed its concerns about the low level of school attendance of Roma/Gypsy children. In more general terms, the Committee found a need for more effective measures to combat prejudices against this minority.[52]

Likewise, the UN Committee on Racial Discrimination, in its Concluding Observations on 19 August 1999, mentioned the situation of Roma/Gypsies as a subject of particular concern. It notes that no improvements had been observed in the high unemployment rates and that educational levels among Roma/Gypsies remained low. According to the Committee, this situation contributes to the continued and unacceptable prevalence of their negative, stereotyped image among the rest of society.[53]

Preschool provision

Only a small number of Roma/Gypsy children attend kindergarten (preschool education). The numbers of Roma/Gypsy children of preschool age (three to six years) who attend kindergarten is three times lower than that of the majority population. According to a study conducted during April and May 1998, only 17 per cent of Roma/Gypsy children aged between three and six years participated in preschool (for the academic year 1997-98) compared with 60 per cent for the population as a whole (for the academic year 1996-97).[54]

Some organisations believe that this low take-up rate of kindergarten provision may have negative effects on school results, because Roma/Gypsy children who do not attend preschool education miss out on preparation for school. This has particular implications for those Roma/Gypsy children whose first language is not Romanian. Some NGOs have responded to this by providing preschool provision specifically for Roma/Gypsy children. For example, Save the Children Romania (*Salvati Copiii*) has run two kindergartens for Roma/Gypsy children.

By contrast, other organisations believe that non-attendance or low attendance of Roma/Gypsy children in preschool formal education does not necessarily have a detrimental impact on the children's future school career. This is based on a certain lack of trust felt by some Roma/Gypsy organisations and families towards preschool formal education. For some it is very difficult to trust an institution which is seen as hostile and discriminatory towards Roma/Gypsy children. Forms of preschool education carried out at home by Roma/Gypsy families are seen by some as equally if not more important than the preschool education provided by the state.

School abandonment and non-attendance

Although there are no precise figures on the number of school-age Roma/Gypsy children, it is generally observed that a large number of Roma/Gypsy pupils leave school early, particularly after the fourth grade, that is from 12-13 years upwards. There have been some attempts to estimate in more detail patterns of enrolment and drop-out. Such research has mainly been done on a sampling basis. Some of the results of this research are reproduced here but we do not claim them to be representative of the situation as a whole.

According to the 1992 national census:
- Roma/Gypsies aged under 16 represented 43 per cent of their group
- 27 per cent of boys and 35 per cent of girls did not complete primary school
- 5 per cent of Roma/Gypsies completed high school
- only half of the children aged seven to ten attended school regularly

- 40 per cent of children under the age of eight do not attend kindergarten or school.

A survey carried out in 1992 recorded that 27 per cent of Roma/Gypsies had never attended school, 5 per cent attended secondary school and less then 1 per cent attended university. It also showed that 51 per cent of Roma/Gypsy children aged ten years attended school regularly, 19 per cent did not attend at all, 16 per cent attended only occasionally and 14 per cent had dropped out.[55]

Further research conducted with a sample of 1,272 families in Bucharest showed that:[56]
- two per cent of Roma/Gypsy children were not enrolled in school
- the school drop-out rate for Roma/Gypsy children was seven per cent compared with one per cent for non-Roma/Gypsy children.

Other research carried out in the school year 1997-98 showed that for children aged between seven and ten years, school participation for the entire population of Romania (including Roma/Gypsies) was 94 per cent. When these figures were disaggregated, however, it showed that school participation for Roma/Gypsy children from the same age-group was only 70 per cent. Similarly, for the age-group 11 to 14 years, school participation for the entire population of Romania was 98 per cent, yet for Roma/Gypsy children was only 68 per cent. Finally, whereas for children as a whole aged between 15 and 18 years school participation was 62 per cent, for Roma/Gypsies it was 21 per cent.[57]

The same research, however, did show an improvement in school participation for Roma/Gypsy pupils between 1992 and 1998. The participation of Roma/Gypsy children aged 7 to 16 years was estimated as being about 5 per cent higher in 1998 than in 1992 for both primary and secondary schools. This could partly be attributed to the fact that in 1994 measures were introduced whereby only those families of children who attended classes could receive their allowance.[58] However, at the time of writing no research has been carried out that explores other factors.

The head-teacher of a school which consists of mostly Roma/Gypsy pupils in Cojomo (a large rural village located in the mountains) explained that it was normal for half of the pupils to be absent at anyone time.[59] It is possible to identify a number of reasons for non-attendance and eventual dropping out on the part of Roma/Gypsies, such as stigmatisation and racist bullying in schools together with the lack of multicultural curricula acknowledging Roma/Gypsy culture identity. Other factors include:
- **Poverty**: some Roma/Gypsy communities live in extreme poverty, for example, in Pata Rat, which is an illegal site located on a rubbish tip. Most children are compelled to work and lack basic infrastructure such as electricity and water. These factors significantly restrict their access to and participation in mainstream schooling. The only educational support of any kind for this particular community is provided by a foreign NGO, *Médecins Sans Frontières*.[60]
- **Poor health**: the Ministry of Health has recently signed an agreement providing free health care for Roma/Gypsies, as part of its strategy for integrating Roma/Gypsies shortly

to be presented to the EU. However, beyond the distribution of cards certifying free medical care, it is not clear at this stage how this will work in practice.[61]

- **Large rural population**: a significant proportion of Roma/Gypsies live in rural communities where, regardless of ethnicity, access to secondary education is often restricted by lack of transport. Schools are also more affected by extreme weather conditions, eg, winter closure. Attending school beyond fourth grade is not viewed as being productive or necessary, particularly within rural communities, due to the particular lack of employment opportunities, and it is often considered to be a burden by those who expect their children to contribute to family income.

Some efforts have been made to address some of these problems. For example, rural schools now have the power to modify the school year structure in accordance with the agricultural calendar. New provisions apply that aim to improve school transport in rural areas. In addition, a special package of measures combining social, material and financial support has been targeted at the Roma/Gypsy population with the aim of securing greater levels of school attendance, thereby facilitating their access to higher education. With more of a focus on Roma/Gypsies specifically, and in particular on those who have abandoned school, the government issued a number of orders. These include orders on the eradication of illiteracy, on overcoming marginalisation and social and professional exclusion and on the organisation of vocational work.[62]

Special schools and childcare institutions

According to Western charities, almost 100,000 children remain institutionalised in Romania. While Roma/Gypsies make up no more than ten per cent of the Romanian population, it is claimed that they account for a much higher percentage of infants in orphanages. Some sources claim that Roma/Gypsy children make up over 80 per cent of the orphanage population.[63]

Children in Romania with special educational needs are also traditionally placed in institutions or "special schools". There are 246 special schools in Romania. The number of children with registered disabilities in special schools is 48,237. The number of students with disabilities included in mainstream schools is 4,822.[64] There is no ethnic breakdown of the special-school student population, and therefore no official data exists on the number of Roma/Gypsies present.

These institutions are differentiated according to the type and degree of disability, eg, speech deficiency, learning difficulties and behavioural problems. They are established at county level, and multidisciplinary commissions are responsible for overseeing the evaluation of children based on criteria approved by the Ministry of Education and Ministry of Health. The selection process is carried out by the Commission of Complex Examination, which is run by the School County Inspectorate. This Commission is organised according to Law 84/1995.[65] Each position in the Commission is gained through public competition; its membership consists of one co-ordinator (psychologist, psycho-pedagogue), two psychologists (specialised in school psychology), one psycho-pedagogue, one medical expert and one social assistant.

Using various tools, such as personality tests (eg, RAVEN) and national standardised tests, the Commission establishes the level and type of disability of the young person in question. On this basis it makes a number of recommendations, including appropriate education, type of special curriculum, personalised intervention programmes and monitoring programmes. On completion of the test, a Certificate of Complex Expertise of Child for School Inspectorate County Notification is drawn up. Based on this notification the child is then registered in a special school.

At Someseni, a school in Cluj Napoca, children identified as having special educational needs are provided for within the secondary school. This is consistent with the policy preferred by the Roma school inspector for that area. In his view there is a fundamental difficulty with the overall system of special schools. He argues that in Romania children attending special schools attract additional funding for both the school and for families. This sets an agenda, which he believes goes against the best interests of the child, since the quality of education is lower and the chances of obtaining future employment are considerably reduced. Thus, although there may be short-term immediate benefits for families, the long-term implications for the children are huge.[66]

Educational reform has included provision for the processes of de-institutionalisation. As part of this, inspectors have been appointed with specific responsibility for children in institutions.

They are required to ensure that there is sufficient co-operation between special-education institutions and mainstream schools to enable smooth transition from the former to the latter. One model is to integrate a few children with special needs into each class, whilst at the same time reducing absolute class sizes. Another model is to establish classes of 8-12 pupils with special needs within mainstream schools. Teacher training includes guidance on working with such children, and specialised classroom back-up (eg, speech therapists) is made available within mainstream establishments.

The National Agency for the Protection of Children's Rights, established by the Emergency Ordinance No. 192/1999, plays a central role in this. It aims to de-institutionalise children, create a range of preventive services, support the further development of foster care and alternative family placements, and develop strategies to prepare children for independence.

Registration in schools

Birth registration and initial school enrolment are issues that often arise when discussing access to education for Roma/Gypsy children. Documentation such as identification documents, birth certificates or civil marriage certificates are required for gaining access to many public services, including education, welfare benefits, health services, public housing and property rights.

Numerous domestic and international organisations have expressed concern about the increasing number of Roma/Gypsy children whose birth has not been registered with the

Romanian authorities and who lack any form of identification. According to the 1992 census, seven per cent of Roma/Gypsy children did not have a birth certificate. Since then some progress has been made with the issue of birth certificates and thus registration in schools.[67] Recent studies show, however, that five per cent of Roma/Gypsies living in Romania still do not have a birth certificate and four per cent of Roma/Gypsies over the age of 14 do not have identity cards.[68] For those Roma/Gypsy communities that are nomadic or at least semi-nomadic, registration issues pose a particular problem.

In 1995, authorities charged with the protection of minors reported that more than 2,500 of the children institutionalised each year (many of whom are Roma/Gypsies) were missing identity documents. The families of children lacking identity documents are not entitled to receive the child-support allowance (approximately $US4 per month). A significant proportion of the more than five million children who *do* receive child allowance are Roma/Gypsies, and these families depend heavily on these child-support allowances, which form a significant proportion of the family income.[69]

It is estimated that between 1,200 and 6,000 Roma/Gypsies might be stateless in Romania after giving up their Romanian citizenship in hopes of being granted asylum in Western countries.[70] As discussed earlier, there are particular bureaucratic obstacles associated with Roma/Gypsy children returnees, which prevents them from returning to school. Readmission policies are complex and make it difficult to register at schools.

Language provision

Given that a large proportion of the Roma/Gypsy population in Romania speaks Romanes, the issue of language provision has dominated much of the debate about meeting the educational needs of Roma/Gypsies. Although in many Roma/Gypsy homes children are raised to speak Romanes as their mother tongue, this does not preclude the learning of Romanian. Most, if not all, Roma/Gypsy children therefore are bilingual if not multilingual. However, rather than addressing issues to do with bilingual teaching and learning, and the skills and sensitivities required on the part of teachers, debates and legislation focus instead on whether and if so how the Romanes language should be taught in schools. For example, the state's efforts at securing fuller "social integration" of Roma/Gypsies, have been mainly concerned with a school programme that offers the opportunity to learn Romanes. There is an option of devoting four hours a week to teaching Romanes in years 1-4, and three hours a week in years 5-12.

The study of Romanes in Romanian schools began in 1990, and special classes for Romani language and literature teachers were established in three teacher-training colleges in Bucharest, Bacâu and Tèrgu-Mures. Students on the programme include not only young people of Roma/Gypsy origin, but also Romanians who have elected to go on to work as teachers in schools with a majority of Roma/Gypsy pupils. After 1992, Romanes was also introduced into primary-school teacher training.[71] In 1998-99, the government established a department of Romani language and literature within the Faculty of Foreign Languages at the University of Bucharest, with places for ten students.[72] In 2000, the Ministry for National Education reported that 4,200 pupils in 37 counties were studying Romanes and that there were 60 Roma/Gypsy language teachers, a rise from 159 pupils and 8 teachers in 1997-98 (see Table 11.3).[73]

Mr Gheorghe Sarau a new inspector for Roma/ Gypsy education is seen by many as contributing to the rising numbers of Roma/ Gypsies receiving education in their mother tongue as well as the numbers of Roma/Gypsy teachers. According to his figures, there were 200 Roma/ Gypsy teachers, out of whom:

- 60 participated in a three-week training course for Romani language and methodological and

Table 11.3 Situation of pupils belonging to national minorities attending schools where teaching is provided in Romanian, who also (by request) study their mother tongue, 1997/98 and 1999/2000

Mother tongue	Total establishments 1997/98	1999/2000	Total pupils 1997/98	1999/2000	Total teaching staff 1997/98	1999/2000
Ukrainian	51	81	7,213	8,132	50	39
Russian (Lipoveni)	18	16	1,547	1,630	13	29
Turkish	46	54	2,212	3,133	62	48
Polish	12	10	398	397	8	13
Bulgarian	5	4	460	478	5	17
Serbian	6	11	251	381	13	14
Slovakian	2	3	37	88	3	4
Czech	5	6	139	123	6	6
Croatian	7	7	557	539	8	10
Greek	3	4	77	193	3	4
Gypsy (Roma)	3	210	159	4,200	8	60
Armenian	2	1	56	11	2	1
Italian	2	1	43	19	2	1
German	2	9	66	519	2	28
Other/not known		24		2,845		82
Total	164	441	13,215	22,688	185	356

Source: Romanian Report on the Framework Convention on the Protection of National Minorities and The Ethos of Education for National Minorities in Romania 1999/2000 School Year, Ministry for National Education in Romania, 2000.

didactic training. This took place in the
summer of 1999 at Satu Mare and was
organised by Sarau with financial support from
the government, FSD Bucharest and FSD Cluj
Napoca Branch

- 45 participated in similar training at
  Calimanesti organised by Sarau with money
  from the Ministry of National Education, the
  UK and French Embassies and Romani CRISS
- 30 of those who completed the course in
  Satu Mare (1999) participated in a
  methodological-didactical module offered
  by Soros Open Network Education 2000+
  at Sinaia in July 2000.

In 2001, the Ministry of National Education
and UNICEF are expected to organise a third
training session on Romani language for a further
90 teachers.

Projects aimed at teaching Romanes are often the
product of individual initiative rather than state
input. A typical example is that of the School
ROMROM, a class for Roma/Gypsy children
held at the home of a teacher from Caracal.
A number of NGO initiatives have also
developed aimed at supporting the study of
the Romani language in schools or centres of
extra-school educational assistance (these run
before or after the official daily school
programme). At present some mainstream
schools offer courses in Romanes for those
Roma/Gypsy children whose parents request it.
However, Romanes is still not the teaching
language in other school disciplines. Those classes
that do exist in Romanes are only a result of
initiatives on the part of individual Roma/Gypsy
teachers. They do not receive any support or

recognition from the official public school
authorities.

In terms of formal teacher training in relation
to intercultural education, universities including
Bucharest are encouraged to take measures to
organise the study of languages and literature
of national minorities, including Romanes.[74]
However, the programme of the teacher training
college in Bucharest shows a number of
shortcomings. First, the programmes seem very
theoretical. Secondly, there seems to be no
concern for civic education although books on
this subject have been introduced at the lower and
upper levels of secondary school. Thirdly, it
appears that there are no elements for identifying
and being aware of differences and similarities
between people, or their consequences at the
social and personal level.[75] Finally, training
primary-school teachers to be aware of equal-
opportunities and discrimination issues is not a
permanent feature of their initial training. If these
issues are tackled, it seems to be only on an *ad hoc*
basis.[76] Ultimately, it remains that although there
has been a significant increase in the number of
students receiving teaching in Romanes as
part of overall schooling, there are still no units
specifically designed for the teaching of Romanes
as there are for other minorities (see Table 11.4).

NGOs are proving to be important actors in the
field of teacher training. Save the Children
Romania, for example, organised, five training
courses in 2000 in Brasov, Tèrgu-Mures, Sibiu,
Mangalia and Baia Mare. This training was for
188 teachers working with Roma/Gypsy children
from 34 counties. It aimed to give teachers
information about Roma/Gypsy history, culture

Table 11.4 Schools in Romania by languages of tuition, 1999/2000

Language of tuition	Total number of schools		Total number of pupils	
	No.	%	No.	%
Hungarian	2,388	9%	193,635	5%
German	277	1%	18,353	0.4%
Ukrainian	18	0.06%	892	–
Serbian	31	0.1%	1,066	–
Slovak	35	0.1%	1,323	–
Czech	3	0.02%	159	–
Croatian	3	0.01%	114	–
Roma/Gypsy	0	–	0	–
Total	2,755	10%	215,542	5.2%

and traditions, and help contribute to a positive change in the overall approach towards Roma/Gypsy children. The Project on Ethnic Relations also organised a series of training activities in Tèrgu-Mures for Roma/Gypsy and non-Roma/Gypsy teachers who have Romani children in their classrooms. These seminars provided an opportunity for teachers to learn about the language and cultural traditions of Roma/Gypsies as well as different teaching methodologies for multicultural classrooms.[77] However, it is difficult to assess within the scope of the report how effective such training is in the long term, in the absence of any formal evaluation.

Increased importance is also being attached to co-operation between Romanian authorities and NGOs working in the field of textbooks on Roma/Gypsy education and culture. A collection of Roma/Gypsy literary texts (for years one to four) was first published during the 1995-96 academic year. The Educational Publishing House has since published a special textbook to support the teaching of Romanes, and the Ministry of Education has prepared a curriculum for years one to four. It is estimated that at present there are over 200 textbooks, studies, dictionaries, research and other material on the issue of Roma/Gypsies in Romanian, Romani and Hungarian languages.[78] For example, there is a multilingual "Communication Manual" for the first year of study, which has had a print run of about 20,000. There are also some texts in the Romani language for years two to four (20,000 copies), a Romani language text by Gheorghe Sarau for grades five to eight (5,000 copies), a primer, published in September 2001 (2,000 copies), and an arithmetic text (experimental basis only). There is still no authoritative textbook on Romani history and culture, in spite of the fact that there is an officially agreed curriculum for this subject.

No in-depth research into the impact of such textbooks has so far been carried out. Roma/Gypsy organisations have requested that the Ministry of Education organise and support the establishment of a working group to evaluate the use of such textbooks, consisting of both Roma/Gypsy and non-Roma/Gypsy education experts. The Ministry of Education is currently conducting a large impact study of textbooks and teacher training with the Institute of Educational Sciences and school professionals. However, this does not include a focus on Romani textbooks.[79]

In spite of the production of textbooks on Romani language, the process of standardising Romanes for this purpose has encountered a number of difficulties. The main difficulty is that a wide variety of dialects is spoken among Roma/Gypsy groups across Romania. For example, in Lungani, a small, heavily Roma/Gypsy-populated rural village in northern Romania, a particular

dialect of Romanes is spoken as the first language. A series of textbooks were introduced to the local school, written in Romanes. However, the Romanes used in these textbooks was not the same dialect, and therefore significantly limited their use in this context.[80]

As well as the need to be sensitive to different Romani dialects, the content of curricula must also be reviewed. So far, efforts in respect to this have been far from fruitful. It seems that the current Romanian textbooks and curricula hardly refer, if at all, to children belonging to ethnic groups other than the majority. Little information is provided on personalities from minority groups or on how minorities have contributed to Romanian history.[81] In particular it appears that many aspects of Roma/Gypsy history are hidden from school curricula in a number of ways:[82]

- Romani words (eg, *gadjo, mishto, nasol*) which are used by both Roma/Gypsies and

Romanians are not acknowledged in dictionaries or textbooks and are considered at best as slang.

- The history of Roma/Gypsy slavery is not mentioned at all.
- Aspects of Roma/Gypsy customs and their way of life are not referred to.
- Images of children in textbooks reflect only the majority population.

The reformulation of curricula, examinations, textbooks and other education policies, from before and since 1991, are carried out by relatively small teams of "experts". Continuing in this tradition, working groups consisting mostly of three to five national experts, sometimes more, are currently solely responsible for designing the course syllabuses for the new curriculum. These teams usually consist of Romanian and foreign specialists, with little widespread or substantive participation from either practitioners or from members of minority communities.[83]

The 1999 amendments to the Education Law included further provisions designed to improve access to education for minorities, with special emphasis on the needs of Roma/Gypsies. Universities can now be established with teaching provided in a minority language backed up by the provision of textbooks in that language. Notwithstanding governmental efforts in this field, in the absence of self-referential education, education policies regarding Roma/Gypsy children seem to be still generating stigma in schools and reinforcing negative perceptions of the "other". For example, mixed classes introduced in schools in Calvini and Vaslui,

although aimed at avoiding segregation, served to reinforce it. With the underlying aim being to bring all pupils in line with Romanian culture and norms, no attempt was made to form links with members of the Roma/Gypsy community and, in particular, the parents. As a result, most local Roma/Gypsy children do not attend.

However, this is not limited to practice on the ground. The overall education policy of the Romanian government seems still to be dominated by assimilative overtones, where the emphasis for change is placed with the "out-group", in this case Roma/Gypsies, rather than with the majority society and systems. The main goal of the Ministry of Education seems to be concerned only with ensuring attendance of Roma/Gypsy children in either mainstream schools or Roma/ Gypsy-specific schools. No emphasis is placed on injecting schools with multicultural values, or with introducing Romanes language, culture and history to the pupil population as a whole. There is no move towards alternative pedagogy or equal education opportunities respecting cultural differences.

As a result, problems soon emerge with the practical application of such legislation. For example, in response to the legislation that stipulates the right for Roma/Gypsy pupils to receive tuition in Romanes for a certain number of hours per week, school principals often find various ways to prevent its implementation. Anecdotal evidence suggests that some school principals try to convince Roma/Gypsy parents that the Romanes language is useless for their children, whilst others threaten to cut their school allowance if parents insist that their children learn Romanes. The refusal to allow classes in Romanes has also occurred at higher levels. For example, the School Inspectorate for the Calarsai County rejected an application from the Mihai-Viteazul school to teach the Romanes language.[84]

The following breakdown of teaching staff according to teaching language in Table 11.5 shows there are still no Roma/Gypsy teachers in mainstream schooling, despite the increase in the number of Roma/Gypsy teachers hired specifically for language tuition.

Whilst preservation of the Romanes language is important, the debate rarely, if at all, focuses on the skills required for teaching bilingual and multilingual children. In 1997-98, the only bilingual units were for Turkish-Tartar students. One argument is that parents have a responsibility to their children to raise them to speak in the principal language in which they are to be educated. However, this fails to take into account that Roma/Gypsy parents themselves may not have passed through the education system. On the other hand there are some who advocate an increased level of teaching at all grades in the Romanes language, placing an emphasis on the establishment of Roma/Gypsy-specific secondary schools. This latter policy proposal is problematic, however, as it can further reinforce separation, isolation and a two-tier education system.

Table 11.5 Teaching staff by level and teaching language in pre-university education 1999/00

Teaching language	Overall total	Preschool teachers	Primary-school teachers	Secondary-school teachers
Total	311,335	36,648	62,858	211,829
Total minorities	15,708	2,807	3,894	9,007
Hungarian	14,186	2,474	3,463	8,249
German	1,212	269	333	610
Ukrainian	57	17	15	25
Serbian	76	11	19	46
Bulgarian	6	6	0	0
Slovakian	139	24	55	60
Czech	17	3	8	6
Croatian	15	3	1	11

NGO practice in the area[85]

It has been estimated that over half the funding for Romanian NGOs originates from foreign donors. It is only in recent years that some local funders have started to provide small grants to NGOs. These Romanian donor agencies, however, still rely on raising their funds from abroad. Limited central government funds are available to NGOs in some areas of health and social care and youth work. However, funding procedures are still relatively *ad hoc*. While a legal framework for the funding of NGOs by local government exists, funds are very limited and their allocation suffers from many of the same problems experienced at central level.[86]

This trend seems to be most apparent in the field of education. For instance, the initiatives described in this section are delivered by NGOs only. Typically, projects are funded by external donors on a 12-month funding cycle that may or may not be renewed. Yet there is reluctance on the part of the government to fund such NGO activities. As a result, a climate of uncertainty exists for teachers, parents and pupils involved in these projects.

Grants and loans from external sources for education development in Romania are substantial on a per capita basis and in relation to the levels received by neighbouring countries in Central and Eastern Europe. A study prepared by the Institute for Educational Sciences estimates that the equivalent of more than $US500 million has been committed to education in Romania in recent years. The largest among these commitments are from the World Bank and the EU PHARE Programme.[87] Florin Moisa, Executive President of the Resource Centre for Roma Communities in Romania, has stated that 2 million euros had been allocated to Romania through the PHARE programme for the period April/May 2000 to September/October 2001, aimed specifically at the improvement of the Roma situation in Romania.[88] At the time of writing, however, the government had not yet implemented any strategies for allocating this money, which according to Moisa is due to the lack of political will. According to Monica Dvorski, Programmes Director of Centre Education 2000+, in March 2001 the government had so far not allocated any funding to NGOs working in the area of education.[89]

In addition to this, the short-term nature of NGO funding in Romania presents particular problems for developing services in communities such as those described above. Engaging with such communities takes time. This is especially true in light of the transient nature of many communities, and the lack of community structure and identifiable leadership in some. Underpinning the lack of long-term engagement is the fact that donors are often uninterested in promoting services in communities where severe and multiple problems exist and success is difficult to demonstrate. As several of the early projects are coming to a close, it will be important to ensure that there are clear follow-up and exit strategies from the external agencies, and plans for the sustainability of project impact and scaling up of programmes where appropriate.[90]

Centre Education 2000+ – a macro-project

Between 1998 and 2000, the Open Society Foundation Romania, in partnership with the Netherlands National Institute for Curriculum Development and the MATRA programme, ran an ambitious macro-project, "Equal opportunities for Roma children through school and school-related activities". It was concerned with developing models of school improvement and education reform that would not only be suitable for local implementation, but could also be replicated in other contexts. In addition, the project sought to promote bilateral communication and co-operation amongst institutions and agencies responsible for the implementation of education reform relevant to Roma/Gypsies at a local level.

In the first year, 12 schools were selected in communities with large numbers of Roma/Gypsies. A further 17 schools joined the project in the second year. The schools were generally representative of the Romanian education system, ie, schools from both urban and rural areas with a mixture of homogeneous and heterogeneous school populations. Schools were encouraged to meet with each other to develop a management style that enabled them to meet the specific educational needs of local communities. A focus was placed on local decision-making and accountability, with a view to enhancing the awareness of and access to education for young Roma/Gypsies. Specific attention was given to co-operative learning as opposed to competition, intercultural education and oral history. Parental involvement was actively encouraged and remedial teaching was seen to demonstrably assist Roma/Gypsy children with their low self-esteem. The schools were primarily viewed as pilots from which it was hoped good practice could be disseminated to other schools, but also to other spheres of social provision relevant to Roma/Gypsy communities. In addition, the project has produced a first reader in Romanes together with a range of publications for teachers offering examples of "good practice".[91]

Catalina Ulrich, one of the programme co-ordinators for the project, believes the most significant problem currently faced by Roma/Gypsy children is low self-esteem, and that the greatest challenge to their effective participation in schooling is the need to establish links with and facilitate the involvement of the parents.[92] At the launch of their new programme, "Improving Education for Roma Focus on Romania", she also highlighted a number of other issues, such as the importance of the children and parents involved having a sense of ownership of the programme. One of the ways in which they have gone some way in achieving this is by using mainly materials produced by Roma/Gypsies themselves.

The overall objective of the new initiative is to support education for Roma in accordance with their specific needs. In particular, it aims to encourage co-operation between governmental and non-governmental bodies in education and actively to involve communities in school life. As well as providing five preselected schools with grants for equipment and teaching materials, it will offer a series of "teacher guides" on topics such as "Intercultural Education", "Classroom Management" and "Remedial Teaching". It is funded under the Stability Pact Initiative for South-Eastern Europe. The funds for the project ($US150,000) were donated by the Austrian Ministry of Foreign Affairs and will cover the running costs for 2001. However, the project's reliance on short-term funding and the lack of institutional sustainability continues to pose the greatest threat to its continued effectiveness.

Fundatia Familia Si Ocrotireas Copilului – a micro-project

Fundatia Familia Si Ocrotireas Copilului (FOC) is an NGO operating in Ferentari. This is an illegal settlement situated in Sector 5 of Bucharest. It has a population of about 400, nearly all of whom identify themselves as Roma. The community and, in particular, its children face multiple social problems as a result of both extreme poverty and discrimination.

Through the school, and in partnership with the community members, FOC aims to operate a holistic approach in working with children and families at risk of extreme marginalisation. Although most of the children with whom the project works are Roma/Gypsies, they are not exclusively so. Although operational in the area since 1995, FOC has only recently turned its attention specifically to the role of schooling.

FOC provides an integrated service to the community and employs social workers, educators and counsellors, backed up by a group of volunteers. Within the local school, FOC provides a separate classroom in which it gives half-day education for two groups of 15 pupils. These pupils are identified as being either at risk of abandoning school or, having done so, have decided to return to school, but require additional support in returning. Because FOC is located within the community, interventions are agreed on a contractual basis between FOC, the child and the family. The schools are not part of this process, although they give full discretion and support to FOC in meeting the aims of the project.

Educational input is broadly defined and delivered on a small-group or individual basis, with content determined by the needs of the individual child. Teaching children to read and write is considered a basic objective. Considerable emphasis is placed upon social education and the development of interpersonal skills. The project does not receive any governmental funding, but relies entirely on foreign donors for its income. It is currently funded on a short-term basis by *Terre Des Hommes* and hopes to attract finance from UNICEF in 2001.

The Center for Education and Professional Development – Step-by-Step, Open Society Foundation

The Center for Education and Professional Development is a member of the Soros Open Network and is focused on implementing the Step-by-Step programme, an alternative model of educational provision for 0-13 year olds. This new method of education rests on the idea that the intellectual development of children starts from the nursery and has to be guided by both the family and educational institutions.[93]

The programme was first introduced in Romanian schools in 1996. A number of schools in all but seven counties in Romania have adopted this approach. More recently, Step-by-Step has been introduced to schools where at least 60 per cent of the pupils are Roma/Gypsies. Key features of the approach include individualised learning, social education, work in small activity groups and the ongoing involvement of parents within the formal school context. Step-by-Step also provides a midday meal to children. This is significant in light of the fact that school children in Romania are expected to provide their own lunches.

The Step-by-Step programme has been established in the Prahova county in a number of schools. For example, in September 2000, Step-by-Step started a kindergarten class in Poina Varbilau, a small rural village some 30km from the main town, Ploiesti. About 80 per cent of the population are Roma/Gypsies. This particular community does not speak Romanes and when parents were consulted on whether their children should be taught Romanes, they felt it to be more useful for them to learn English.

At the time of writing, the class catered for 31 children, 20 of whom were Roma/Gypsies. The teacher, a local resident, received special training in the Step-by-Step methodology. The involvement of parents is seen as vital. Parents helped establish the project by decorating the classroom, and are responsible for its upkeep. The classroom also doubles up as "parents' room". Parents accompany children on school trips and involve themselves in classroom activities. The programme was seen as an opportunity for helping to develop parenting skills, which were encouraged with the help of booklets translated from Dutch.

Ploiesti also has a large Roma/Gypsy population. Unlike the Roma/Gypsies in Poina Varbilau, this community leads a semi-nomadic lifestyle. At the state kindergarten, 31 out of the total 44 pupils were Roma/Gypsies. When first attending the school, Roma/Gypsy children tended to feel more isolated than most. Methods of small-group activity were therefore used. Many children came from homes that lacked basic facilities such as toilets or running water, so it was felt that basic skills associated with these needed to be incorporated into the learning.

The school, in accordance with the Step-by-Step methodology, actively encourages parental involvement in the school. However, such activities contravene legislation which purports to ban Roma/Gypsy parents on the grounds of "health and safety". For example, the "sanitary police" had recently visited the school and wanted to impose an on-the-spot fine, thus revealing one example of legislated bad practice that reinforces discrimination.

A Step-by-Step kindergarten programme had also been established within a secondary school in Ploiesti. The school, which caters for 467 pupils, about a third of whom are Roma/Gypsies, covers the 8-14/15 age range. The Step-by-Step kindergarten class within this had 28 children, 17 of whom were Roma/Gypsies. Unusually, this particular class had two teachers instead of one. The class worked in activity groups with the active participation of parents. According to the teachers, the response of Roma/Gypsy parents was mixed: while some seemed highly motivated in promoting their children's education, others seemed scared of the knowledge and abilities that their children would acquire. The children themselves, when interviewed, expressed much enthusiasm for the school.[94]

Salvati Copiii – Save the Children Romania

Salvati Copiii has developed a national plan of action aimed at supporting the interests of Roma/Gypsy children (see box below). This has been agreed upon by various Roma/Gypsy and non-Roma/Gypsy organisations, and by some governmental institutions. The ultimate objective is for this plan to be incorporated into the Romanian government's national strategy on Roma/Gypsies. The plan has been sent to all relevant ministries, including the Education Ministry.

According to its preamble, the plan is based on the principle of a real democracy, including the provision of equal rights, chances and opportunities for all citizens and children. It recognises that children belonging to minority

---

Salvati Copiii's National Plan of Action

- All educational provision should be made by the authorities in consultation with Roma/Gypsy representatives, in order to make education appropriate and relevant. In the national programmes in support of Roma/Gypsy children, elected representatives from Roma/Gypsy communities should be included in order to represent the interests of Roma/Gypsy children. Where possible, Roma/Gypsy children and adults should be included as well. The responsibility for implementing these provisions lies with the Ministry of National Education, the school inspectorates of the counties, Roma/Gypsy NGOs and Roma/Gypsy communities.

- Educational authorities, Roma/Gypsy and non-Roma/Gypsy NGOs should work together to train teachers for preschool and school education, and to incorporate an intercultural curriculum. The responsibility for implementing this lies with the Ministry of National Education, school inspectorates of the counties and NGOs.

- Action should be taken to promote the value of education among Roma/Gypsy families. Support and advice facilities should be set up close to the settlements of Roma/Gypsy communities. The responsibility for implementing this will lie with school inspectorates of the counties, school units, NGOs, the Alliance for Roma/Gypsy Unity and the Department for Child Protection.

- Cultural institutions should be responsible for the publication of teaching materials concerning Roma/Gypsy history, culture and traditions. Such institutions should be the Ministries of Culture and National Education, the Department for the Protection of Minorities and NGOs.

- The curriculum should include information about Roma/Gypsy history and culture. Those responsible should be the Ministry of National Education and Roma/Gypsy NGOs. Due to the fact that at certain times of year Roma/Gypsies and children accompany their parents to work in other areas, these children should be accepted by schools in those areas, on the basis of an operative correspondence between school units. Implementation of this proposal should be carried out by the Ministry of National Education, school inspectorates of the counties and school units.

- It is essential that children retain knowledge and understanding of their mother tongue. Therefore all kindergartens should make this available through appropriate support, including bilingual materials and Romani teachers of Roma/Gypsy origin. This process should be continued at all stages of the educational system, according to pupils' requests. The responsibility for implementing this lies with the Ministry of National Education, school inspectorates of the counties, Roma/Gypsy NGOs and Roma/Gypsy communities.

- In recognition of the strong oral culture of Roma/Gypsy communities, broadcasting authorities should be urged to schedule educational programmes in the Romani language at times accessible to children. The broadcasting authorities, national television, commercial broadcasters, the Ministry of National Education and NGOs should be responsible for this.

communities have the right to their own culture, religion and language in order to have access to all public services.

The preamble estimates that about half of the Roma/Gypsy population of school age do not attend school on a regular basis; some of these children have never attended school and a very small percentage ever reaches higher education. The result is a high rate of illiteracy, which affects all aspects of Roma/Gypsy life. The preamble

claims that Roma/Gypsy families' attitude towards education is generally one of reticence, based on a fear that their own children will suffer because of the attitudes of other children and teachers. It also acknowledges that there is still a widespread lack of information on the Romanes language, history and culture in school books and curricula for children belonging to the majority of the population.

• School authorities and Roma/Gypsy NGOs together should find the best solutions for school evaluation and orientation. Roma/Gypsy children who have not had access to preschool education should be enrolled, one year before their school age, in preparatory classes. Responsible bodies should be the school inspectorates of the counties, school units and kindergartens, Roma/Gypsy NGOs and Roma/Gypsy communities.

• Roma/Gypsy children should be integrated in mainstream education. In special cases, Article 8 of the Education Law, concerning transport to the nearest school, would apply. Those responsible should be the education authorities and Roma/Gypsy NGOs.

• Children and adolescents who failed education at the prescribed age should have the opportunity to attend part-time courses in schools as close as possible to their homes. The Ministry of National Education, school inspectorates of the counties, school units and Roma/Gypsy communities should be responsible for implementing this.

• Teachers who have Roma/Gypsy children in their classes should receive specific training. The Ministry of National Education, school inspectorates of the counties, teachers' clubs, and county centres for psychic and pedagogical assistance should be responsible for this.

• Based on NGO proposals, the Ministries of Culture and National Education should plan and allot funds in order to preserve Roma/Gypsy culture and the Romani language, by stimulating specific talents and organising in schools certified technological courses for Roma/Gypsy traditional professions. Responsible bodies should be the Ministry of Culture, the Ministry of National Education, the Ministry of Youth and Sports and NGOs.

• The provision of school and professional training for Roma/Gypsy children is the base for their future social integration, and will give them the chance to find better places to work. Ultimately, this will lead to the improvement of Roma/Gypsy families' standards of living.

The National Plan of Action also sets a strategy for the protection and promotion of Roma/Gypsy identity and culture. Because of the widespread racist attitudes and labelling of Roma/Gypsy children, it calls for a media campaign to combat stereotypes, discrimination against Roma/Gypsies and other forms of xenophobia and intolerance. This campaign will be carried out by television and radio broadcasts, governmental institutions, NGOs and journalists. Finally, the National Plan of Action also includes a strategy for health issues.

Save the Children Romania organises teacher training for teachers working with Roma/Gypsy children (as discussed previously). It also runs different projects for Roma/Gypsy children, such as:

- kindergartens for Roma/Gypsy children in Tecuci and Sanger-Mures
- classes in the Romanian language for children in a school in Craiova

- an information caravan that goes to Roma/Gypsy communities in five counties offering information on the rights of Roma/Gypsy children
- education on non-discrimination in three counties
- the production of several publications for Roma/Gypsy children, including the UN Convention on the Rights of the Child in the Romani language.

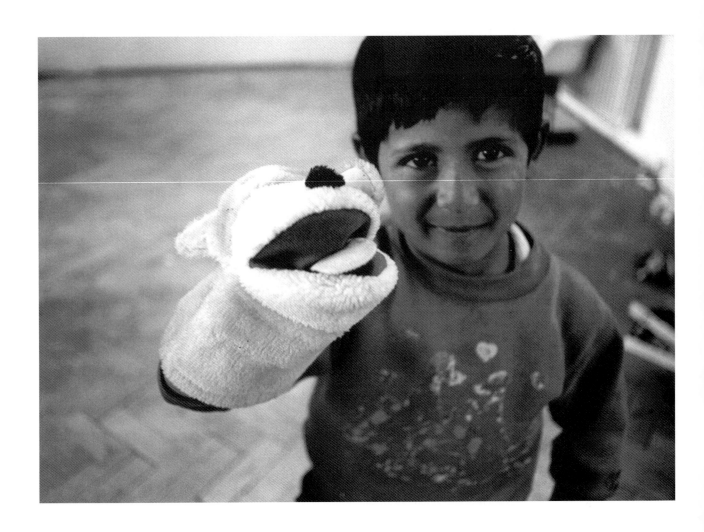

Voices of Roma/Gypsy children

These interviews are taken from the transcript of the film *Equal Chances* produced by *Salvati Copiii*, Save the Children Romania. Interviews were conducted with 10 Roma/Gypsy communities during the period April – May 1998.

"What grade are you in?"
"1st grade."
"And how old are you?"
"I'm 12."

"How old are you?"
"I'm 14."
"Do you still go to school?"
"No."
"How many grades did you finish in school?"
"Six."
"And how long have you been going to the garbage pit?"
"Since I was a little kid... I've been going to both – to school and to the pit... since I was 5."

"I pick cherries. My mother washes them and in the evening after school, I go and sell them."
"Where?"
"Here, in Mangalia."
"But, why do you sell cherries?"
"To buy notebooks, shoes, clothes..."

"Do you enjoy school?"
"I enjoy it, but I don't have the things I need to go, we don't have the money for books and notebooks."

"What is the most important thing for you?"
"To learn! It's good to learn..."

"Why?"
"Because if I didn't learn, I wouldn't know anything."

"Do you enjoy school?"
"Yes."
"Why do you like it?"
"I like reading."

"Sometimes, we feel sad because we have such a horrible school. Others have lovely schools... but we have an ugly school."
"Why are the other schools lovely?"
"They have central heating and beautiful desks."

"How do the teachers talk to you?"
"'Go to hell!' 'Shut up!'... They hit our hands with a stick, pull our hair ..."

"Do you have any Romanian friends?"
"Yes."
"And Roma ones?"
"Yes, both Roma and Romanians."
"Who do you get along with the best?"
"All of them. I have no problems with any of them."

"Would you prefer to be Romanian, English or French?"
"No! A... a Romanian Roma."

"The Magyar [Hungarian] children at school treat us badly."
"Why don't you have Magyar classmates?"
"Because they stay away from the Roma and they don't speak to us at all."
"Are you in separate classes?"
"Yes."

"Can you speak Romani?"
"No, there is no one here to speak Romani to. No one speaks it in our village."

"Would you like to go to school?"
"Yes."
"And what would you like to learn at school?"
"To learn, to read..."

"If one of the children gets ill, we carry them on our back up to the ambulance."
"How far?"
"5km."

"There are 20 boys and girls in Colt'u who can't read or write. They are 16 to 20 years old."
"And did they go to school?"
"Yes, they went to school here, in the village, to the Hungarian school. But they didn't learn a word of Hungarian."

"Would you like to read and write?"
"Yes, very much."
"Why?"
"Because here, in our community, I do activities with the children... we put on plays about the life and customs of the Roma people. We've even taken our theatre group to Bucharest. I would like to write down my ideas by myself. But I have to ask someone to spend hours with me to write down my ideas on what I want to do with the children."

These interviews were conducted by Charlie Bell during the period November – December 2000 as part of the research for the report, with the help of Veronica Vasilescu, Ioana Herseni, Ioana Puscascu and Catalin Ganea.

C, 8 years old

"Do you have brothers and sisters?"
"I had a brother and a sister. Both died. I have one brother. He is in the fifth grade now."
"And what do you like about school?"
"They teach us to write. We eat. They tell us stories. We can sit on the chair and say something new every day. We learn poems."
"And do you have any special friends?"
"Everybody. All the boys and all the girls."
"Do you sometimes miss school?"
"Yes, sometimes I'm ill."
"And what do you want to do when you are older?"
"I want to be like my father. I want to wash cars."

A group of 8-18 year olds, attending a special remedial project part-funded by two NGOs, but located in a secondary school in Iasi

"So why have you taken this second chance to return to education?"
"I was in Germany. They did not provide education for us there."

"I need to read and write in order to get my driving licence."

"I want to emigrate and my chances are better if I know some things."

"I want to be a doctor, teacher or lawyer to help Roma people."

A special class in the Someseni secondary school in Cluj

"What don't you like about school?"
"When our teacher shouts at us."

A 15 year old attending the FOC project at School No. 136, Ferentari, Bucharest

"How many children in this class are Roma?"
"We do not discriminate by ethnicity here. We face the same problems and live in the same community. Yes, we have problems that are common to us all. You must understand that to focus on our race will divert the authorities from finding the solutions to these problems."

A 17 year old attending a vocational school in Cluj

"What do you know about the new anti-discrimination ordinance that has recently been introduced? Do you think it will help Roma people?"
"Sure we know about it. But it is just a law. We will have problems when we want to get a job, but here at school we are treated equally and fairly."

Another member of the same class

"Is it helpful to have teaching in the Romani language?"
"No. None of us speak it. It is only spoken by the old people aged over 70. We are Romanian. The Romani language will not help us get jobs."

A group of Roma/Gypsy students at Iasi University

"If you were Minister of Education for a day what changes would you make to promote education for Roma?"
"I would not want to be Minister for Education. Our education system is fine. I would prefer to be Minister of Finance and allocate money to implement it effectively."

"I would make education to eighth grade compulsory for all Roma and hold parents accountable for ensuring that their children attended school. Yes, that would be a priority."

"Having reached University you have obviously faced and overcome considerable discrimination. Do you face discrimination here?"
"Most of us have been lucky. Our parents have money and have supported us. We do not face discrimination at University. Well, that's not true. We receive too much positive discrimination from the staff and sometimes that gives us problems with the other students."

"And what about teaching in the Romani language?"
"It is good to preserve our culture but it is of little practical use."

"Yes, I do not speak Romani, but I would like my son to be able to."

Recommendations

Given that Romania has ratified:
- the International Covenant on Civil and Political Rights (ratified 9 December 1974, entered into force 23 March 1976)
- the International Covenant on Economic, Social and Cultural Rights (ratified 9 December 1974, entered into force 3 January 1976)
- the International Convention on the Elimination of All Forms of Racial Discrimination (ratified 15 September 1970, entered into force 15 October 1970)
- the Convention on the Rights of the Child (ratified 28 September 1990, entered into force 28 October 1990)

- the Convention Against Discrimination in Education, 1960 (ratified 1964)
- the International Convention on the Elimination of All Forms of Racial Discrimination, 1965 (ratified 1970)
- the European Convention for the Protection of Human Rights and Fundamental Freedoms (ratified 20 June 1994, entered into force the same date)
- Protocols Nos. 1 to 10 to the Convention for the Protection of Human Rights and Fundamental Freedoms (ratified 10 June 1994)
- Protocol No. 11 to the Convention for the Protection of Human Rights and Fundamental Freedoms, on the restructuring of the control mechanism established by the Convention (ratified 1 August 1995)
- the European Framework Convention for the Protection of National Minorities (ratified 11 May 1995, entered into force 1 February 1998)

and that it has signed but not yet ratified:
- the European Charter for Regional or Minority Languages (signed 17 July 1995)

Save the Children recommends that:

The Government of Romania

- Implements the international obligations stemming from the different international treaties it has ratified.
- Ratifies the European Charter for Regional or Minority Languages.
- Invites the Special Rapporteur on the Right to Education to conduct a field mission in order to assess the shortcomings of the Romanian education system, in particular with regard to the right to education of Roma/Gypsy children.
- Includes in the legislation adequate provisions banning discrimination in the sphere of education, providing effective remedies for victims of discriminatory treatment.
- Clarifies the statistical data regarding the Roma/Gypsy population, and related figures such as the number of Roma/Gypsy children attending school and their attainment.
- Amends current legislation in order to ensure the teaching in and of the Romani language and the establishment of specific educational institutions providing education for Roma/Gypsy identity (Roma/Gypsy history, culture, arts, etc), supported by adequate financial resources.
- Develops a partnership on an equal basis with Roma/Gypsy representatives in shaping education policies for Roma/Gypsies and ensures Roma/Gypsies equal participation in implementing and evaluating such policies and processes.
- Supports, including by sufficient financial resources, a self-referential education policy to include:
  - programmes to eradicate stigmas and develop self-esteem among Roma/Gypsy children, including multicultural programmes in the Children's Clubs
  - kindergartens in Roma/Gypsy communities and the development of preschool education
  - education in the mother tongue, by progressively teaching in the Romani language, supporting the devlopment of teaching materials in the Romani language and supporting the development of appropriate teacher training.

– the establishment in schools of counselling centres for Roma/Gypsy parents and of programmes for Roma/Gypsy parents to take part in school processes and decisions

– the development of ethnic-identity assertion and anti-discrimination programmes for institutionalised Roma/Gypsy children and other Roma/Gypsy children in difficulty

– the development of distance education for Roma/Gypsy and rural communities, by supporting the development of teaching materials and communication networks in the country and abroad, encouraging educational activities within the international Roma/Gypsy network.

• Supports, including by sufficient financial resources, intercultural education to include:

– a national campaign of intercultural education and the prevention of racial discrimination in schools

– compulsory intercultural education for teachers

– compulsory anti-racial/intercultural education in schools

– adequate training in intercultural education, for children of the majority, teachers and other education professionals, for public servants, police and army staff

– adoption of multicultural school curricula and the development of teaching materials, including textbooks on civic/anti-racial education and Roma history/culture

– training for school mediators

– promoting the participation of Roma/Gypsy parents in schools

– intercultural permanent/adult education, including through the mass media.

The international organisations, including the UN Commission on Human Rights, the Special Rapporteur on the Right to Education and the Special Rapporteur on Contemporary Forms of Racism, Racial Discrimination, Xenophobia and Related Intolerance, and the European Union

- Closely monitor the international obligations undertaken by the Romanian government in respect of the right to education, with particular attention to the right to education of Roma/Gypsy children.

Romania: Notes on the text

1 For some Roma organisations and other human-rights groups, the ethnic designation of Rom (pl. Roma, adj. Romani) is a matter of self-identification and self-determination. Therefore, members of Roma associations have recommended the use of these terms. Some of the Romani organisations also recommend the use of the double "Rr", which corresponds more specifically to its pronunciation in the *Kalderash* dialect. Notwithstanding these linguistic justifications, the government, in order to avoid what it claims to be confusion between the ethnic designation and other patronymic stems such as Romania, Rome, etc, has used the double "Rr" spelling. This report, in order to be consistent with the report as a whole, uses the terms "Roma/Gypsy" or "Roma/Gypsies", recognising that *Țigani* is still used by some communities and that not all those groups who identify themselves as Roma use the "Rr" spelling.

2 *Țigani* was the official term used in the 1992 census.

3 Elena si Catalin Zamfir, *Tiganii Intre Ignorare si Igrijorare (Gypsies: Between Ignorance and Anxiety)*, Editura Alternative, 1993.

4 Elena Marushiakova and Vesselin Popov, "Historical and Ethnographic Background: Gypsies, Roma , Sinti" in Will Guy (ed) *Between Past and Future: the Roma of Central and Eastern Europe*, University of Hertfordshire Press, 2001, and Viorel Achim, *Țiganii în istoria Românieie (A History of Gypsies in Romania)*, Editura Enciclopedicâ, Bucharest, 1998.

5 Unpublished research of Romani Criss cited by Elena Marushiakova and Vesselin Popov in their comments to this report.

6 *Rudari* are one of the groups of Romanian-speaking Gypsies (often with a non-Rom consciousness) that are found throughout Europe. They are also referred to in other contexts as *Karavlahs* (in Bosnia and Herzegovina, for example) and *Boyashi/Boyasha* (in Croatia, for example).

7 Elena Marushiakova and Vesselin Popov, "Historical and Ethnographic Background: Gypsies, Roma, Sinti." in Will Guy (ed) *Between Past and Future, the Roma of Central and Eastern Europe*, University of Hertfordshire Press, Spring 2001.

8 World Bank, *Romania. Current Political Situation*, 16 January 2001.

9 European Roma Rights Centre, *Sudden Rage at Dawn – Violence Against Roma in Romania*, September 1996.

10 European Commission, *Regular Report on Progress towards Accession, Romania*, 8th November 2000.

11 Mihaela Tesliuc and Lucian Pop, *Poverty, Inequality and Social Protection*, International Management Foundation, Bucharest, December 2000.

12 Ina Zoon, *On the Margins: Roma and Public Services in Romania, Bulgaria and Macedonia*, edited by Mark Norman Templeton, OSI, New York, 2001.

13 "Roma still Knocking on Europe's Closed Doors", *Transitions*, Vol. 4, No. 4, September 1997.

14 Romanian National Youth Policy, *European Steering Committee for Youth – 26th meeting*, Budapest 25 – 27 October 2000, Evaluation Report by the International Group of Experts.

15 World Bank, *Hidden Challenges to Education Systems in Transition Economies*, September 2000, p. 38.

16 World Bank, *Hidden Challenges to Education Systems in Transition Economies*, September 2000, p. 38.

17 Delia Grighore in her comments for this report.

18 OSI and the Central European University Centre for Policy Studies (CPS), *EU Accession Project: Roma Minority in Romania*, country report, forthcoming.

19 Nicolae Gheorghe *et al* and PERRAC – the Advisory Rromani Council of the Project on Ethnic Relations, *"Rrom[ani people]" or "Țigan" (pronn [tsigan])?*, a draft working document (updated March 2000 DG 123) prepared for the International Seminar on Tolerance organised by the Council of Europe, the Romanian government and ODIHR-OSCE, Bucharest, 23-26 May 1999.

20 Exchange rate: $US1.00 = 28,001.00 Romanian lei (on 23 May 2001)

21 Government of Romania, Department for Protection of National Minorities, Bucharest, 2000.

22 N Gheorghe, N Bitu, J Tanaka and S Stefanescu, "Policy-making on Roma in Central and Eastern European Countries: Inventory, Challenges, Commitments, Good Practices and Weaknesses", in Embassy of Finland in Romania, *International Expert Symposium on Roma Questions*, 28-29 January 2000, Cluj-Napoca, Romania, 2000.

23 OSI and CPS, EU *Accession Project: Roma Minority in Romania*, country report, forthcoming.

24 European Commission, *Regular Report from the Commission on Progress towards Accession, Romania*, October 1999.

25 World Bank, *Romania Weekly Updates*, November/December 2000.

26 World Bank, *Romania Weekly Updates*, January 2001.

27 Zsolt Istvan Mato, "Minorities in Romania Granted Language Rights", in *Transitions Online*, 22-26 January 2001.

28 BBC Monitoring, "Romania's Mayor Reportedly Refuses to Apply Minority-language Passages of Law", text of report made on 21 April by Hungarian TV, 23 April 2001; BBC Monitoring, "Far-Right Romanian Mayor Plans Minority Headcount", Bucharest, 27 April 2001.

29 OSI and CPS, EU *Accession Project: Roma Minority in Romania*, country report, forthcoming.

30 See World Education Forum, *Romania Country Report*, 2000, for a more detailed elaboration.

31 OSI and CPS, *EU Accession Project: Roma Minority in Romania*, country report, forthcoming.

32 C Bîrzea, F Anghel, M Balica *et al*, *Romania: Education for All*, Ministry of National Education and Institute For Sciences of Education, Bucharest, 1999.

33 UNICEF TransMONEE Report, *Romania*, UNICEF Innocenti Research Centre, Italy, 2000.

34 OECD, *Reviews of National Policies for Education: Romania*, 2000.

35 World Bank, "Trends in Education Access and Financing during the Transition in Central and Eastern Europe", *Technical Paper* No. 361, April 1997.

36 Ioana Herseni (co-ordinator), Mircea Badesc *et al*, *The Romanian System of Education*, Balkan Society for Pedagogy and Education, 1999.

37 World Bank, "Trends in Education Access" (see note 35).

38 UNICEF TransMONEE Report, *Romania*, UNICEF Innocenti Research Centre, Italy, 2000.

39 OECD, *Reviews of National Policies for Education. Romania*, 2000.

40 World Bank, "Trends in Education Access" (see note 35).

41 World Bank, "Trends in Education Access" (see note 35).

42 OECD, *Reviews of National Policies for Education. Romania*, 2000.

43 World Bank, "Trends in Education Access" (see note 35).

44 World Bank, "Trends in Education Access" (see note 35).

45 UNICEF TransMONEE Report, *Romania*, UNICEF Innocenti Research Centre, Italy, 2000.

46 Fieldwork carried out in Romania in Nov-Dec 2000.

47 Delia Grighore in her comments for this report.

48 Delia Grighore in her comments for this report

49 Based on fieldwork carried out in Romania Nov-Dec 2000.

50 Romanian Report at the Stockholm Forum "Combating Intolerance", Stockholm, 29-30 January 2001.

51 Save the Children Romania in its comments for this report.

52 See: CRC/C/15/Add.16, 7 February 1994.

53 See: A/54/18, paras. 272-290, 19 August 1999.

54 OSI and CPS, *EU Accession Project: Roma Minority in Romania*, country report, forthcoming.

55 Bucharest University, Department of Sociology, Psychology, Pedagogy and Social Work, the Romanian Academy, the National Institute of Economic Research, the Research Institute of the Quality of Life, *The Romany Population. Socio-Economic Situation and Co-ordinates of a Support Programme*, 1993.

56 Fundatia Internationala pentru Copil si Familie, the Association "Tanara Generatie a Romilor" and UNICEF Romania, *An Evaluation Survey of Barriers between Family and School in a District of Bucharest*.

57 Mihai Surdu, *Education Policy for the Gypsy (Roma) Population in Romania*, Research Support Scheme, 2000.

58 Mihai Surdu, *Education Policy for the Gypsy (Roma) Population in Romania* (see note 57).

59 Fieldwork carried out in Romania Nov-Dec 2000.

60 Fieldwork carried out in Romania Nov-Dec 2000.

61 Central Europe Online Romania "Roma to Get Free Health Care in Romania", Agence France Press, 2.5.01.

62 Order Nos: 3633/13.04.1999, 4231/18.08.1999 and 4318/30.08.1999 respectively. See: L. Murvai (co-ordinator), Leman Ali *et al*, *The Ethos of Education for National Minorities in Romania 1999/2000 School Year*, Ministry for National Education in Romania, 2000.

63 Ruth Sorelle, *Romania's Forgotten Children*, International Association of Physicians in AIDS Care, 1998.

64 Information provided by Stefan Popenici, Adviser to the Minister of Education, 30-31 March 2001.

65 Republished Chapter VI-art. 41-46 OMEN no. 4216/17.08.1999.

66 Interview with a Roma Inspector as part of fieldwork carried out in Romania in Nov-Dec 2000.

67 See: A/54/18, paras. 272-290, 19 August 1999.

68 OSI and CPS, *EU Accession Project: Roma Minority in Romania*, country report, forthcoming.

69 OSI and CPS, *EU Accession Project* (see note 68).

70 OSI and CPS, *EU Accession Project* (see note 68).

71 L Murvai (co-ordinator), Leman Ali *et al*, *The Ethos of Education for National Minorities in Romania 1999/2000 School Year*, Ministry for National Education in Romania, 2000.

72 C Ulrich, *Study Case 2: Social and Educational Inclusion of Rroma Children*. Language of teaching was entirely or partially the maternal language in 10 per cent of kindergartens, 9 per cent of primary schools, 10 per cent of lower secondary education and 12 per cent of upper secondary education. In these schools it seems there were 20,045 Magyar teachers, 995 German teachers, 234 Slovak teachers and 2,250 of other minorities.

73 L Murvai (co-ordinator), *The Ethos of Education* (see note 71).

74 L Murvai (co-ordinator), *The Ethos of Education* (see note 71).

75 M Miroiu, "The Gender Dimension of Education in Romania", *SOCO Project Paper* No. 83, Vienna, 2000.

76 M Miroiu, "The Gender Dimension" (see note 75).

77 See: www.romnews.com.

78 Gheorghe Sarau has set up a virtual library (http://www.edu.ro/mino.htm and click *invatamant pentru romi*).

79 Information provided by Stefan Popenici, Adviser to the Minister of Education, 30-31 March 2001.

80 Fieldwork carried out in Romania Nov-Dec 2000.

81 Delia Grighore in her comments for this report.

82 Delia Grighore in her comments for this report.

83 UNICEF TransMONEE Report, *Romania*, UNICEF Innocenti Research Centre, Italy, 2000.

84 Case study provided by Save the Children Romania, 2000.

85 We are aware that there are numerous other good NGOs working in this area, such as Wasdass Foundation, Satra Astra, Aven Amentza, the Phoenix Foundation and the Intercultural Institute. Within the constraints of this report it was simply not possible to discuss the work of all NGOs.

86 V Dakova, B Dreossi, J Hyatt and A Socolovschi, *Review of the Romanian NGO Sector: Strengthening Donor Strategies*, Charity Know How and Charles Stewart Mott Foundation, November 2000.

87 UNICEF TransMONEE Report, *Romania*, UNICEF Innocenti Research Centre, Italy, 2000.

88 In a paper addressed to the Centre Education 2000+ Conference in March 2001. The Resource Centre for Roma Communities is the institution responsible for the administration of the Partnership Fund for Roma (a component of the PHARE programme "The Improvement of the Roma Situation") in Romania.

89 Centre Education 2000+ Conference – Improving Education for Roma – Focus Romania", 30-31 March 2001, Sinaia, Romania.

90 Centre Education 2000+ Conference – Improving Education for Roma – Focus Romania", 30-31 March 2001, Sinaia, Romania.

91 Report on Centre Education 2000+ Conference "Improving Education for Roma – Focus Romania", 30-31 March 2001, Sinaia, Romania; Centre Education 2000+ information pack, Bucharest, 2000.

92 *Open Society Chronicle*, A Newsletter of Soros Open Network Romania, No. 1, Feb-Mar 2001, p. 5; interview carried out during fieldwork in Romania Nov-Dec 2000.

93 *Open Society Chronicle*, A Newsletter of Soros Open Network Romania, No. 1, Feb-Mar 2001, p. 2.

94 Interviews conducted with teachers and children as part of fieldwork carried out in Nov-Dec 2000.

Selected references and resources

General

J-P Liégeois and N Gheorghe, *Roma/Gypsies: A European Minority*, Minority Rights Group International, London, 1995.

Will Guy (ed), *Between Past and Future: the Roma of Central and Eastern Europe*, University of Hertfordshire Press, 2001.

Ina Zoon, *On the Margins: Roma and Public Services in Romania, Bulgaria and Madedonia*, edited by Mark Norman Templeton, OSI, New York, 2001.

Albania

AEDP, "An Education Development Strategy for Albania", Albanian Education Development Project, 1999.

Children's Human Rights Centre of Albania, *The Forgotten Children*, 1999.

ERRC (European Roma Rights Centre), "No record of the case. Roma in Albania", *Country Reports*, No. 5, June 1997.

M Gjokutaj, "The Needs of Roma Children for Education", in *Se Bashku*, Albanian Education Development Project Newsletter, 1999, pp. 18-24.

A Hazizaj, "A New Law for the Protection of Children's Rights in Albania", in CRCA *Revista*, No. 3, January 1999, pp. 58-63.

Human Rights Watch/Helsinki, *Human Rights in Post-Communist Albania*, March 1996.

D Renton, *Child Trafficking in Albania*, Save the Children, March 2001.

UNICEF, *Children's Situation in Albania*, 1999.

Bosnia and Herzegovina

Centre for Protection of the Rights of Minorities, Sarajevo, *Status of the Roma in Bosnia and Herzegovina (Survey Results)*, Sarajevo, 1999.

Helsinki Citizen's Assembly and Roma Associations from Tuzla Canton, *Analysis on the Current Status of the Roma Returnees to Tuzla Canton*, 1999.

International Crisis Group, *Is Dayton Failing?*, 1999.

International Crisis Group, *Rule of Law in Public Administration*, 1999.

Ombudsmen of the Federation of Bosnia and Herzegovina, *Report on Human Rights Situation in the Federation of BiH for 1999*, Sarajevo, February 2000, Chapter VII – Protection of the Rights of the Child.

UNDP, *Human Development Report: Bosnia and Herzegovina 1998*, Chapter VII – Education.

UNDP, *Human Development Report: Bosnia and Herzegovina 2000: Youth*.

Bulgaria

Human Rights in Bulgaria, *Annual Reports of the Bulgarian Helsinki Committee*, Sofia, 1994-2000.

Human Rights Project, *Annual Reports*, Sofia, 1994-2000.

Human Rights Project, "Program for equal participation of Roma in public life of Bulgaria", *Roma Rights in Focus*, Newsletter of Human Rights Project. No. 10, 1998.

I Koleva (ed), *Konceptsia za socializatsia na detsa ot romski proizhod v neravnostoyno socialno polozhenie* [A Concept for Socialising Children of Roma Origin with an Unequal Social Status], UNICEF, Sofia, 1994.

Hr Kyuchukov, "Preparation for the Education of Gypsy Children in Bulgaria", *Journal of the Gypsy Lore Society* (Ser. 5) 2:1 (1992), pp. 147-155.

Hr Kyuchukov, *Podgotovka za ogramotyavane v uslovia na bilingvisam* [Preparation for Literacy in a Bilingual Situation], Sofia University, 1994.

Hr Kyuchukov, "The Communicative Competence of Romany (Gypsy-speaking) Children in Bulgarian Discourse in a Classroom Situation", *International Journal of Psycholinguistics* (Osaka) 10:1 (1994), pp. 41-46.

Hr Kyuchukov, "Bilingualism and Bilingual Education in Bulgaria", *European Journal of Intercultural Studies* 6:1 (1995), pp. 56-60.

Hr Kyuchukov, "Turkish and Gypsy Children Learning Bulgarian, Psycholinguistic Aspects of Second Language Acquisition in a Multicultural Environment", (PhD Thesis), University of Amsterdam, 1995.

Hr Kyuchukov, *Romani Children and Their Preparation for Literacy. A Case Study*, University of Tilburg, 1995.

Hr Kyuchukov (ed), *Ovladiavaneto na balgarskia ezik ot uchenitsi romi I-IV klas. (Resultati ot edno nauchno izsledvane)* [Mastering of Bulgarian Language from Roma Children in I-IV Class. (The Results from one Academic Survey)], Club'90, Sofia, 1997.

Hr Kyuchukov, *Lingvodidaktichni problemi na obuchenie pri ranen bilingvism. Avtoreferat za prisazhdane na obrazovatelna i nauchna stepen "doktor"* [Lingual and Didactical Problems of Education among Early Bilingualism], Sofia, 1997.

Hr Kyuchukov, *Psiholingvistichni aspekti na rannia bilinvism.(Varhu mateerial ot balgarski, turski i romski ezik).* [Psycholinguistical Aspects for the Early Bilingualism (on the Materials of Bulgarian, Turkish and Roma Languages)], Balkanska fondatsia za mezhdukulturno obrazovanie i razbiratelstvo, Sofia, 1997.

E Marushiakova, "Vulnerability of the Children of the Gypsy Ethnic Community", in *Nationwide Situation Analysis of Bulgaria's Children and Families*, UNICEF, New York, 1992, pp. 63-72.

E Marushiakova and V Popov, "The Cultural Traditions of the Gypsies in Contemporary Bulgaria and the Attitude of the State and Local Authorities Towards Them", in *Gypsies in the Locality*, Council of Europe Press, Strasburg, 1994, pp. 111-16.

E Marushiakova and V Popov, " 'Gypsy Schools' in Bulgaria", *Promoting Human Rights and Civil Society in Central and Eastern Europe*, Newsletter of the International Helsinki Federation for Human Rights 4 (1994): 5.

E Marushiakova and V Popov, "Gypsy Minority in Bulgaria – literacy, policy and community development (1985-1995)", *Alpha 97*, Culture Concepts Publishers, Toronto, & UNESCO Institute for Education, Hamburg, 1997, pp. 37-56.

E Marushiakova and V Popov, *Gypsies (Roma) in Bulgaria*, Peter Lang Verlag, Frankfurt am Main, 1997, pp. 41-42.

Y Nunev, *Romsko dete i negovata semeina sreda* [Roma child and its family environment], International Centre for Minority Studies and Intercultural Relations, Sofia, 1998.

Rezultati ot prebroyavaneto na naselenieto. Tom I – Demografski charakteristiki [The Results from the People Census, Vol. 1 – Demographic Characteristic], Natsionalen statisticheski institut, Sofia, 1994, p. 194.

The Roma in Bulgaria: Collaborative Efforts between Local Authorities and Nongovernmental Organizations. Lom, Bulgaria, April 24-25, 1988, Report, Project on Ethnic Relations, Princeton, 1998.

Y Thonden, *Children of Bulgaria: Police Violence and Arbitrary Confinement*, Human Rights Watch, New York, 1996.

I Tomova, *The Gypsies in the Transition Period*, International Centre for the Minority Studies and Intercultural Relations, Sofia, 1995.

R Valchev (ed), *Kniga za mezhdukulturno satrudnichestvo* [Book of Intercultuural Collaboration], Centre "Open Education", Sofia, 1999.

T Zang, *Destroying ethnic identity. The Gypsies of Bulgaria*, A Helsinki Watch Report, New York, 1991.

Croatia

Balent, "The experience of the Centre for Social Work in Čakovec", *Roma in Croatia Today (Romi u Hrvatskoj danas)*, Group for the Direct Protection of Human Rights, Zagreb, 1998.

Dominić, *Roma: People and/or Social Problem?* Undergraduate dissertation, School of Social Work, University of Zagreb, 1997.

ECRI (European Commission Against Racism and Intolerance), *Report on Croatia*, 9 November 1999.

ERRC (European Roma Rights Centre), *Field Report: the ERRC in Croatia*, 1998.

Glas Roma, *Education and Upbringing of Romany Children in Croatia*, 1994.
> Chapters in this publication include:
> Bogdan, "Romany National Community in the Republic of Croatia"
> Hrvatić, "Towards a Conceptualisation of a Croatian Educational Model for Roma Children"
> Pintarić *et al*, "Socio-economic Influence on the Success (or Failure) of Roma Children in School"
> Pleše, "Education of Roma in the Drnje Primary School"

Government Office for National Minorities, *Report*, 1999.

Hrvatić and Ivančić, The Historical and Social Characteristics of Roma in Croatia, *Journal for General Social Issues* 9(2-3) (In Croatian language *Društvena istraživanja*), 2000.

Ringold, *Roma and the transition in Central and Eastern Europe*, World Bank, 2000.

Štambuk, "Roma in Croatia in the Nineties", *Journal for General Social Issues* 9(2-3) (In Croatian language *Društvena istraživanja*), 2000.

FR of Yugoslavia: Serbia

G Basić, *Položaj manjina u SR Jugoslavija* (Position of Minorities in FR Yugoslavia), in Collected papers: *Položaj manjina u Saveznoj Republici Jugoslavija*, Serbian Academy of Sciences and Arts: Conferences, Volume LXXXIV, Department of Social Sciences, Book 19.

D Djordjević, *Romi – nase komsije* (Roma – Our Neighbours), sociological-ethnological study of Roma, Niš, April 2000.

Helsinki Committee for Human Rights in Serbia, *Minorities in Serbia*, Belgrade, 2000.

A Mitrovic and G Zajic, *Decenija s Romima u Masurici* (A Decade with Masurica Roma), in *Društvene promene i položaj Roma* (Social Changes and the Position of Roma), Serbian Academy of Sciences and Arts, Belgrade, 1993.

Pact for Peace and Stability in South-Eastern Europe, *Thematic Reviews of Education Policy – Serbia*, Task Force for Education, June 2001.

R Roksandić and V Pesić (eds), *Ratnistvo, patriotizam, patrijarhalnost* (Martialism, Patriotism, Patriarchalism), analysis of elementary school textbooks, Belgrade, 1994.

M Samardžić, *Položaj manjina u Vojvodina* (Position of Minorities in Vojvodina), Centar za antiratnu akciju, Belgrade, 1998.

Society for the Promotion of Romani Settlements and Institute of Criminological and Sociological Studies, *Mali London, romsko naselje u Pančevu, Problemi i moguća rešenja* (Mali London, Romani settlement in Pančevo, Problems and Possible Solutions), Belgrade, 1999.

FR of Yugoslavia: Montenegro

B Jakšic, *Life of Displaced Kosovo Roma in Montenegro (Podgorica and Nikšić) and Possibilities for Integration*, Belgrade-Podgorica, 2000.

M Lutovac, *Romi u Crnoj Gori* (Roma in Montenegro), Društvo prijatelja knjige, Ivangrad, 1987.

Montenegrin Constitution Chapter 5, *Special Rights of Members of National and Ethnic Groups, Službeni list RCG*, No. 48/92.

Z Tasić. The findings of Tasić, an activist of *Grupa Margo*, were published in *Republika*, Belgrade, 2000 and *Matica Crnogorska*, Podgorica, 2001. His paper *Romi u Crnoj Gori – status i perspektive* (Roma in Montenegro – Status and Prospects) was not published in its entirety.

Vrela (newspaper for refugees and displaced persons in Montenegro).

FR of Yugoslavia: Kosovo

Z Andjelkovic, S Scepanovic and G Prlincevic, *Days of Terror (in the Presence of the Internal Forces)*, Centre for Peace and Tolerance, Belgrade, 2000.

ERRC, *Roma in the Kosovo Crisis*, online at http://errc.org/publications/indices/kosovo. shtml

N Holtey, *Zwei Reisen zur Erkundung der Lage der Ashkali und Roma im Kosovo* (in German), 22 February 2000, available online at: www.bndlg.de/~wplarre/na000302.htm

Human Rights Watch, *Abuses against Serbs and Roma in the New Kosovo*, August 1999, available at www.hrw.org/hrw/reports/1999/kosov2/

H Islami, *Demographic Reality in Kosova*, Kosovo Information Centre in 1994.

H Islami, *Evolucioni dhe Transicioni Demografik* (in Albanian), Dukagjini Press, Peja/Pec, 1999.

Kosovo Education Centre, *Education in Kosova: Figures and Facts*, Prishtina, November 2000.

Minority Studies Society Studii Romani, *Identity Formation among Minorities in the Balkans: the cases of Roms, Egyptians and Ashkali in Kosovo*, Sofia, 2001.

OSCE, *Kosovo/Kosova As Seen, As Told, Part IV: The Impact of the Conflict on Communities and Groups in Kosovo Society: Kosovo "Gypsies" (Maxhupet) – Roma*, available online at www.osce.org/kosovo/reports/hr/part1/ch20.htm

T Peric, "Kosovo Roma today: violence, insecurity, enclaves and displacement", in *Roma Rights* No. 1, 2000, http://errc.org/ rr_nr1_2000/kosovo.shtml.

A Pipa and S Repishti (eds), *Studies on Kosova*, Columbia University Press, New York, 1984.

P Polansky, *The Gypsies of Kosova: A Survey of their Communities after the War*, available online at www.decani.yunet.com/gypsies.html

P Srivastava, *Discussion Paper on the Results of Phase 1 of the Roma/Ashkalia Education Program and Implications for Future Program Design*, IRC, 24 May 2000.

P Srivastava, *Program for Roma and Ashkalia Education (PRAE) Final Program Report*, IRC, January 2001.

UNHCR/OSCE *7th Joint Assessment of the Situation of Ethnic Minorities in Kosovo (period covering October 2000 to February 2001)*, available online, together with previous such reports, at: www.osce.org/ kosovo/publications

UNICEF, *Building a Vision for Pilot Schools in Kosovo: The conceptual framework*, UNICEF Kosovo discussion paper, 2001.

UNICEF, *Education Situation Report No. 1: Bringing Children Back to School in Kosovo*, Prishtina, 27 July 1999.

UNMIK DES draft paper *Preliminary Policy Development and Action Plan for Non-Serb Minorities*, 11 December 2000.

World Bank, "Education" chapter in *Kosovo, Federal Republic of Yugoslavia: Economic and Social Reforms for Peace and Reconciliation*, 1 February 2001. Available online at: http://www.seerecon.org/Kosovo/ KosovoDonorPrograms/WBEconReport/ wb-kosovo-econreport.htm

Former Yugoslav Republic of Macedonia

Committee on the Elimination of Racial Discrimination, *Concluding Observations on the former Yugoslav Republic of Macedonia* (CERD/C/304/ Add. 38).

ECRI (European Commission against Racism and Intolerance), *Second Report on the Former Yugoslav Republic of Macedonia*, adopted on 16 June 2000, Strasburg, 2001.

ERRC (European Roma Rights Centre), *Pleasant Fiction: the Human Rights Situation of Roma in Macedonia*, Country Report Series, No.7, Budapest, 1998.

ERRC, *Written Comments of the European Roma Rights Centre (ERRC) Concerning the Former Yugoslav Republic of Macedonia, For Consideration by the European Commission against Racism and Intolerance in Strasbourg in June 1998*, 1998.

Human Rights Watch/Helsinki, *A Threat to Stability: Human Rights Violations in Macedonia,* Human Rights Watch, New York, 1996.

Divina Lakinska-Popovska, *Vulnerability of Roma children in the Municipality of Shuto Orizari,* UNICEF, United Nations Children's Fund and the World Bank, unpublished, 2000.

Ministry of Education, *Draft Strategy for Development of Education in the Republic of Macedonia,* 2000.

Ministry of Education, *Information about the Current Condition in the Education of Minorities in the Republic of Macedonia,* 1999.

Ministry of Education, UNESCO *Education for All Report – 2000,* August 1999, p. 2.

Open Society Institute, the Institute for Educational Policy, *Roma in the Education System of Macedonia: A Problem Analysis:* IEP OSI Budapest, forthcoming.

H Poulton, *The Roma in Macedonia: A Balkan Success Story?,* RFE/RL Research Report, Vol. 2, 1993.

Project on Ethnic Relations, *State Policies Toward the Roma in Macedonia, Oct. 13-14, 2000, Skopje, Macedonia,* PER Publications, New Jersey, 2000.

Romania

C Bîrzea, F Anghel, M Balica *et al, Romania: Education for All,* Ministry of National Education and Institute For Sciences of Education, Bucharest, 1999.

Embassy of Finland in Romania, *International Expert Symposium on Roma Questions,* 28-29 January 2000, Cluj-Napoca, Romania, 2000.

European Roma Rights Centre, *Sudden Rage at Dawn – Violence Against Roma in Romania,* September 1996.

Ioana Herseni (co-ordinator), Mircea Badesc *et al, The Romanian System of Education,* Balkan Society for Pedagogy and Education, 1999.

Mariea Ionescu and Sorin Cace, *Best Practice in Rroma Communities,* Open Society Foundation and Resource Centre for Rroma Communities, Bucharest, 2000.

L Murvai (co-ordinator), Leman Ali *et al, The Ethos of Education for National Minorities in Romania 1999/2000 School Year,* Ministry for National Education in Romania, 2000.

National Agency for the Protection of Children's Rights, *The National Strategy for Child Welfare 2000-2003,* 2000.

OECD, *Reviews of National Policies for Education: Romania,* 2000.

OSCE *Report on the Situation of Roma and Sinti in the OSCE Area,* 7 April 2000.

UNICEF and Department of Child Protection, *Situatii Copilului si a Familiei in Romania 1993 – 1997*. (The Situation Of Children And Families in Romania 1993-1997), 1997.

UNICEF TransMONEE Report, *Romania*, UNICEF Innocenti Research Centre, Italy, 2000.

World Bank, *Romania. Current Political Situation*, 16 January 2001.

World Bank, *Hidden Challenges to Education Systems in Transition Economies*, September 2000.

World Education Forum, *Romania Country Report*, 2000.

Acknowledgements

We wish to acknowledge the donors for this project without whom this work would not have been possible, namely the Swiss and US State Departments under the auspices of the Stability Pact for South-Eastern Europe Quick Start Package, Save the Children UK, UNICEF and KulturKontakt.

The following country reports were funded under the auspices of the Stability Pact for South-Eastern Europe: Albania, Bosnia and Herzegovina, Bulgaria, Croatia, Federal Republic of Yugoslavia (Serbia, Montenegro and Kosovo), Former Yugoslav Republic of Macedonia and Romania. KulturKontakt also provided co-finance for the Federal Republic of Yugoslavia: Serbia report. Save the Children UK funded the following country reports: Czech Republic, Finland, Greece, Hungary, Italy, Slovakia and the United Kingdom. Finally, the Slovakia country report was co-financed by SCF-UK and the UNICEF Regional Office for the CEE/CIS and Baltic States.

Save the Children would like to thank the project team, which has been responsible for this project. The team consisted of Maria Andruszkiewicz, Kath Pinnock, Federica Donati, Patricia Coelho and Olga Nakajo-Widder. Special thanks is owed to Martin Kovats, Elena Marushiakova and Vesselin Popov, who have been involved in various aspects of the report and have offered continued and invaluable support from its beginning in 1999.

Save the Children UK would especially like to thank the many individuals and organisations who have contributed in a number of ways to this report from both within and outside of Save the Children UK. These include (in no particular order): Angus Bancroft, Michelle Lloyd, Richard Morran, Margaret Thompson, David Simpson, Richard Powell, David Norman, Patti Strong, Angela Pudar, Olivera Damjanović, Rasa Sekulovic, Ardian Gojani, Madeleine Tearse, Judy Lister, Poppy Szaybo, Martin Emerson, Piero Colacicchi and Miralena Mamina.

We would also like to thank all those who read and commented on early drafts of *Denied a Future?*, including John Beauclerk, Professor Françoise Hampson, Professor Katarina Tomasevski, and Sigmund Karlstrom. We are also grateful to all those who read the final report which, together with some of the above, included Chris Cuninghame, Marion Molteno, Michelle Stratford, Frances Ellery, Robert Mangham and Ravi Wickremasinghe.

Contributors to the *Denied a Future?* reports

Editor Kath Pinnock

Roma/Gypsy and Traveller education: An overview of the issues
Martin Kovats

Photography Poppy Szaybo
[Images – Italy and Hungary: Andrew Williams]

Country reports: South-Eastern Europe

Albania
Co-authors: Altin Hazizaj and staff at the Children's Human Rights Centre for Albania; and Federica Donati

Bosnia and Herzegovina
Editor: Allison Smith
Contributors: Prof. dr Neđo Milićević, Mr Petar Đaković, Ms Ljiljana Mijović MA, Zdravo da ste (Hi Neighbour) Banja Luka; Budi moj prijatelj (Be my Friend) Sarajevo

Bulgaria
Co-Authors: Elena Marushiakova and Vesselin Popov

Croatia
Co-Authors: Ramiza Mehmedi and Jasmina Papa

FR Yugoslavia: Overview
Author: Alex Anderson

FR Yugoslavia: Serbia
Author: Humanitarian Law Centre, Belgrade

FR Yugoslavia: Montenegro
Author: Humanitarian Law Centre, Belgrade

FR Yugoslavia: Kosovo
Author: Alex Anderson
Contributor: Avdullah Qafani

FYR of Macedonia
Author: Martin Demorovski

Romania
Editors: Kath Pinnock and Federica Donati
Contributors: Charlie Bell, Save the Children Romania, Sorin Cace and Delia Grighore

Biographies of authors (in alphabetical order)

Alex Anderson was an Amnesty International Researcher in 1999-2000, conducting field investigations in Hungary and Bulgaria and is scheduled to become Caucasus Researcher for Human Rights Watch from Autumn 2001. His experience of Kosovo predates the war. In 1997, he worked in OSCE election observation missions and researched a MA dissertation on the Kosovar Albanian civil resistance. Earlier, he managed aid projects and researched for TV documentaries in the former Soviet Union.

Maria Andruszkiewicz is Programme Development Officer for Save the Children's UK/Europe region and is a leading member of the *Denied a Future?* project team. Before joining Save the Children she worked in Central and Eastern Europe and the former Soviet Union in the field of consumers' rights and NGO and Small and Medium-sized Enterprise (SME) development.

Martin Demorovski is an independent Romani consultant who works for different Romani and non-Romani international NGOs as well as intergovernmental organisations. He is currently doing work for the European Roma Rights Centre-Budapest, The OSCE-ODIHR Contact Point for Roma and Sinti Issues, and the Council of Europe. One of the main priorities in his work is reporting and writing articles about Romani issues.

Federica Donati was Human Rights Adviser for Save the Children UK and a leading member of the *Denied a Future?* project team. She is now Assistant Programme Officer for UNICEF in New Delhi, India.

Dr Martin Kovats completed a PhD on 'The Development of Roma Politics in Hungary' at the University of Portsmouth. He is now an Honorary Research Fellow at the Centre for Russian and East European Studies, University of Birmingham. He has published on Roma and minority issues in academic journals in both the UK and Hungary.

Elena Marushiakova is a scholar at the University of Leipzig and co-chair of *Studii Romani*, a Minority-Studies NGO based in Sofia, Bulgaria. She is a specialist in the field of ethnography with particular reference to Roma/Gypsies in South-Eastern Europe.

Ramiza Mehmedi is a social pedagogue and founder of the Roma Women's NGO 'Better Future' in Croatia. She has a long-standing commitment to challenging educational disadvantage and discrimination faced by Roma in Croatia.

Jasmina Papa is a social worker and political scientist, and has been involved in many community-development initiatives with Roma groups in Croatia.

Dr Kath Pinnock is UK/Europe Policy and Research Officer for Save the Children UK. As well as being a leading member of the project team for *Denied a Future?*, she does work around participatory research methods. Her PhD explored the role of Roma/Gypsies in the non-governmental sector in Bulgaria 1989-1997, and she has published articles on the non-governmental sector and Roma/Gypsy organisations in Eastern Europe as well as on EU policy and welfare issues.

Vesselin Popov is a scholar at the Ethnographical Institute and Museum of Bulgaria Academy of Sciences and co-chair of *Studii Romani*, a Minority-Studies NGO based in Sofia, Bulgaria. He is a specialist in the field of ethnography with particular reference to Roma/Gypsies in South-Eastern Europe.

Allison Smith is a barrister specialising in international law and human rights. She has also worked in many conflict and post-conflict countries carrying out fact-finding missions, including Kosovo.

Poppy Szaybo is a professional photographer and runs photographic projects with Gypsy/Traveller and refugee children across Europe, including the UK. She is also a cultural projects adviser for organisations such as London Arts and the British Council. Currently, she is curating an exhibition of Romani art for the University of Hertfordshire and is also working on a number of projects as part of *Denied a Future?* for Save the Children UK.

The Humanitarian Law Centre is a non-governmental organisation based in Belgrade, and also has offices in Montenegro and Kosovo. They carry out legal analysis, campaign work and media-monitoring on issues relating to human rights abuses for minorities, internally displaced persons, and refugees.

The Children's Human Rights Centre of Albania is a non-governmental organisation based in Tirana. It aims to protect and develop children's rights in Albania based on the UN Convention for the Rights of the Child. Members of CRCA are lawyers, physicians, journalists, and sociologists with specialist knowledge of children's rights and issues.